On the morning of the 20th, a male manga artist was reported dead in his home. Upon finding him, the investigators gave him some water and a banana that was found at the scene and he gradually recovered. Two months later, he was released into the mountains. Here's *World Trigger* volume 12.

—Daisuke Ashihara, 2015

Daisuke Ashihara began his manga career at the age of 27 when his manga *Room 303* won second place in the 75th Tezuka Awards. His first series, *Super Dog Rilienthal*, began serialization in *Weekly Shonen Jump* in 2009. *World Trigger* is his second serialized work in *Weekly Shonen Jump*. He is also the author of several shorter works, including the one-shots *Super Dog Rilienthal*, *Trigger Keeper* and *Elite Agent Jin*.

WORLD TRIGGER VOL. 12
SHONEN JUMP Manga Edition

STORY AND ART BY DAISUKE ASHIHARA

Translation/Lillian Olsen
Touch-Up Art & Lettering/Annaliese Christman
Design/Sam Elzway
Editor/Marlene First

Printed in the U.S.A.

Published by VIZ Media, LLC
P.O. Box 77010
San Francisco, CA 94107

10 9 8 7 6 5 4 3 2 1
First printing, September 2016

www.viz.com

PARENTAL ADVISORY
WORLD TRIGGER is rated T for Teen and is
recommended for ages 13 and up. This volume
contains fantasy violence.
ratings.viz.com

www.shonenjump.com

WORLD TRIGGER

DAISUKE ASHIHARA

12

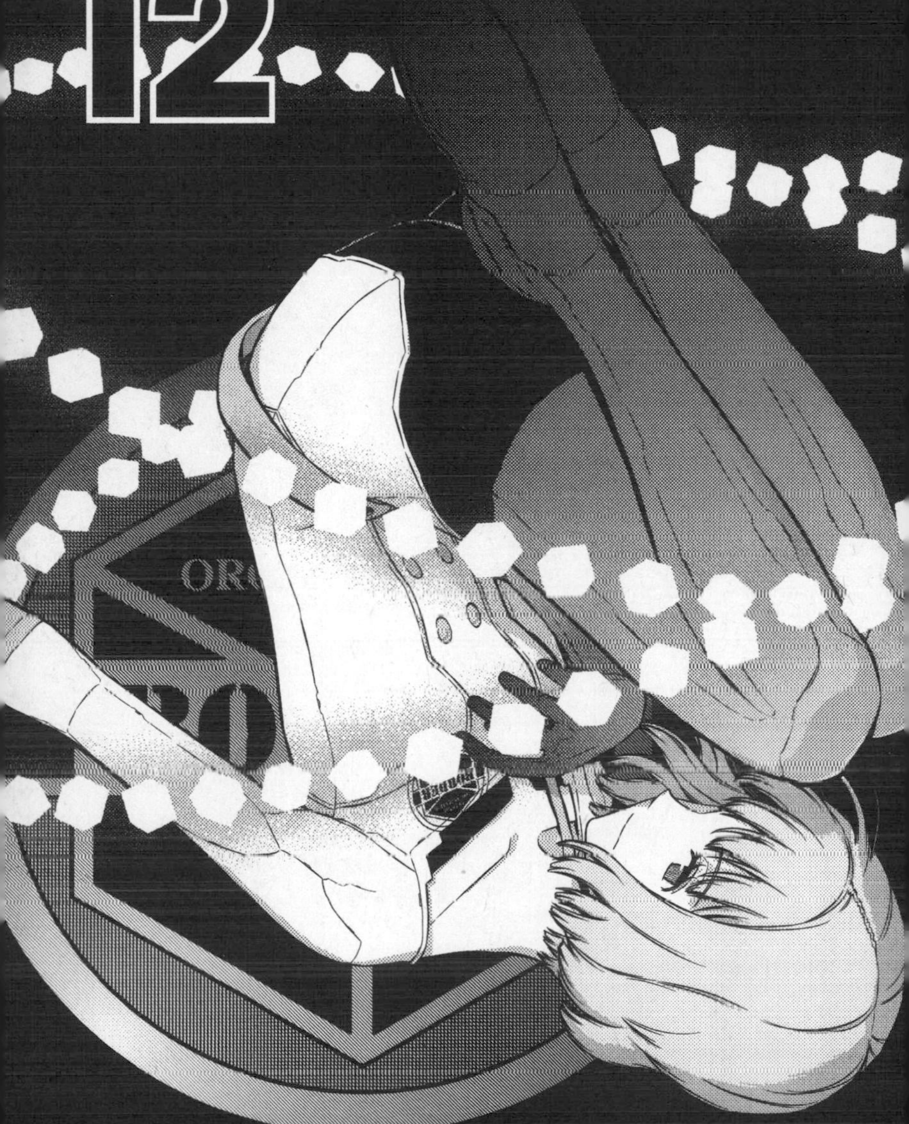

SHONEN JUMP MANGA EDITION

WORLD TRIGGER DATA BASE

BORDER

An agency founded to protect the city's peace from Neighbors.

S-Rank Black Trigger Users (i.e. Tsukihiko Amo)

A-Rank (Elite) — Away teams selected from here (Arashiyama, Miwa squads)

Promoted in Rank Wars

B-Rank (Main force) — Agents on defense duty must be at least B-Rank (Tamakoma-2)

Promoted at 4,000 solo points

C-Rank (Trainees) — Use trainee Triggers only in emergencies (Izuho Natsume)

TRIGGER

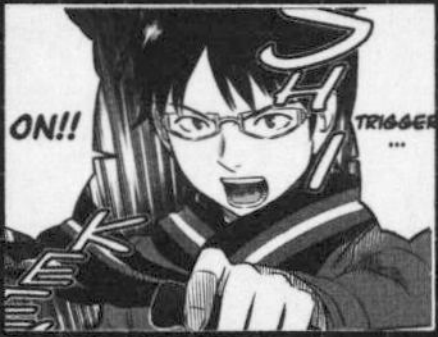
TRIGGER...
ON!!

A technology created by Neighbors to manipulate Trion. Used mainly as weapons, Triggers come in various types.

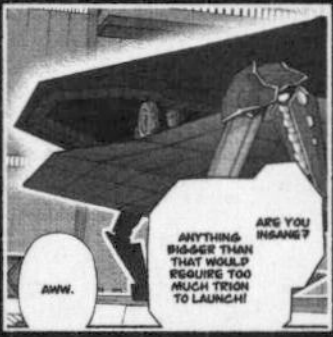
ARE YOU INSANE?
ANYTHING BIGGER THAN THAT WOULD REQUIRE TOO MUCH TRION TO LAUNCH!
AWW.

◀ Away mission ships also run on Trion.

POSITIONS

Border classifies them into three groups: Attacker, Gunner and Sniper.

Attacker

Close-range attacks. Weapons include: close-range Scorpions that are good for surprise attacks, the balanced Kogetsu sword, and the defense-heavy Raygust.

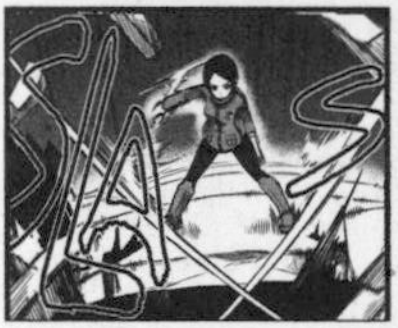

Gunner

Shoots from mid-range. There are several types of bullets, including multipurpose Asteroids, twisting Vipers, exploding Meteors, and tracking Hounds. People who don't use gun-shaped Triggers are called Shooters.

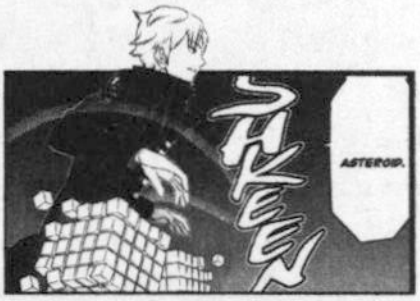
ASTEROID.

◀ Osamu and Izumi are Shooters.

Sniper

Fires from a long distance. There are three sniping rifles: the well-balanced Egret, the light and easy Lightning, and the powerful but unwieldy Ibis.

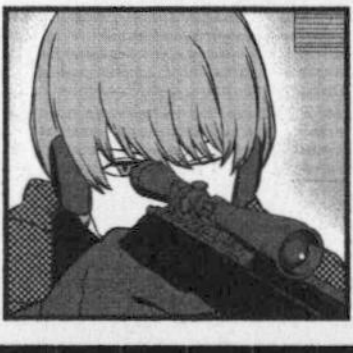

Operator

Supports combatants by relaying information such as enemy positions and abilities.

RANK WARS

Practice matches between Border agents. Promotions in Border are based on good results in the Rank Wars and defense duty achievements.

B-Rank agents are split into top, middle, and bottom groups. Three to four teams fight in a melee battle. Defeating an opposing squad member earns you one point and surviving to the end nets two points. Top teams from the previous season get a bonus.

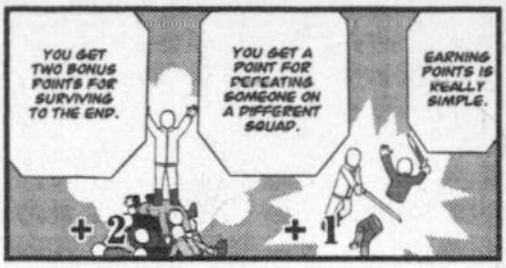
EARNING POINTS IS REALLY SIMPLE.
YOU GET A POINT FOR DEFEATING SOMEONE ON A DIFFERENT SQUAD.
+1
YOU GET TWO BONUS POINTS FOR SURVIVING TO THE END.
+2

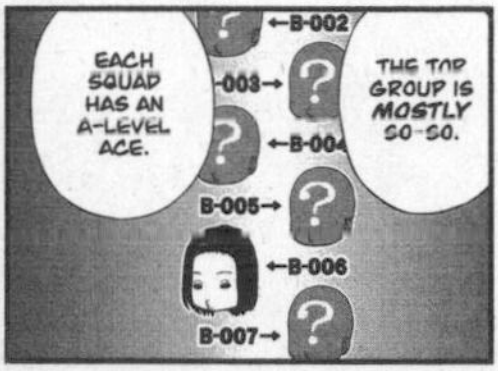
THE TOP GROUP IS MOSTLY SO-SO.
EACH SQUAD HAS AN A-LEVEL ACE.
←B-002
-003→
←B-004
B-005→
←B-006
B-007→

B-Rank middle groups have set strategies. Top groups all have an A-Rank level ace.

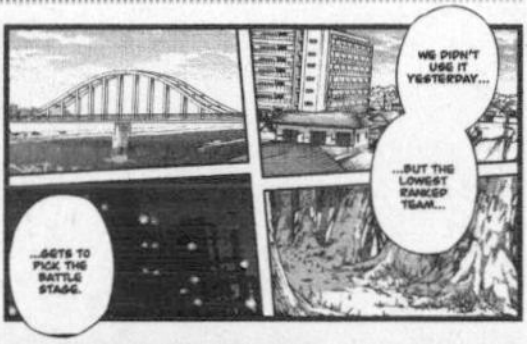
WE DIDN'T USE IT YESTERDAY...
...BUT THE LOWEST RANKED TEAM...
...GETS TO PICK THE BATTLE STAGE.

The lowest-ranked team in each match gets to pick the stage.

A-Rank

Top two B-Rank squads get to challenge A-Rank.

B-Rank

Agents ▶ (B-Rank and above) can't fight trainees (C-Rank) for points.

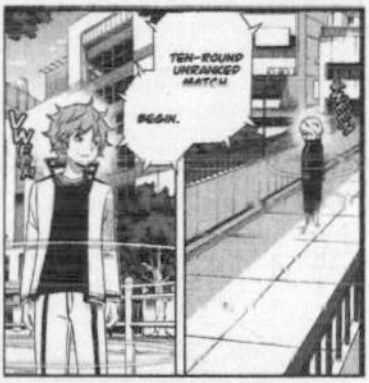
TEN-ROUND UNRANKED MATCH
BEGIN.

C-Rank Wars are fought through solo matches. Beating someone with more points than you gets you a lot of points. On the other hand, beating someone with fewer points doesn't get you as many.

C-Rank

STORY

About four years ago, a Gate connecting to another dimension opened in Mikado City, leading to the appearance of invaders called Neighbors. After the establishment of the Border Defence Agency, people were able to return to their normal lives.

Osamu Mikumo is a junior high student who meets Yuma Kuga, a Neighbor. Yuma is targeted for capture by Border, but Tamakoma branch agent Yuichi Jin steps in to help. He convinces Yuma to join Border instead, then gives his Black Trigger to HQ in exchange for Yuma's enlistment. Now Osamu, Yuma and Osamu's friend Chika work towards making A-Rank together.

Aftokrator, the largest military nation in the Neighborhood, begins another large-scale invasion! Border succeeds in driving them back, but over thirty C-Rank trainees are kidnapped in the process. Border implements more plans for away missions to retrieve the missing Agents.

Tamakoma-2 enters the Rank Wars to be chosen for the away team. They win their first match with flying colors as well as the second match against Suwa and Arafune squads. The third match has an unexpected stage picked by Nasu squad, and Ko Murakami's side effect will make the fight all the more difficult.

WORLD TRIGGER CHARACTERS

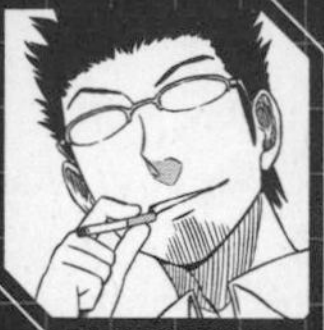

TAKUMI RINDO

Tamakoma Branch Director.

TAMAKOMA BRANCH

Understanding toward Neighbors. Considered divergent from Border's main philosophy.

TAMAKOMA-2

Tamakoma's B-Rank squad, aiming to get promoted to A-Rank.

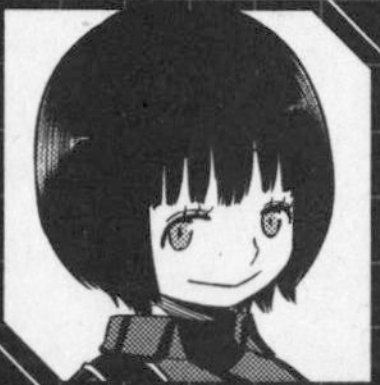

CHIKA AMATORI

Osamu's childhood friend. She has high Trion levels.

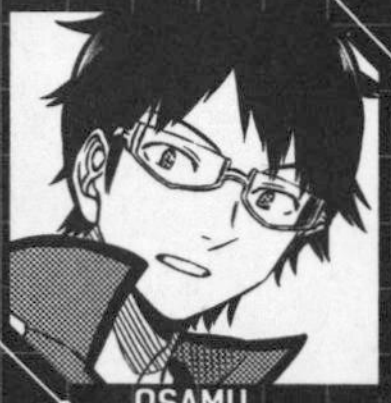

OSAMU MIKUMO

Ninth-grader who's compelled to help those in trouble. Captain of Tamakoma-2 (Mikumo squad).

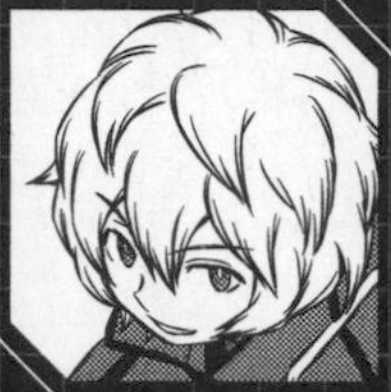

YUMA KUGA

A Neighbor who carries a Black Trigger.

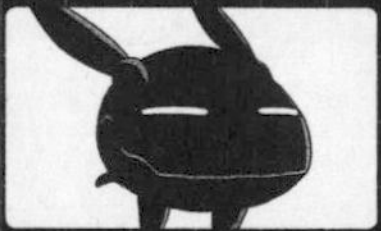

REPLICA

Yuma's chaperone. Missing after recent invasion.

TAMAKOMA-1

Tamakoma's A-Rank squad.

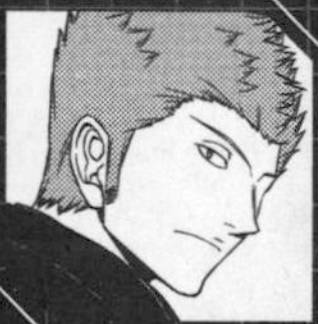

REIJI KIZAKI

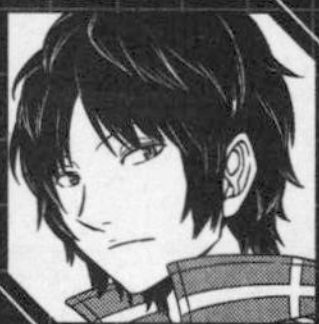

KYOSUKE KARASUMA

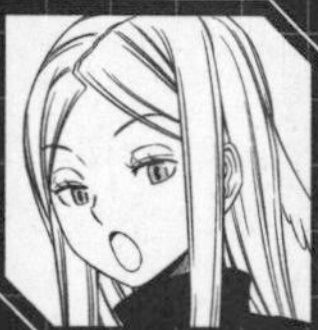

KIRIE KONAMI

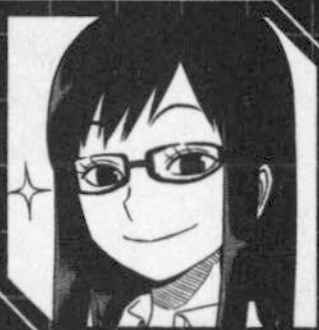

SHIORI USAMI

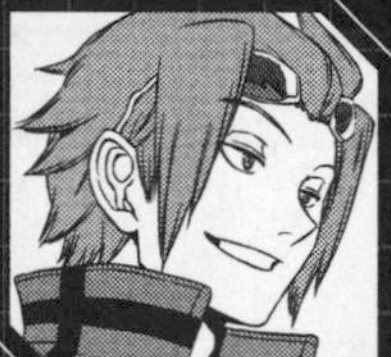

YUICHI JIN

Former S-Rank Black Trigger user. His Side Effect lets him see the future.

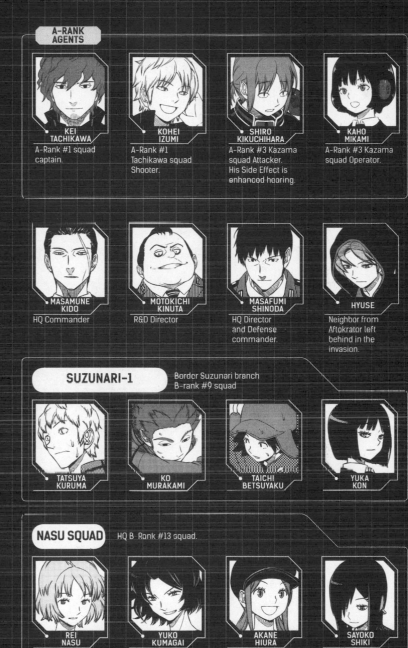

A-RANK AGENTS

KEI TACHIKAWA
A-Rank #1 squad captain.

KOHEI IZUMI
A-Rank #1 Tachikawa squad Shooter.

SHIRO KIKUCHIHARA
A-Rank #3 Kazama squad Attacker. His Side Effect is enhanced hearing.

KAHO MIKAMI
A-Rank #3 Kazama squad Operator.

MASAMUNE KIDO
HQ Commander

MOTOKICHI KINUTA
R&D Director

MASAFUMI SHINODA
HQ Director and Defense commander.

HYUSE
Neighbor from Aftokrator left behind in the invasion.

SUZUNARI-1
Border Suzunari branch B-rank #9 squad

TATSUYA KURUMA

KO MURAKAMI

TAICHI BETSUYAKU

YUKA KON

NASU SQUAD
HQ B-Rank #13 squad.

REI NASU

YUKO KUMAGAI

AKANE HIURA

SAYOKO SHIKI

WORLD TRIGGER
CONTENTS

12

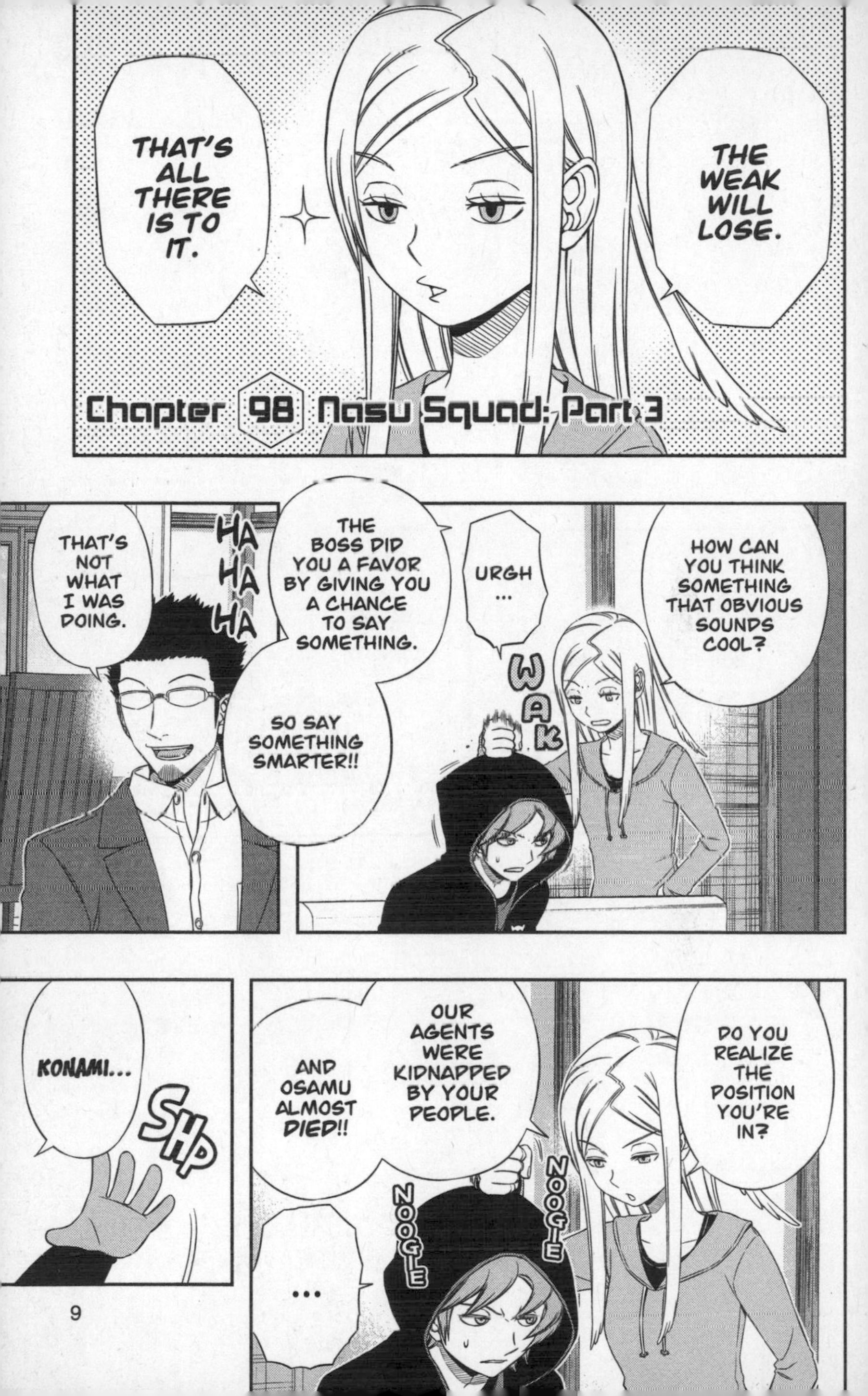
THE WEAK WILL LOSE.
THAT'S ALL THERE IS TO IT.
Chapter 98 Nasu Squad: Part 3
HOW CAN YOU THINK SOMETHING THAT OBVIOUS SOUNDS COOL?
URGH ...
WAK
THE BOSS DID YOU A FAVOR BY GIVING YOU A CHANCE TO SAY SOMETHING.
SO SAY SOMETHING SMARTER!!
HA HA HA
THAT'S NOT WHAT I WAS DOING.
DO YOU REALIZE THE POSITION YOU'RE IN?
NOOGIE
OUR AGENTS WERE KIDNAPPED BY YOUR PEOPLE.
AND OSAMU ALMOST DIED!!
NOOGIE
...
SHP
KONAMI...

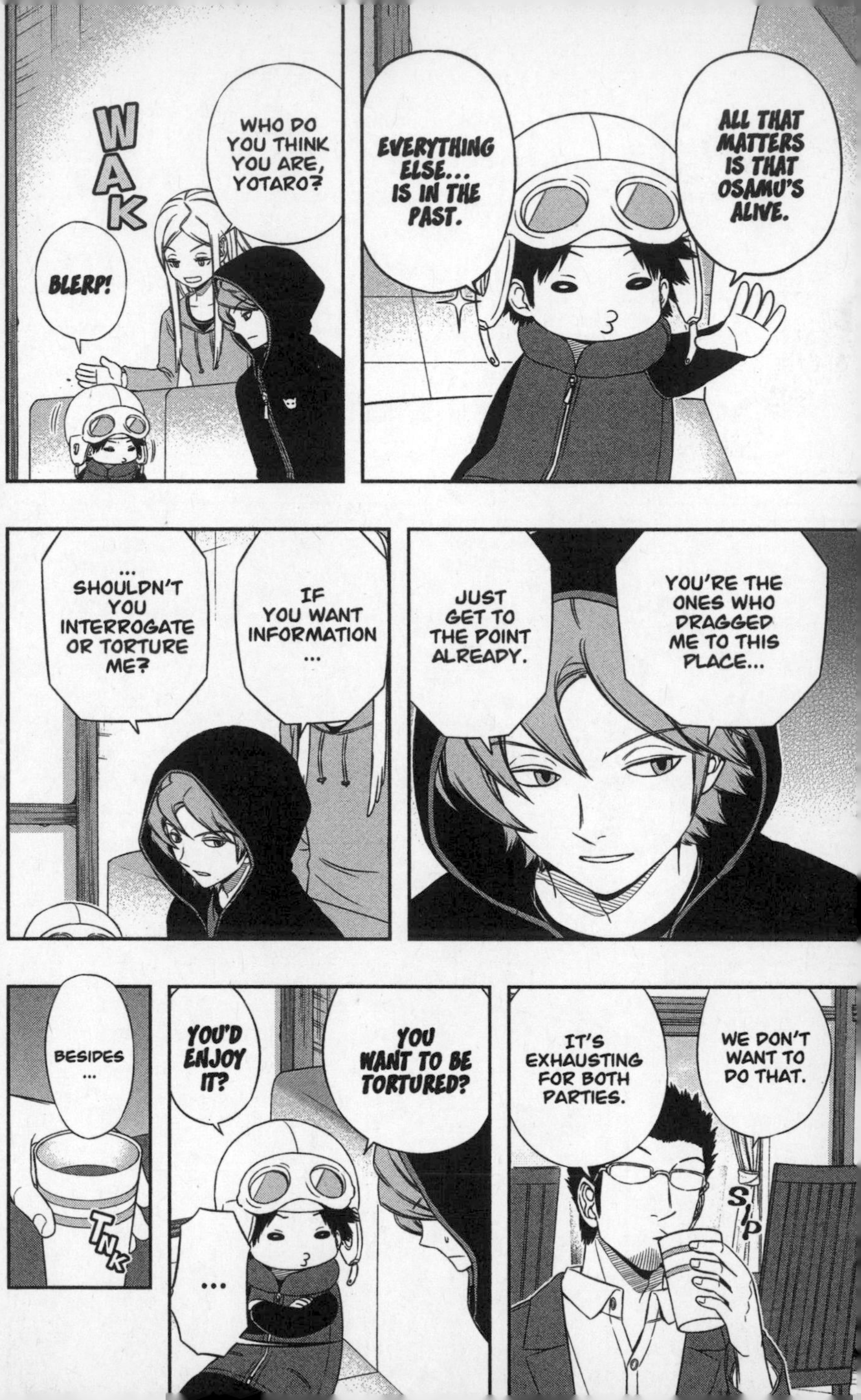
ALL THAT MATTERS IS THAT OSAMU'S ALIVE.
EVERYTHING ELSE... IS IN THE PAST.
WHO DO YOU THINK YOU ARE, YOTARO?
WAK
BLERP!
YOU'RE THE ONES WHO DRAGGED ME TO THIS PLACE...
JUST GET TO THE POINT ALREADY.
IF YOU WANT INFORMATION ...
... SHOULDN'T YOU INTERROGATE OR TORTURE ME?
WE DON'T WANT TO DO THAT.
IT'S EXHAUSTING FOR BOTH PARTIES.
SIP
YOU WANT TO BE TORTURED?
YOU'D ENJOY IT?
...
BESIDES ...
TNK

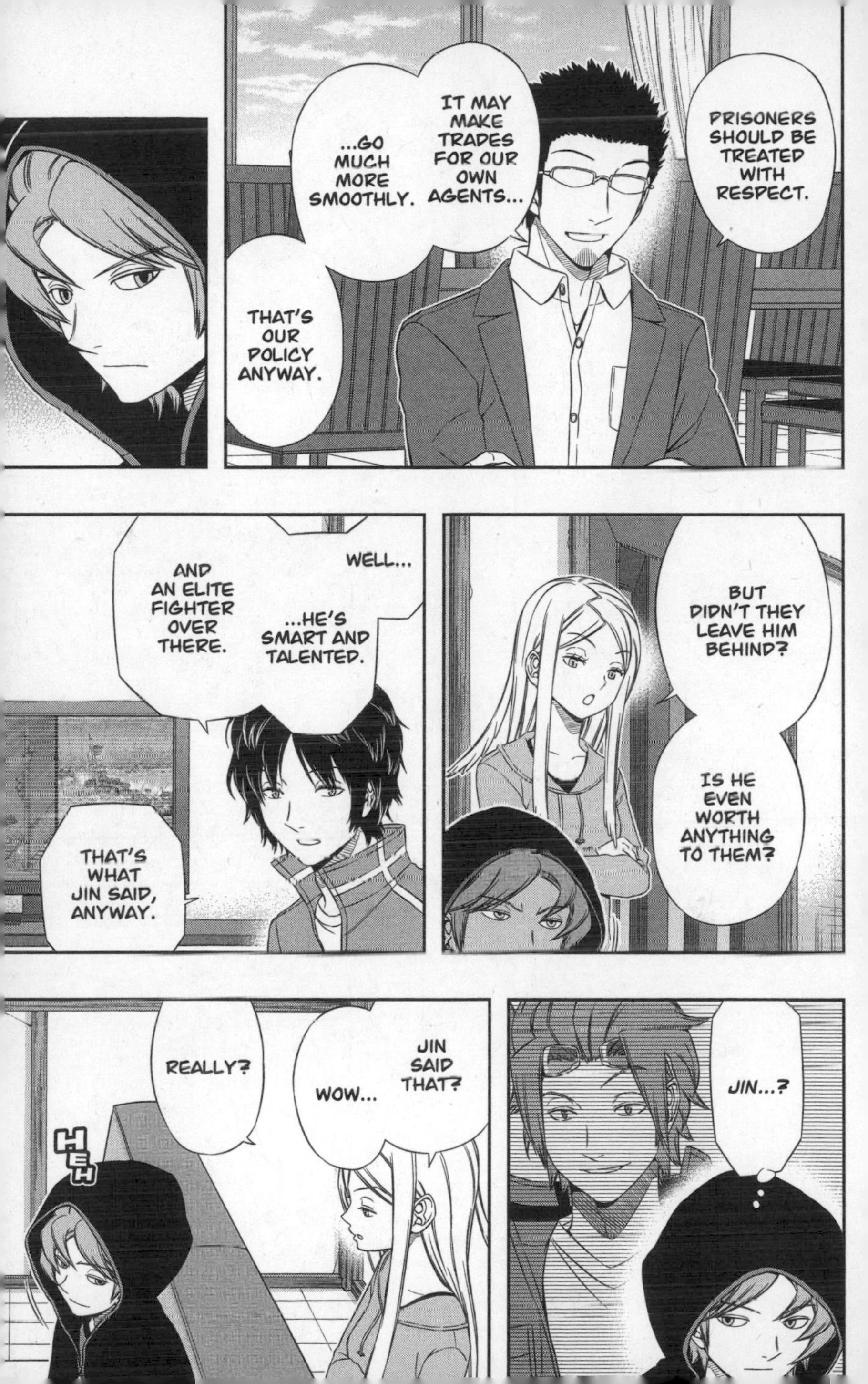
PRISONERS SHOULD BE TREATED WITH RESPECT.
IT MAY MAKE TRADES FOR OUR OWN AGENTS...
...GO MUCH MORE SMOOTHLY.
THAT'S OUR POLICY ANYWAY.
BUT DIDN'T THEY LEAVE HIM BEHIND?
IS HE EVEN WORTH ANYTHING TO THEM?
WELL...
...HE'S SMART AND TALENTED.
AND AN ELITE FIGHTER OVER THERE.
THAT'S WHAT JIN SAID, ANYWAY.
JIN...?
JIN SAID THAT?
WOW...
REALLY?
HEH

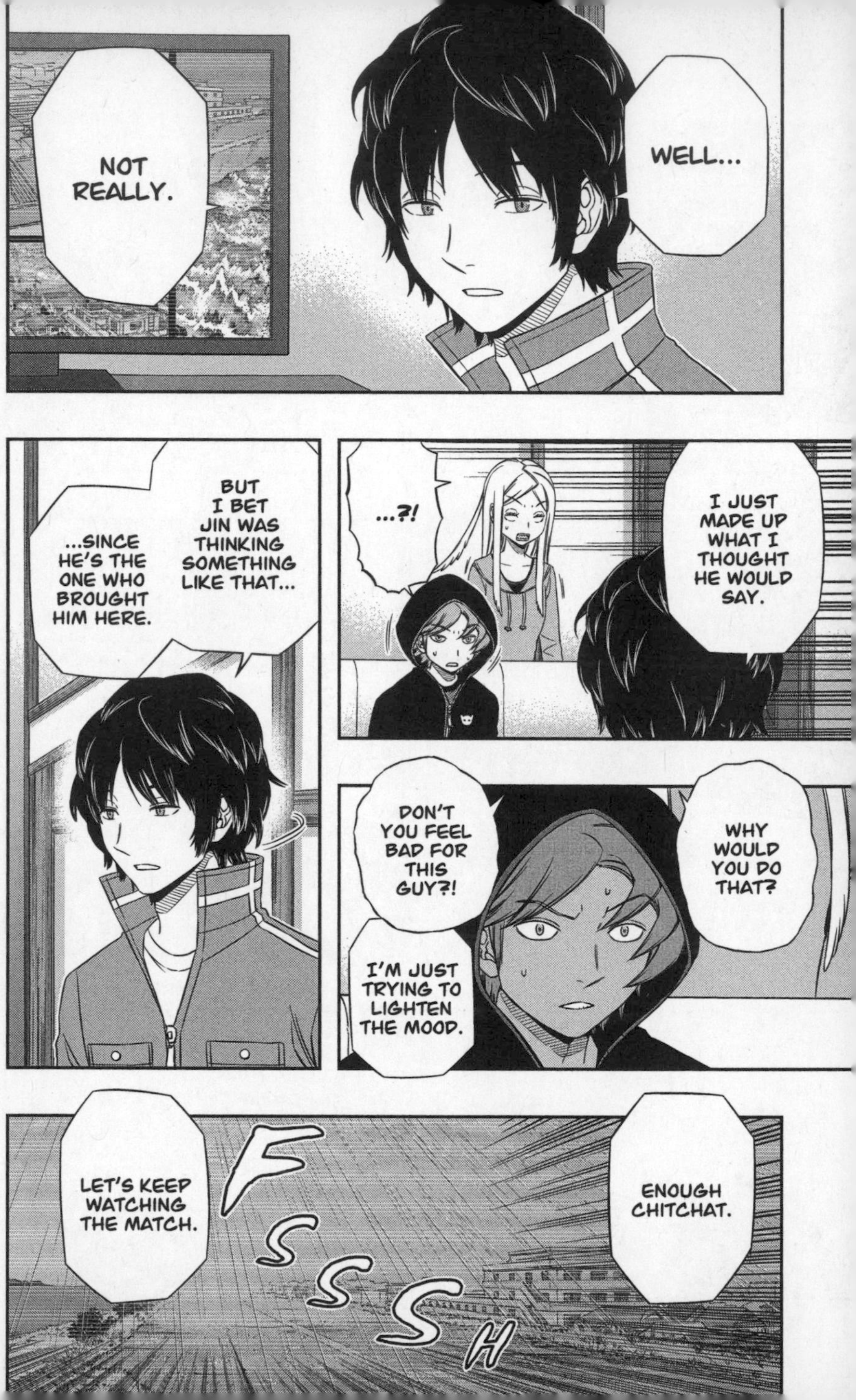
WELL...
NOT REALLY.
I JUST MADE UP WHAT I THOUGHT HE WOULD SAY.
...?!
WHY WOULD YOU DO THAT?
DON'T YOU FEEL BAD FOR THIS GUY?!
I'M JUST TRYING TO LIGHTEN THE MOOD.
BUT I BET JIN WAS THINKING SOMETHING LIKE THAT...
...SINCE HE'S THE ONE WHO BROUGHT HIM HERE.
ENOUGH CHITCHAT.
LET'S KEEP WATCHING THE MATCH.
FSSSH

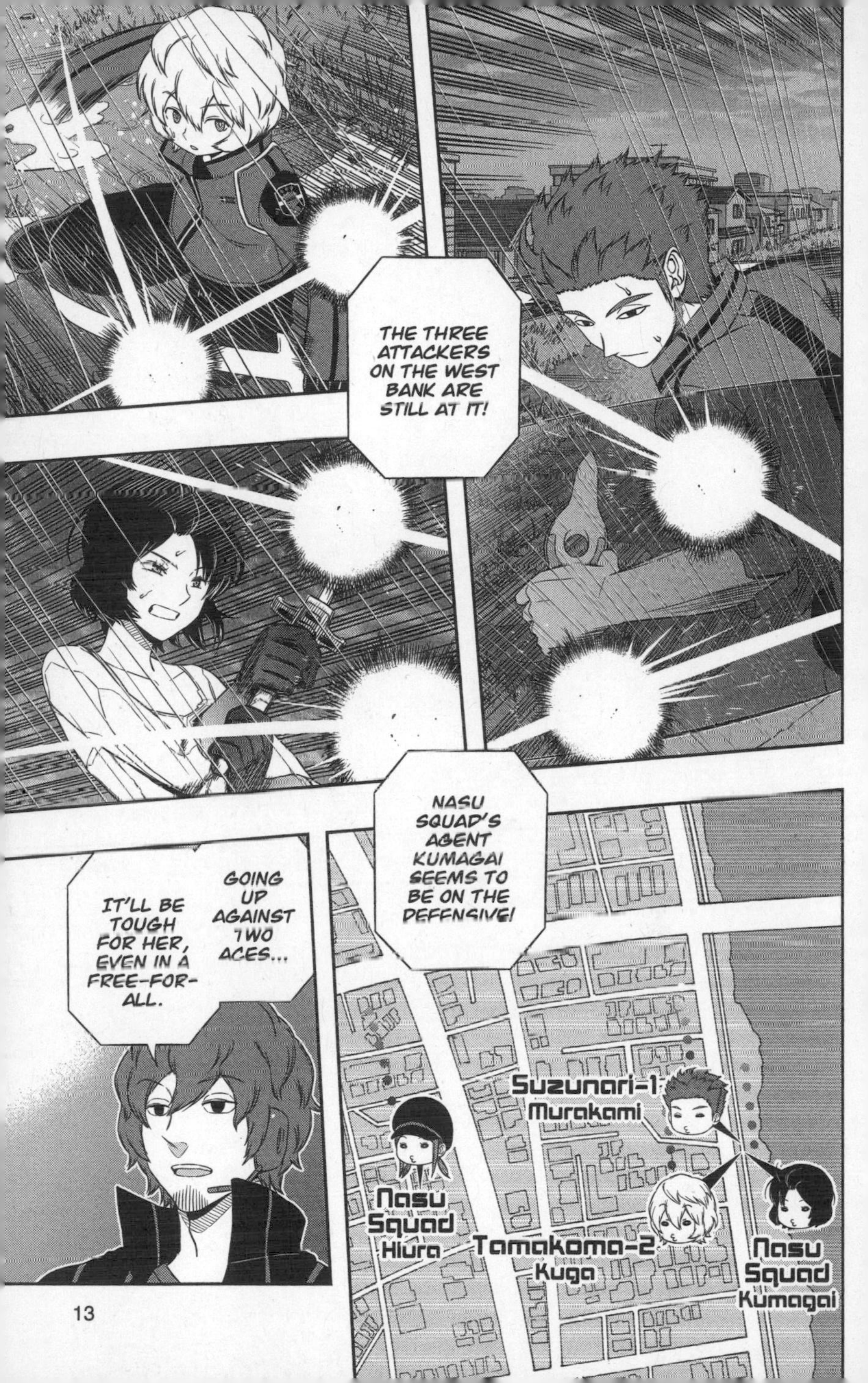
THE THREE ATTACKERS ON THE WEST BANK ARE STILL AT IT!
NASU SQUAD'S AGENT KUMAGAI SEEMS TO BE ON THE DEFENSIVE!
Suzunari-1 Murakami
Nasu Squad Kumagai
Tamakoma-2 Kuga
Nasu Squad Hiura
GOING UP AGAINST TWO ACES...
IT'LL BE TOUGH FOR HER, EVEN IN A FREE-FOR-ALL.

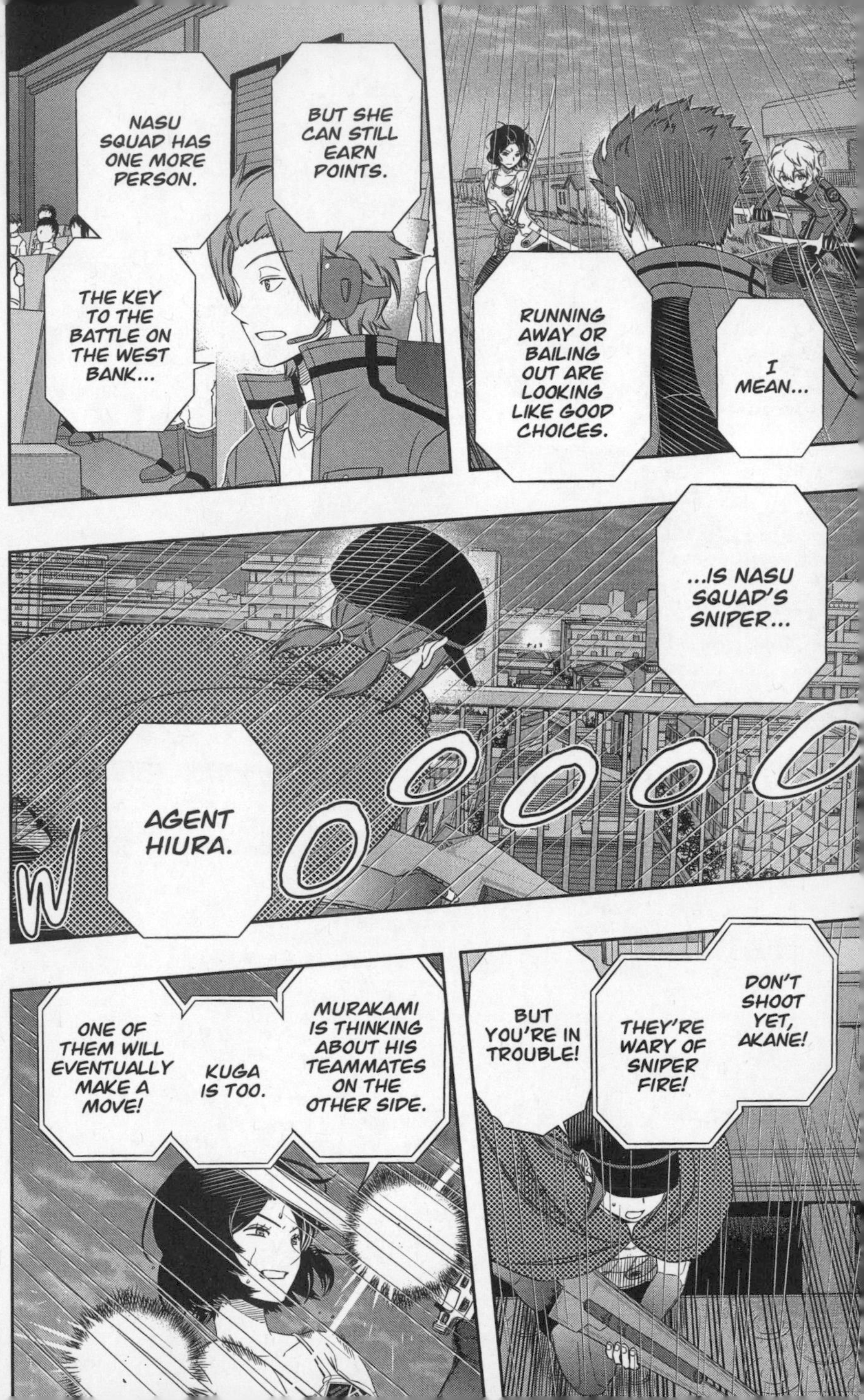
I MEAN...
RUNNING AWAY OR BAILING OUT ARE LOOKING LIKE GOOD CHOICES.
BUT SHE CAN STILL EARN POINTS.
NASU SQUAD HAS ONE MORE PERSON.
THE KEY TO THE BATTLE ON THE WEST BANK...
...IS NASU SQUAD'S SNIPER...
AGENT HIURA.
WOOOOO
DON'T SHOOT YET, AKANE!
THEY'RE WARY OF SNIPER FIRE!
BUT YOU'RE IN TROUBLE!
MURAKAMI IS THINKING ABOUT HIS TEAMMATES ON THE OTHER SIDE.
KUGA IS TOO.
ONE OF THEM WILL EVENTUALLY MAKE A MOVE!

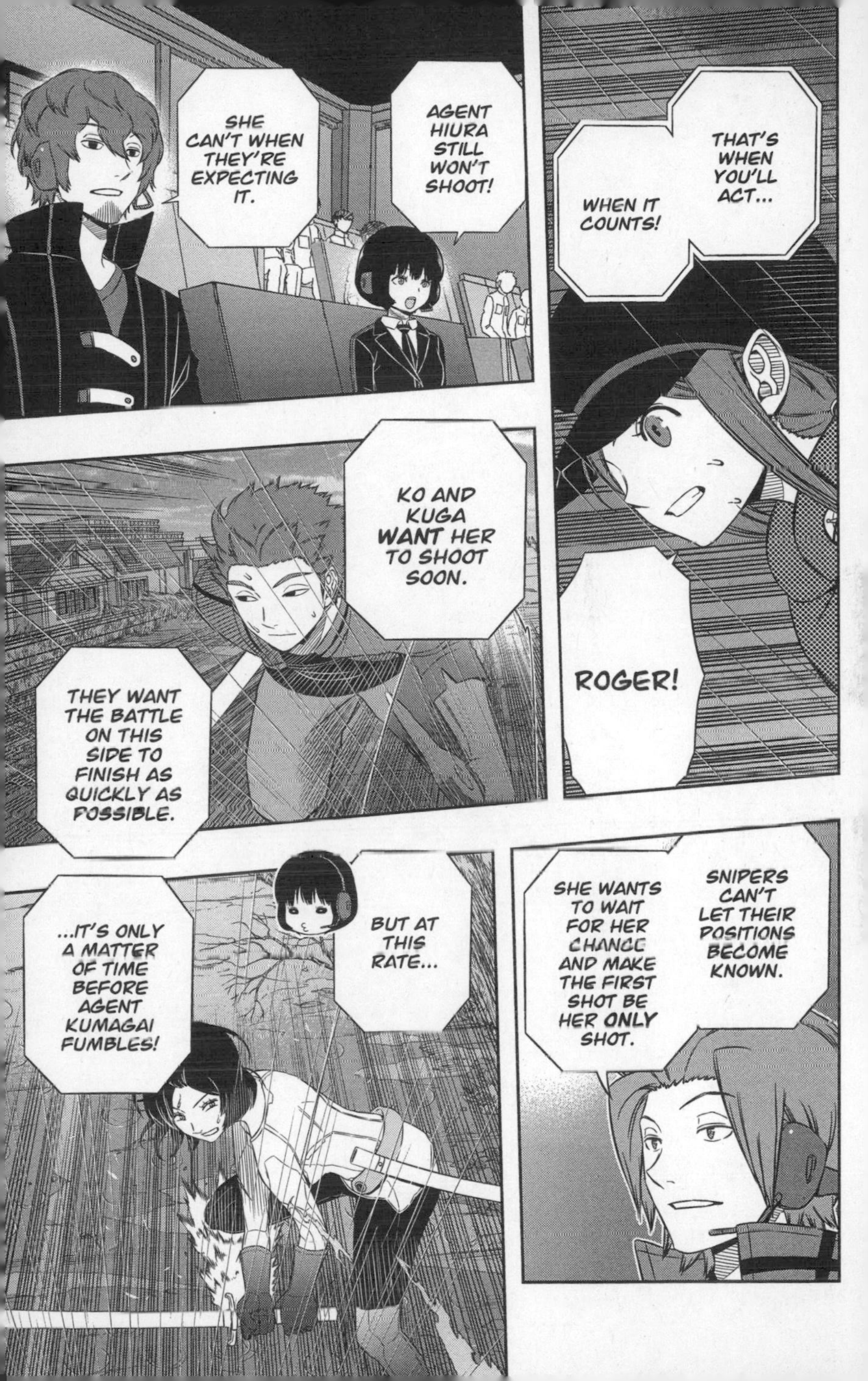
THAT'S WHEN YOU'LL ACT...
WHEN IT COUNTS!
ROGER!
AGENT HIURA STILL WON'T SHOOT!
SHE CAN'T WHEN THEY'RE EXPECTING IT.
KO AND KUGA WANT HER TO SHOOT SOON.
THEY WANT THE BATTLE ON THIS SIDE TO FINISH AS QUICKLY AS POSSIBLE.
SNIPERS CAN'T LET THEIR POSITIONS BECOME KNOWN.
SHE WANTS TO WAIT FOR HER CHANCE AND MAKE THE FIRST SHOT BE HER ONLY SHOT.
BUT AT THIS RATE...
...IT'S ONLY A MATTER OF TIME BEFORE AGENT KUMAGAI FUMBLES!

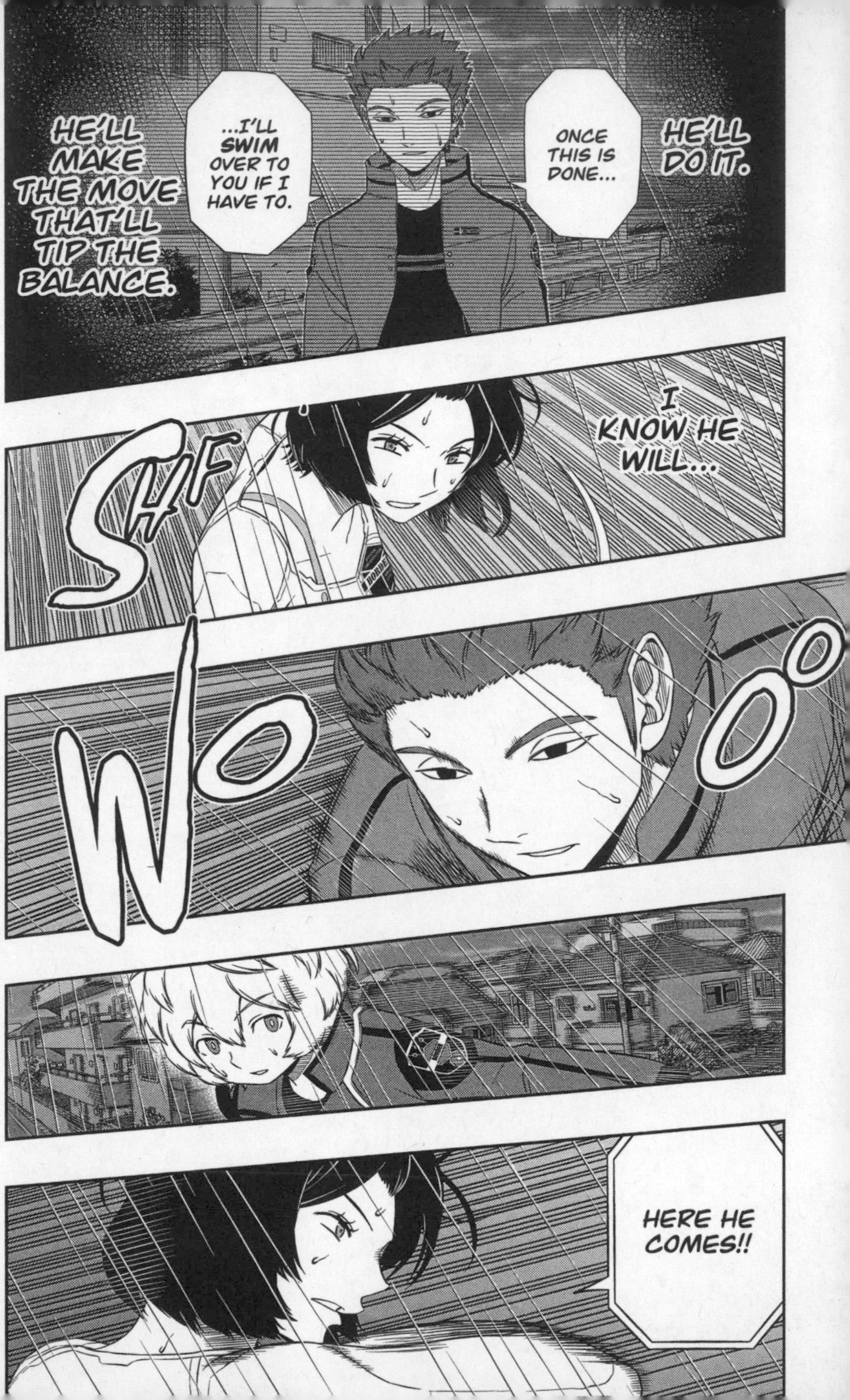

HE'LL DO IT.
ONCE THIS IS DONE...
...I'LL SWIM OVER TO YOU IF I HAVE TO.
HE'LL MAKE THE MOVE THAT'LL TIP THE BALANCE.
I KNOW HE WILL...
SHF
WOOO
HERE HE COMES!!

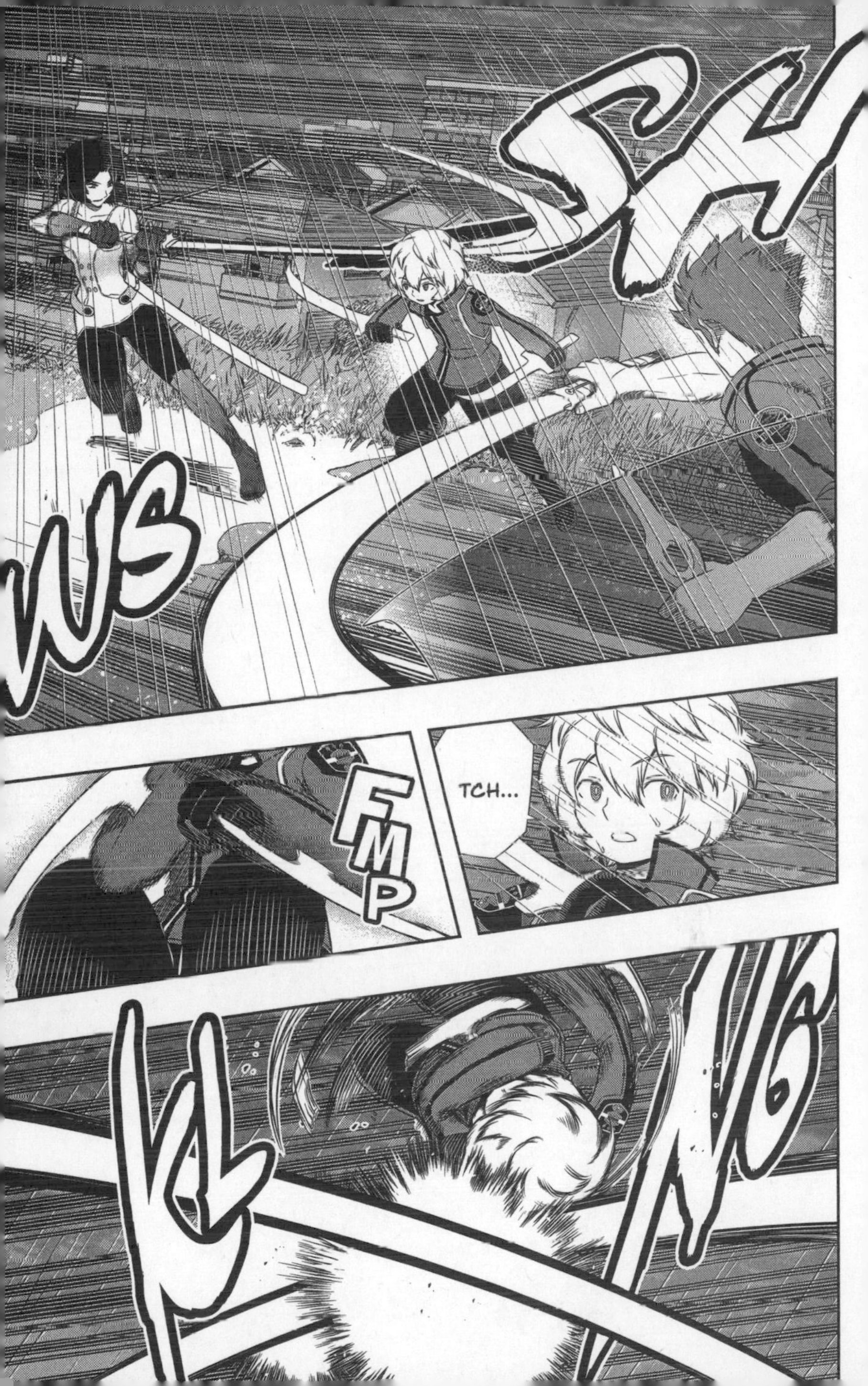
WS
TCH...
FMP
KL
NG

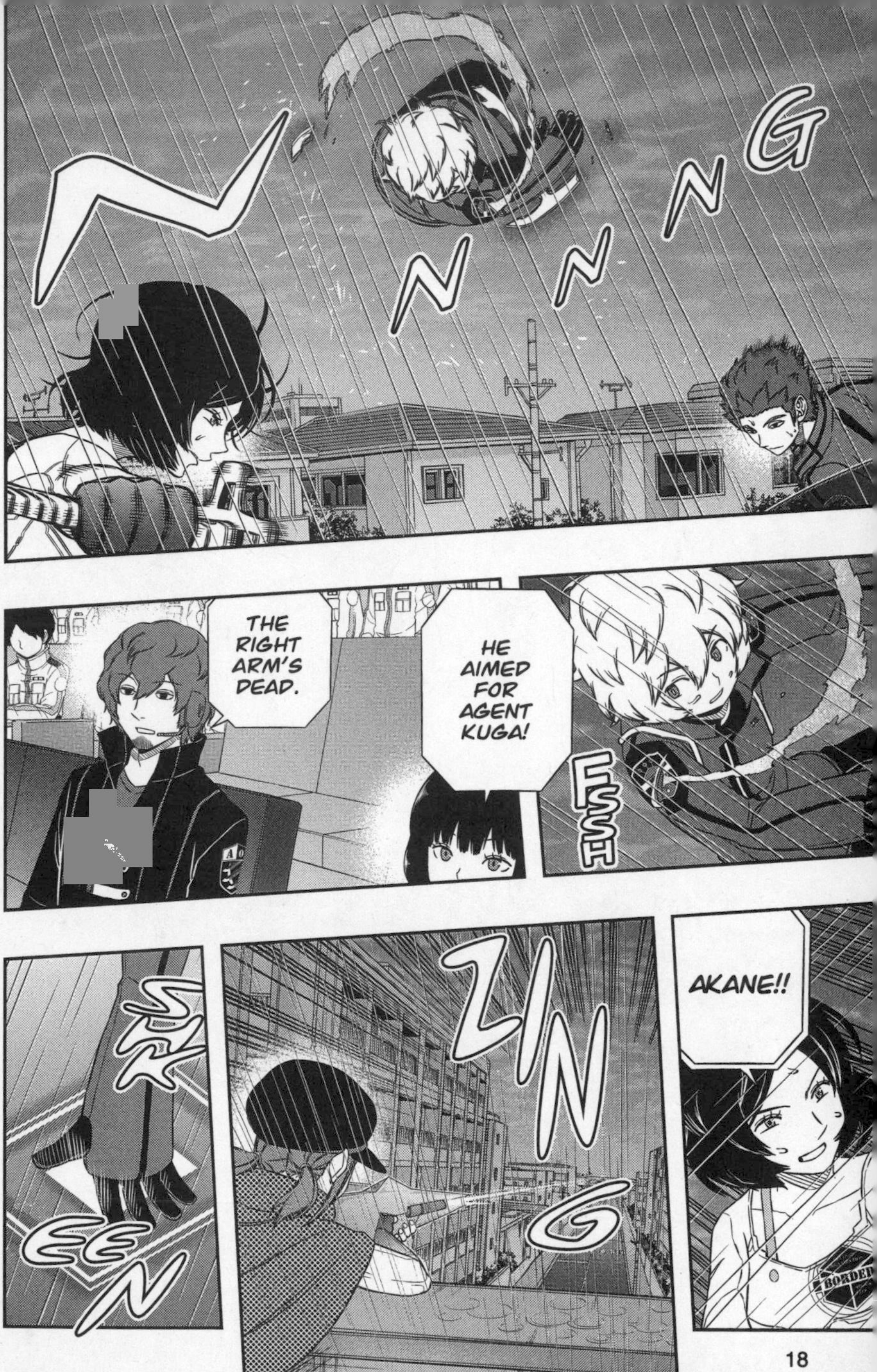
V-NNNG
FSSH
HE AIMED FOR AGENT KUGA!
THE RIGHT ARM'S DEAD.
AKANE!!
ZING
SHKEEN

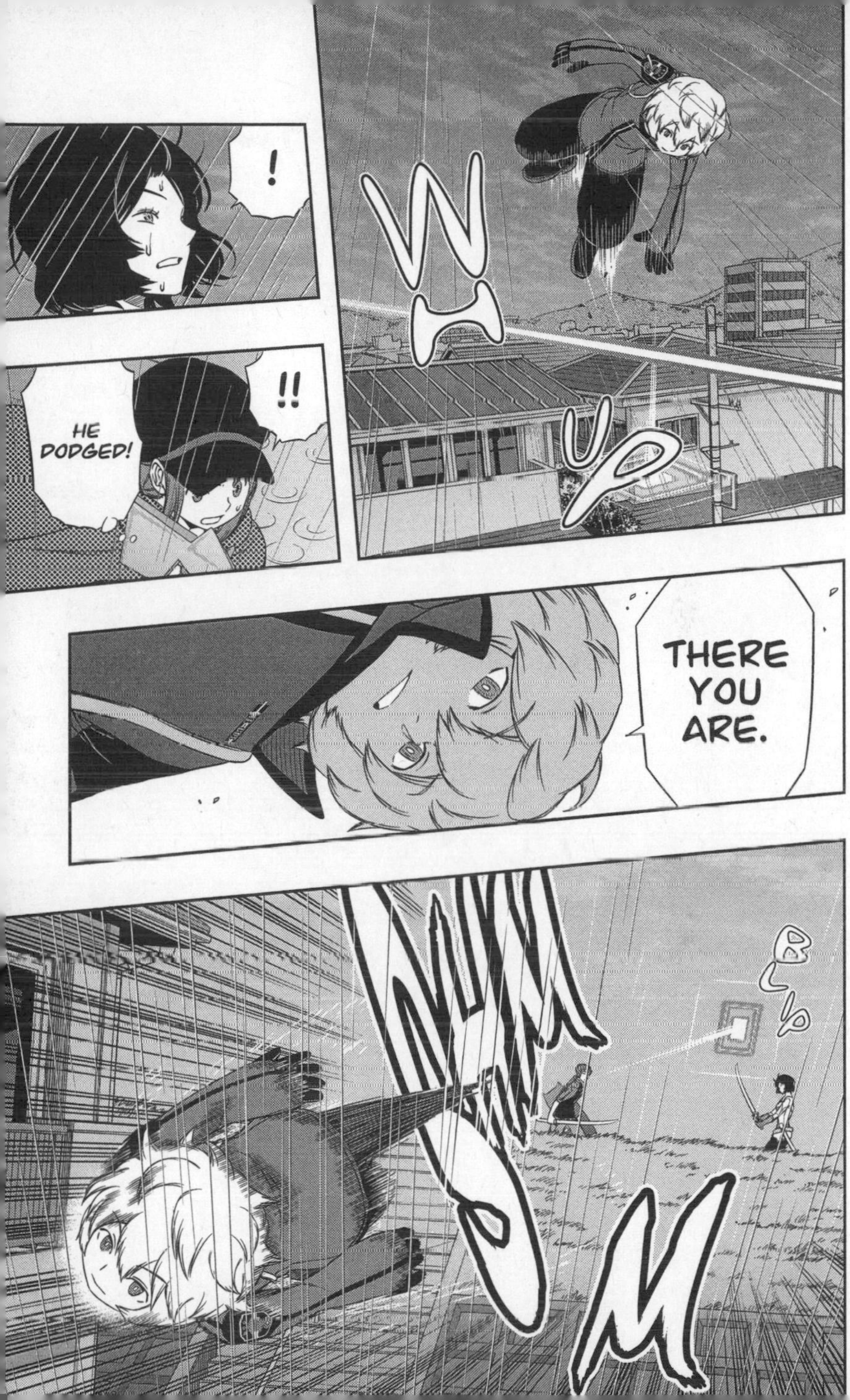
WHUP
!
!!
HE DODGED!
THERE YOU ARE.
BLIP
WHAMM

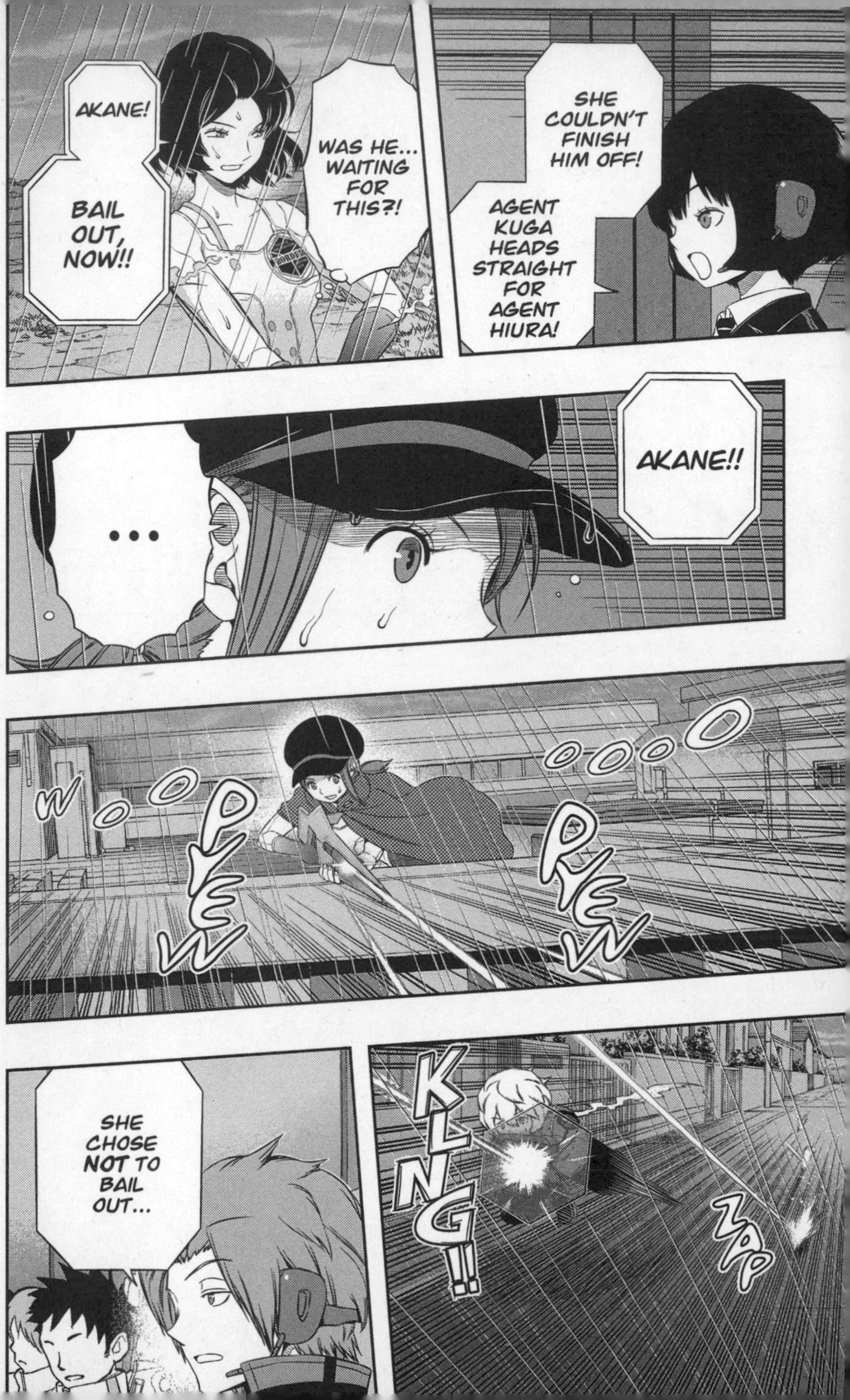

SHE COULDN'T FINISH HIM OFF!
AGENT KUGA HEADS STRAIGHT FOR AGENT HIURA!
WAS HE... WAITING FOR THIS?!
AKANE!
BAIL OUT, NOW!!
AKANE!!
...
OOOOO
WOOO
PYEW
PYEW
KLNG!!
ZAP
SHE CHOSE NOT TO BAIL OUT...

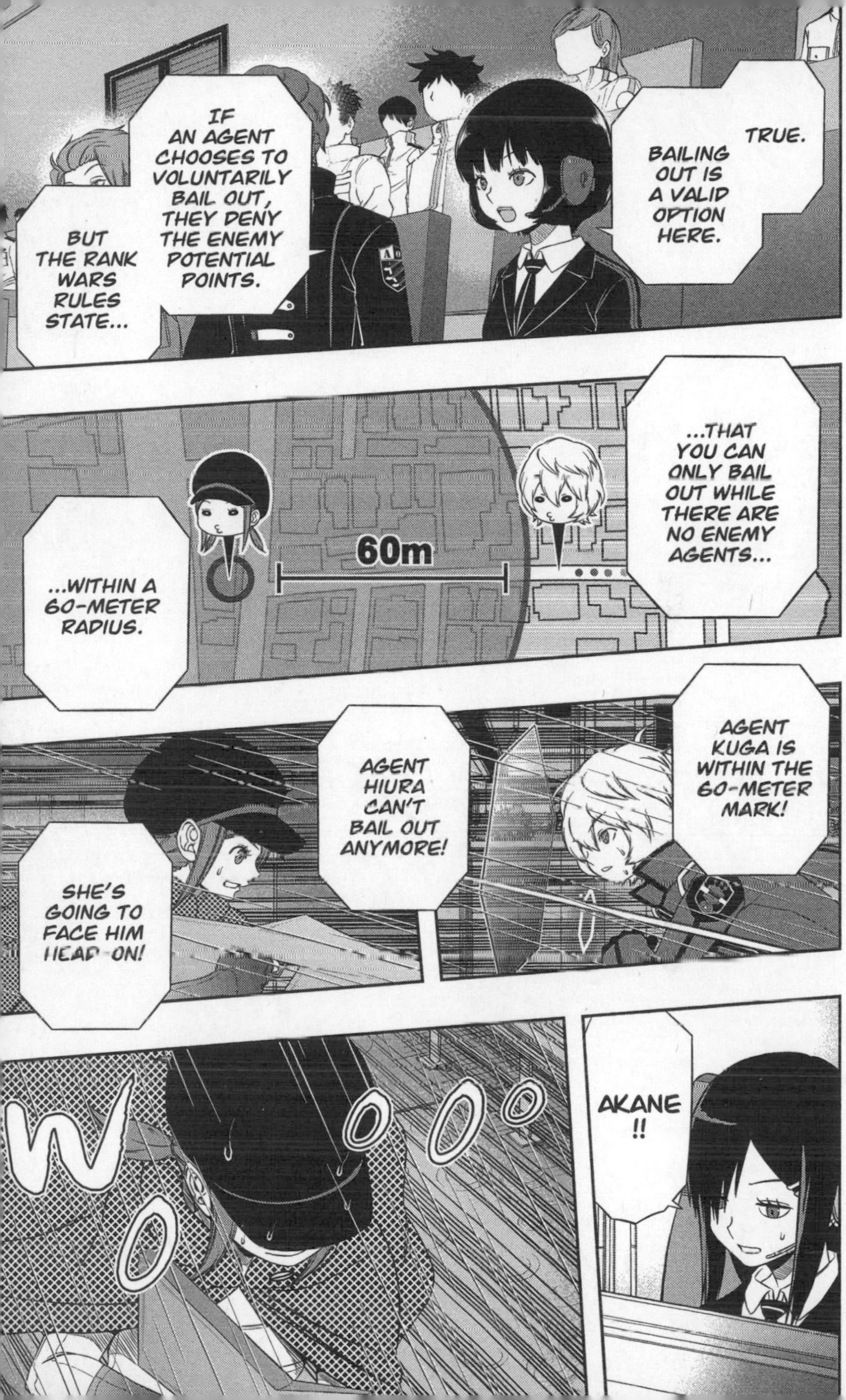
TRUE. BAILING OUT IS A VALID OPTION HERE.
IF AN AGENT CHOOSES TO VOLUNTARILY BAIL OUT, THEY DENY THE ENEMY POTENTIAL POINTS.
BUT THE RANK WARS RULES STATE...
...THAT YOU CAN ONLY BAIL OUT WHILE THERE ARE NO ENEMY AGENTS...
60m
...WITHIN A 60-METER RADIUS.
AGENT KUGA IS WITHIN THE 60-METER MARK!
AGENT HIURA CAN'T BAIL OUT ANYMORE!
SHE'S GOING TO FACE HIM HEAD-ON!
AKANE!!
WOOOO

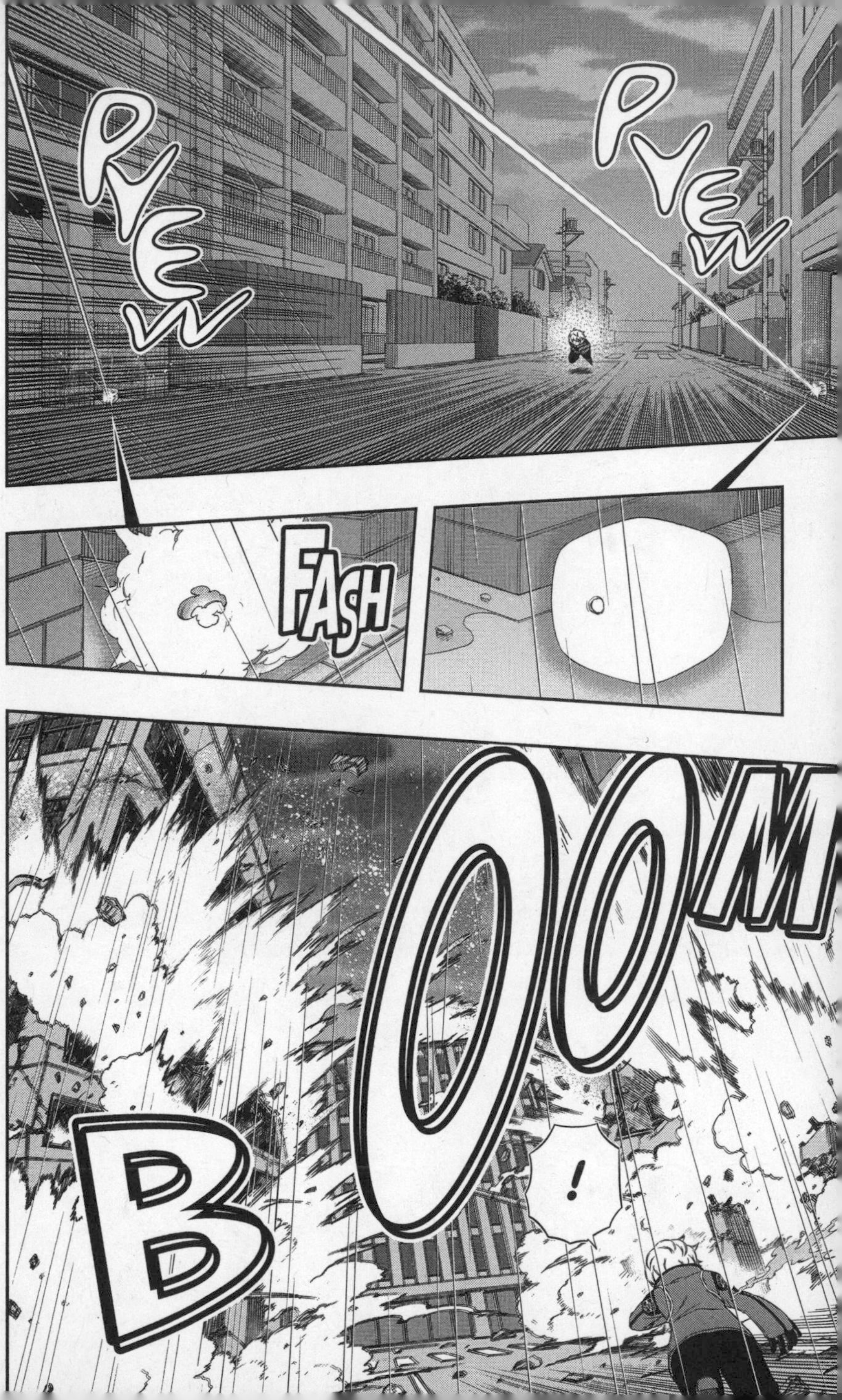
PYEW
PYEW
FASH
BOOM
!

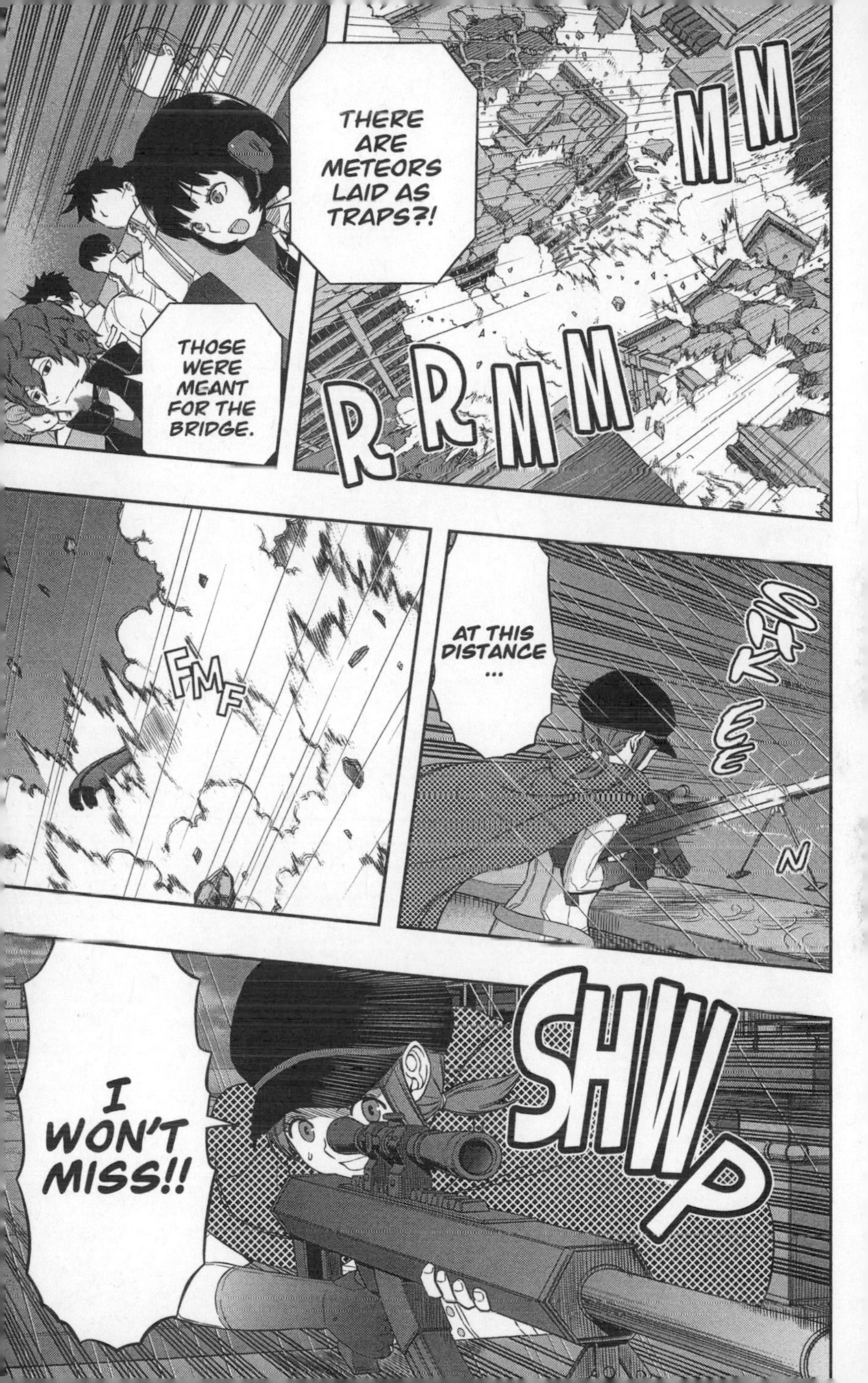
RRMMMM
THERE ARE METEORS LAID AS TRAPS?!
THOSE WERE MEANT FOR THE BRIDGE.
SKREEEN
AT THIS DISTANCE ...
FMF
SHWP
I WON'T MISS!!

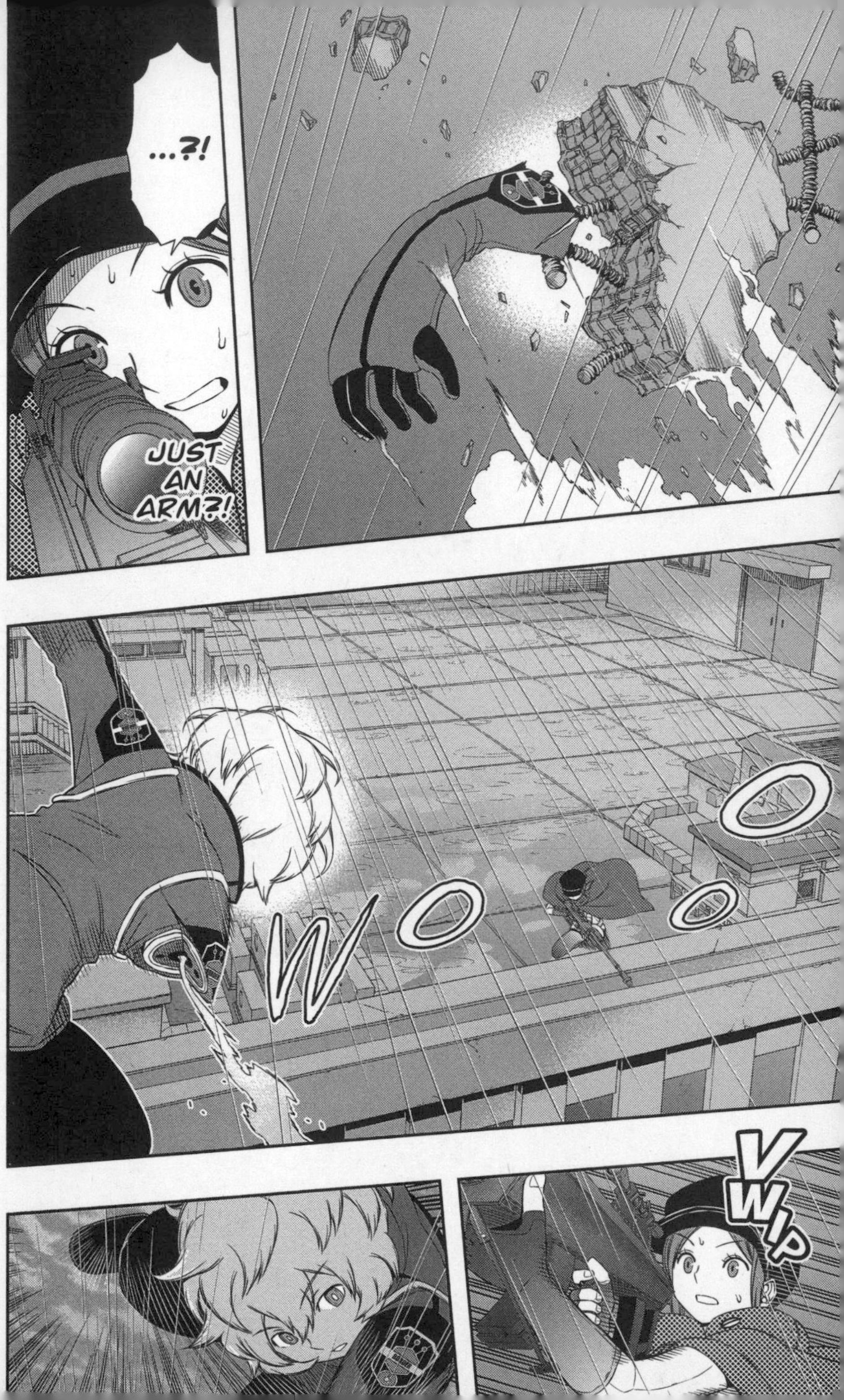
...?!
JUST AN ARM?!
WOOO
VWIP

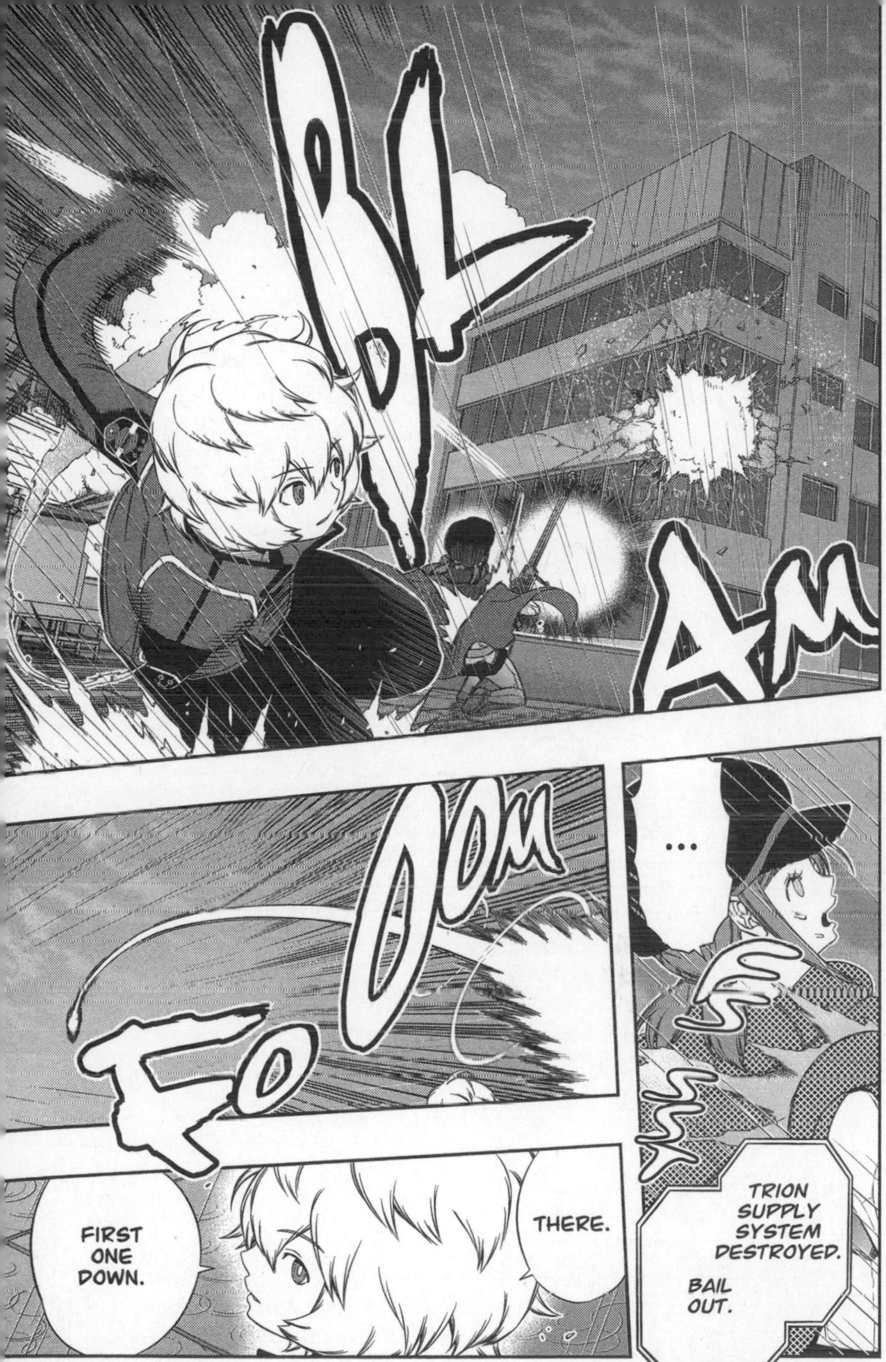
BLAM
...
FOOOM
TRION SUPPLY SYSTEM DESTROYED.
BAIL OUT.
THERE.
FIRST ONE DOWN.

■ **2015 _Weekly Shonen Jump_ 37/38 combined issue cover**
An illustration for the combined issue cover. I was told to draw Yuma with a squirt gun, so I gave him a quick-firing gun with an extra attachment. It's probably too heavy to run with in real life.

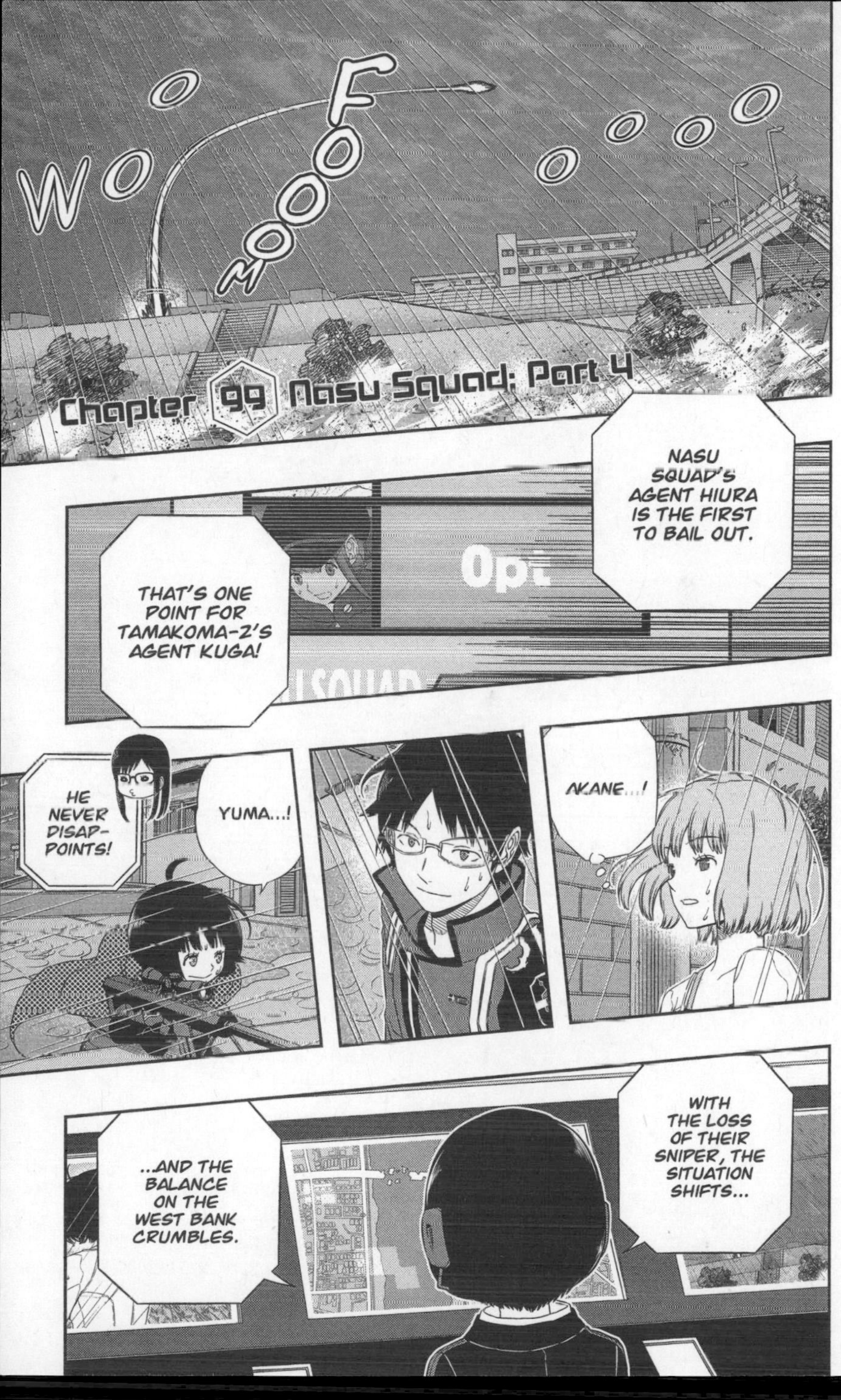
WOOOF
OOOOO
Chapter 99 Nasu Squad: Part 4
NASU SQUAD'S AGENT HIURA IS THE FIRST TO BAIL OUT.
0pt
THAT'S ONE POINT FOR TAMAKOMA-2'S AGENT KUGA!
AKANE...!
YUMA...!
HE NEVER DISAP-POINTS!
WITH THE LOSS OF THEIR SNIPER, THE SITUATION SHIFTS...
...AND THE BALANCE ON THE WEST BANK CRUMBLES.

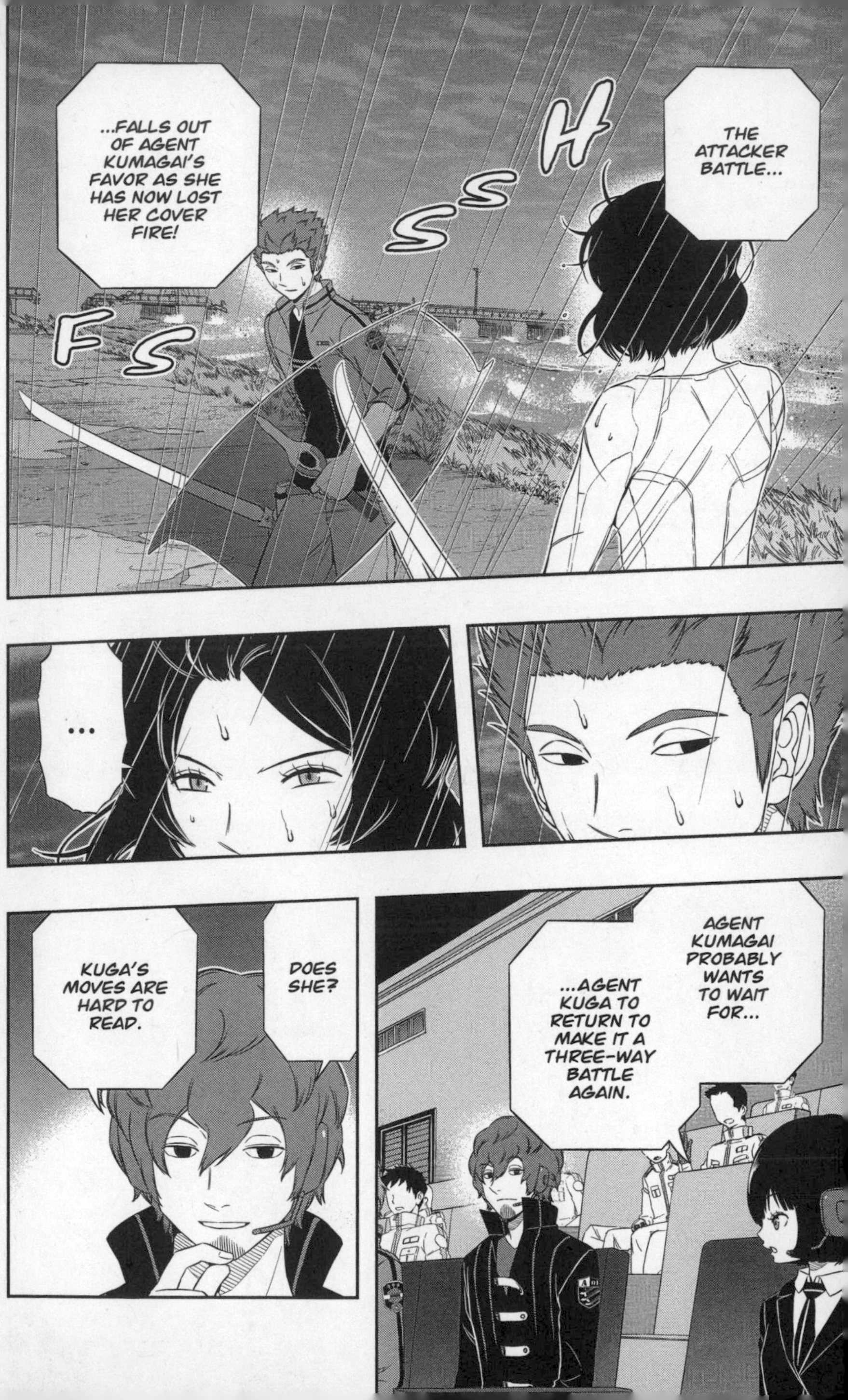
THE ATTACKER BATTLE...
SSSH
...FALLS OUT OF AGENT KUMAGAI'S FAVOR AS SHE HAS NOW LOST HER COVER FIRE!
FS
...
AGENT KUMAGAI PROBABLY WANTS TO WAIT FOR...
...AGENT KUGA TO RETURN TO MAKE IT A THREE-WAY BATTLE AGAIN.
DOES SHE?
KUGA'S MOVES ARE HARD TO READ.

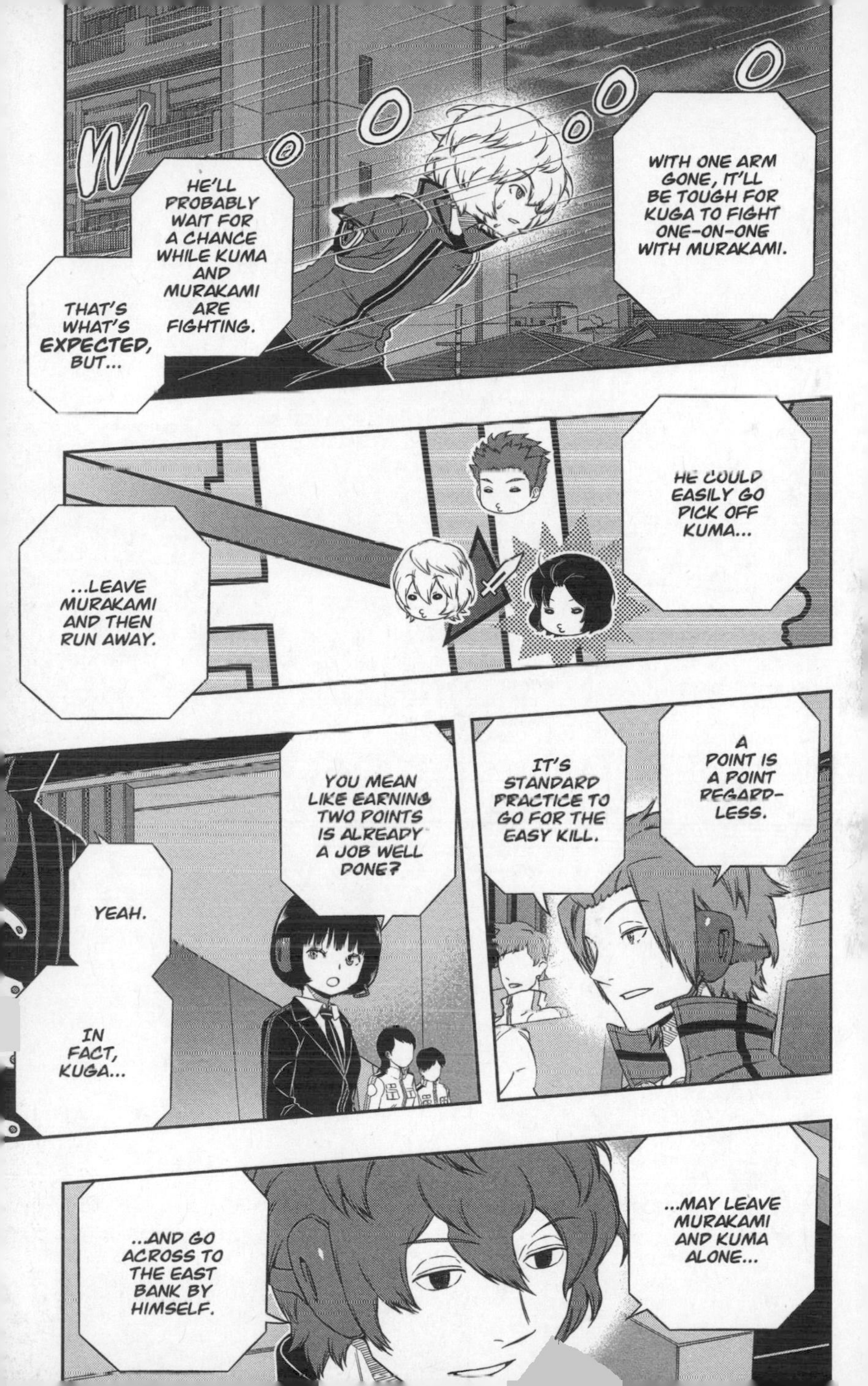
WOOOOOO
WITH ONE ARM GONE, IT'LL BE TOUGH FOR KUGA TO FIGHT ONE-ON-ONE WITH MURAKAMI.
HE'LL PROBABLY WAIT FOR A CHANCE WHILE KUMA AND MURAKAMI ARE FIGHTING.
THAT'S WHAT'S EXPECTED, BUT...
HE COULD EASILY GO PICK OFF KUMA...
...LEAVE MURAKAMI AND THEN RUN AWAY.
A POINT IS A POINT REGARDLESS.
IT'S STANDARD PRACTICE TO GO FOR THE EASY KILL.
YOU MEAN LIKE EARNING TWO POINTS IS ALREADY A JOB WELL DONE?
YEAH.
IN FACT, KUGA...
...MAY LEAVE MURAKAMI AND KUMA ALONE...
...AND GO ACROSS TO THE EAST BANK BY HIMSELF.

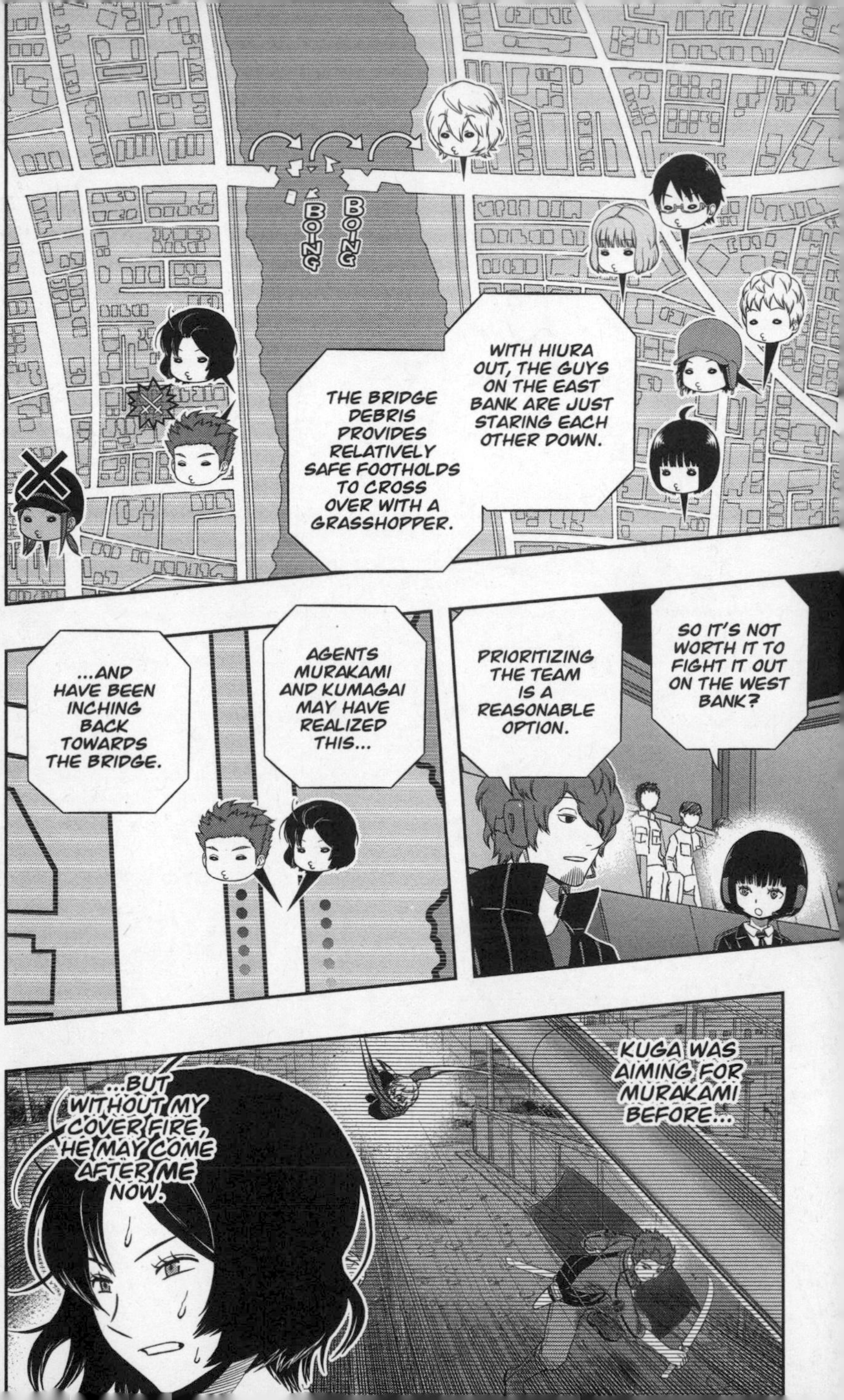
BOING
BOING
WITH HIURA OUT, THE GUYS ON THE EAST BANK ARE JUST STARING EACH OTHER DOWN.
THE BRIDGE DEBRIS PROVIDES RELATIVELY SAFE FOOTHOLDS TO CROSS OVER WITH A GRASSHOPPER.
SO IT'S NOT WORTH IT TO FIGHT IT OUT ON THE WEST BANK?
PRIORITIZING THE TEAM IS A REASONABLE OPTION.
AGENTS MURAKAMI AND KUMAGAI MAY HAVE REALIZED THIS...
...AND HAVE BEEN INCHING BACK TOWARDS THE BRIDGE.
KUGA WAS AIMING FOR MURAKAMI BEFORE...
...BUT WITHOUT MY COVER FIRE, HE MAY COME AFTER ME NOW.

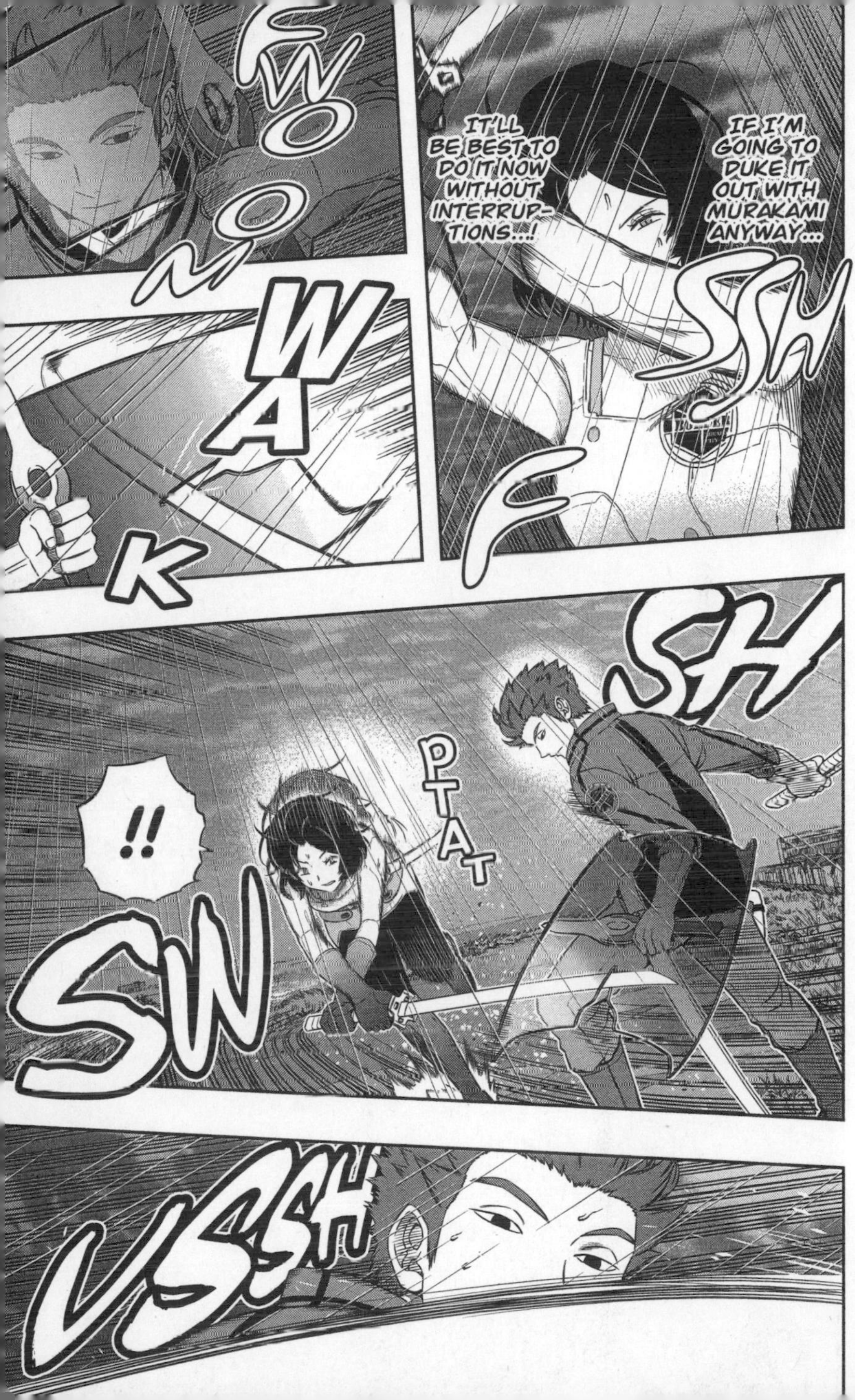
IF I'M GOING TO DUKE IT OUT WITH MURAKAMI ANYWAY...
IT'LL BE BEST TO DO IT NOW WITHOUT INTERRUP-TIONS...!
SSH
F
FWOOM
WAK
SSH
PTAT
!!
SWN
VSSH

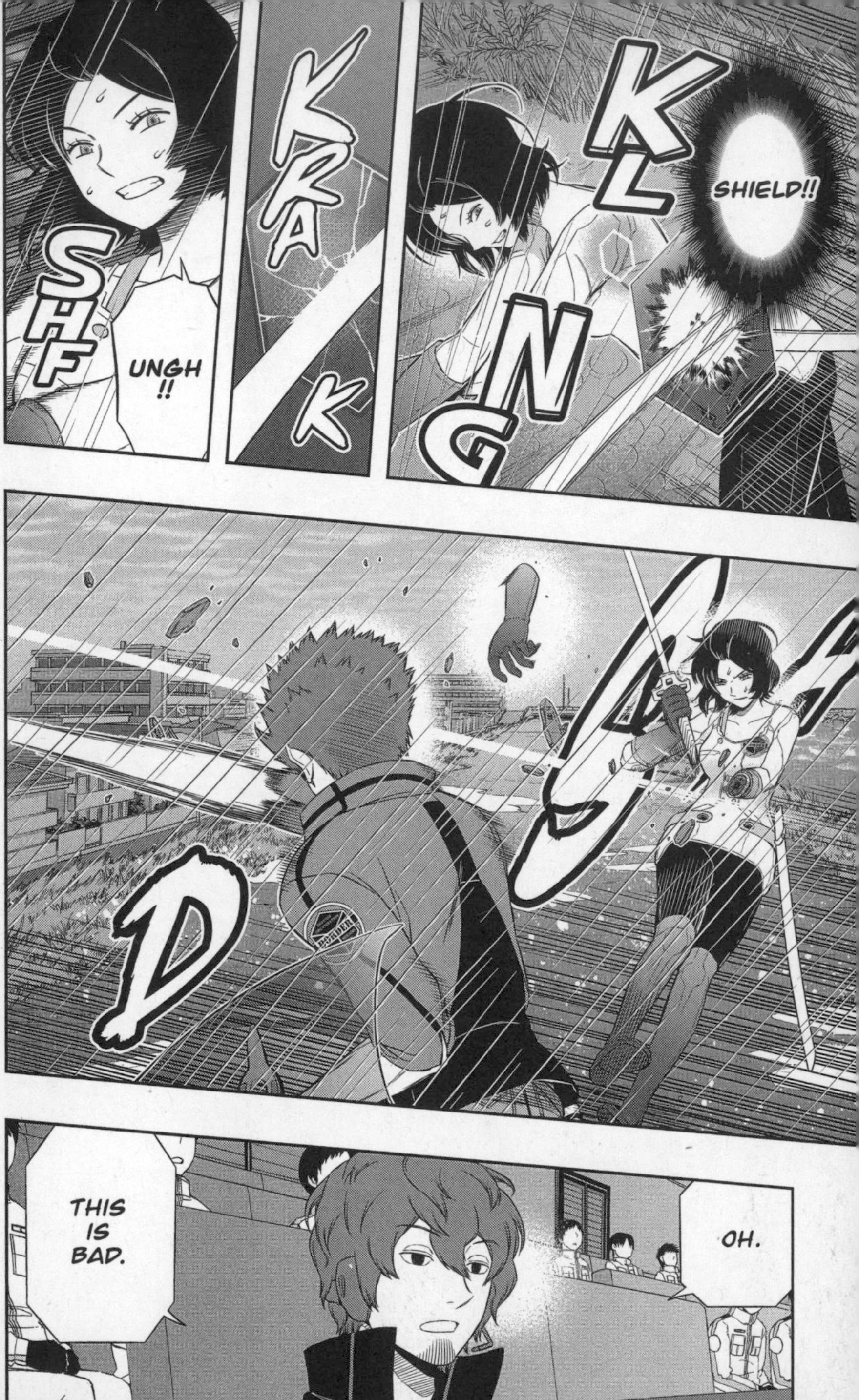
KLNG
SHIELD!!
KRAK
SHF
UNGH!!
D
OH.
THIS IS BAD.

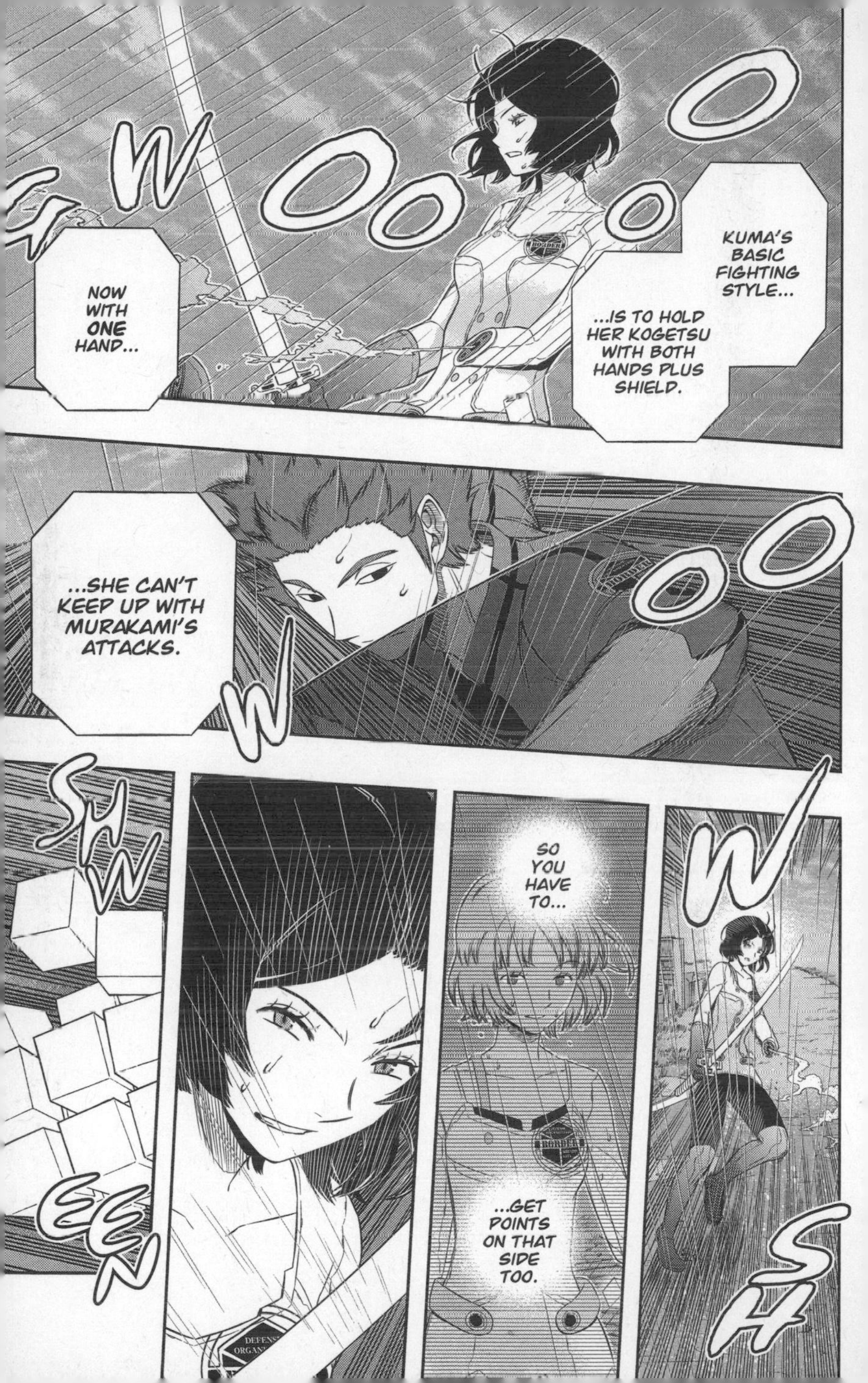
KUMA'S BASIC FIGHTING STYLE...
...IS TO HOLD HER KOGETSU WITH BOTH HANDS PLUS SHIELD.
NOW WITH ONE HAND...
...SHE CAN'T KEEP UP WITH MURAKAMI'S ATTACKS.
SO YOU HAVE TO...
...GET POINTS ON THAT SIDE TOO.

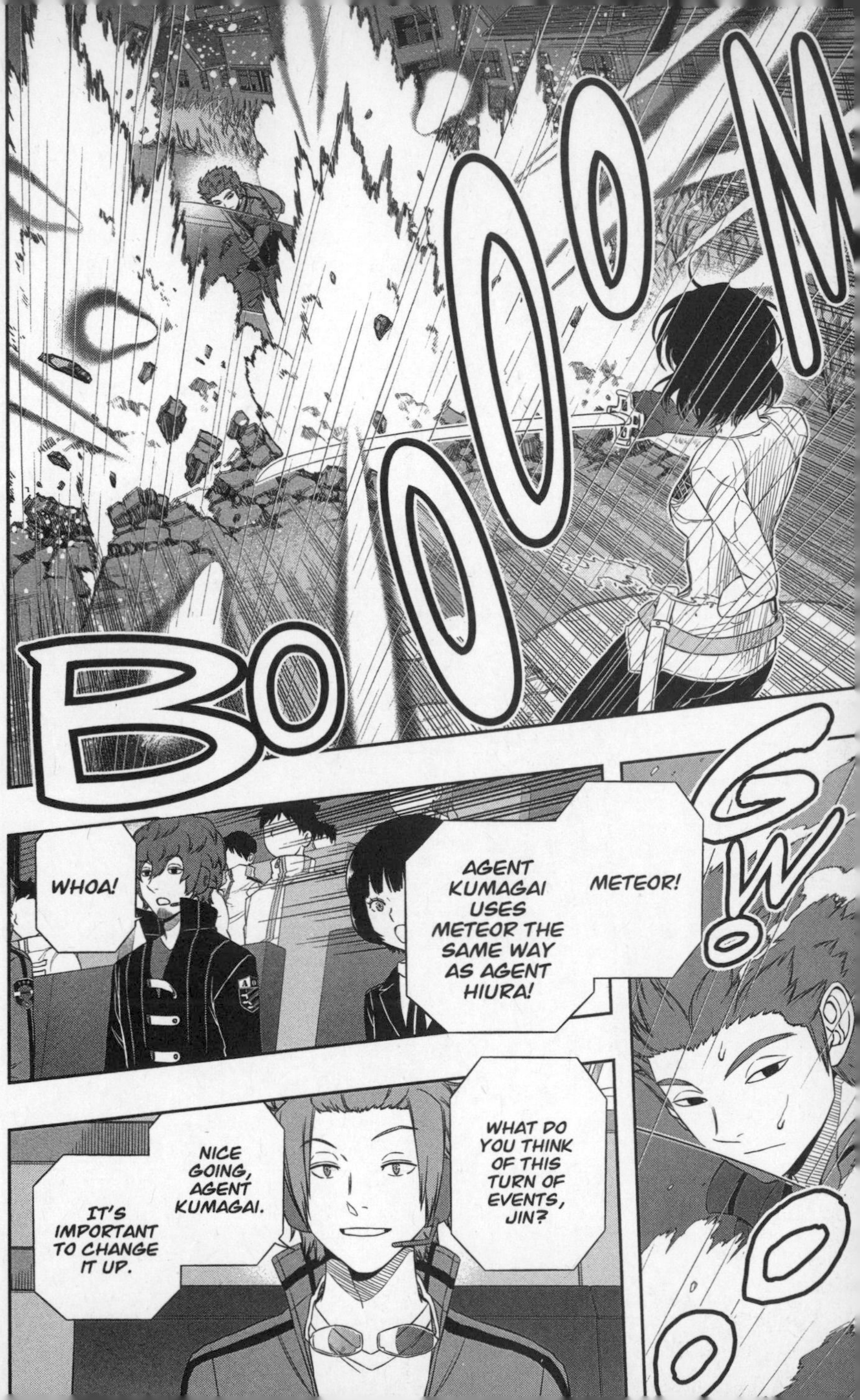
BOOOOOM
GWOOOO
METEOR!
AGENT KUMAGAI USES METEOR THE SAME WAY AS AGENT HIURA!
WHOA!
WHAT DO YOU THINK OF THIS TURN OF EVENTS, JIN?
NICE GOING, AGENT KUMAGAI.
IT'S IMPORTANT TO CHANGE IT UP.

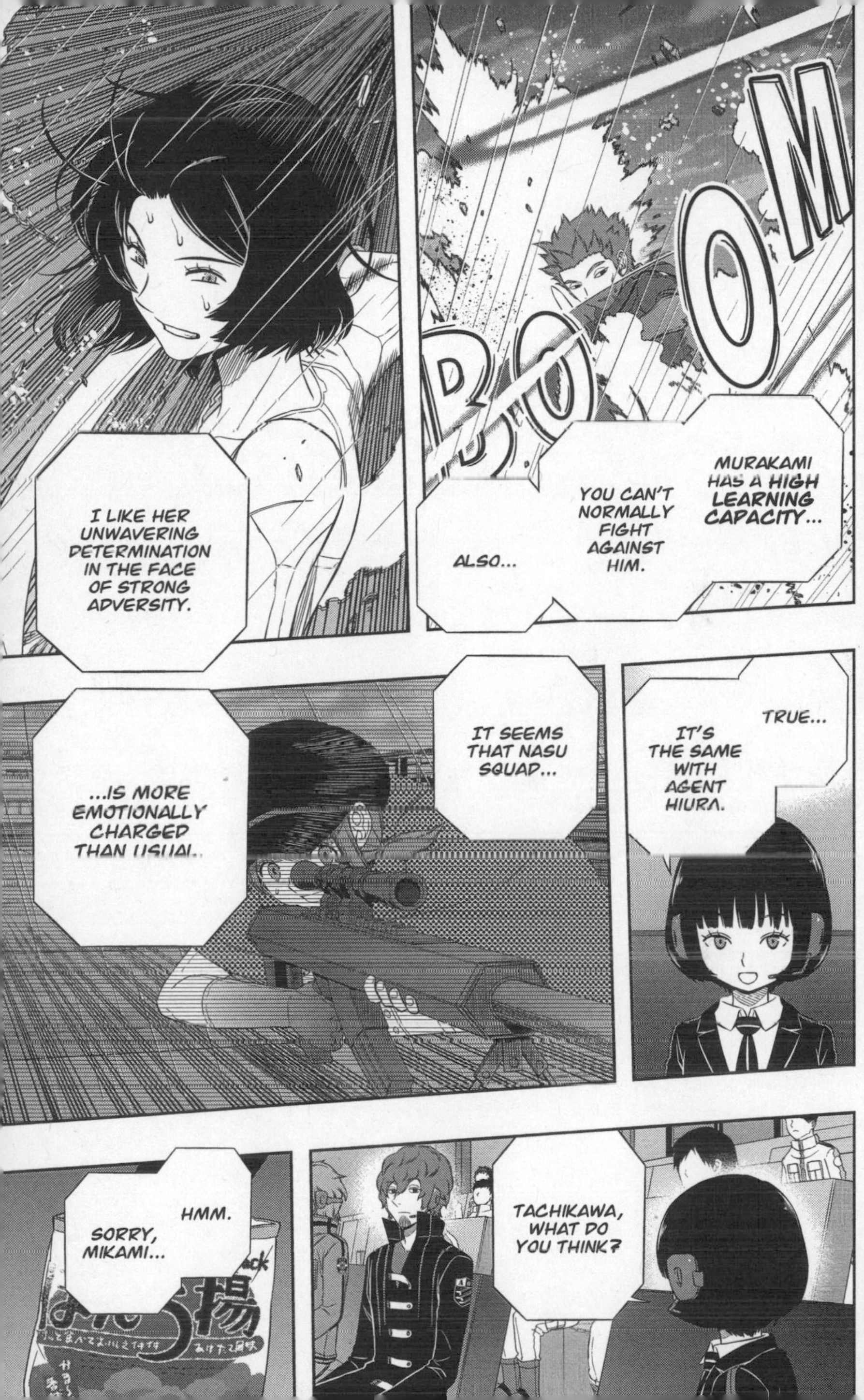
BOOOM
MURAKAMI HAS A HIGH LEARNING CAPACITY...
YOU CAN'T NORMALLY FIGHT AGAINST HIM.
ALSO...
I LIKE HER UNWAVERING DETERMINATION IN THE FACE OF STRONG ADVERSITY.
TRUE...
IT'S THE SAME WITH AGENT HIURA.
IT SEEMS THAT NASU SQUAD...
...IS MORE EMOTIONALLY CHARGED THAN USUAL.
TACHIKAWA, WHAT DO YOU THINK?
HMM.
SORRY, MIKAMI...

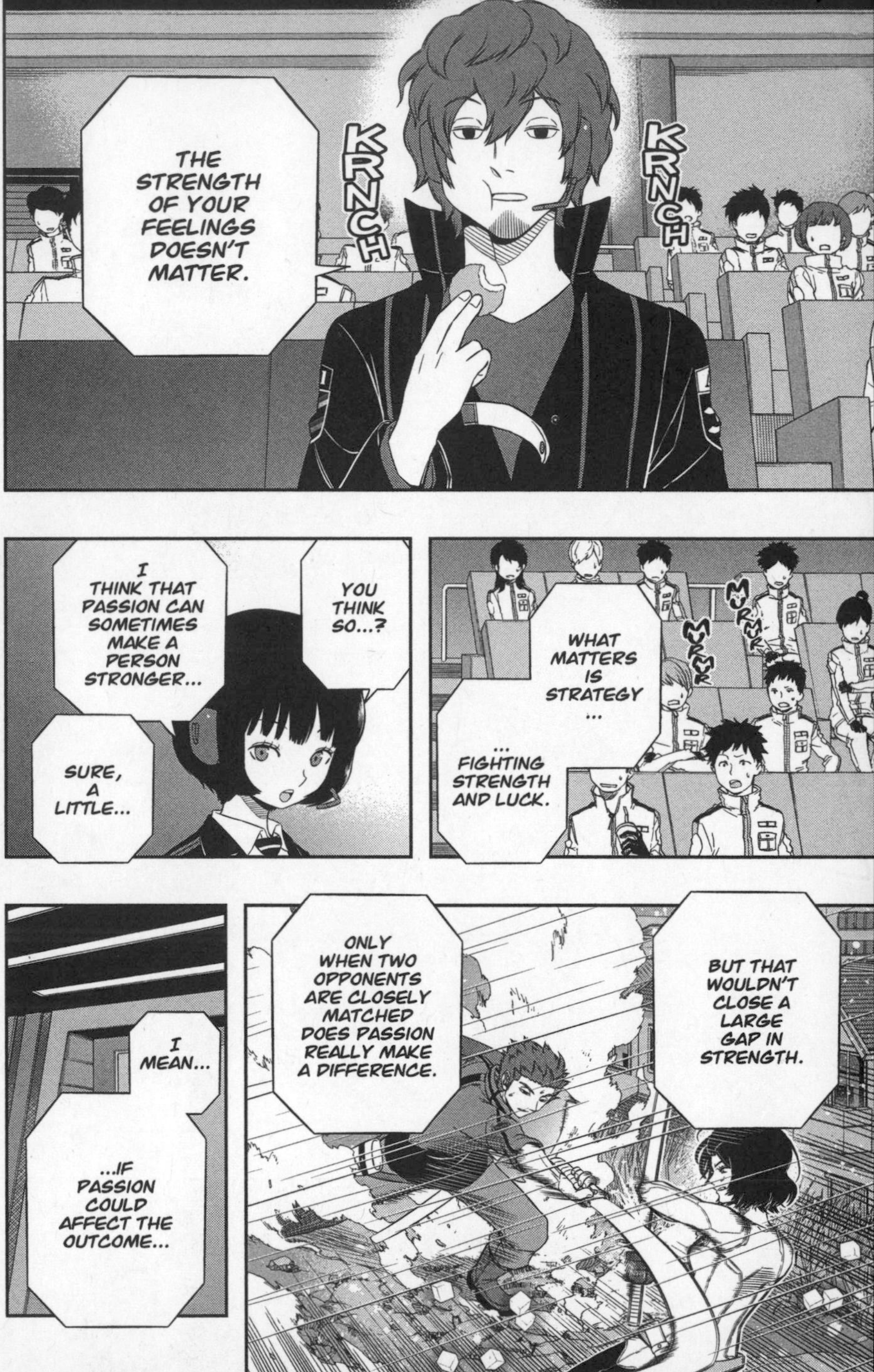
KRNCH
KRNCH
THE STRENGTH OF YOUR FEELINGS DOESN'T MATTER.
MURMUR
MURMUR
WHAT MATTERS IS STRATEGY ...
... FIGHTING STRENGTH AND LUCK.
YOU THINK SO...?
I THINK THAT PASSION CAN SOMETIMES MAKE A PERSON STRONGER...
SURE, A LITTLE...
ONLY WHEN TWO OPPONENTS ARE CLOSELY MATCHED DOES PASSION REALLY MAKE A DIFFERENCE.
BUT THAT WOULDN'T CLOSE A LARGE GAP IN STRENGTH.
I MEAN...
...IF PASSION COULD AFFECT THE OUTCOME...

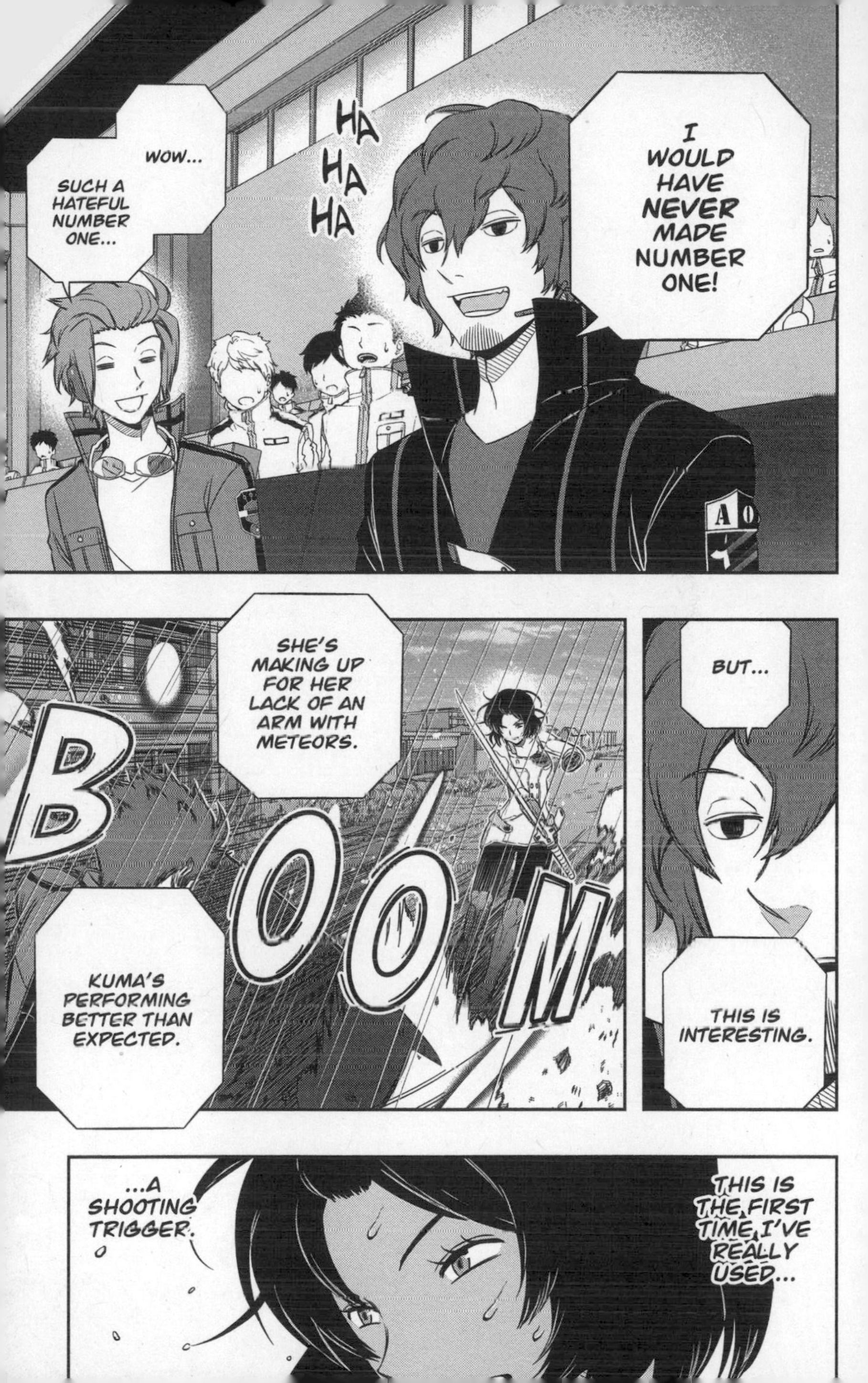
I WOULD HAVE NEVER MADE NUMBER ONE!
HA HA HA
WOW...
SUCH A HATEFUL NUMBER ONE...
BUT...
THIS IS INTERESTING.
SHE'S MAKING UP FOR HER LACK OF AN ARM WITH METEORS.
BOOM
KUMA'S PERFORMING BETTER THAN EXPECTED.
THIS IS THE FIRST TIME I'VE REALLY USED...
...A SHOOTING TRIGGER.

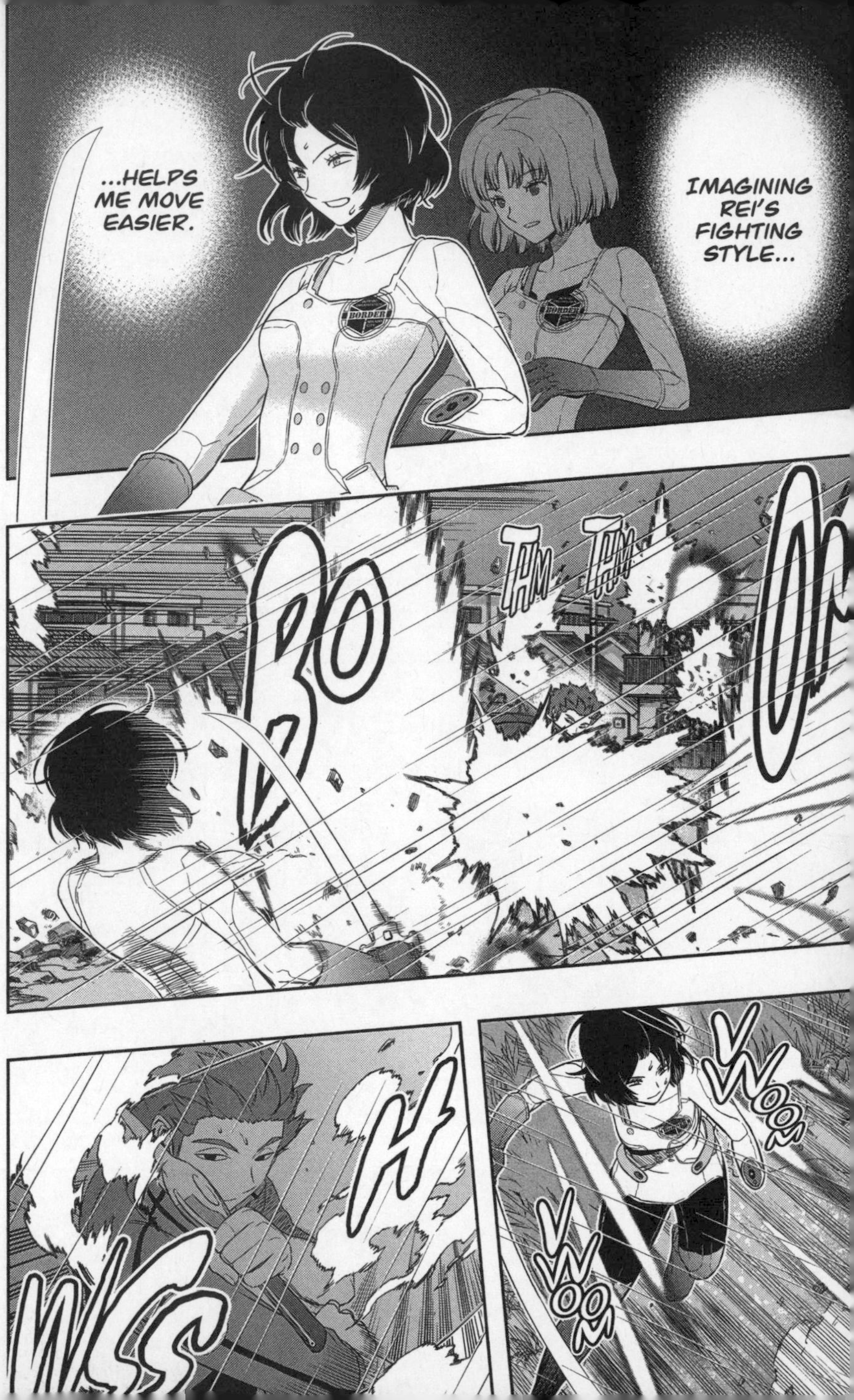
IMAGINING REI'S FIGHTING STYLE...
...HELPS ME MOVE EASIER.
TAM TAM
BO
VWOOM
VWOOM

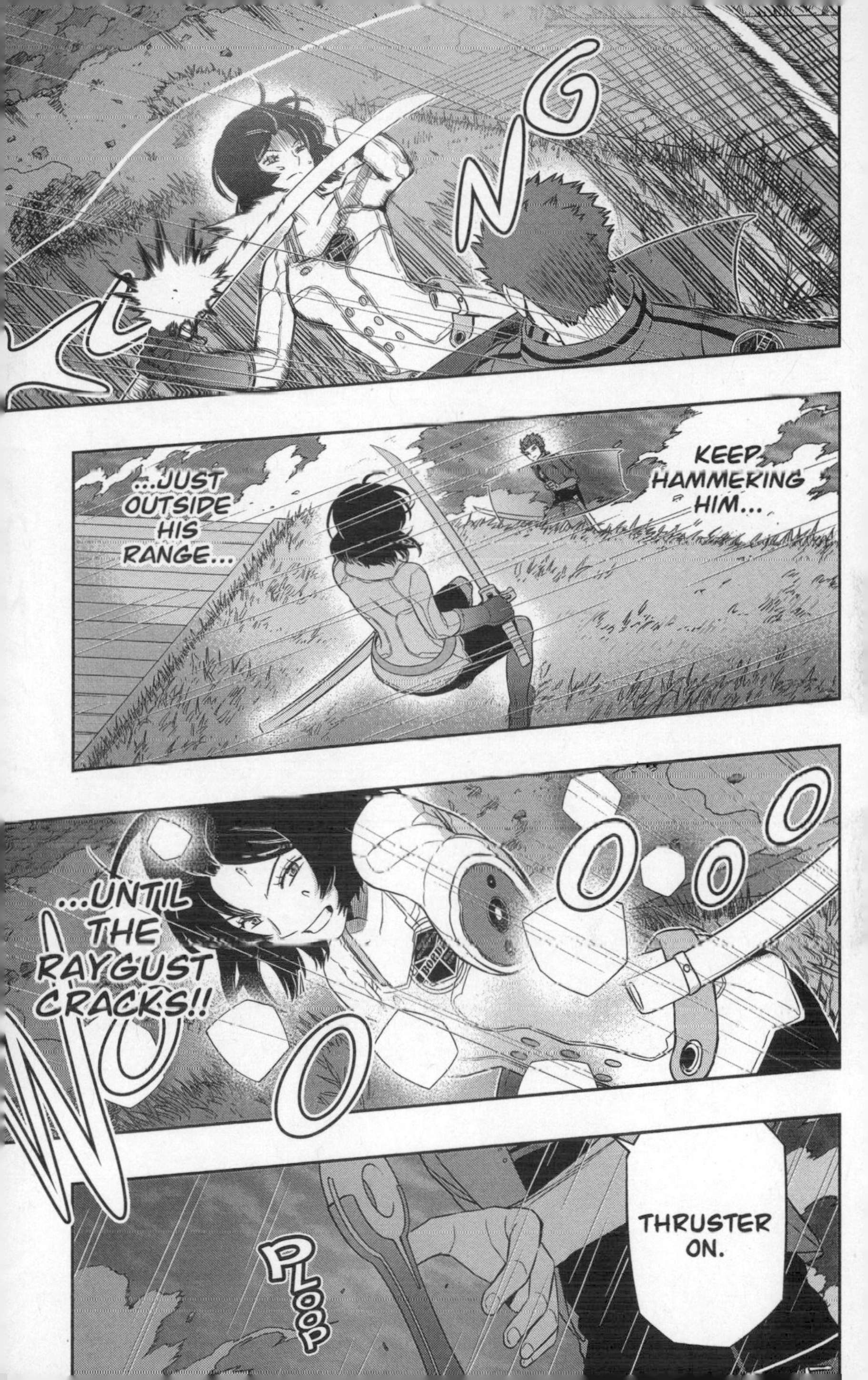
NG
KEEP HAMMERING HIM...
...JUST OUTSIDE HIS RANGE...
...UNTIL THE RAYGUST CRACKS!!
THRUSTER ON.
PLOOP

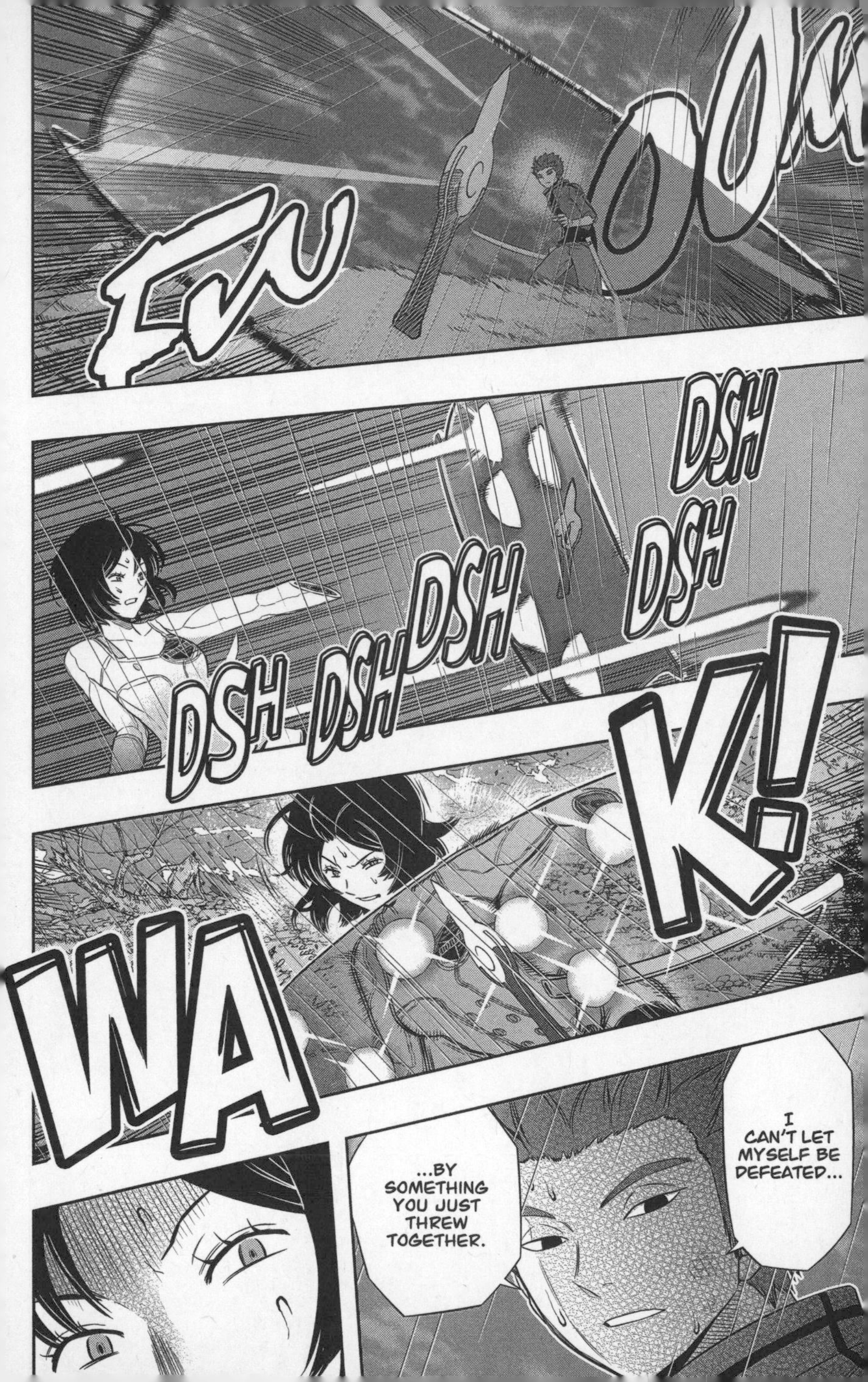

FWOOO
DSH DSH DSH DSH DSH DSH
WAK!
I CAN'T LET MYSELF BE DEFEATED...
...BY SOMETHING YOU JUST THREW TOGETHER.

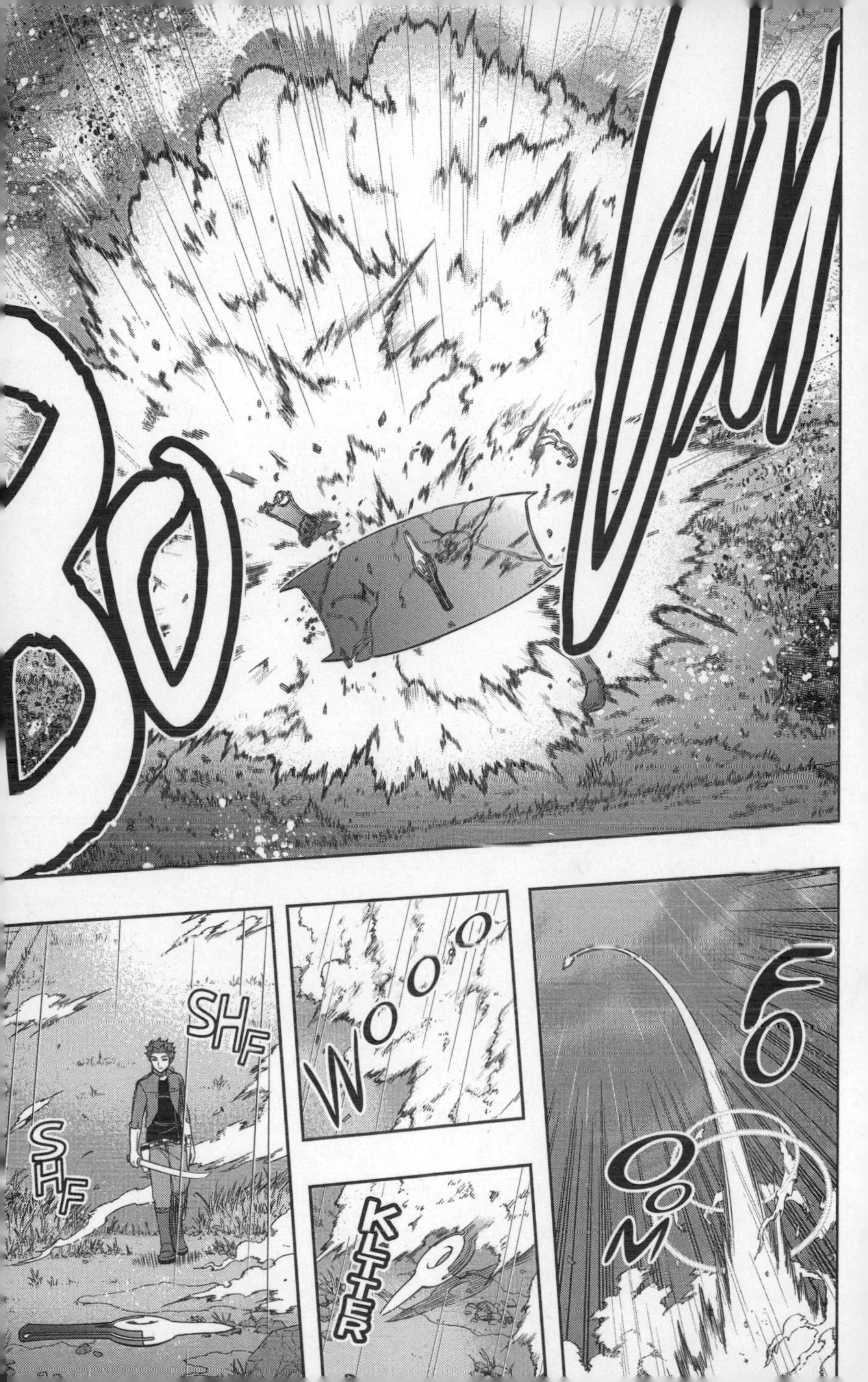

FOOOM
WOOOO
KLITTER
SHF
SHF

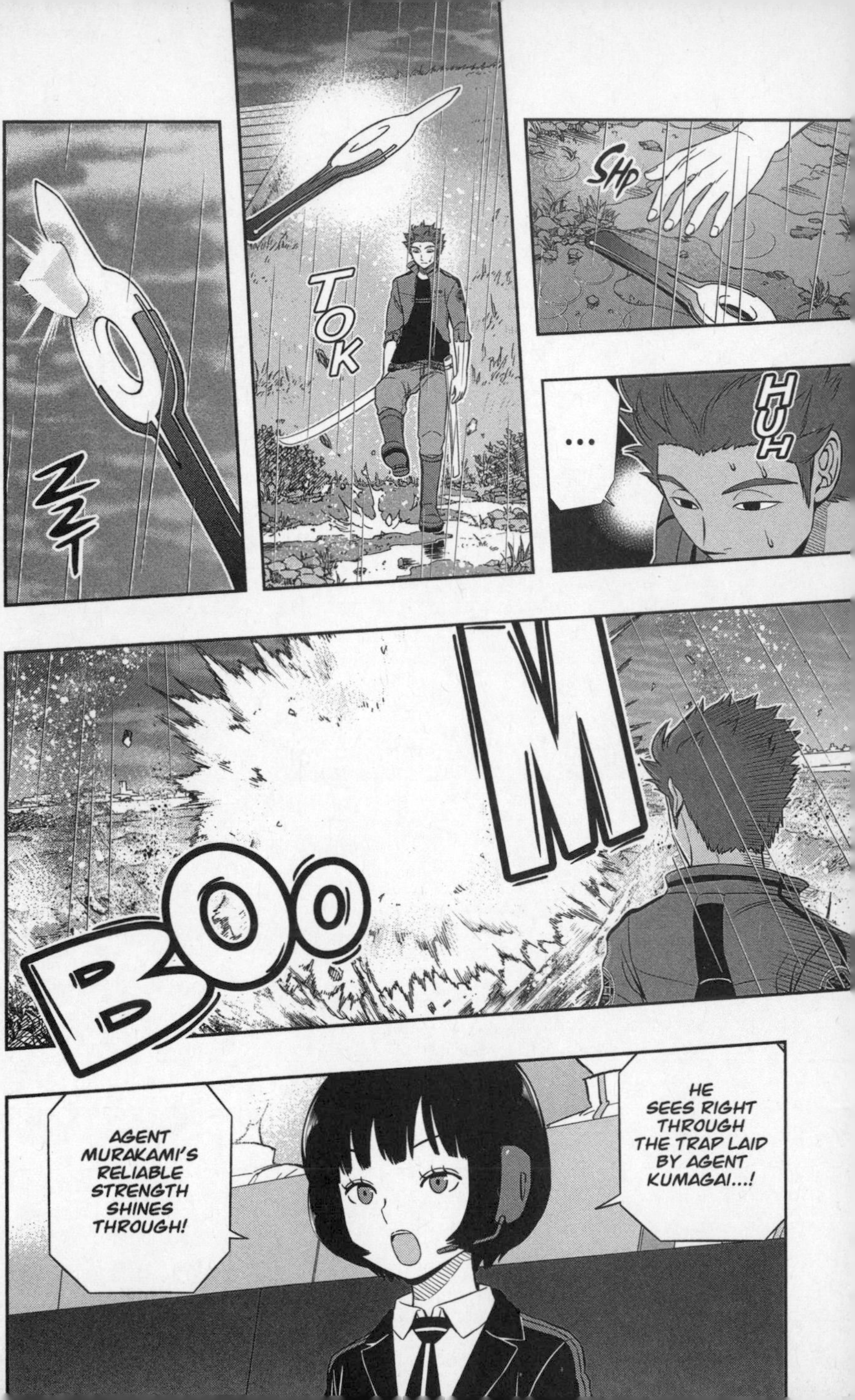

SHP
HUH
...
TOK
ZZZT
BOOOM
HE SEES RIGHT THROUGH THE TRAP LAID BY AGENT KUMAGAI...!
AGENT MURAKAMI'S RELIABLE STRENGTH SHINES THROUGH!

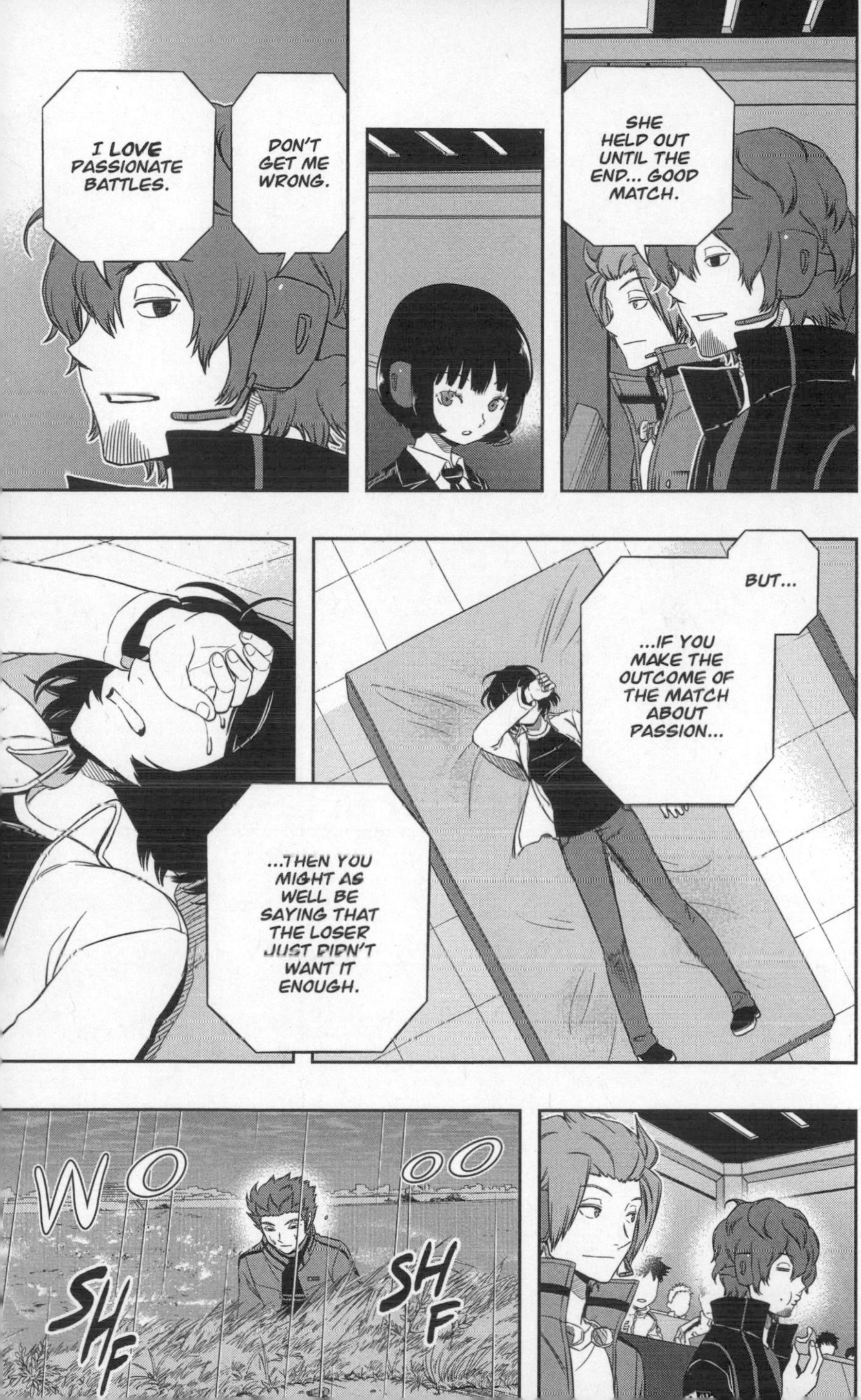
SHE HELD OUT UNTIL THE END... GOOD MATCH.
DON'T GET ME WRONG.
I LOVE PASSIONATE BATTLES.
BUT...
...IF YOU MAKE THE OUTCOME OF THE MATCH ABOUT PASSION...
...THEN YOU MIGHT AS WELL BE SAYING THAT THE LOSER JUST DIDN'T WANT IT ENOUGH.
WOOO
SHF
SHF

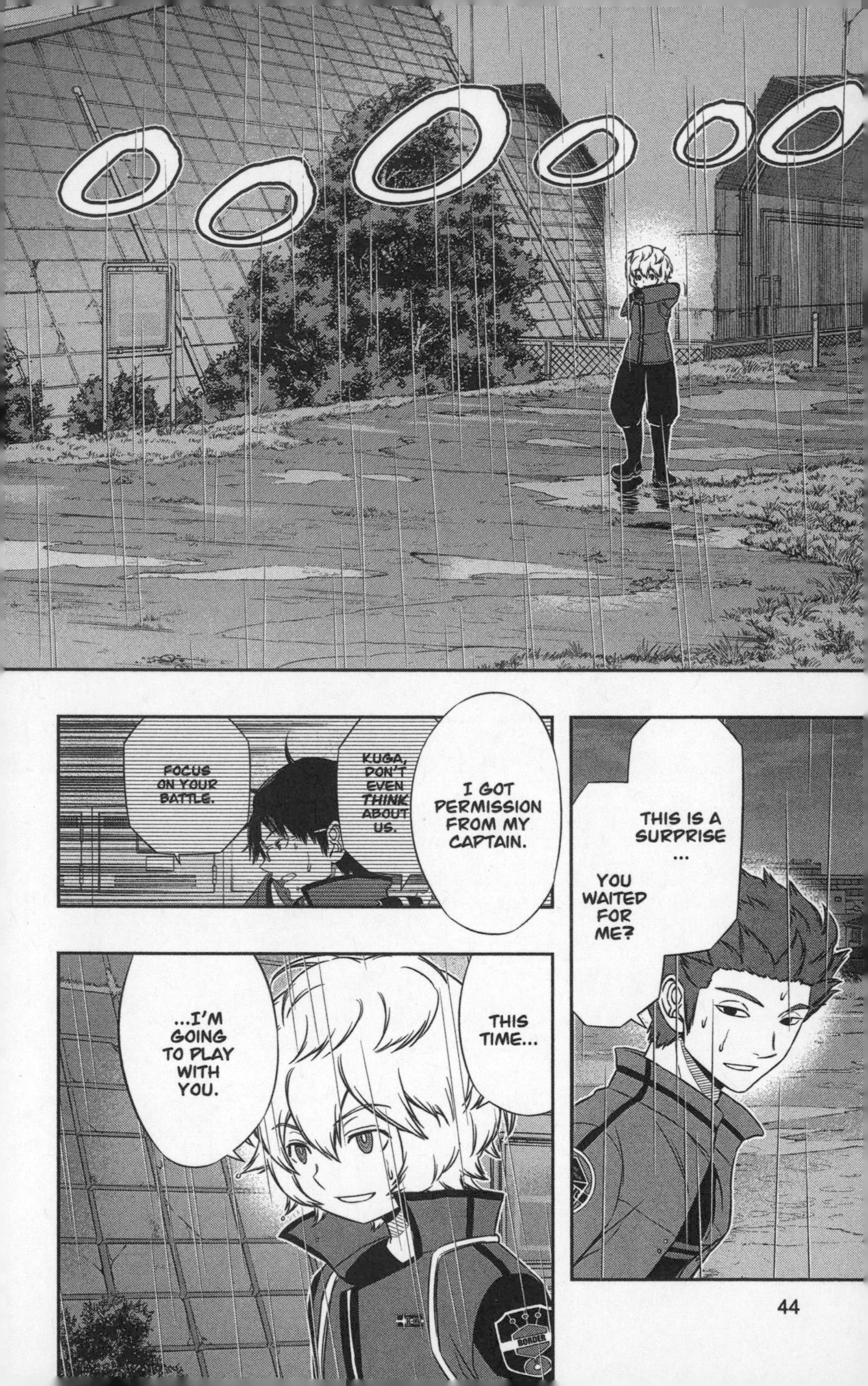
THIS IS A SURPRISE ...
YOU WAITED FOR ME?
I GOT PERMISSION FROM MY CAPTAIN.
KUGA, DON'T EVEN THINK ABOUT US.
FOCUS ON YOUR BATTLE.
THIS TIME...
...I'M GOING TO PLAY WITH YOU.

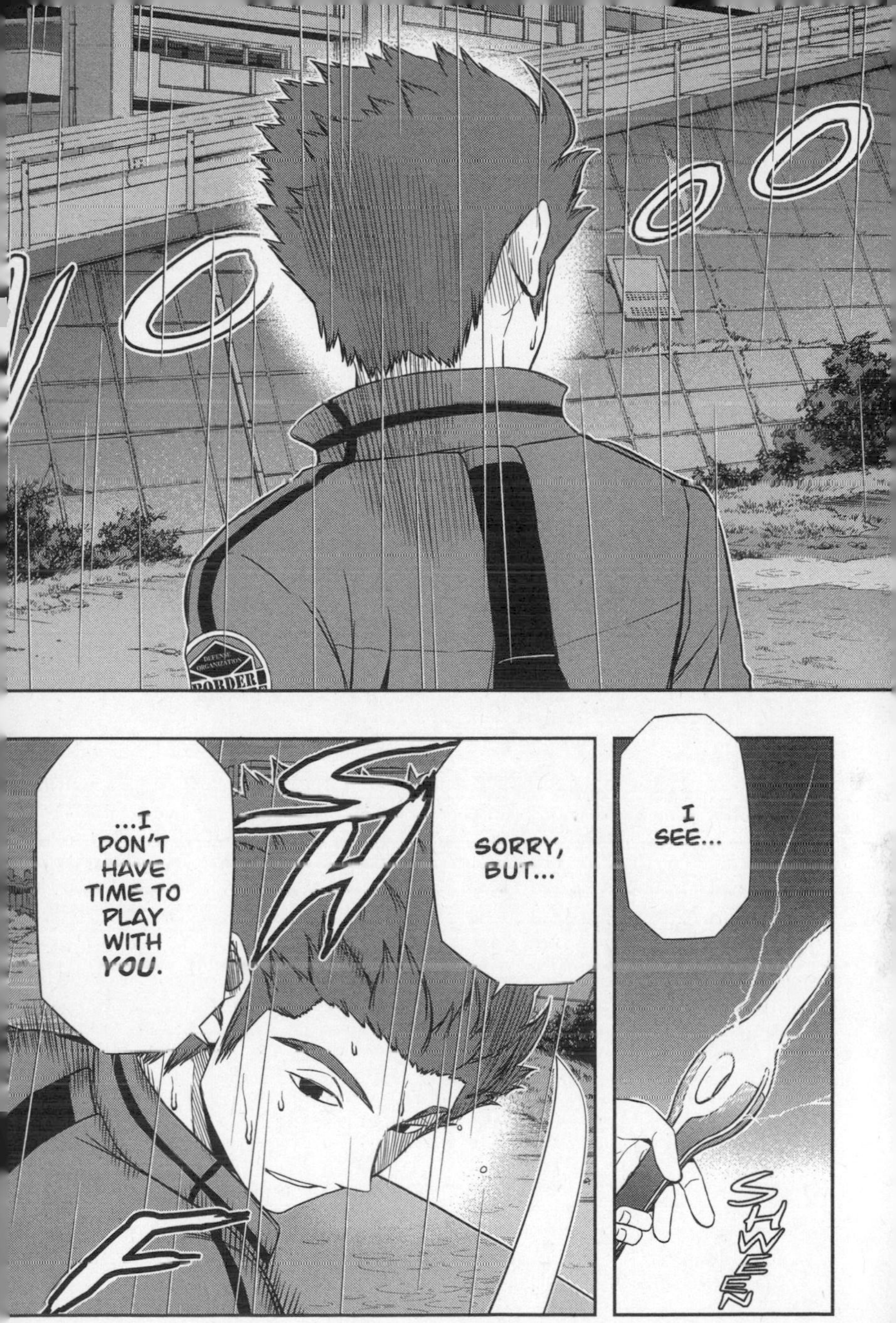
DEFENSE ORGANIZATION
BORDER
I SEE...
SHWEEN
SORRY, BUT...
...I DON'T HAVE TIME TO PLAY WITH YOU.

Suwa Squad Strategy Room

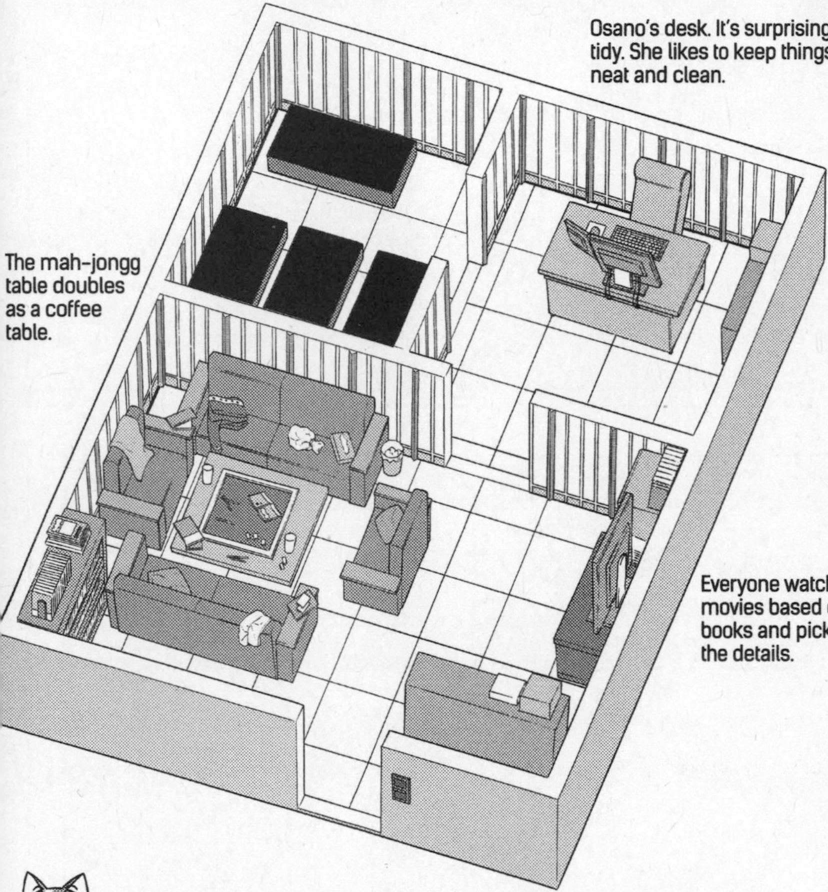
Osano's desk. It's surprisingly tidy. She likes to keep things neat and clean.
The mah-jongg table doubles as a coffee table.
Everyone watches movies based on books and picks at the details.

Suwa Squad's Strategy Room has a mah-jongg table and Tachikawa, Azuma and Fuyushima come over every night to party. The place is full of personal books and manga—a perfect place for slacking off. Osano doesn't clean up after anyone, so this place would've been disgusting without Tsutsumi.

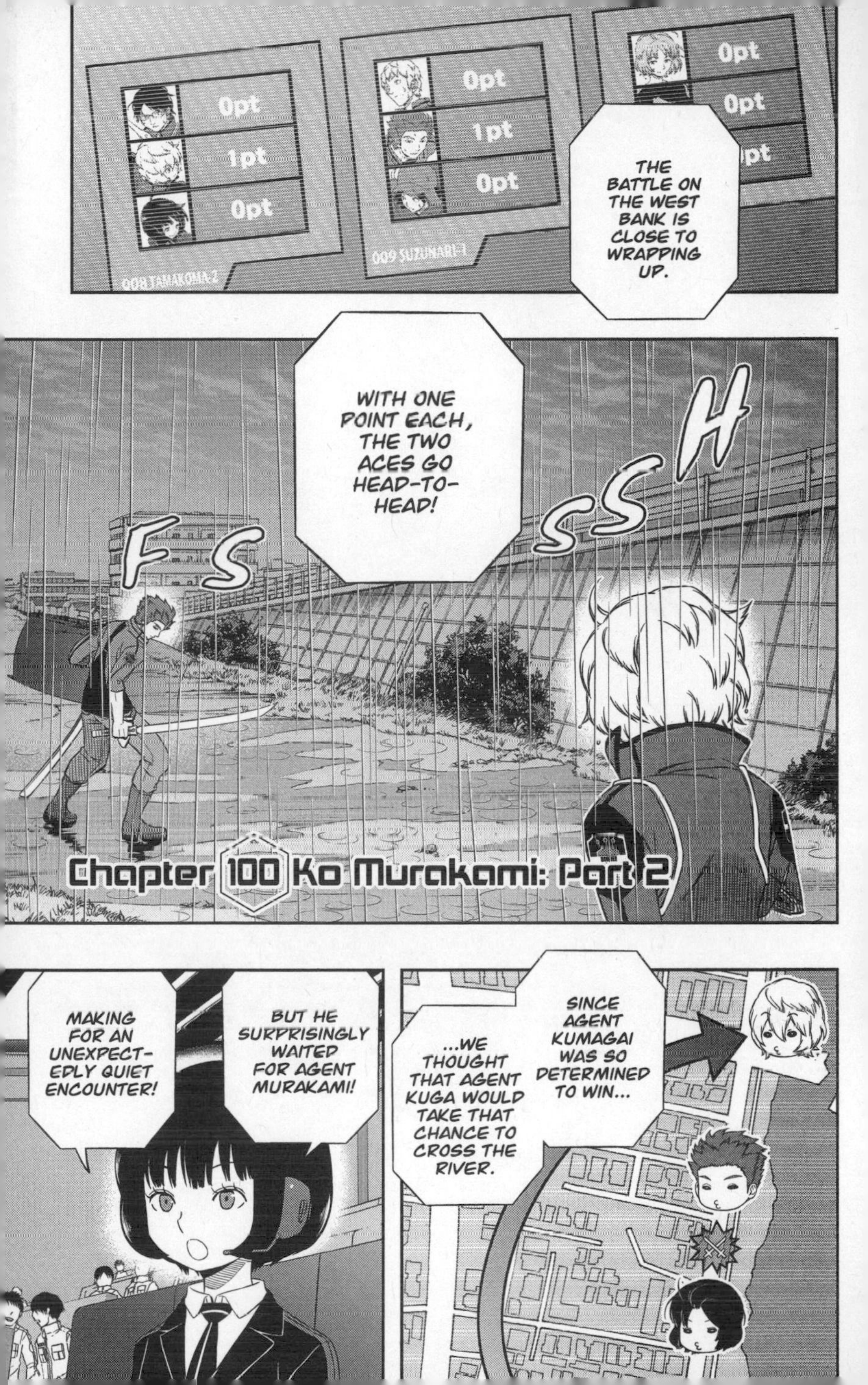
THE BATTLE ON THE WEST BANK IS CLOSE TO WRAPPING UP.
WITH ONE POINT EACH, THE TWO ACES GO HEAD-TO-HEAD!
FSSSH
Chapter 100 Ko Murakami: Part 2
SINCE AGENT KUMAGAI WAS SO DETERMINED TO WIN...
...WE THOUGHT THAT AGENT KUGA WOULD TAKE THAT CHANCE TO CROSS THE RIVER.
BUT HE SURPRISINGLY WAITED FOR AGENT MURAKAMI!
MAKING FOR AN UNEXPECTEDLY QUIET ENCOUNTER!

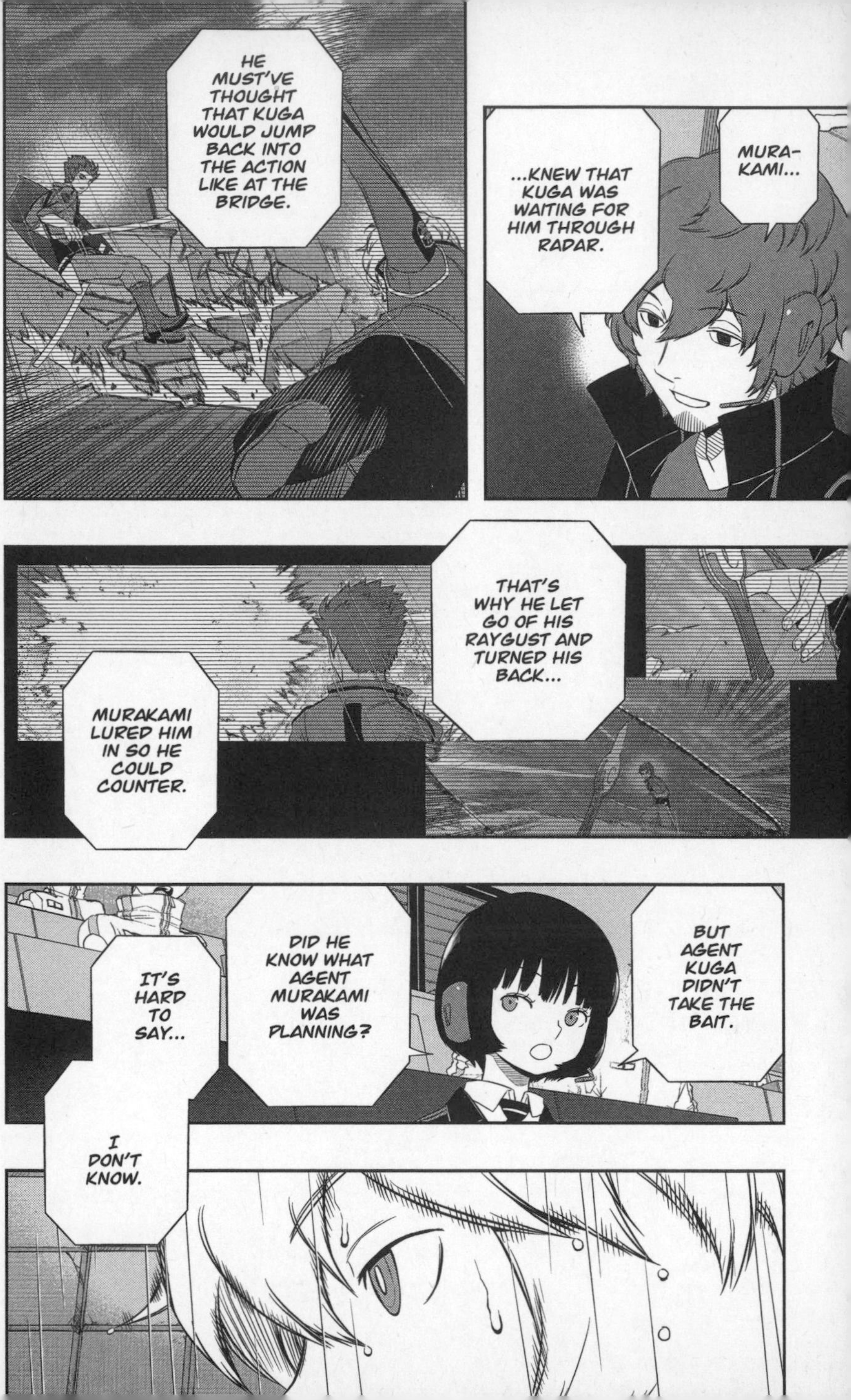
MURA-KAMI...
...KNEW THAT KUGA WAS WAITING FOR HIM THROUGH RADAR.
HE MUST'VE THOUGHT THAT KUGA WOULD JUMP BACK INTO THE ACTION LIKE AT THE BRIDGE.
THAT'S WHY HE LET GO OF HIS RAYGUST AND TURNED HIS BACK...
MURAKAMI LURED HIM IN SO HE COULD COUNTER.
BUT AGENT KUGA DIDN'T TAKE THE BAIT.
DID HE KNOW WHAT AGENT MURAKAMI WAS PLANNING?
IT'S HARD TO SAY...
I DON'T KNOW.

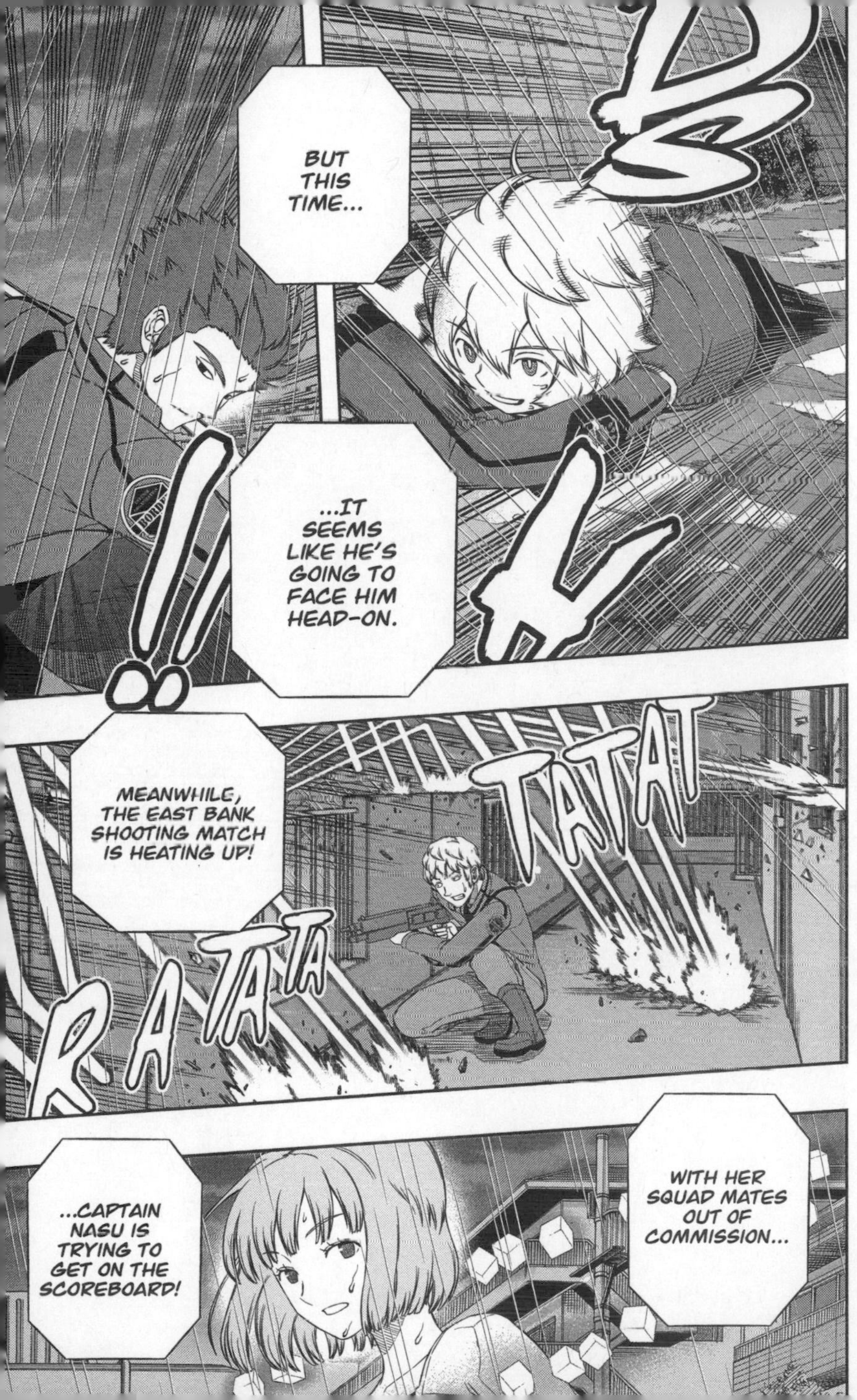

BUT THIS TIME...
...IT SEEMS LIKE HE'S GOING TO FACE HIM HEAD-ON.
!!
TATAT
MEANWHILE, THE EAST BANK SHOOTING MATCH IS HEATING UP!
RATATATA
WITH HER SQUAD MATES OUT OF COMMISSION...
...CAPTAIN NASU IS TRYING TO GET ON THE SCOREBOARD!

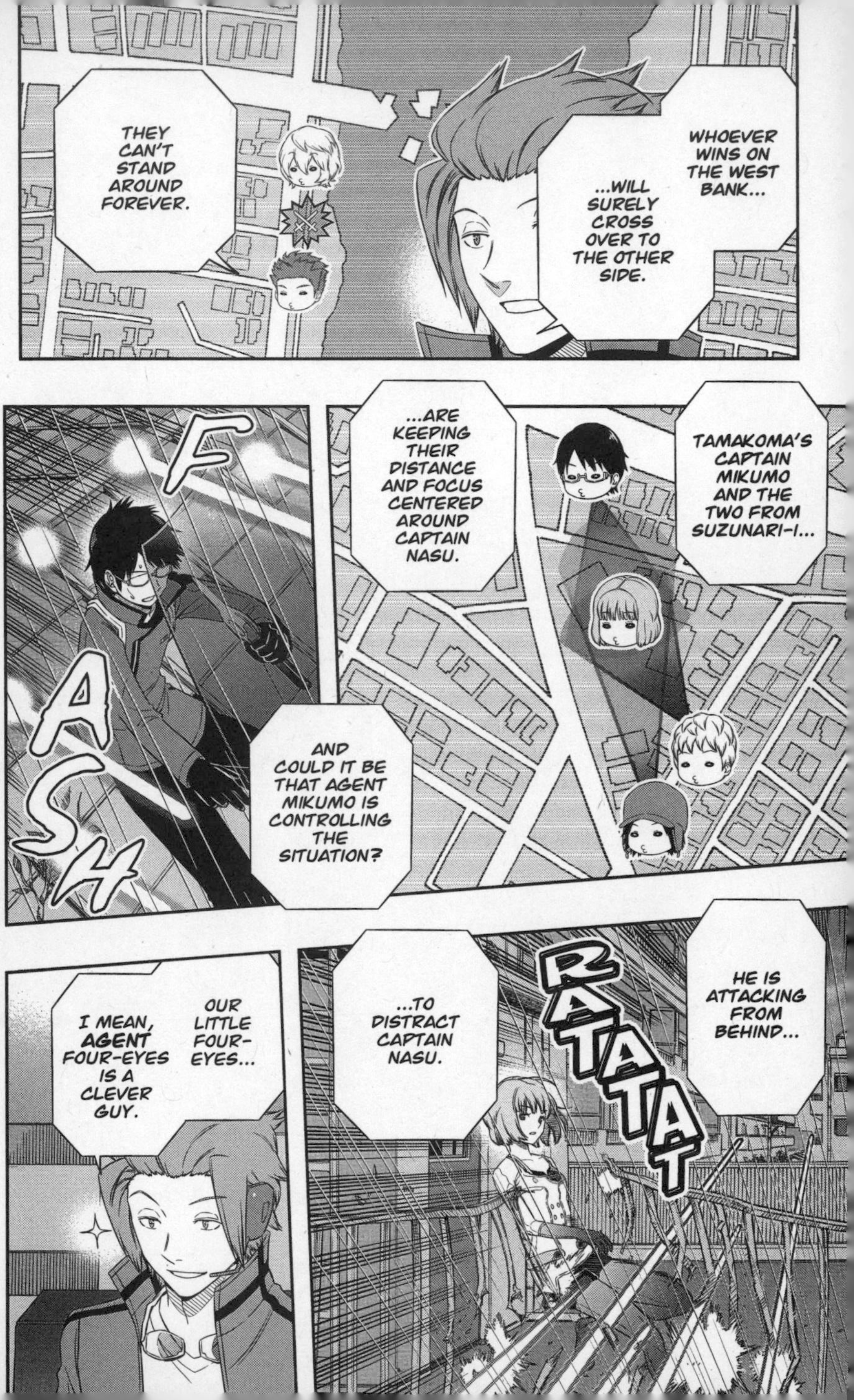
WHOEVER WINS ON THE WEST BANK...
...WILL SURELY CROSS OVER TO THE OTHER SIDE.
THEY CAN'T STAND AROUND FOREVER.
TAMAKOMA'S CAPTAIN MIKUMO AND THE TWO FROM SUZUNARI-1...
...ARE KEEPING THEIR DISTANCE AND FOCUS CENTERED AROUND CAPTAIN NASU.
AND COULD IT BE THAT AGENT MIKUMO IS CONTROLLING THE SITUATION?
FASH
HE IS ATTACKING FROM BEHIND...
RATATAT
...TO DISTRACT CAPTAIN NASU.
OUR LITTLE FOUR-EYES...
I MEAN, **AGENT** FOUR-EYES IS A CLEVER GUY.

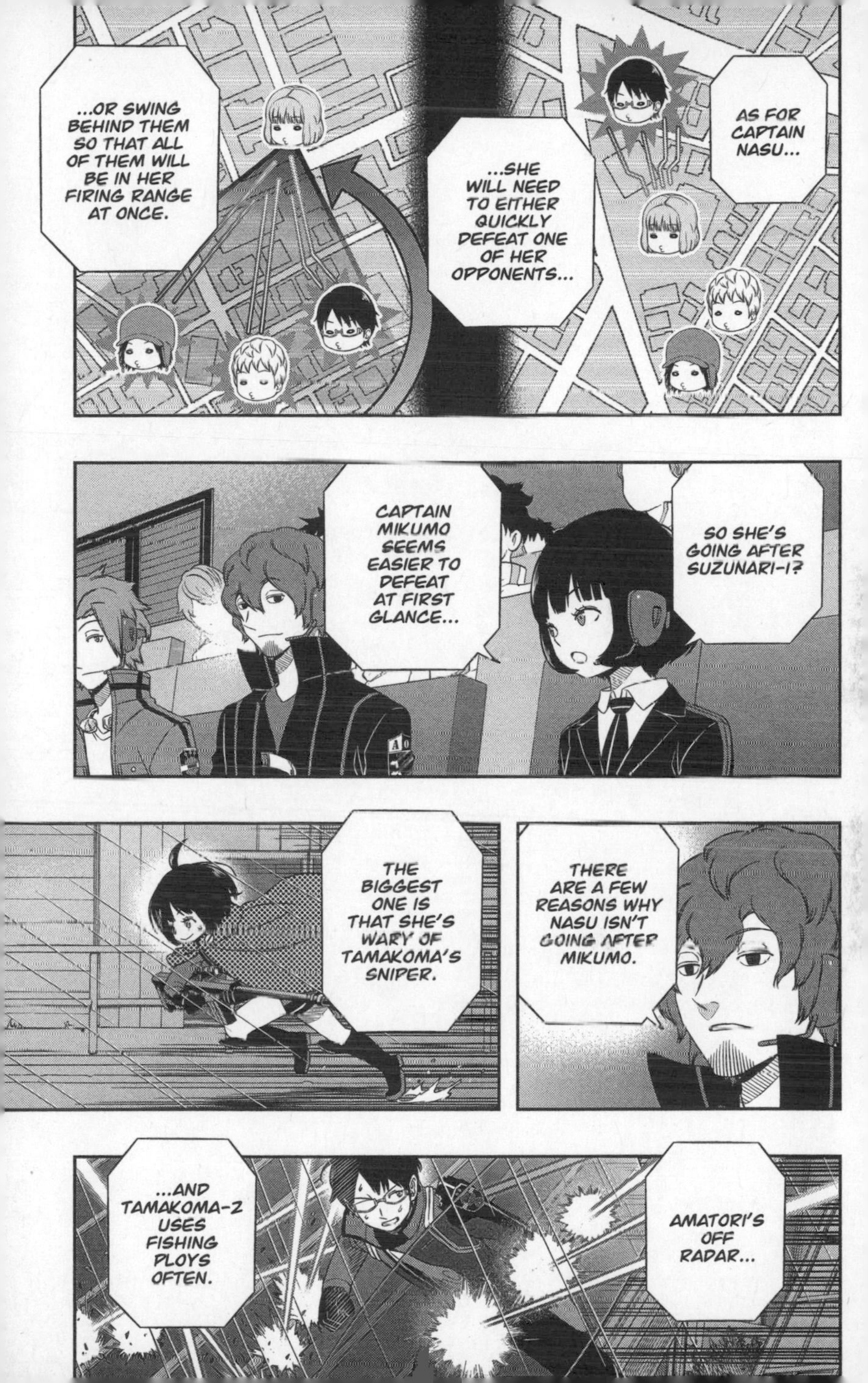
AS FOR CAPTAIN NASU...
...SHE WILL NEED TO EITHER QUICKLY DEFEAT ONE OF HER OPPONENTS...
...OR SWING BEHIND THEM SO THAT ALL OF THEM WILL BE IN HER FIRING RANGE AT ONCE.
SO SHE'S GOING AFTER SUZUNARI-1?
CAPTAIN MIKUMO SEEMS EASIER TO DEFEAT AT FIRST GLANCE...
THERE ARE A FEW REASONS WHY NASU ISN'T GOING AFTER MIKUMO.
THE BIGGEST ONE IS THAT SHE'S WARY OF TAMAKOMA'S SNIPER.
AMATORI'S OFF RADAR...
...AND TAMAKOMA-2 USES FISHING PLOYS OFTEN.

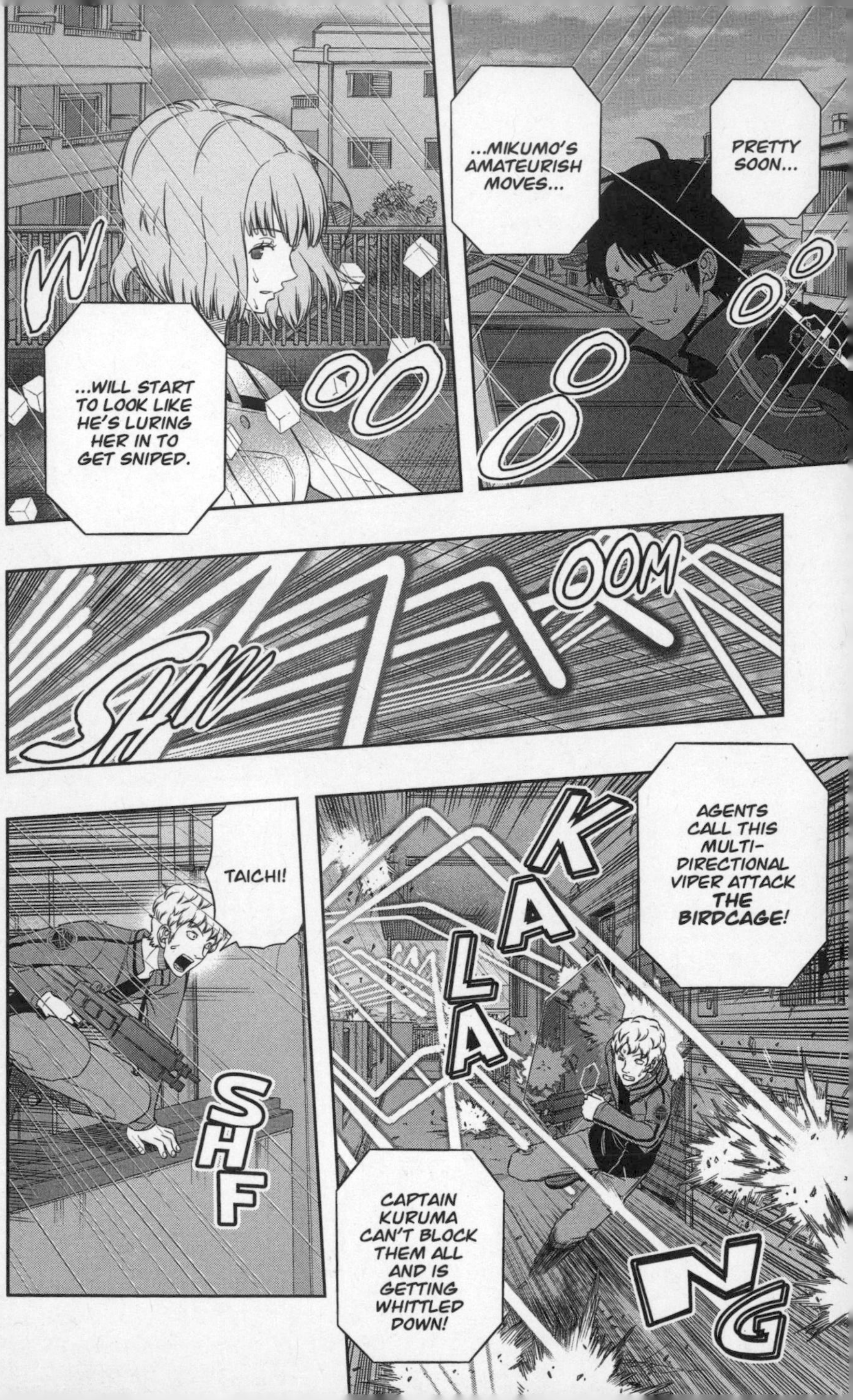
PRETTY SOON...
...MIKUMO'S AMATEURISH MOVES...
WOOOOOOO
...WILL START TO LOOK LIKE HE'S LURING HER IN TO GET SNIPED.
SHOOM
AGENTS CALL THIS MULTI-DIRECTIONAL VIPER ATTACK THE BIRDCAGE!
KALANG
CAPTAIN KURUMA CAN'T BLOCK THEM ALL AND IS GETTING WHITTLED DOWN!
TAICHI!
SHF

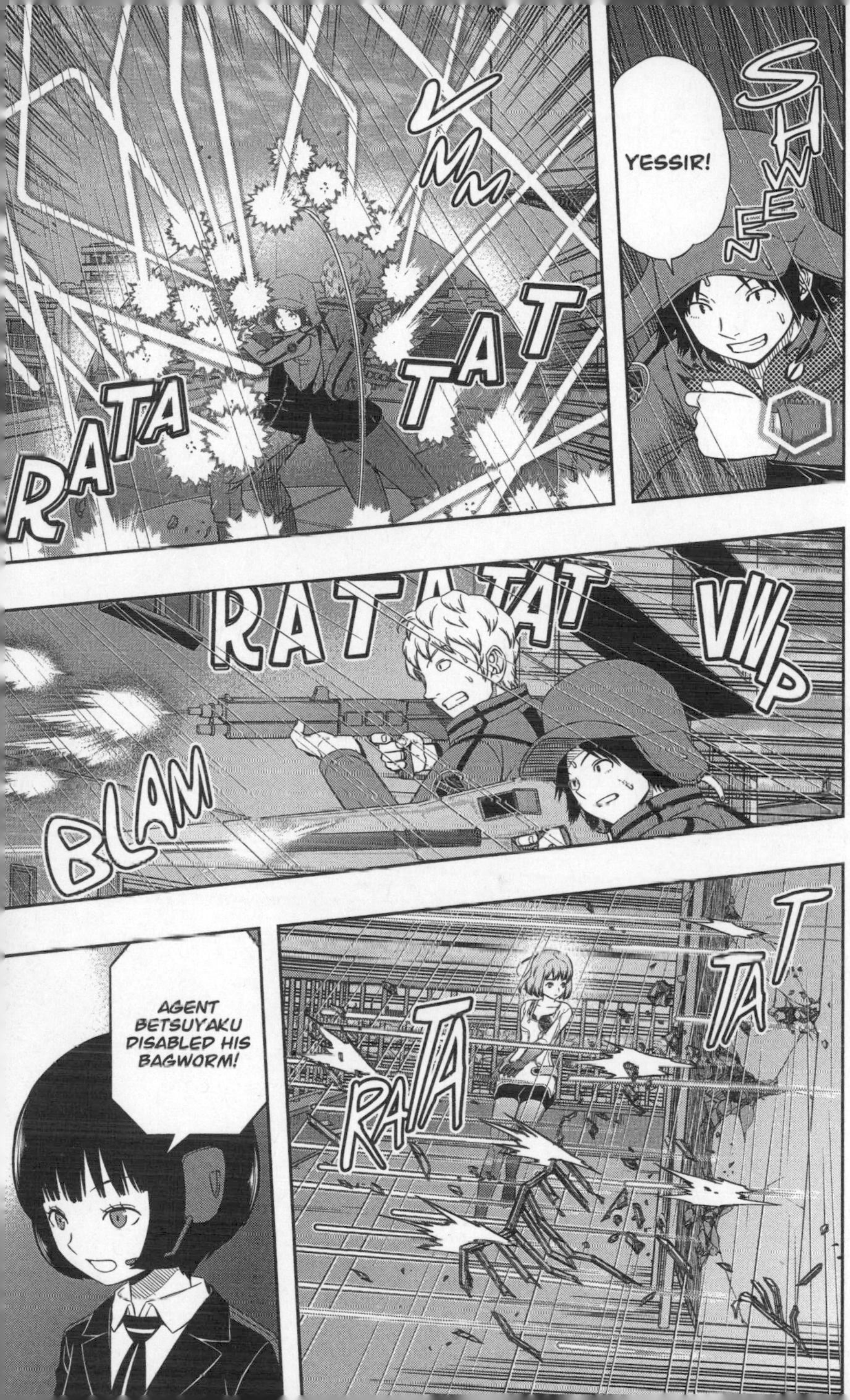
YESSIR!
SHWEEN
VMMM
RATA
TAT
RATATAT
VWIP
BLAM
RATA
TAT
AGENT BETSUYAKU DISABLED HIS BAGWORM!

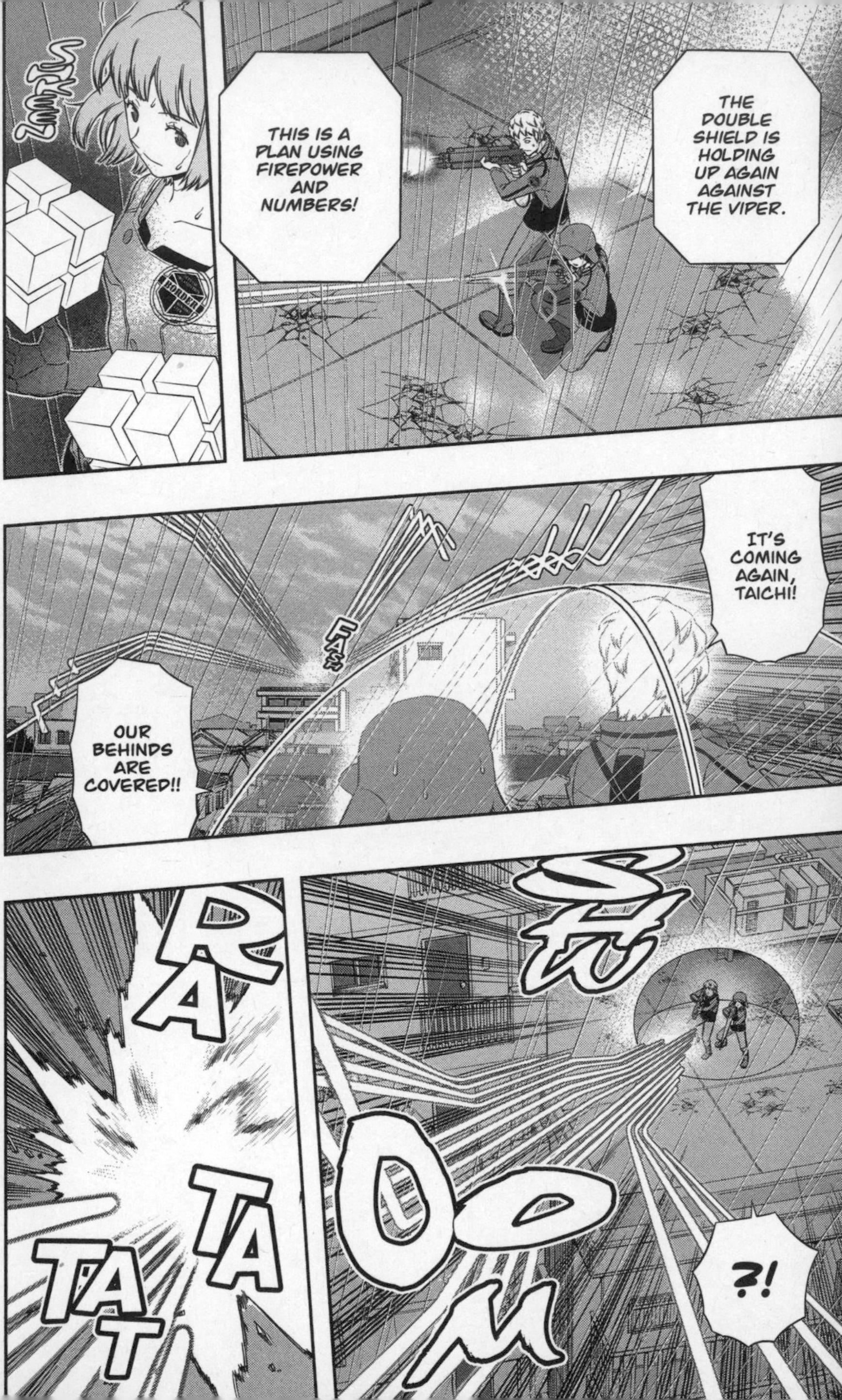
THE DOUBLE SHIELD IS HOLDING UP AGAIN AGAINST THE VIPER.
THIS IS A PLAN USING FIREPOWER AND NUMBERS!
IT'S COMING AGAIN, TAICHI!
FASH
OUR BEHINDS ARE COVERED!!
SHOOM
?!
RATATATAT

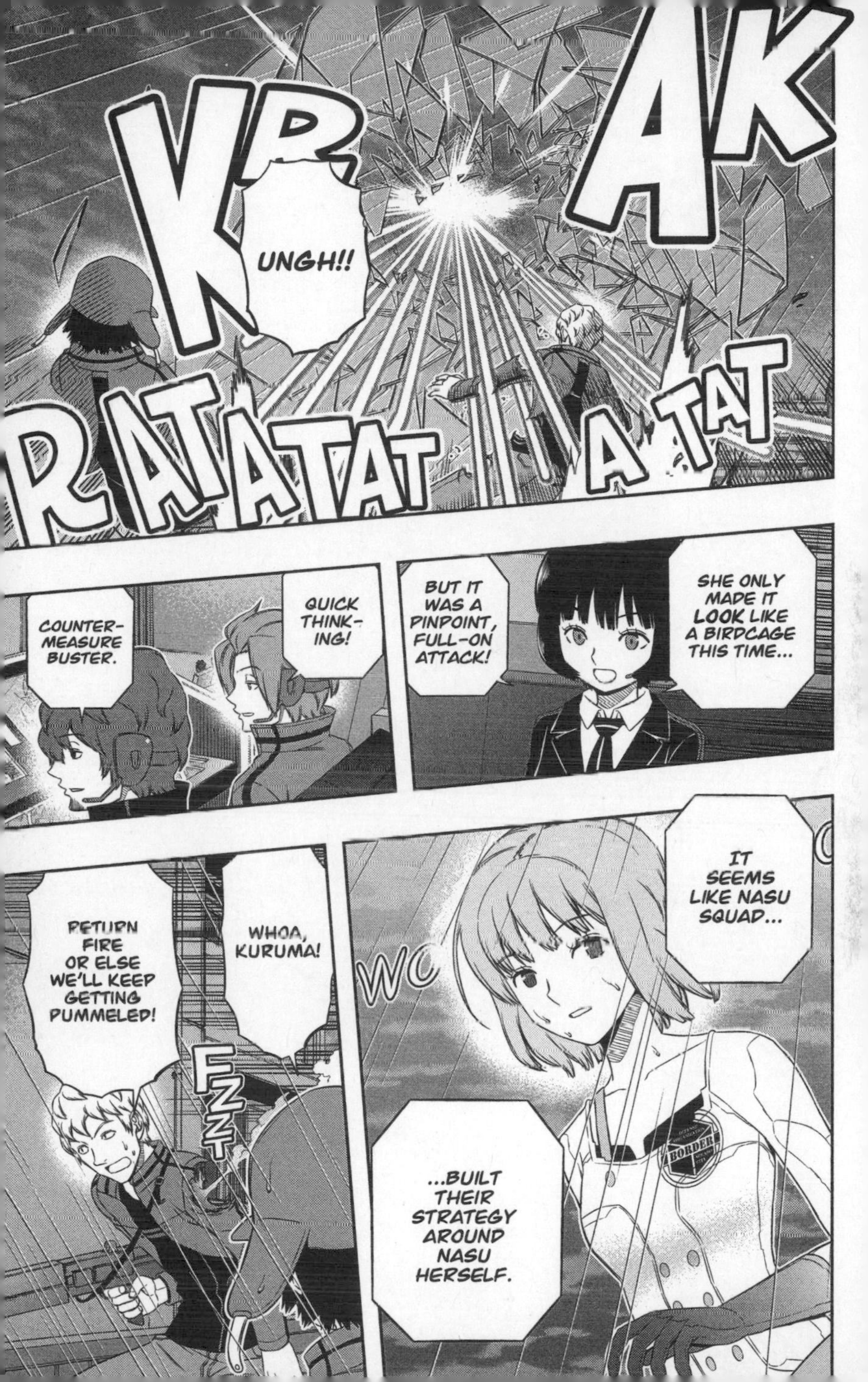
KR AK
UNGH!!
RATATATAT
A TAT
SHE ONLY MADE IT LOOK LIKE A BIRDCAGE THIS TIME...
BUT IT WAS A PINPOINT, FULL-ON ATTACK!
QUICK THINKING!
COUNTER-MEASURE BUSTER.
IT SEEMS LIKE NASU SQUAD...
WO
...BUILT THEIR STRATEGY AROUND NASU HERSELF.
WHOA, KURUMA!
RETURN FIRE OR ELSE WE'LL KEEP GETTING PUMMELED!
FZZT

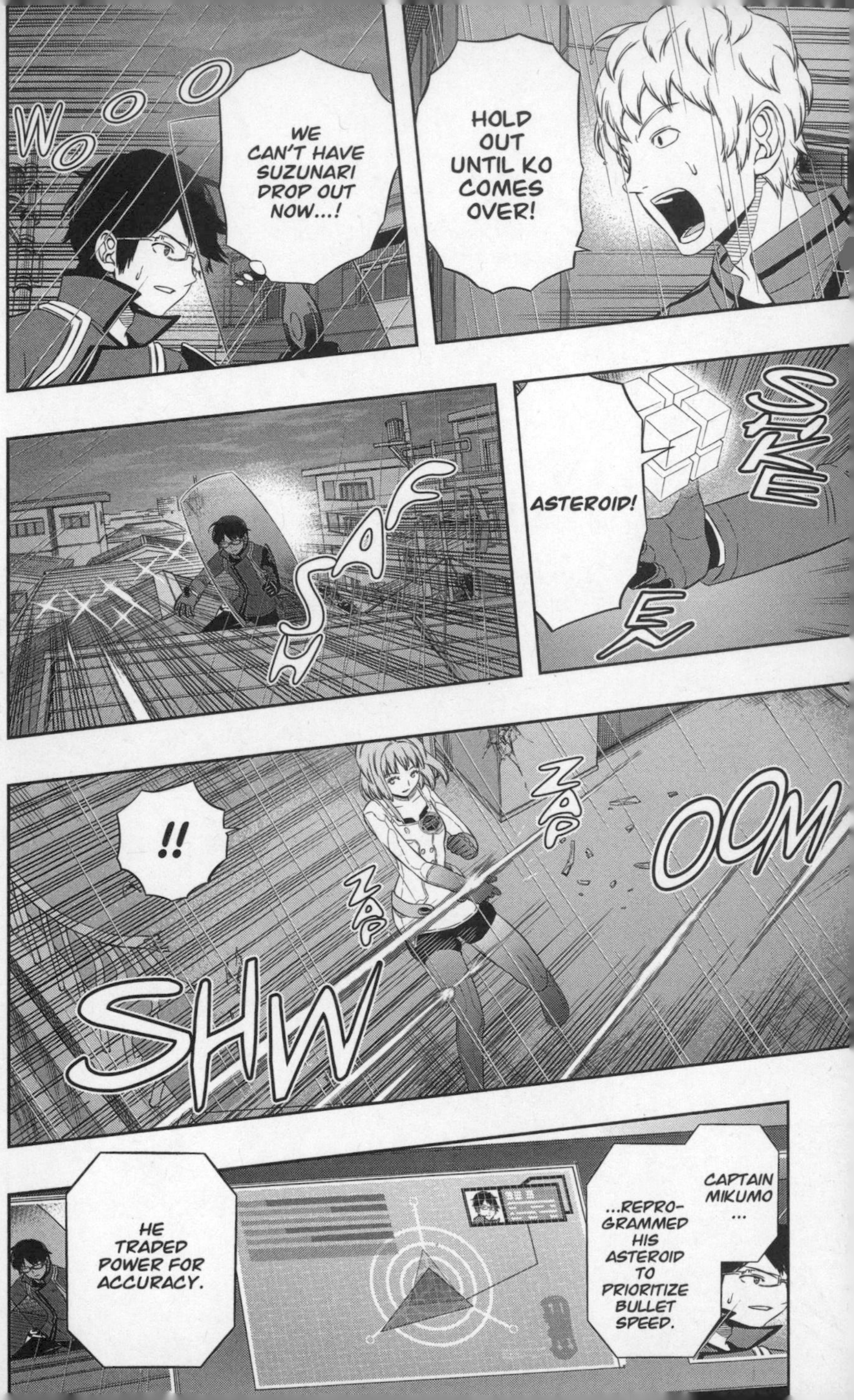
HOLD OUT UNTIL KO COMES OVER!
WE CAN'T HAVE SUZUNARI DROP OUT NOW...!
WOOO
SHKE
ASTEROID!
E
FASH
OOM
ZAP
!!
ZAP
SHW
CAPTAIN MIKUMO...
...REPROGRAMMED HIS ASTEROID TO PRIORITIZE BULLET SPEED.
HE TRADED POWER FOR ACCURACY.

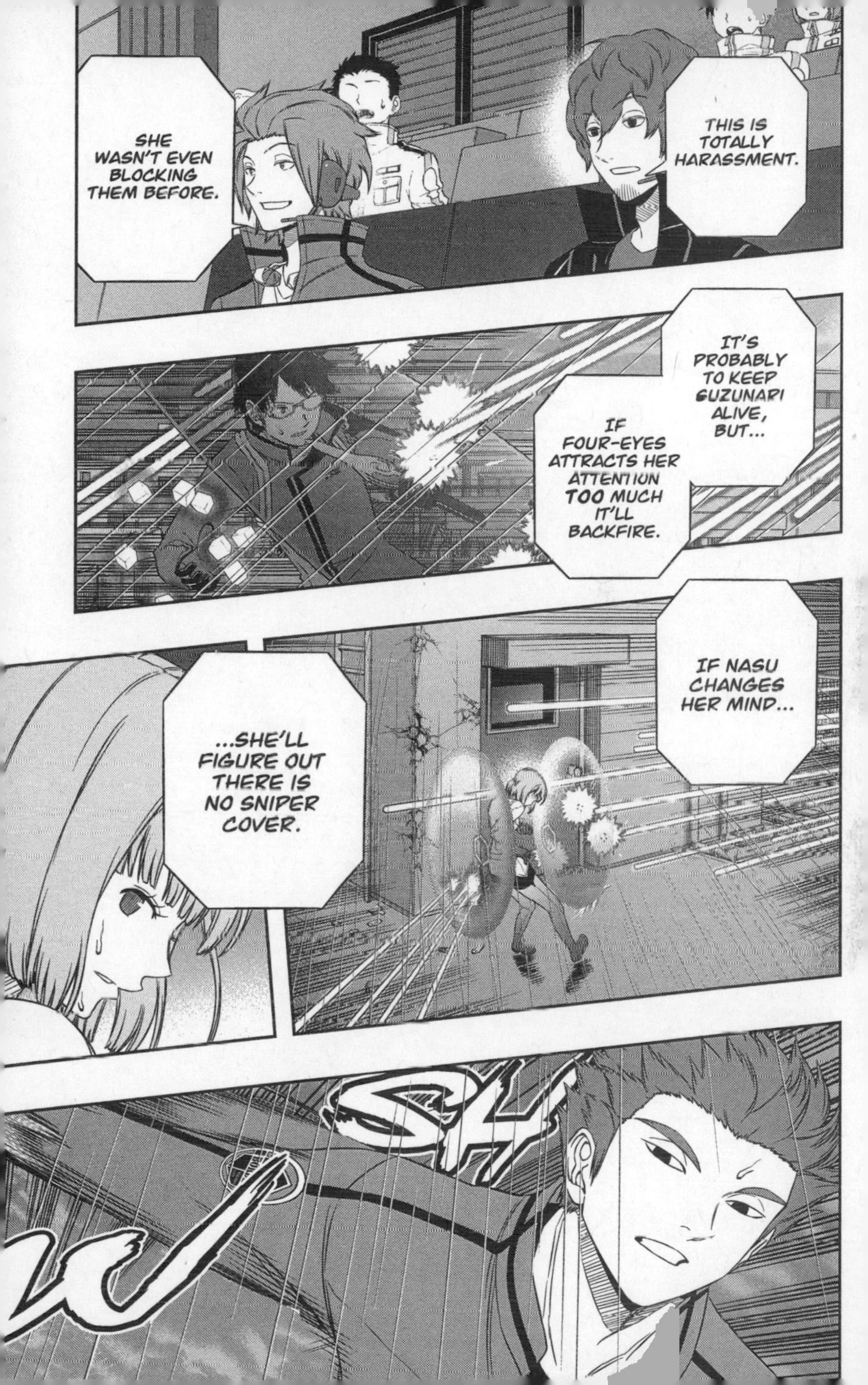
THIS IS TOTALLY HARASSMENT.
SHE WASN'T EVEN BLOCKING THEM BEFORE.
IT'S PROBABLY TO KEEP GUZUNARI ALIVE, BUT...
IF FOUR-EYES ATTRACTS HER ATTENTION TOO MUCH IT'LL BACKFIRE.
IF NASU CHANGES HER MIND...
...SHE'LL FIGURE OUT THERE IS NO SNIPER COVER.

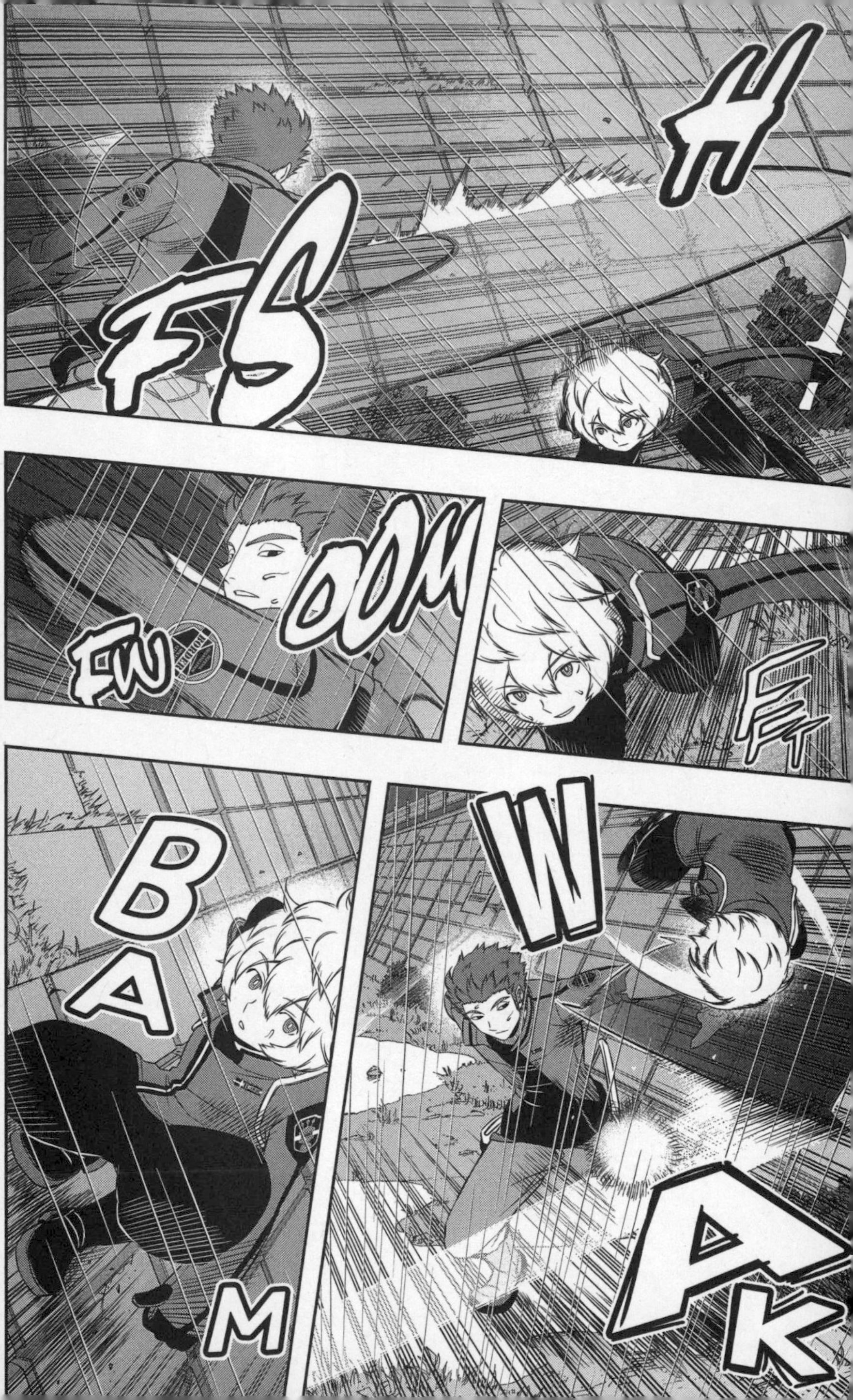
FSH
FFT
FWOOM
WAK
BAM

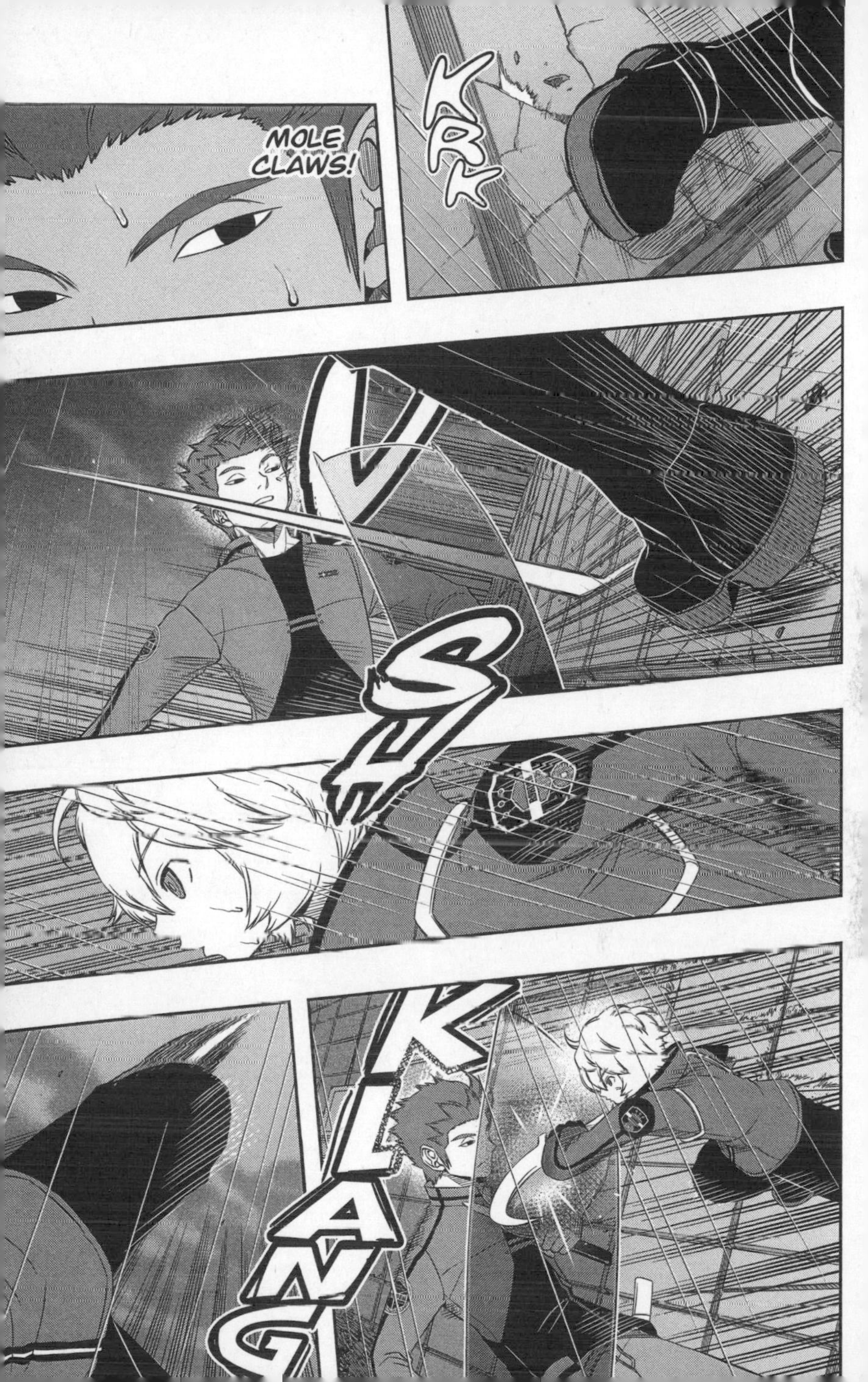
KRK
MOLE CLAWS!
SH
KLANG

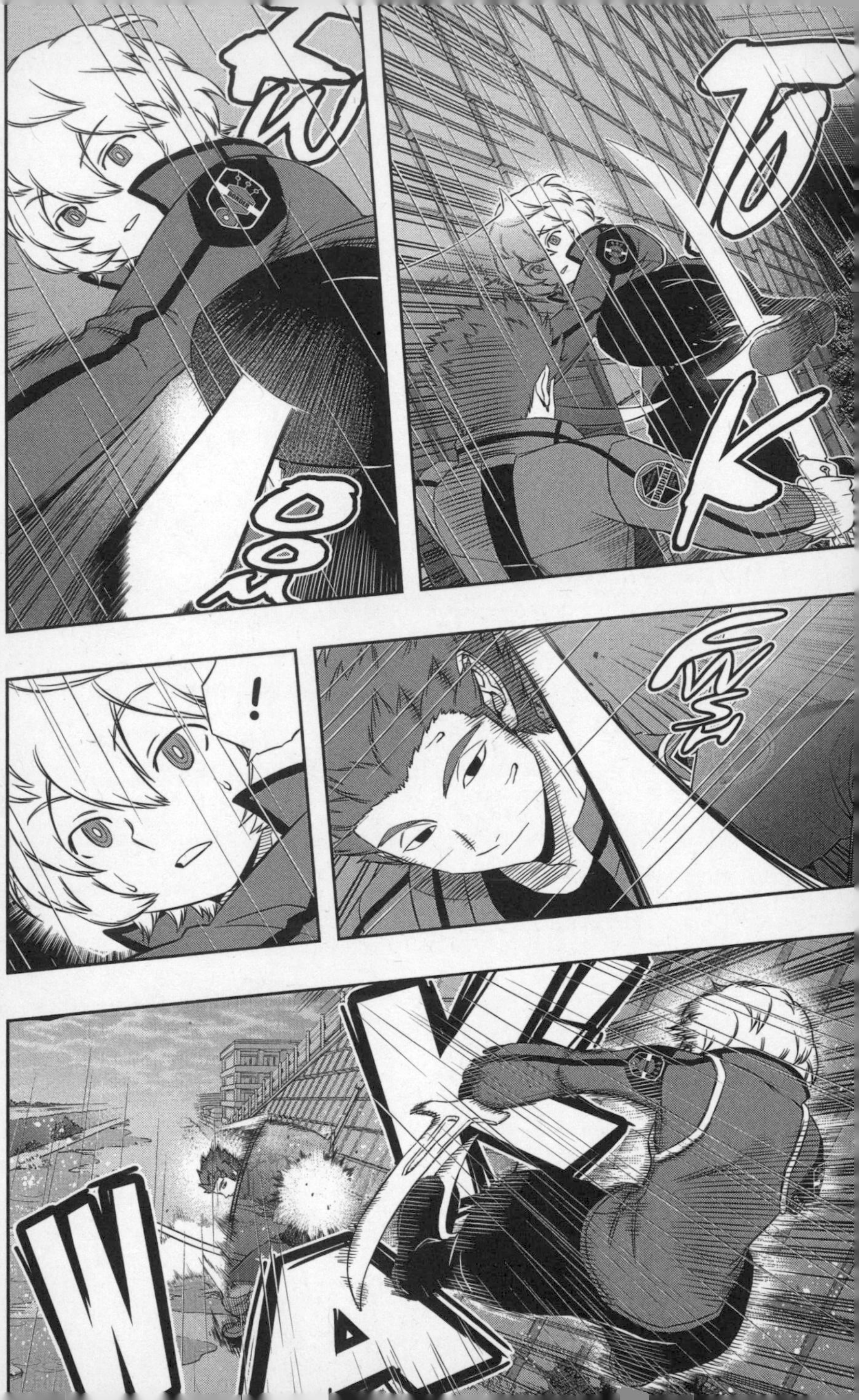
TOK
SWSH
!

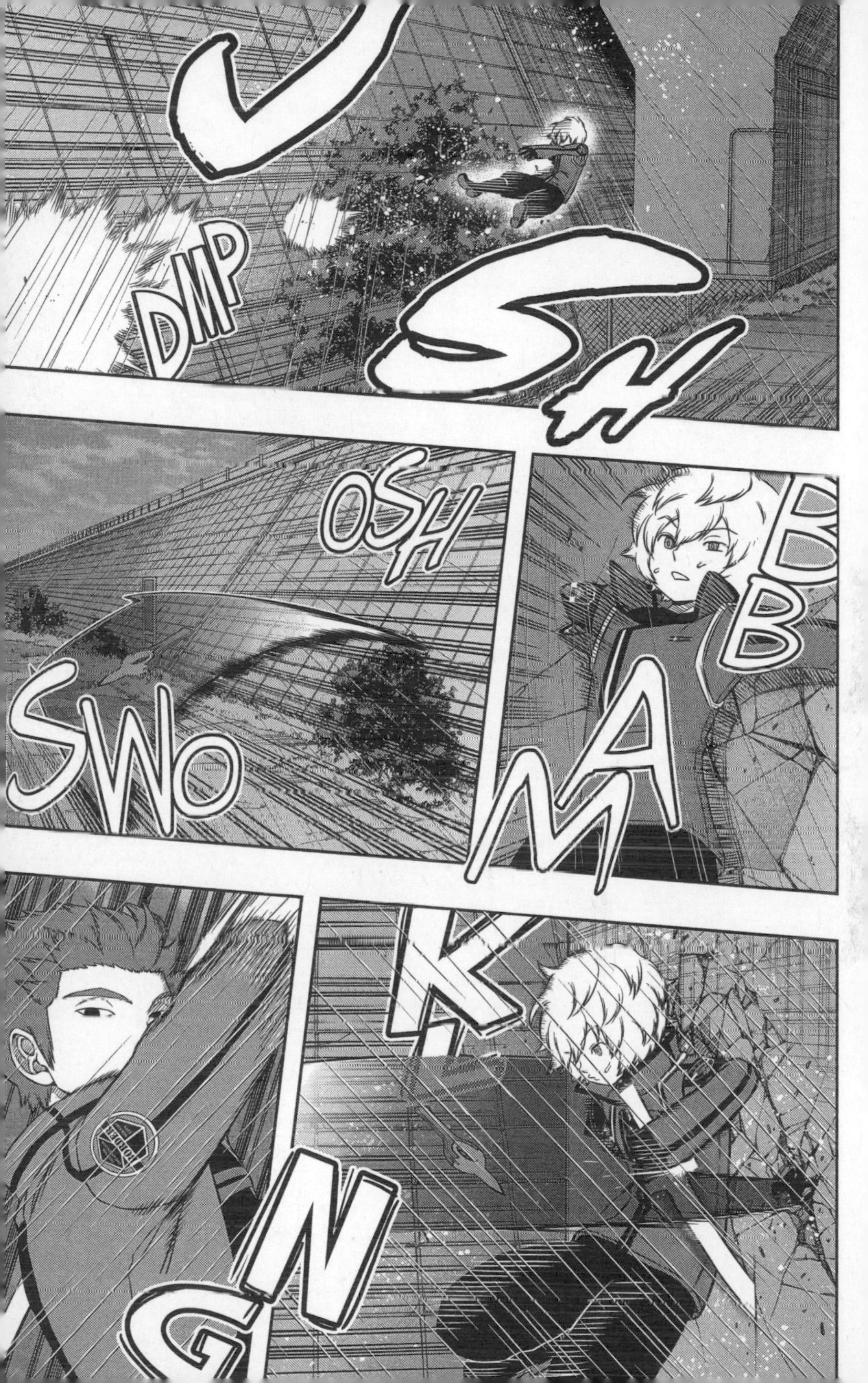
SH
DMP
BBAMM
OSH
SWO
K
NG

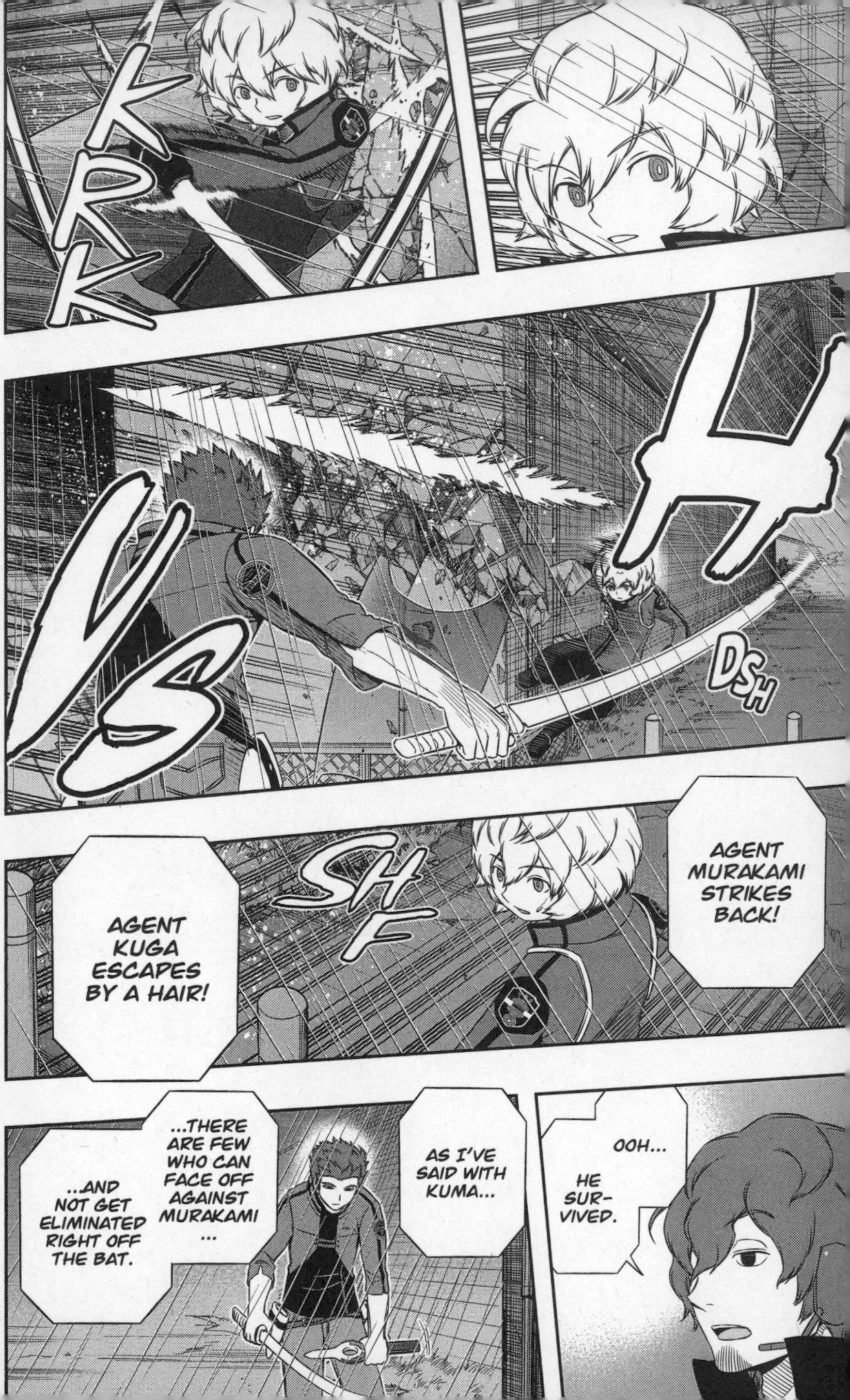
KRK
DSH
AGENT MURAKAMI STRIKES BACK!
SHF
AGENT KUGA ESCAPES BY A HAIR!
OOH...
HE SUR-VIVED.
AS I'VE SAID WITH KUMA...
...THERE ARE FEW WHO CAN FACE OFF AGAINST MURAKAMI...
...AND NOT GET ELIMINATED RIGHT OFF THE BAT.

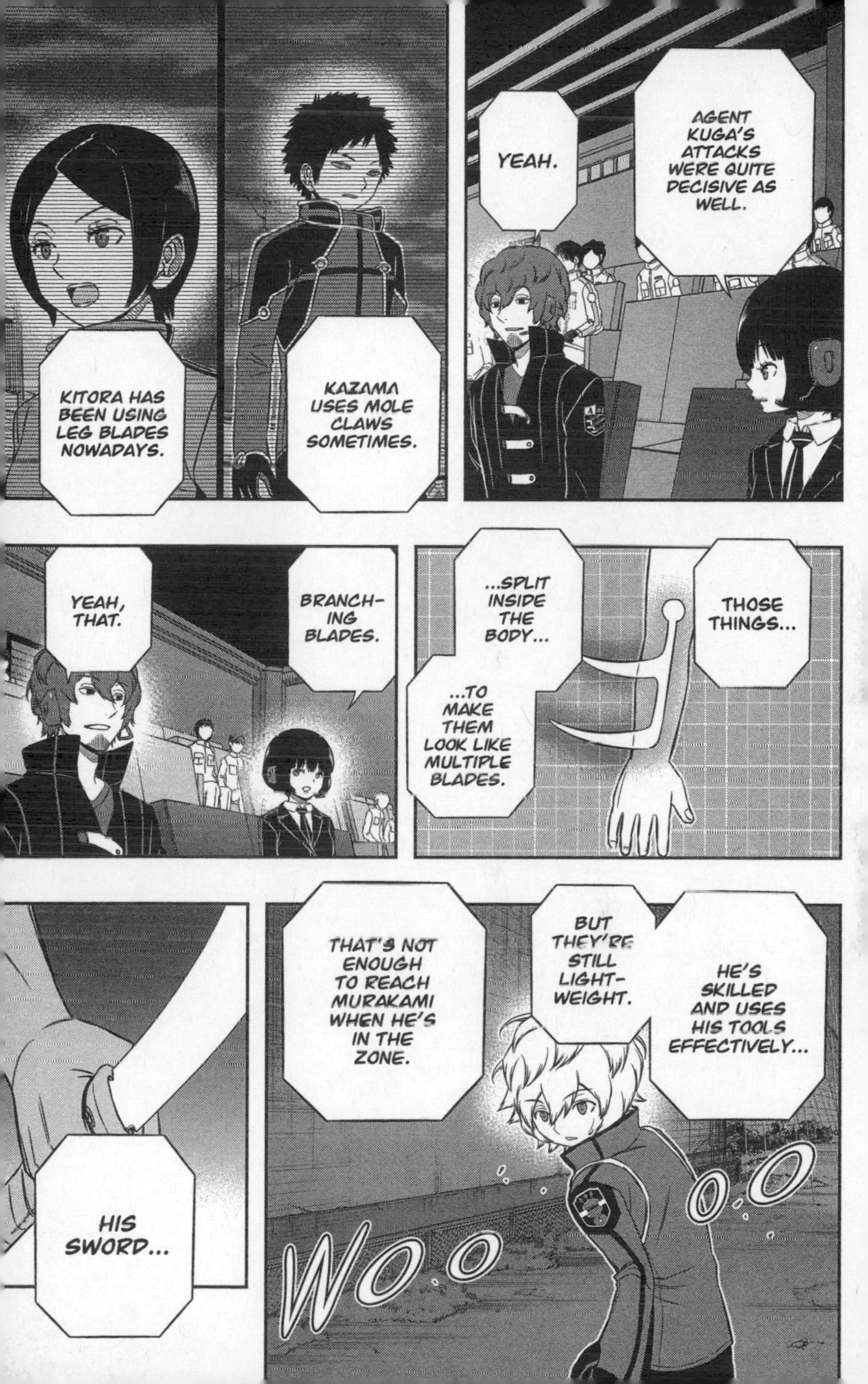
AGENT KUGA'S ATTACKS WERE QUITE DECISIVE AS WELL.
YEAH.
KAZAMA USES MOLE CLAWS SOMETIMES.
KITORA HAS BEEN USING LEG BLADES NOWADAYS.
THOSE THINGS...
...SPLIT INSIDE THE BODY...
...TO MAKE THEM LOOK LIKE MULTIPLE BLADES.
BRANCH-ING BLADES.
YEAH, THAT.
HE'S SKILLED AND USES HIS TOOLS EFFECTIVELY...
BUT THEY'RE STILL LIGHT-WEIGHT.
THAT'S NOT ENOUGH TO REACH MURAKAMI WHEN HE'S IN THE ZONE.
WOOOOO
HIS SWORD...

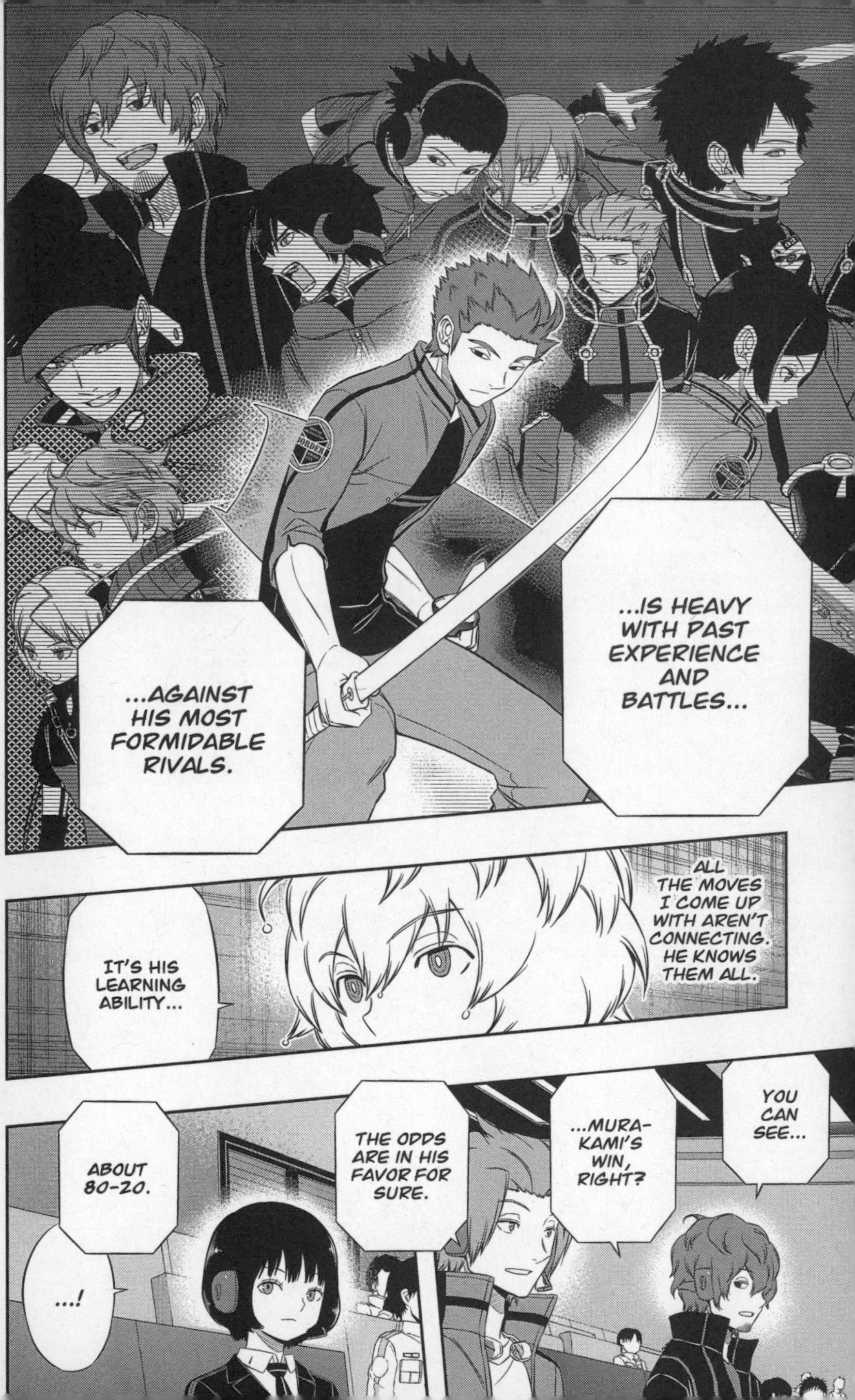
...IS HEAVY WITH PAST EXPERIENCE AND BATTLES...
...AGAINST HIS MOST FORMIDABLE RIVALS.
ALL THE MOVES I COME UP WITH AREN'T CONNECTING. HE KNOWS THEM ALL.
IT'S HIS LEARNING ABILITY...
YOU CAN SEE...
...MURA-KAMI'S WIN, RIGHT?
THE ODDS ARE IN HIS FAVOR FOR SURE.
ABOUT 80-20.
...!

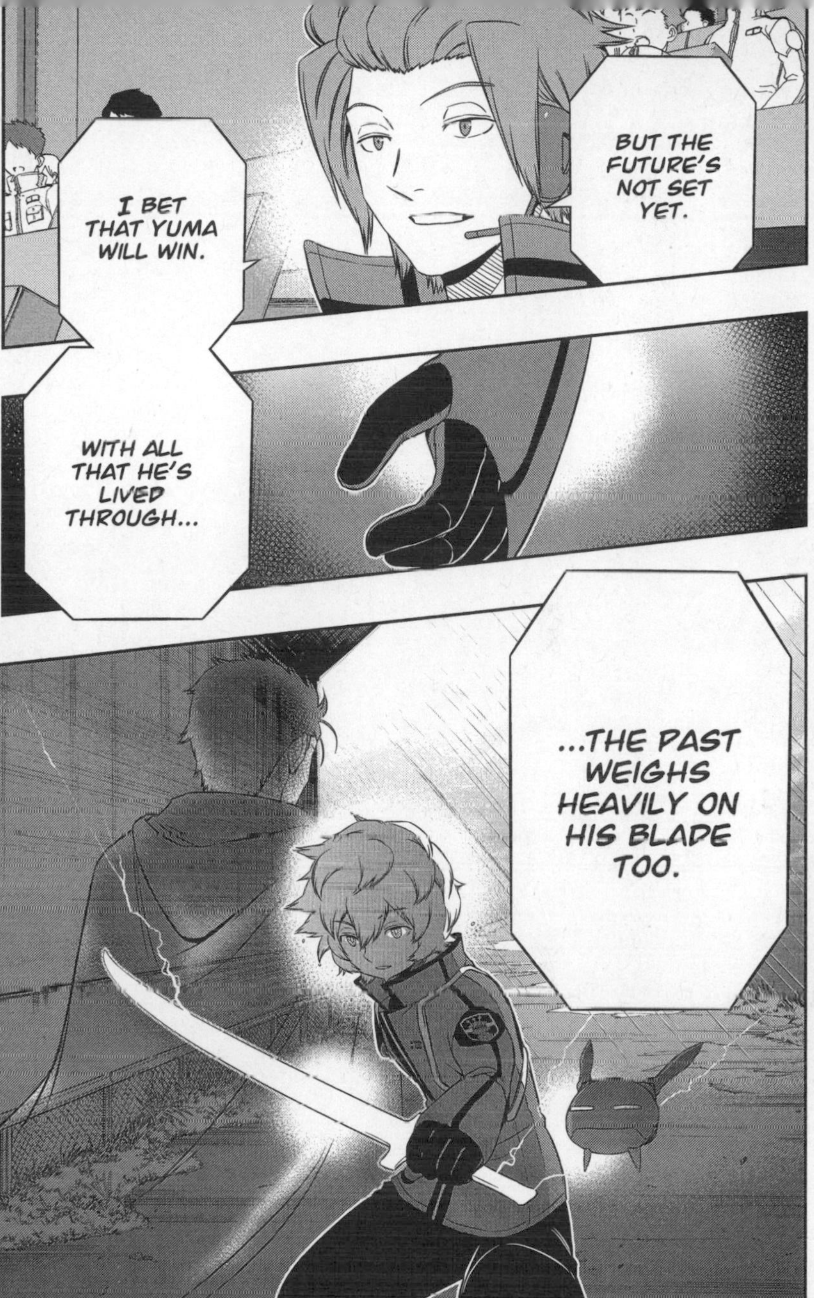
BUT THE FUTURE'S NOT SET YET.
I BET THAT YUMA WILL WIN.
WITH ALL THAT HE'S LIVED THROUGH...
...THE PAST WEIGHS HEAVILY ON HIS BLADE TOO.

Arafune Squad Strategy Room

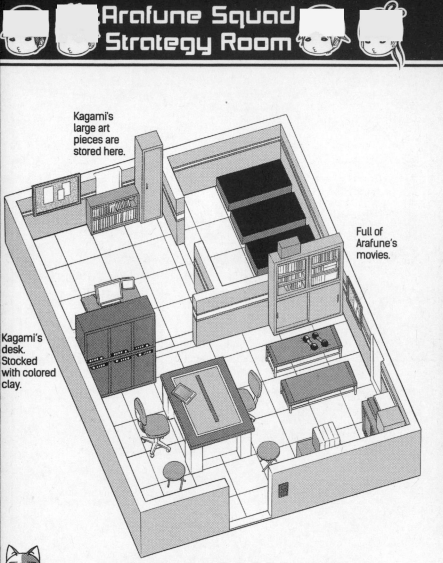

Kagami's large art pieces are stored here.
Full of Arafune's movies.
Kagami's desk. Stocked with colored clay.

Arafune Squad's Strategy Room. Everyone brought in weight-training machines, hammocks, strange statues, a large-screen projector, etc. until the place was a mess. It forced Arafune to restrict the amount of personal items in the room. It has since been streamlined into a "working office."

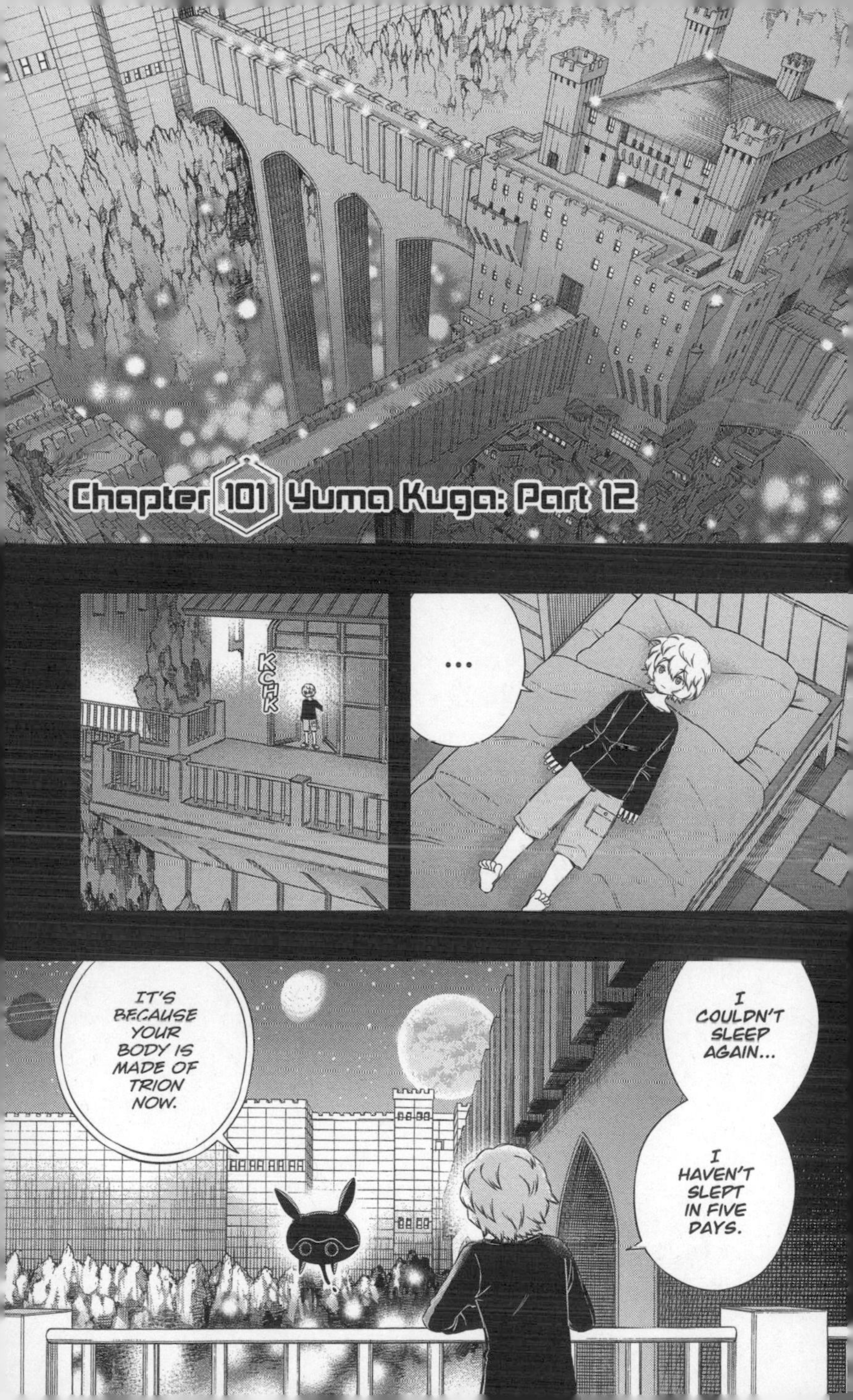

Chapter 101 Yuma Kuga: Part 12
...
KCHK
I COULDN'T SLEEP AGAIN...
I HAVEN'T SLEPT IN FIVE DAYS.
IT'S BECAUSE YOUR BODY IS MADE OF TRION NOW.

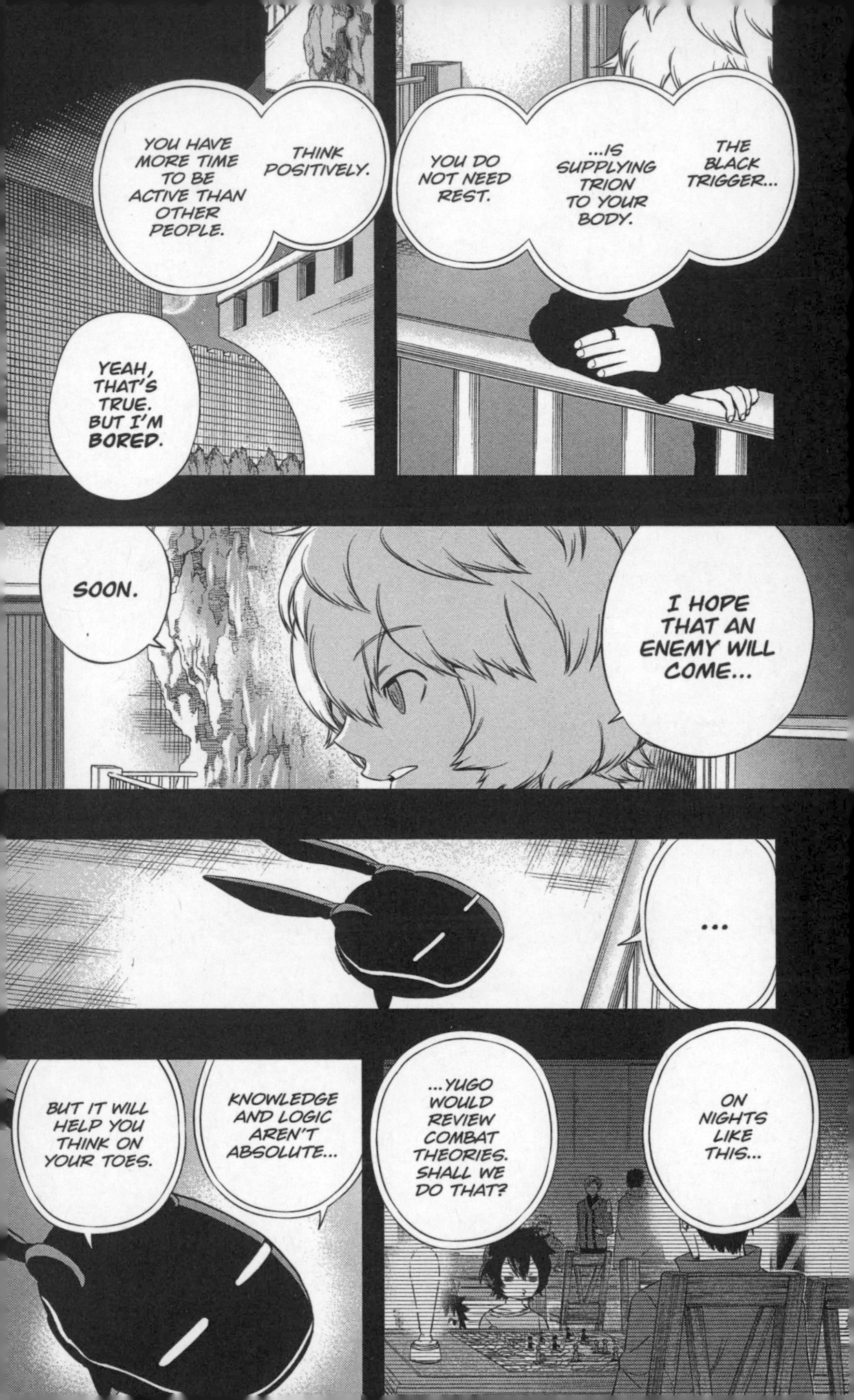
THE BLACK TRIGGER...
...IS SUPPLYING TRION TO YOUR BODY.
YOU DO NOT NEED REST.
THINK POSITIVELY.
YOU HAVE MORE TIME TO BE ACTIVE THAN OTHER PEOPLE.
YEAH, THAT'S TRUE. BUT I'M BORED.
I HOPE THAT AN ENEMY WILL COME...
SOON.
...
ON NIGHTS LIKE THIS...
...YUGO WOULD REVIEW COMBAT THEORIES. SHALL WE DO THAT?
KNOWLEDGE AND LOGIC AREN'T ABSOLUTE...
BUT IT WILL HELP YOU THINK ON YOUR TOES.

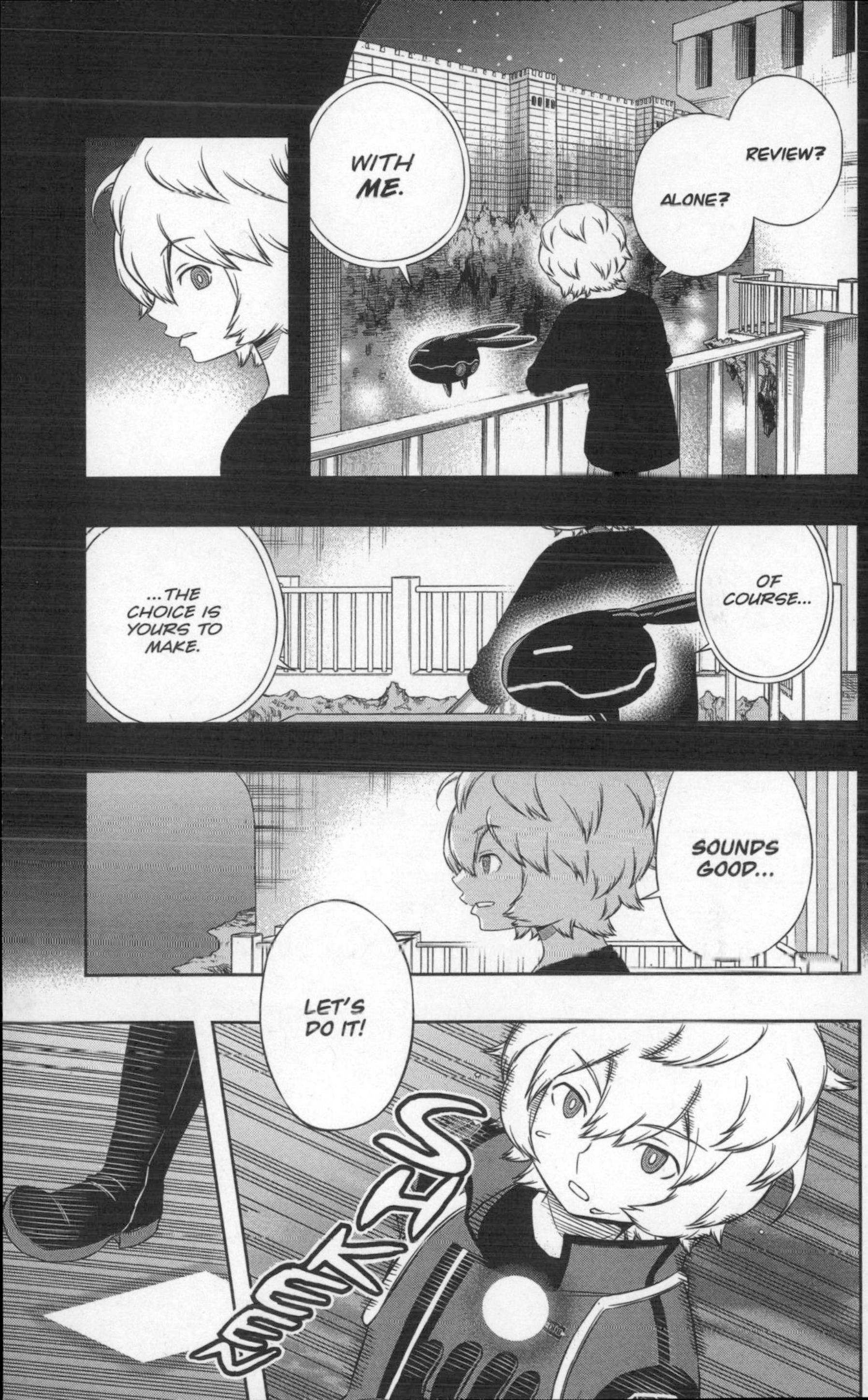
REVIEW?
ALONE?
WITH ME.
OF COURSE...
...THE CHOICE IS YOURS TO MAKE.
SOUNDS GOOD...
LET'S DO IT!

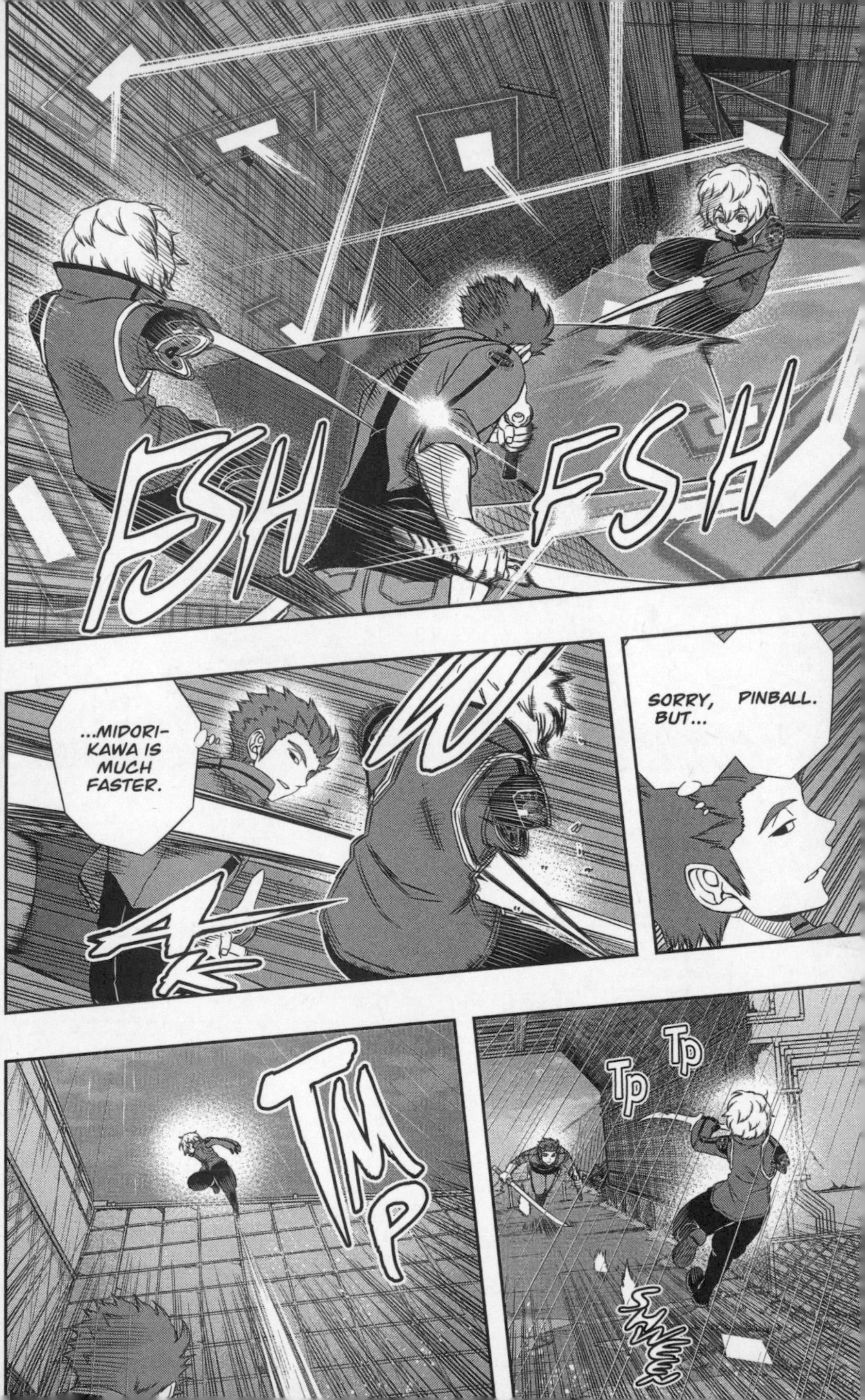
FSH
FSH
SORRY, PINBALL. BUT...
...MIDORI-KAWA IS MUCH FASTER.
Tp
Tp
TMP

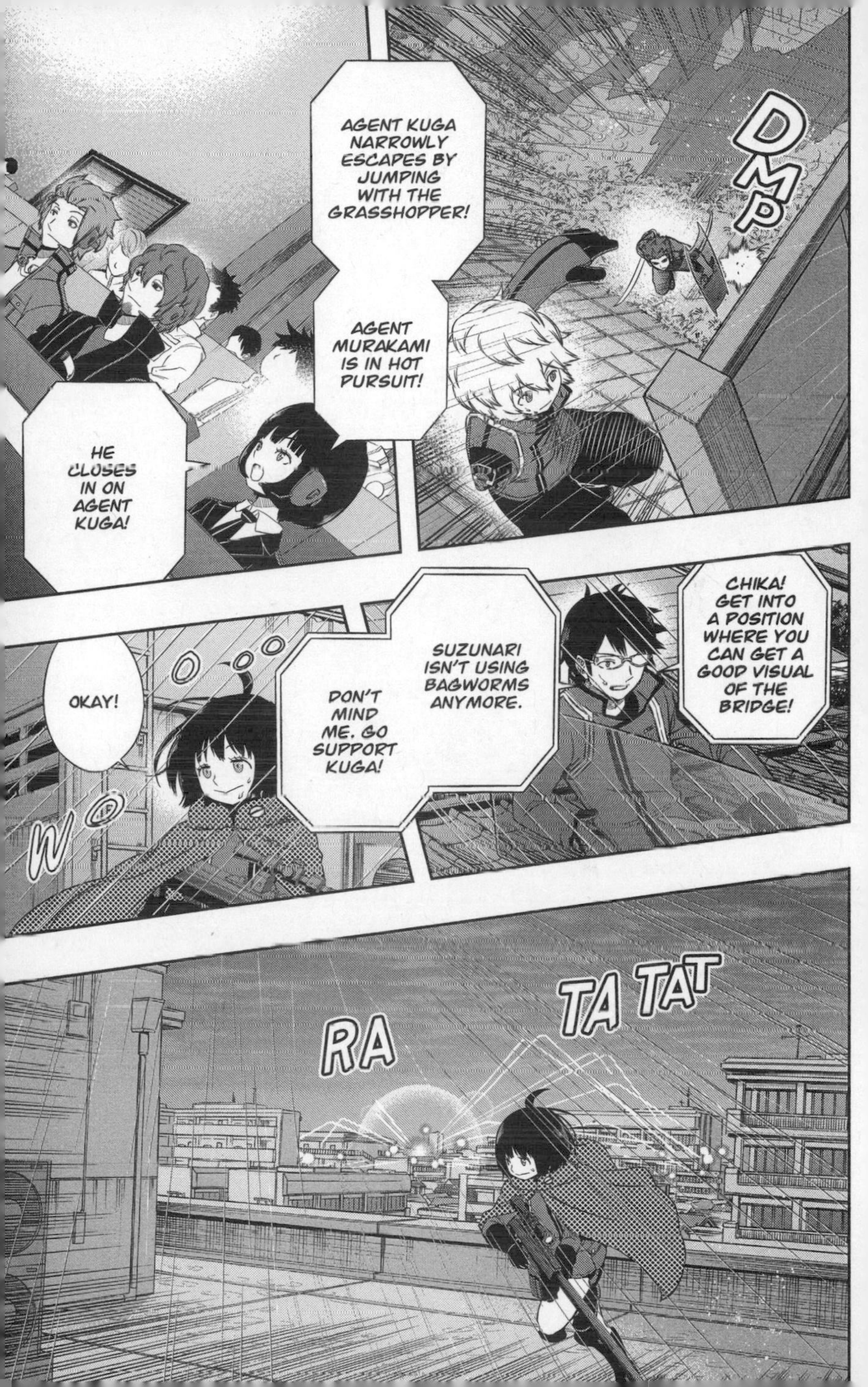
DMP
AGENT KUGA NARROWLY ESCAPES BY JUMPING WITH THE GRASSHOPPER!
AGENT MURAKAMI IS IN HOT PURSUIT!
HE CLOSES IN ON AGENT KUGA!
CHIKA! GET INTO A POSITION WHERE YOU CAN GET A GOOD VISUAL OF THE BRIDGE!
SUZUNARI ISN'T USING BAGWORMS ANYMORE.
DON'T MIND ME. GO SUPPORT KUGA!
WOOOO
OKAY!
TA TAT
RA

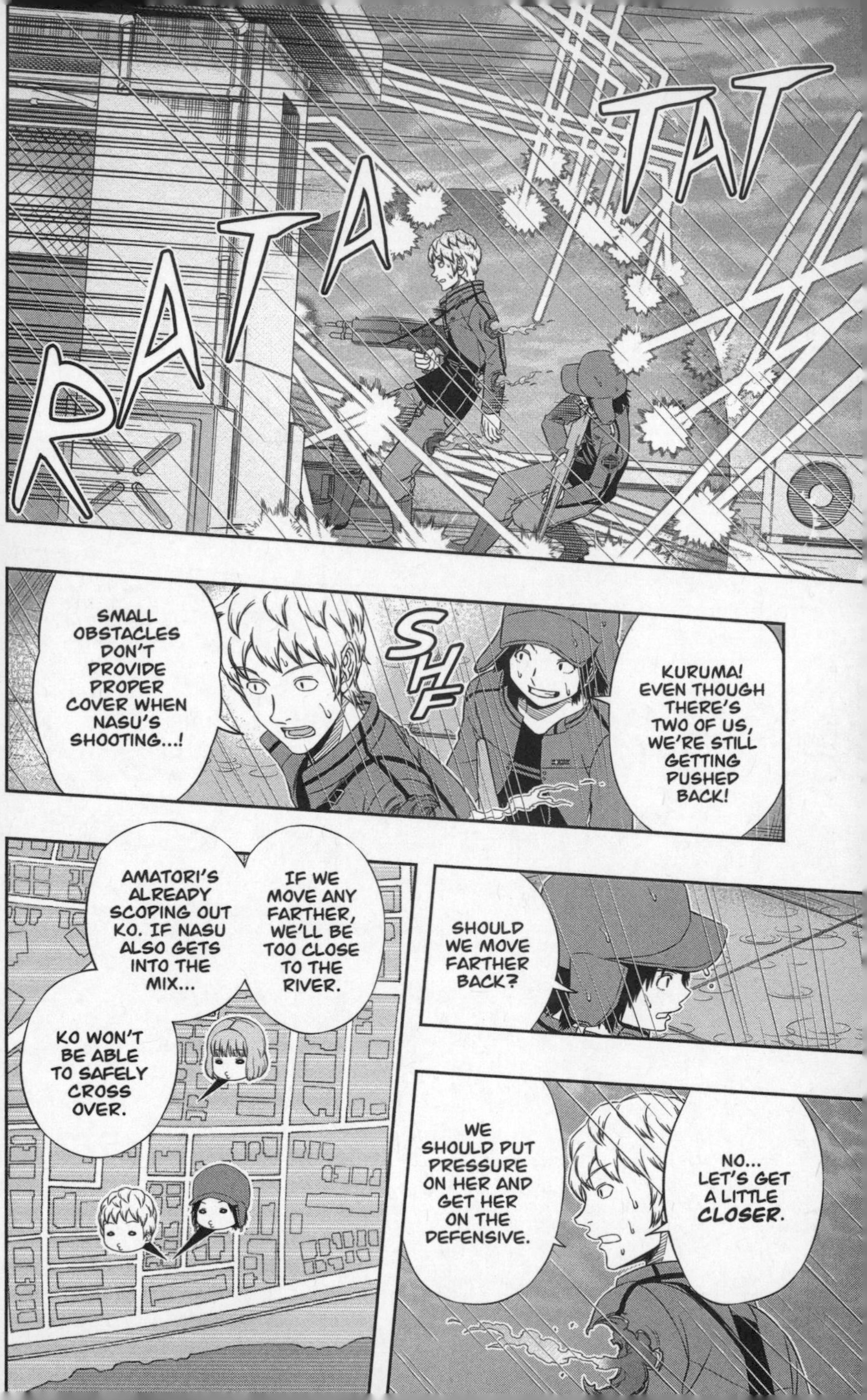
RATATATAT
KURUMA! EVEN THOUGH THERE'S TWO OF US, WE'RE STILL GETTING PUSHED BACK!
SHF
SMALL OBSTACLES DON'T PROVIDE PROPER COVER WHEN NASU'S SHOOTING...!
SHOULD WE MOVE FARTHER BACK?
NO... LET'S GET A LITTLE CLOSER.
WE SHOULD PUT PRESSURE ON HER AND GET HER ON THE DEFENSIVE.
IF WE MOVE ANY FARTHER, WE'LL BE TOO CLOSE TO THE RIVER.
AMATORI'S ALREADY SCOPING OUT KO. IF NASU ALSO GETS INTO THE MIX...
KO WON'T BE ABLE TO SAFELY CROSS OVER.

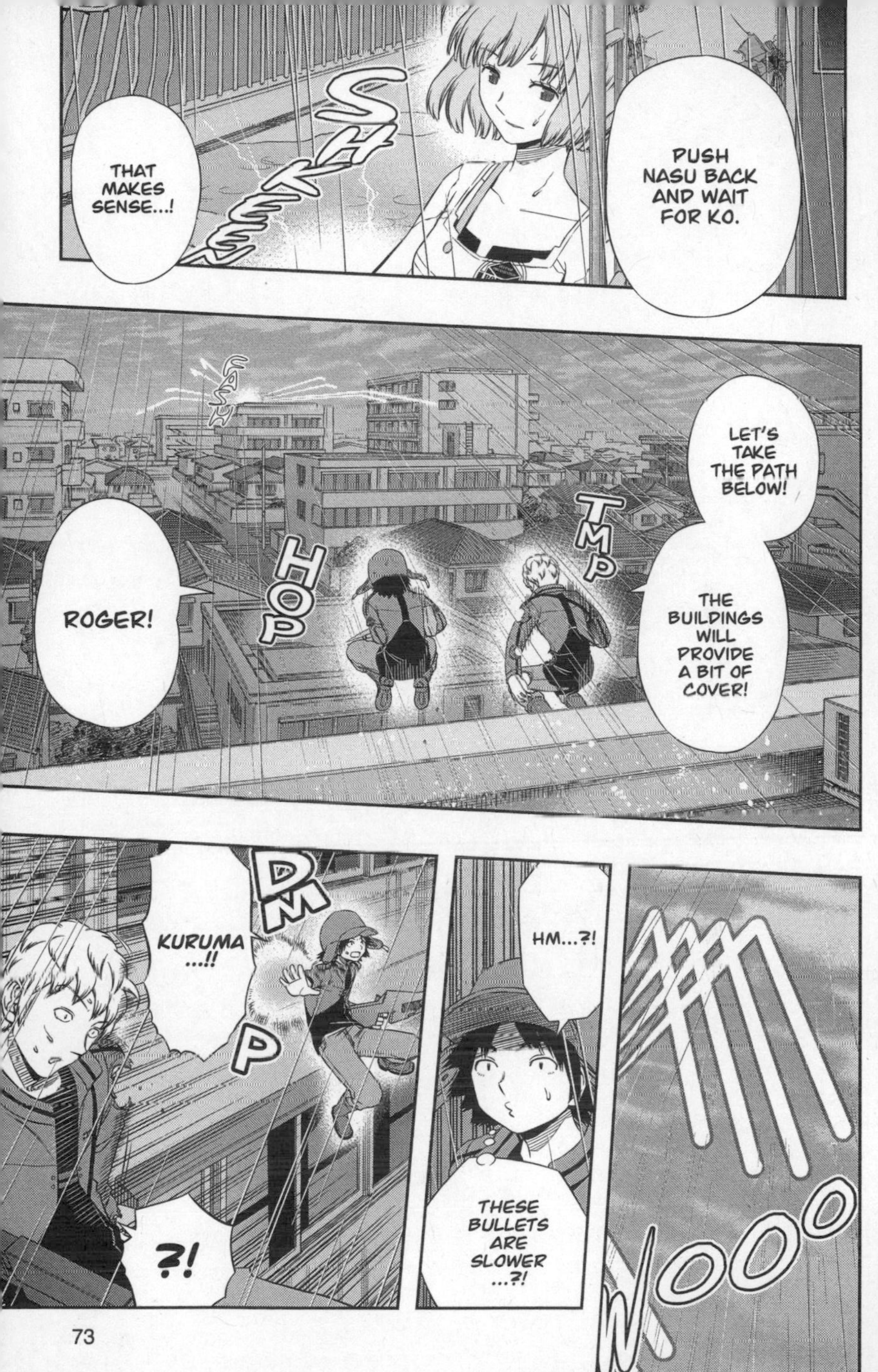
PUSH NASU BACK AND WAIT FOR KO.
SHKEEN
THAT MAKES SENSE...!
LET'S TAKE THE PATH BELOW!
THE BUILDINGS WILL PROVIDE A BIT OF COVER!
TMP
HOP
FASH
ROGER!
WOOO
HM...?!
THESE BULLETS ARE SLOWER ...?!
DM
KURUMA ...!!
P
?!

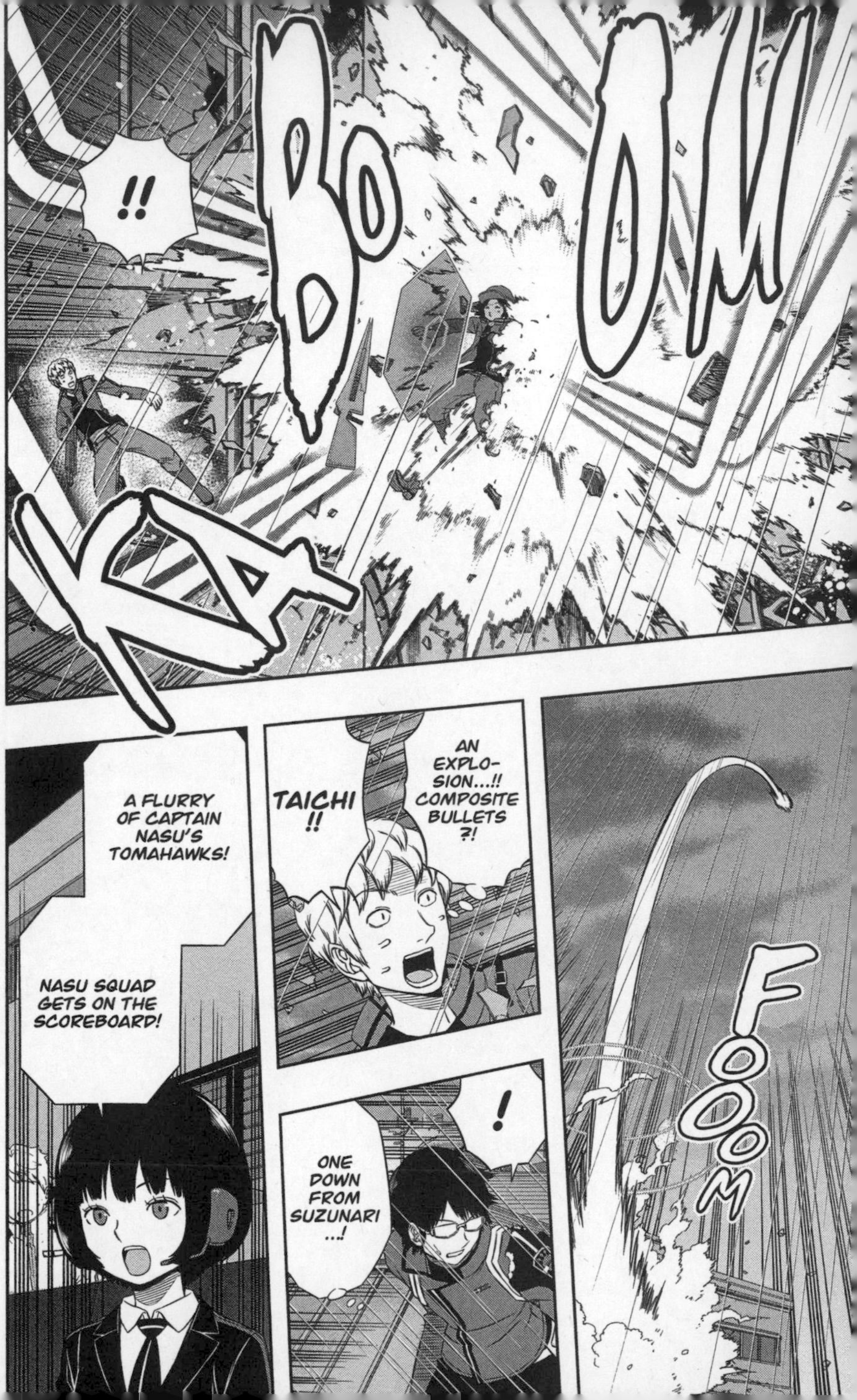
BOOM
!!
KA
FOOOOM
AN EXPLOSION...!! COMPOSITE BULLETS?!
TAICHI!!
!
ONE DOWN FROM SUZUNARI...!
A FLURRY OF CAPTAIN NASU'S TOMAHAWKS!
NASU SQUAD GETS ON THE SCOREBOARD!

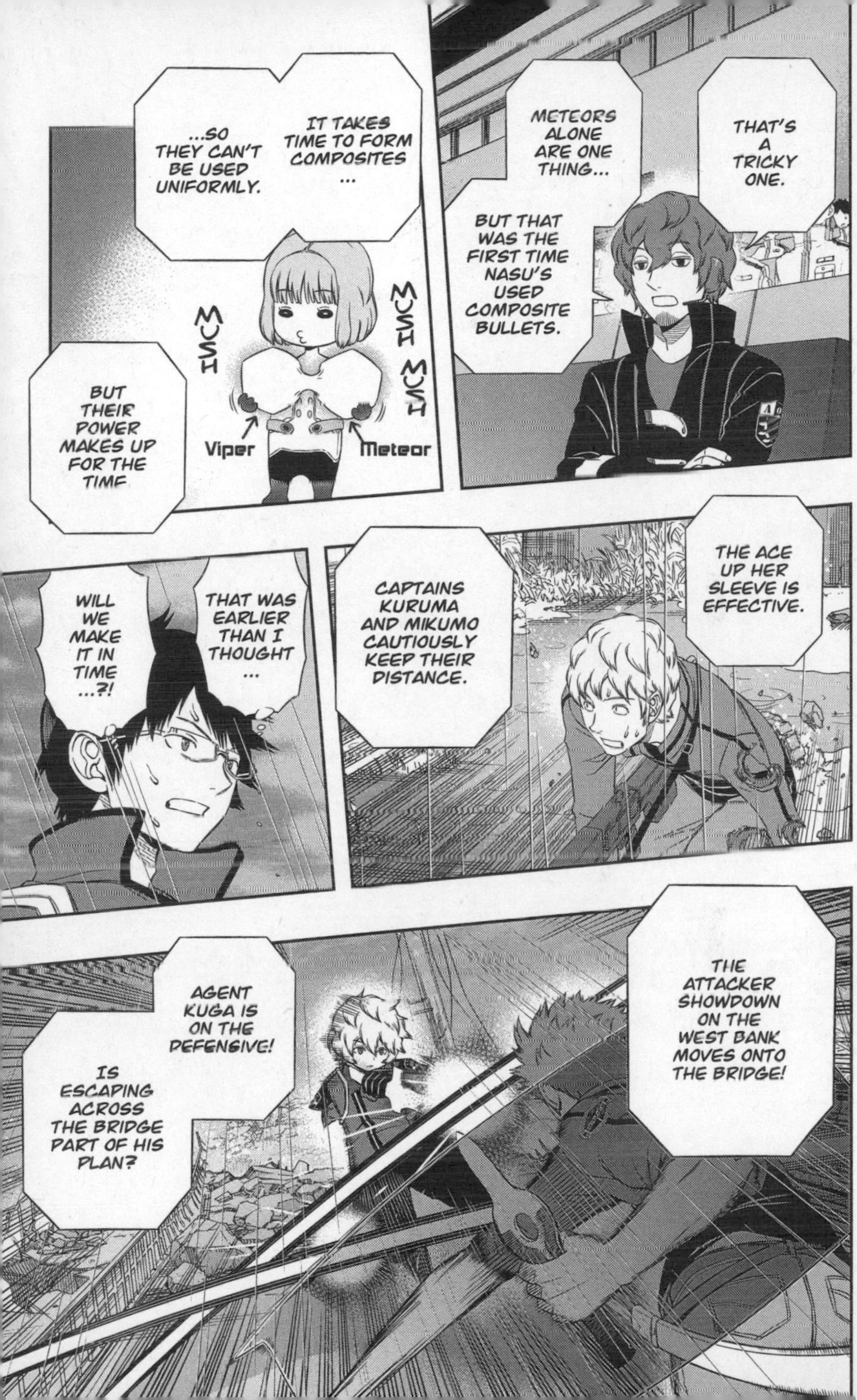
THAT'S A TRICKY ONE.
METEORS ALONE ARE ONE THING...
BUT THAT WAS THE FIRST TIME NASU'S USED COMPOSITE BULLETS.
IT TAKES TIME TO FORM COMPOSITES...
...SO THEY CAN'T BE USED UNIFORMLY.
MUSH MUSH
MUSH
Viper
Meteor
BUT THEIR POWER MAKES UP FOR THE TIME
THE ACE UP HER SLEEVE IS EFFECTIVE.
CAPTAINS KURUMA AND MIKUMO CAUTIOUSLY KEEP THEIR DISTANCE.
THAT WAS EARLIER THAN I THOUGHT...
WILL WE MAKE IT IN TIME...?!
THE ATTACKER SHOWDOWN ON THE WEST BANK MOVES ONTO THE BRIDGE!
AGENT KUGA IS ON THE DEFENSIVE!
IS ESCAPING ACROSS THE BRIDGE PART OF HIS PLAN?

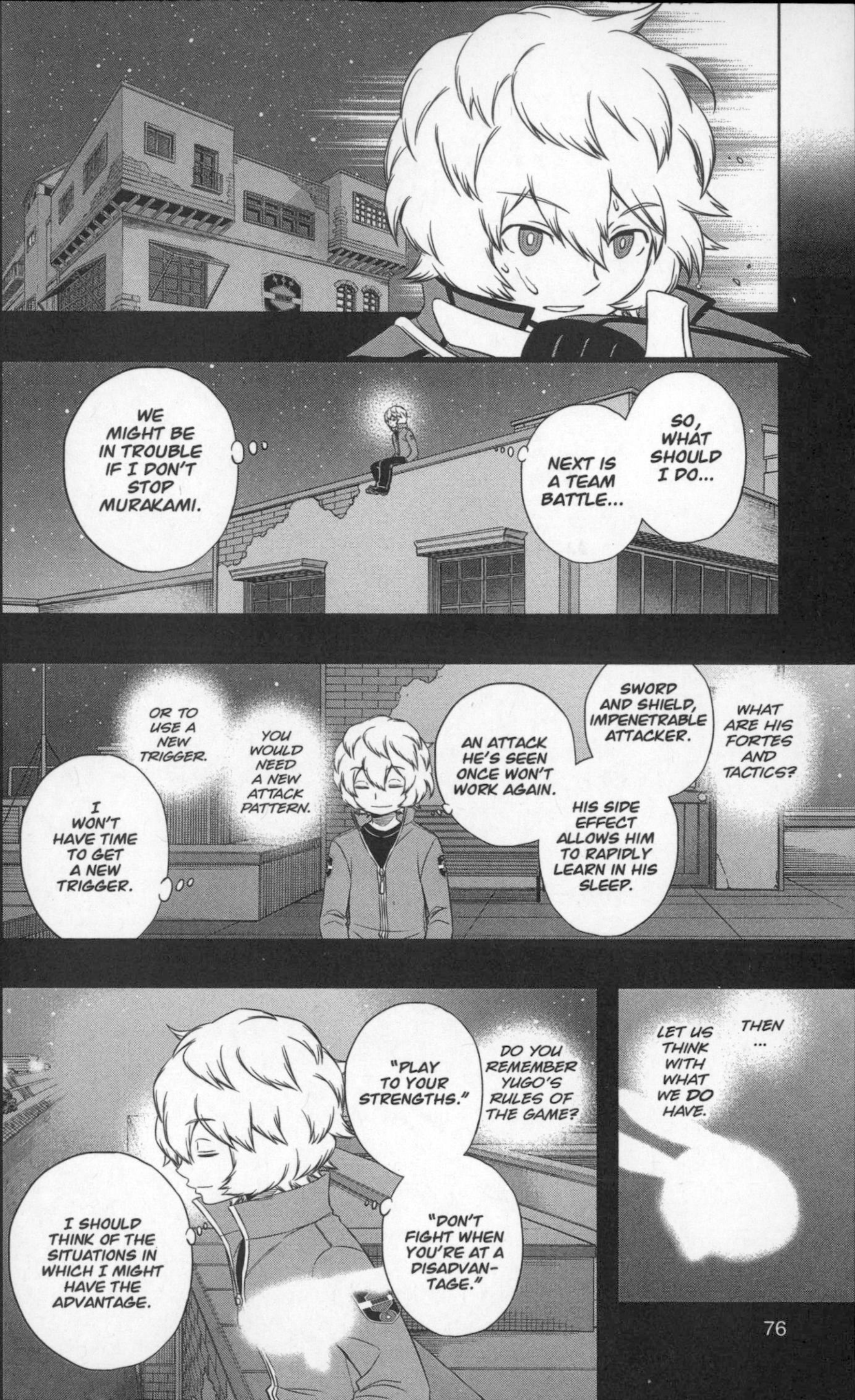
SO, WHAT SHOULD I DO...
NEXT IS A TEAM BATTLE...
WE MIGHT BE IN TROUBLE IF I DON'T STOP MURAKAMI.
WHAT ARE HIS FORTES AND TACTICS?
SWORD AND SHIELD, IMPENETRABLE ATTACKER.
HIS SIDE EFFECT ALLOWS HIM TO RAPIDLY LEARN IN HIS SLEEP.
AN ATTACK HE'S SEEN ONCE WON'T WORK AGAIN.
YOU WOULD NEED A NEW ATTACK PATTERN.
OR TO USE A NEW TRIGGER.
I WON'T HAVE TIME TO GET A NEW TRIGGER.
THEN ...
LET US THINK WITH WHAT WE DO HAVE.
DO YOU REMEMBER YUGO'S RULES OF THE GAME?
"PLAY TO YOUR STRENGTHS."
"DON'T FIGHT WHEN YOU'RE AT A DISADVANTAGE."
I SHOULD THINK OF THE SITUATIONS IN WHICH I MIGHT HAVE THE ADVANTAGE.

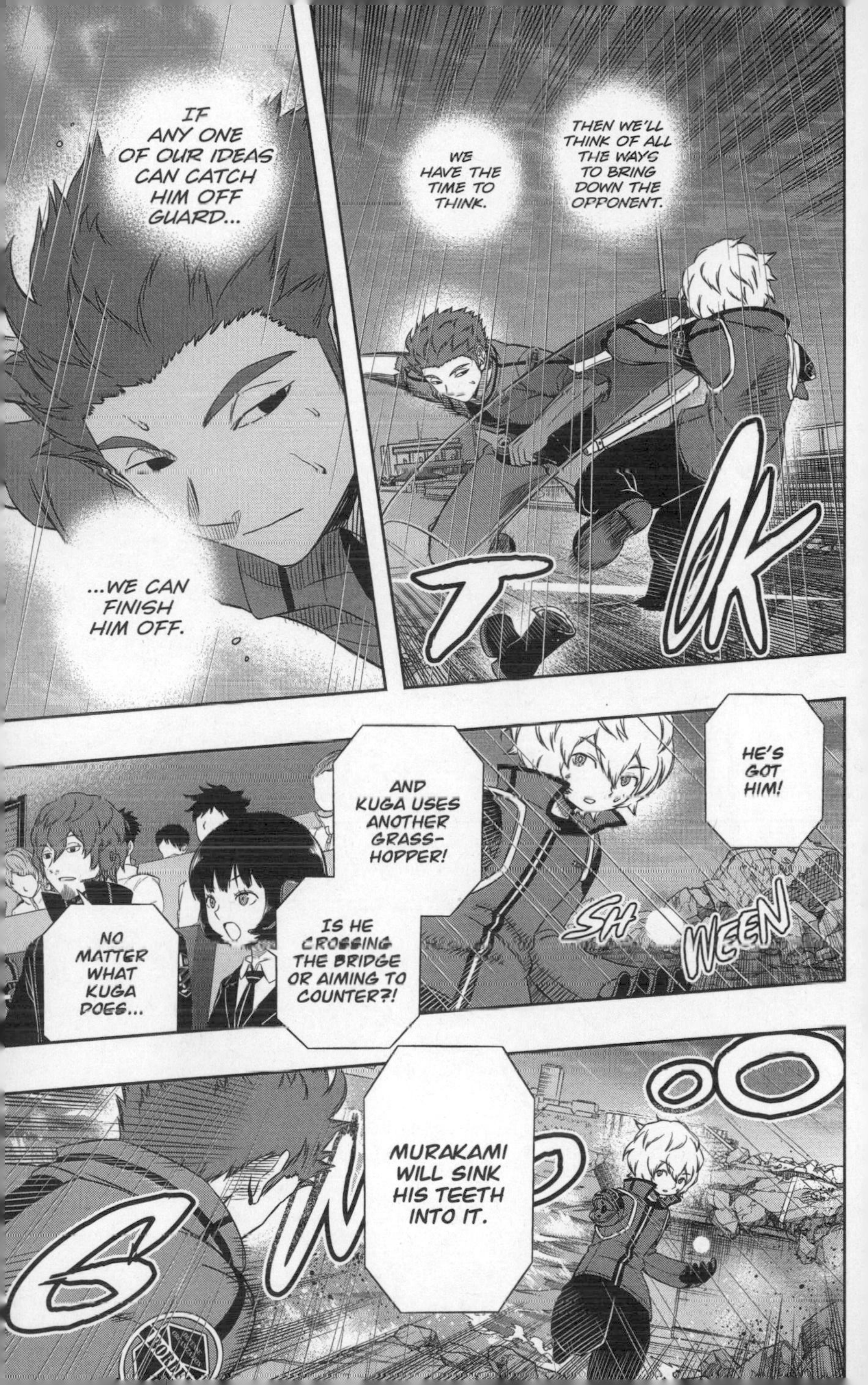
THEN WE'LL THINK OF ALL THE WAYS TO BRING DOWN THE OPPONENT.
WE HAVE THE TIME TO THINK.
TOK
IF ANY ONE OF OUR IDEAS CAN CATCH HIM OFF GUARD...
...WE CAN FINISH HIM OFF.
HE'S GOT HIM!
AND KUGA USES ANOTHER GRASS-HOPPER!
SHWEEN
IS HE CROSSING THE BRIDGE OR AIMING TO COUNTER?!
NO MATTER WHAT KUGA DOES...
OO
MURAKAMI WILL SINK HIS TEETH INTO IT.
GWOO

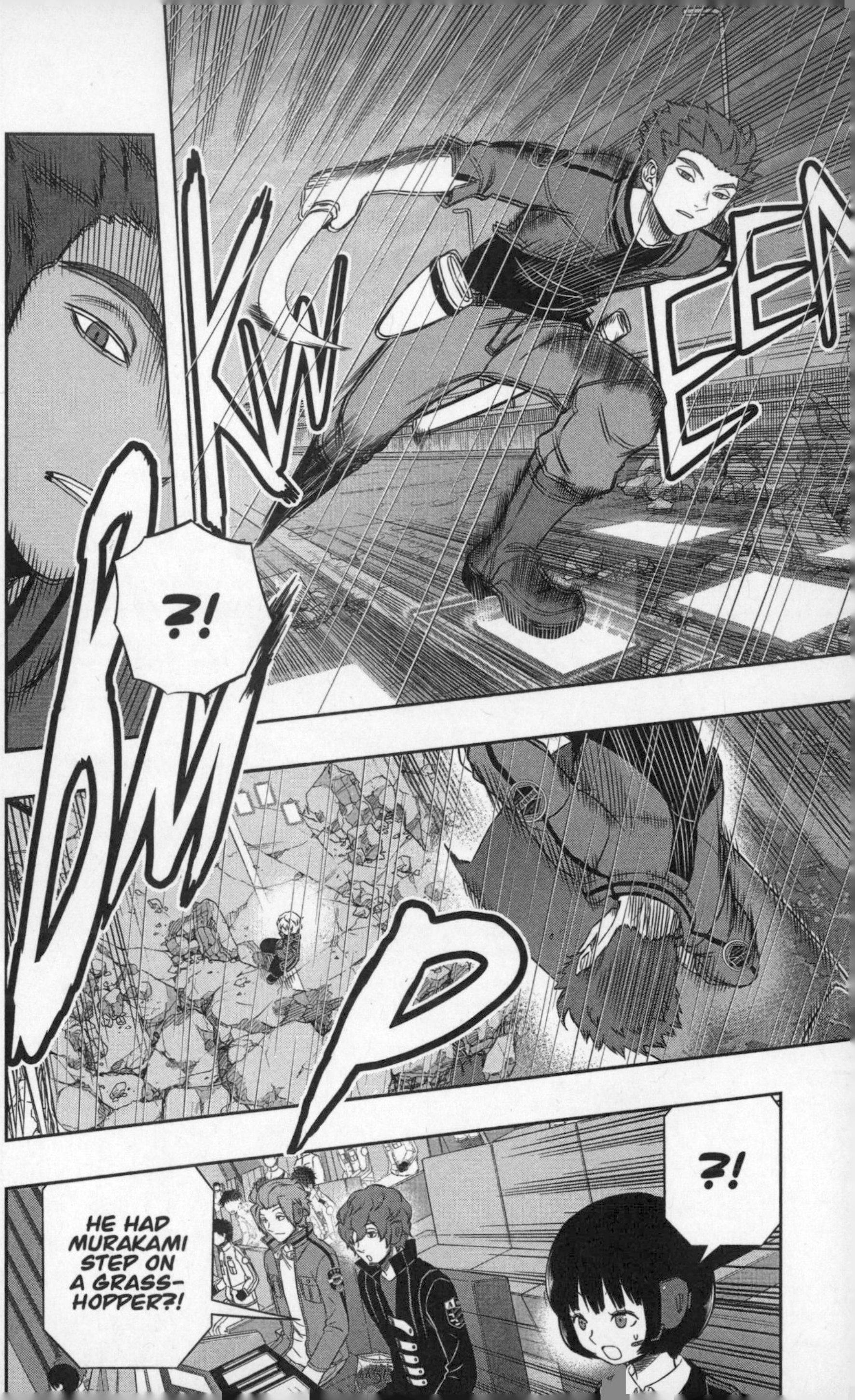
KWEEN
?!
BMP
?!
HE HAD MURAKAMI STEP ON A GRASS-HOPPER?!

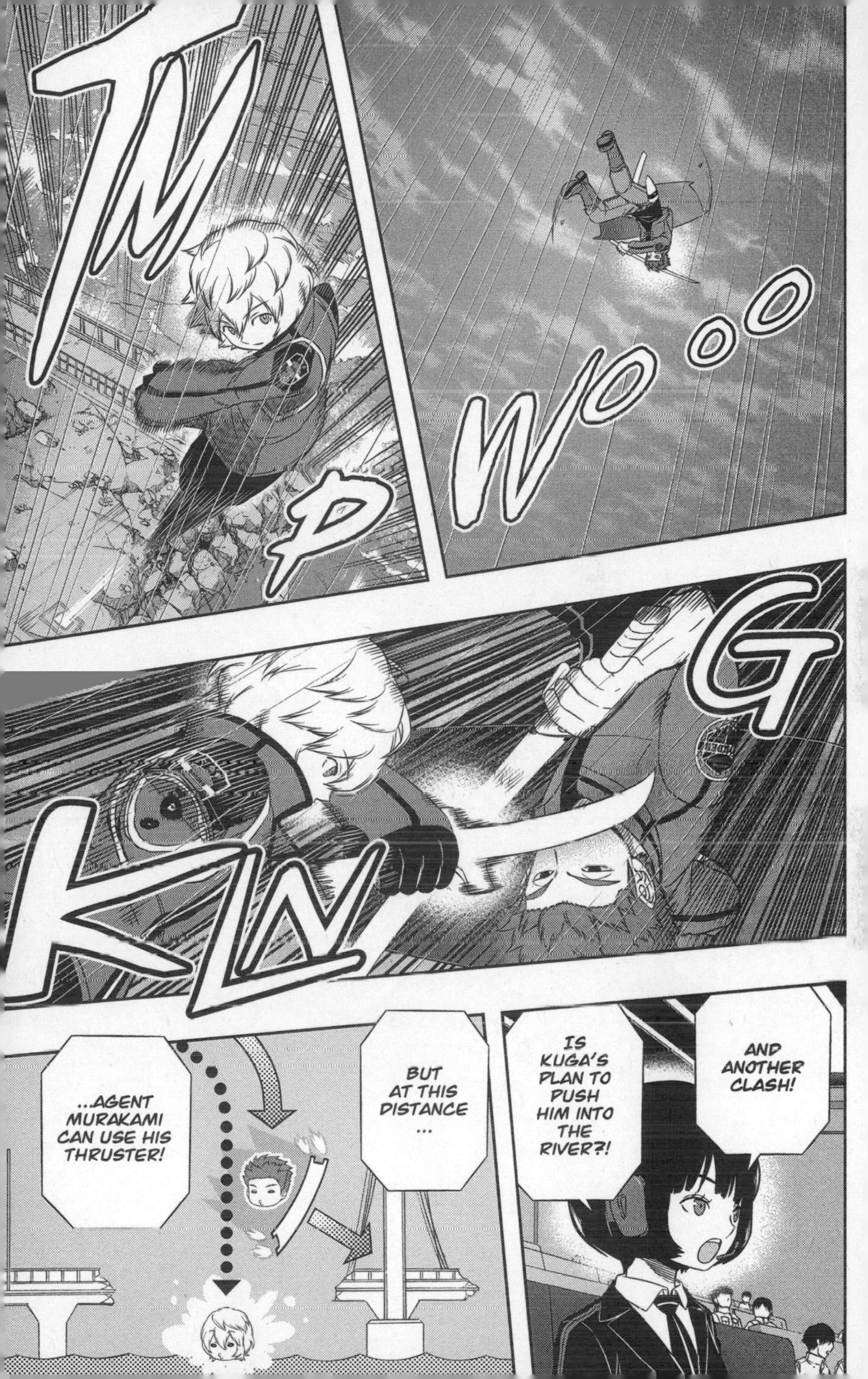
WOOO
TMP
KLNG
AND ANOTHER CLASH!
IS KUGA'S PLAN TO PUSH HIM INTO THE RIVER?!
BUT AT THIS DISTANCE...
...AGENT MURAKAMI CAN USE HIS THRUSTER!

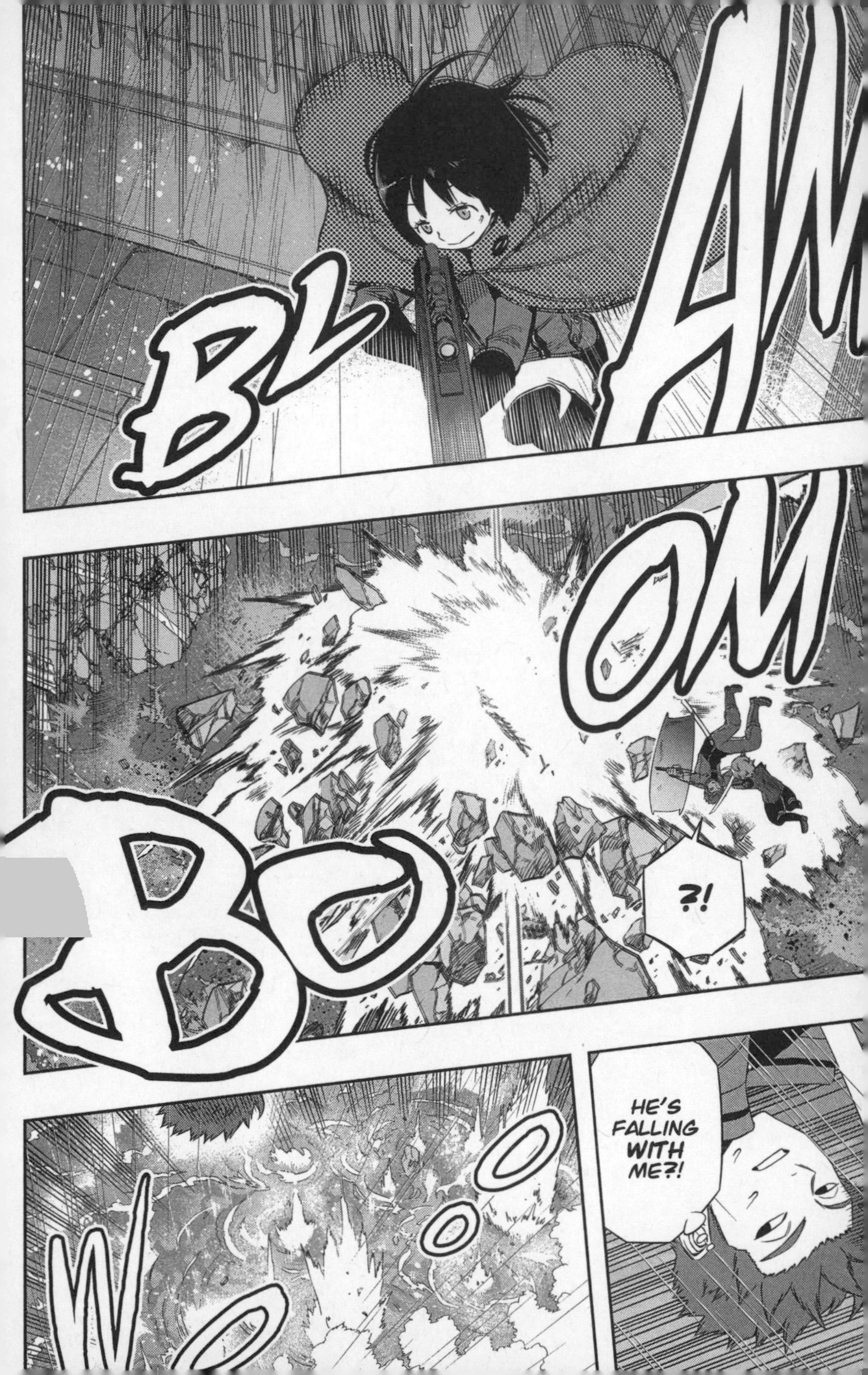
BLAM
BOOM
?!
HE'S FALLING WITH ME?!
WOOO

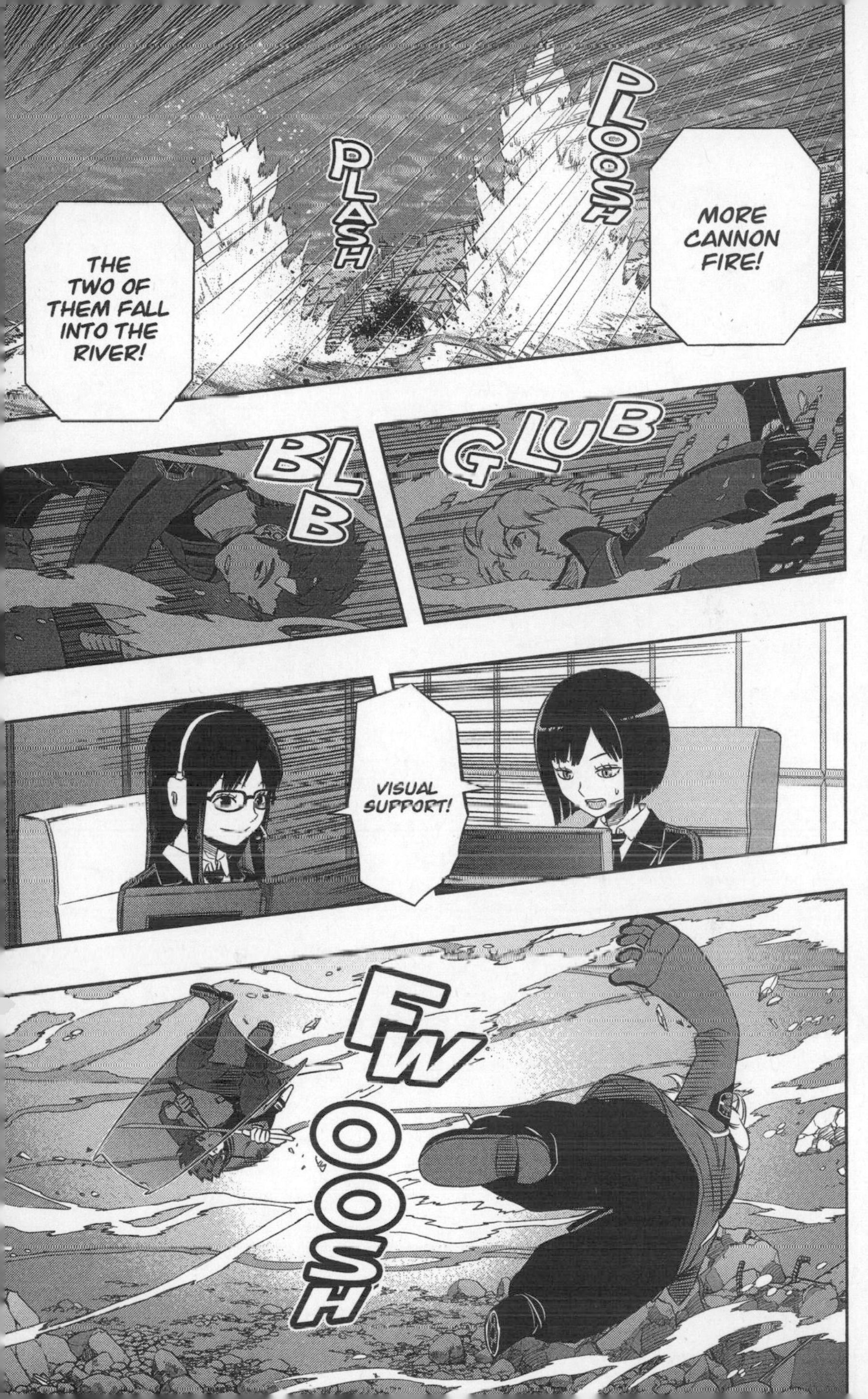
MORE CANNON FIRE!
PLOOSH
PLASH
THE TWO OF THEM FALL INTO THE RIVER!
GLUB
BLB
VISUAL SUPPORT!
FWOOSH

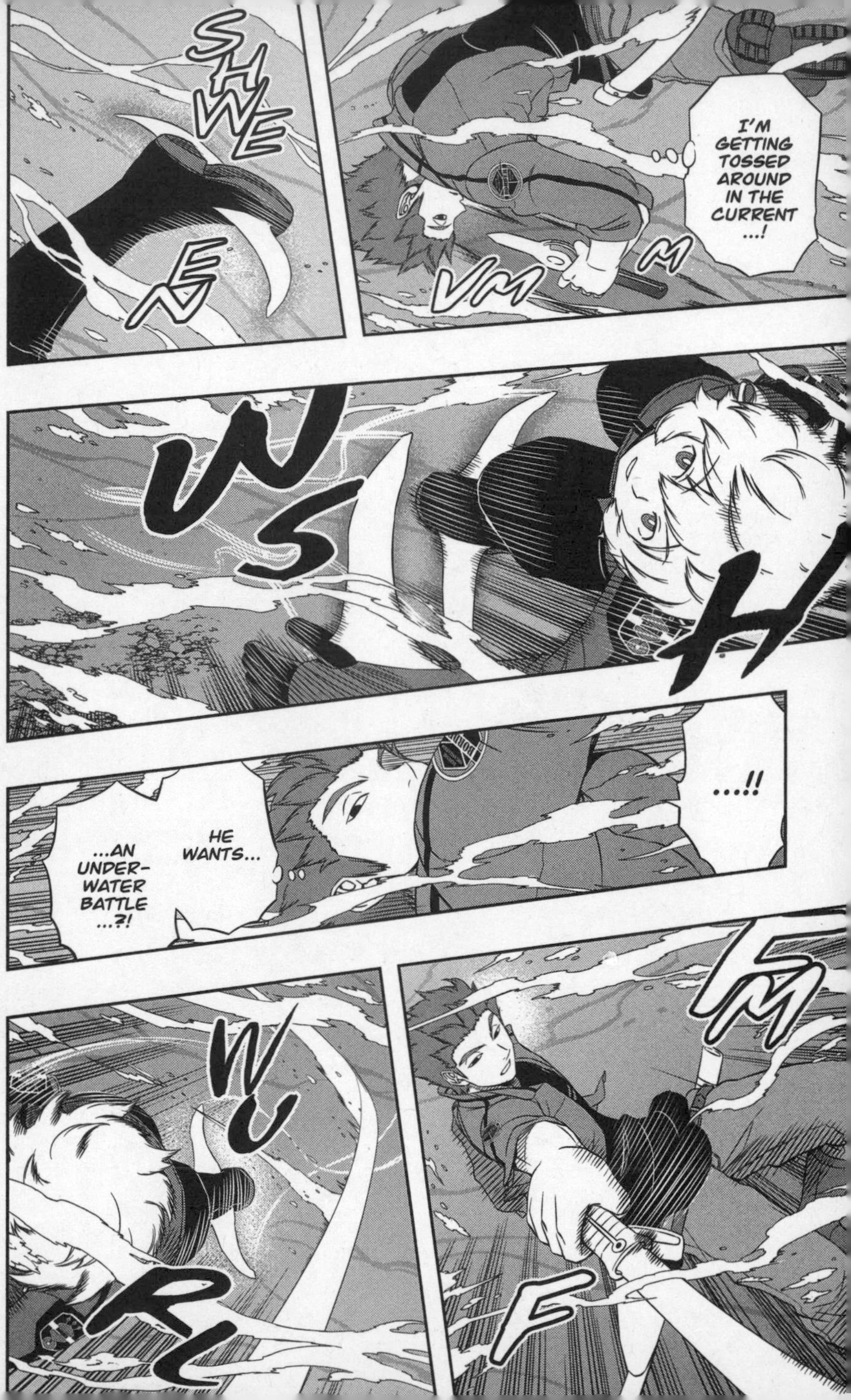
I'M GETTING TOSSED AROUND IN THE CURRENT ...!
VMM
SHWE
EN
WSHH
...!!
HE WANTS...
...AN UNDER-WATER BATTLE ...?!
MM
F
WU
RL

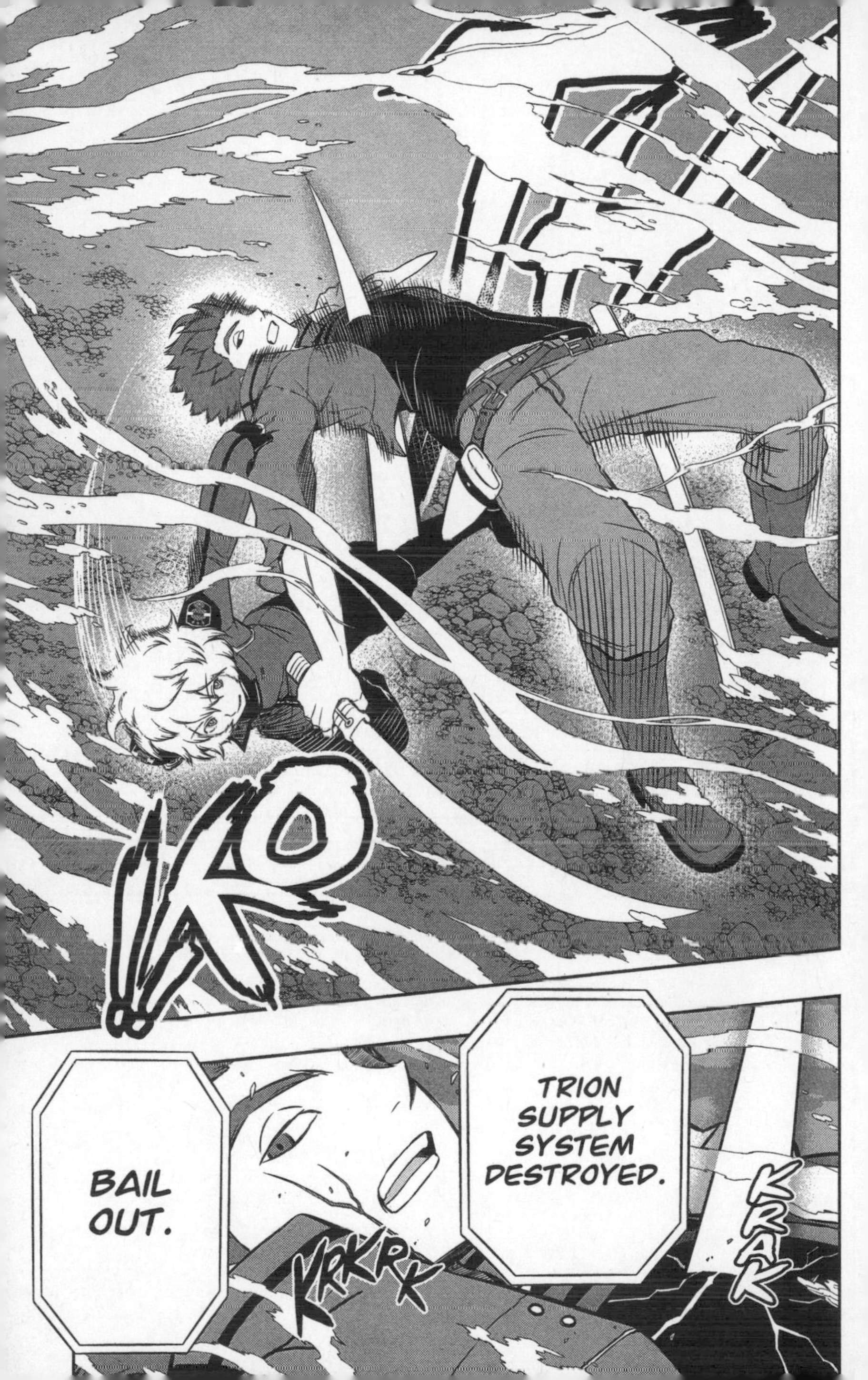
KO
TRION SUPPLY SYSTEM DESTROYED.
KRAK
KRKRK
BAIL OUT.

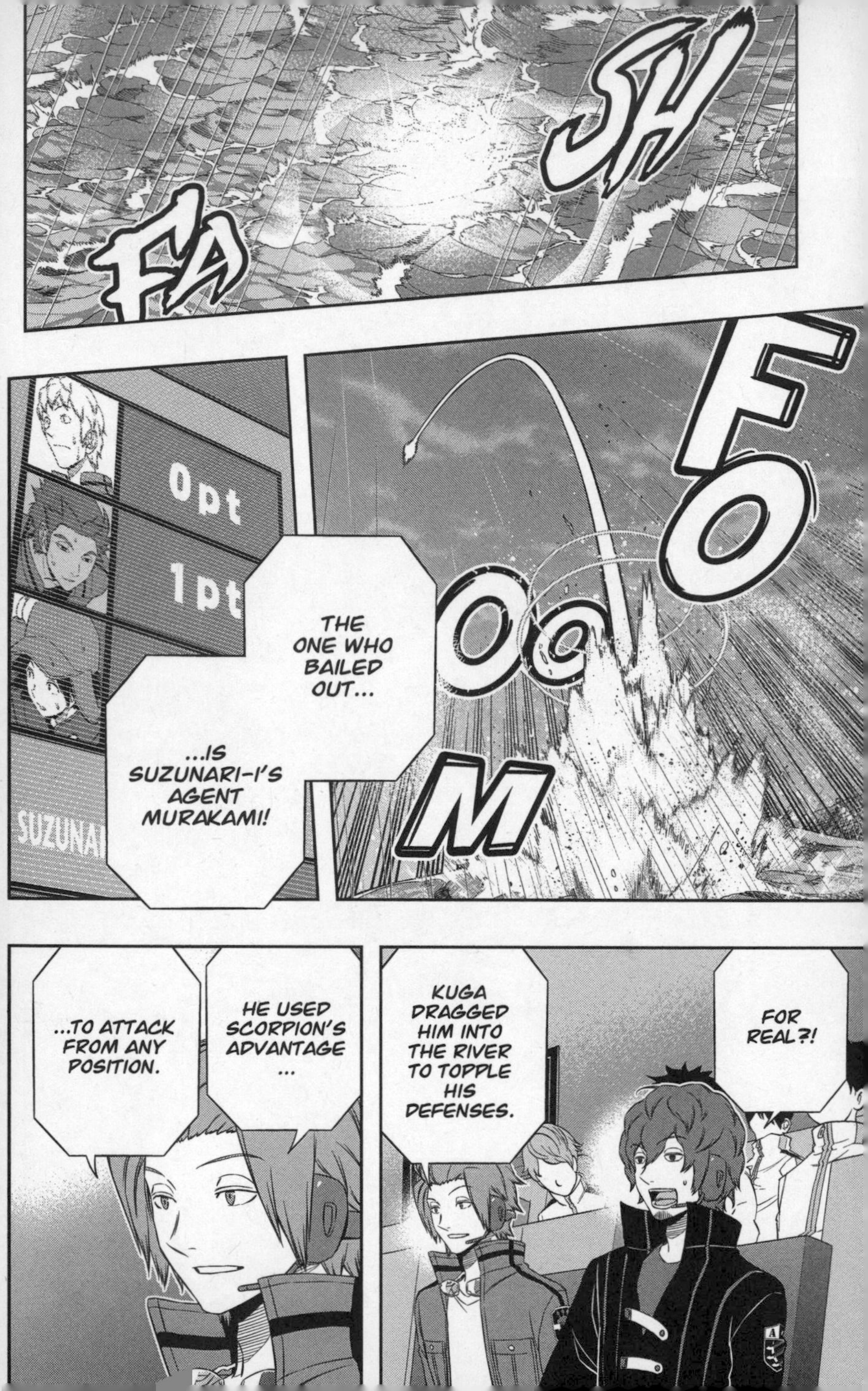
FASH
FOOOM
0pt
1pt
THE ONE WHO BAILED OUT...
...IS SUZUNARI-1'S AGENT MURAKAMI!
FOR REAL?!
KUGA DRAGGED HIM INTO THE RIVER TO TOPPLE HIS DEFENSES.
HE USED SCORPION'S ADVANTAGE...
...TO ATTACK FROM ANY POSITION.

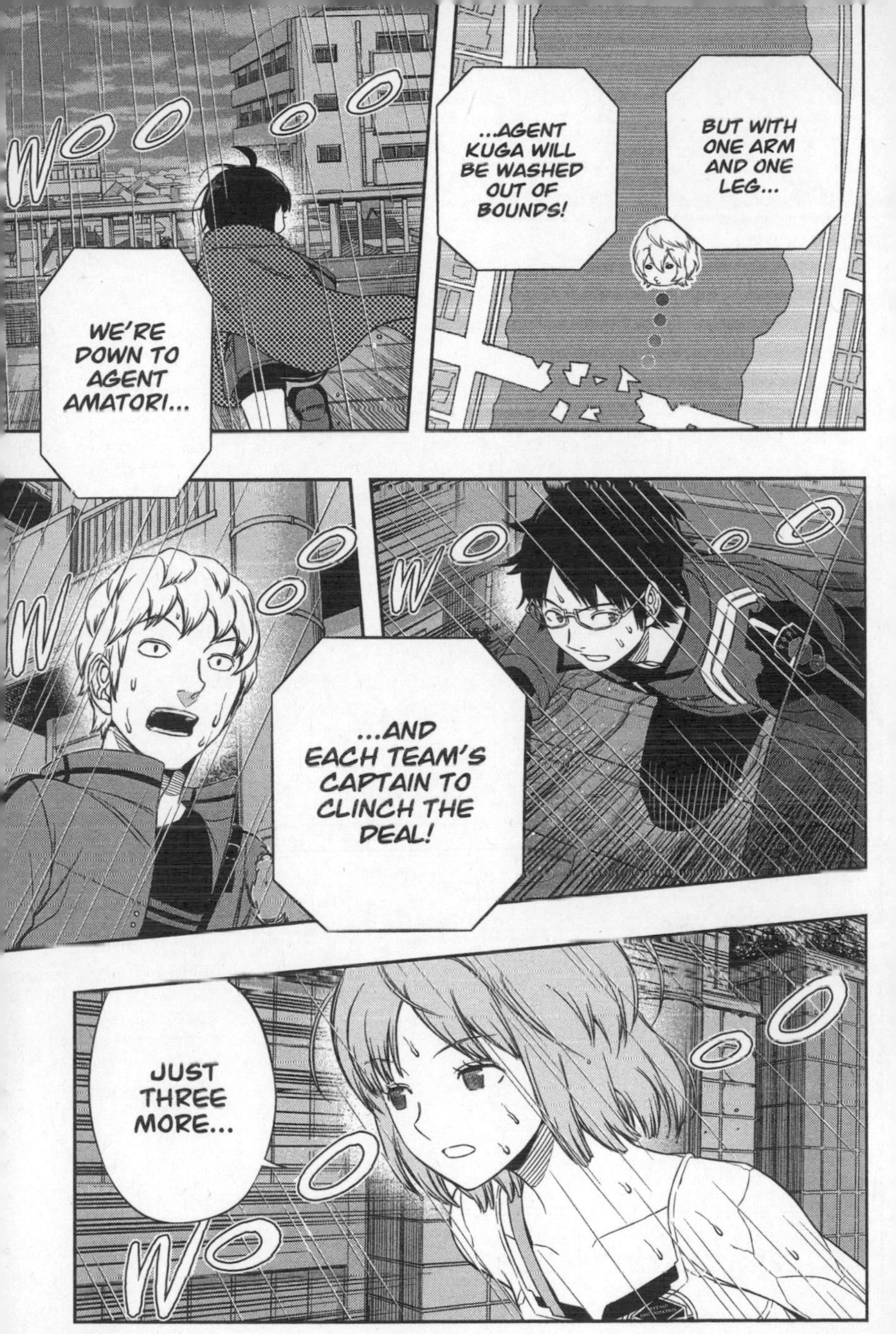
BUT WITH ONE ARM AND ONE LEG...
...AGENT KUGA WILL BE WASHED OUT OF BOUNDS!
WOOOOO
WE'RE DOWN TO AGENT AMATORI...
WOOOO
...AND EACH TEAM'S CAPTAIN TO CLINCH THE DEAL!
WOOO
JUST THREE MORE...
WOOOOO

Suzunari-1 Strategy Room

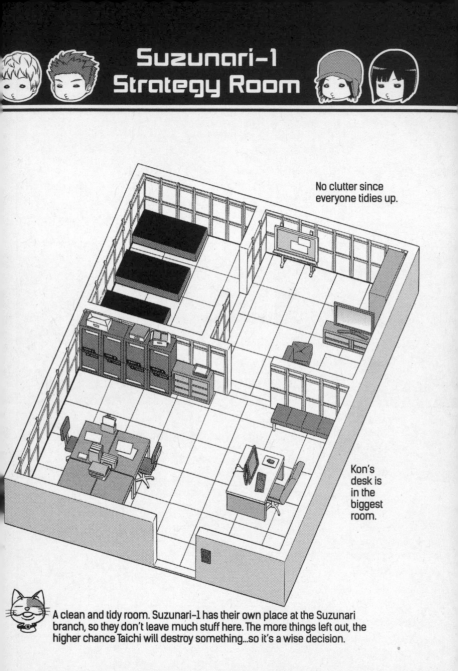

No clutter since everyone tidies up.

Kon's desk is in the biggest room.

A clean and tidy room. Suzunari-1 has their own place at the Suzunari branch, so they don't leave much stuff here. The more things left out, the higher chance Taichi will destroy something...so it's a wise decision.

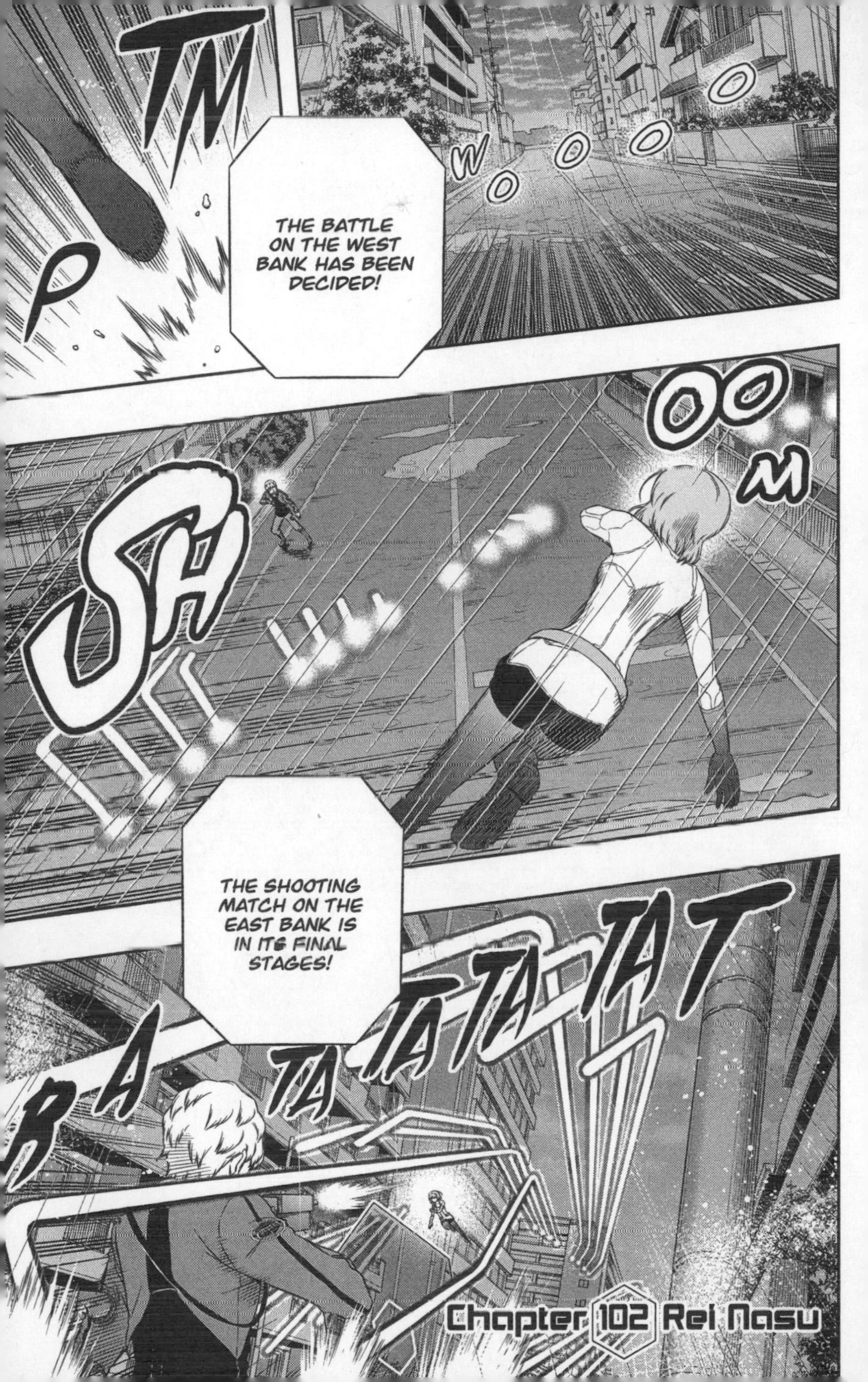
WOOOOO
THE BATTLE ON THE WEST BANK HAS BEEN DECIDED!
TMP
OOM
SH
THE SHOOTING MATCH ON THE EAST BANK IS IN ITS FINAL STAGES!
B A TA TA TA-TA-TAT
Chapter 102 Rei Nasu

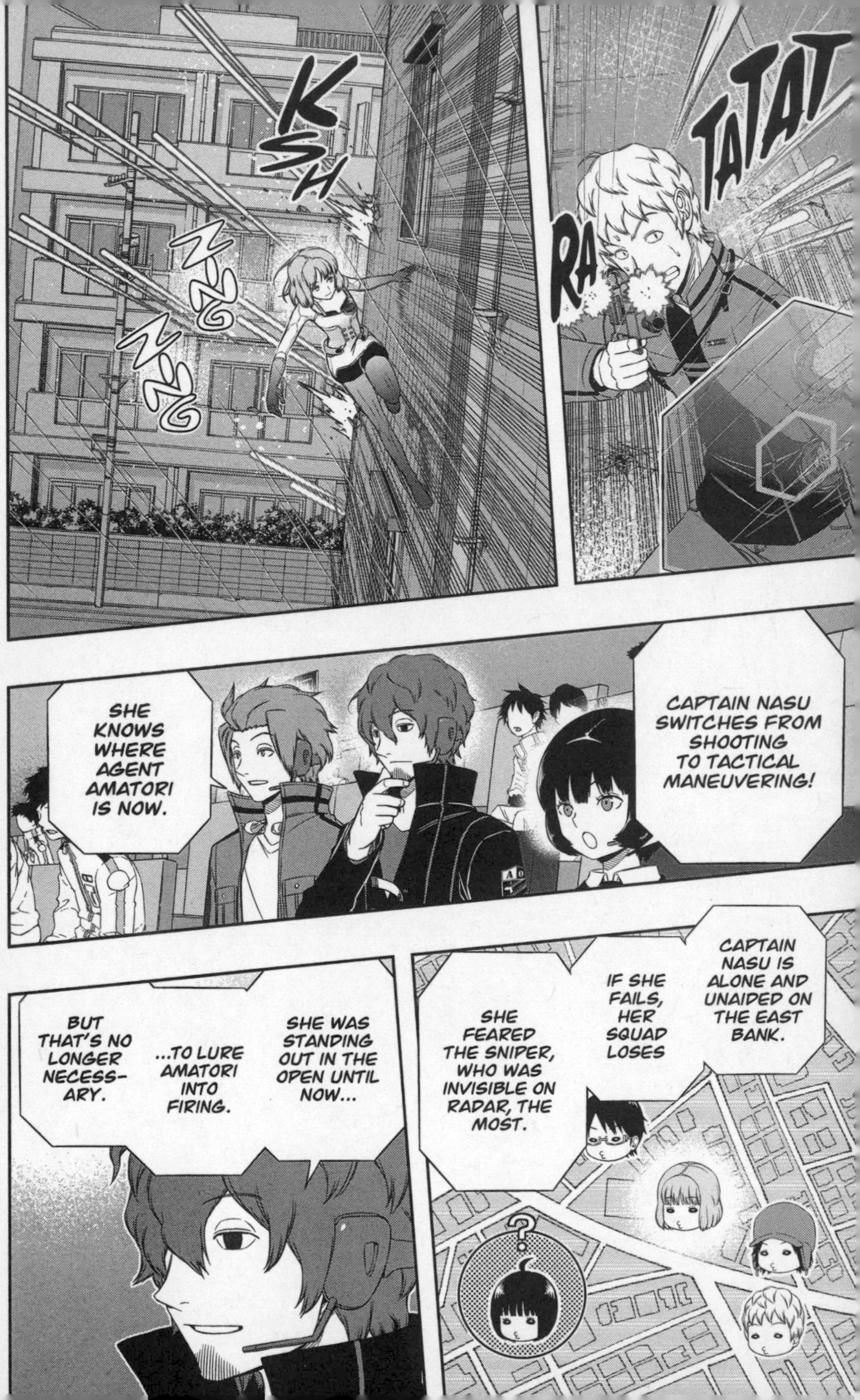
RA
TATAT
KSH
NZG
NZG
CAPTAIN NASU SWITCHES FROM SHOOTING TO TACTICAL MANEUVERING!
SHE KNOWS WHERE AGENT AMATORI IS NOW.
CAPTAIN NASU IS ALONE AND UNAIDED ON THE EAST BANK.
IF SHE FAILS, HER SQUAD LOSES
SHE FEARED THE SNIPER, WHO WAS INVISIBLE ON RADAR, THE MOST.
SHE WAS STANDING OUT IN THE OPEN UNTIL NOW...
...TO LURE AMATORI INTO FIRING.
BUT THAT'S NO LONGER NECESS-ARY.

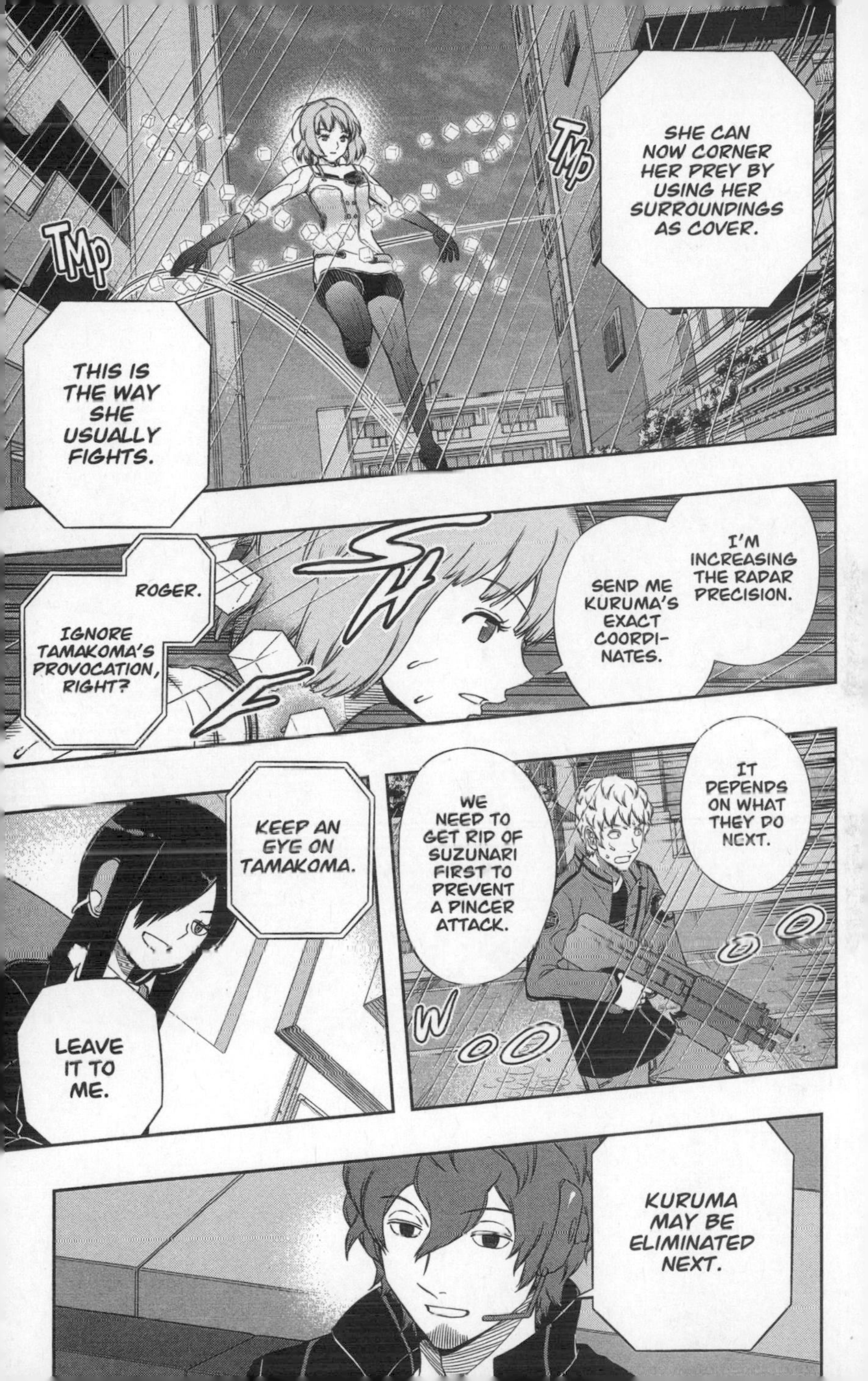
SHE CAN NOW CORNER HER PREY BY USING HER SURROUNDINGS AS COVER.
TMP
TMP
THIS IS THE WAY SHE USUALLY FIGHTS.
I'M INCREASING THE RADAR PRECISION.
SEND ME KURUMA'S EXACT COORDI-NATES.
SHF
ROGER.
IGNORE TAMAKOMA'S PROVOCATION, RIGHT?
IT DEPENDS ON WHAT THEY DO NEXT.
WE NEED TO GET RID OF SUZUNARI FIRST TO PREVENT A PINCER ATTACK.
WOO
KEEP AN EYE ON TAMAKOMA.
LEAVE IT TO ME.
KURUMA MAY BE ELIMINATED NEXT.

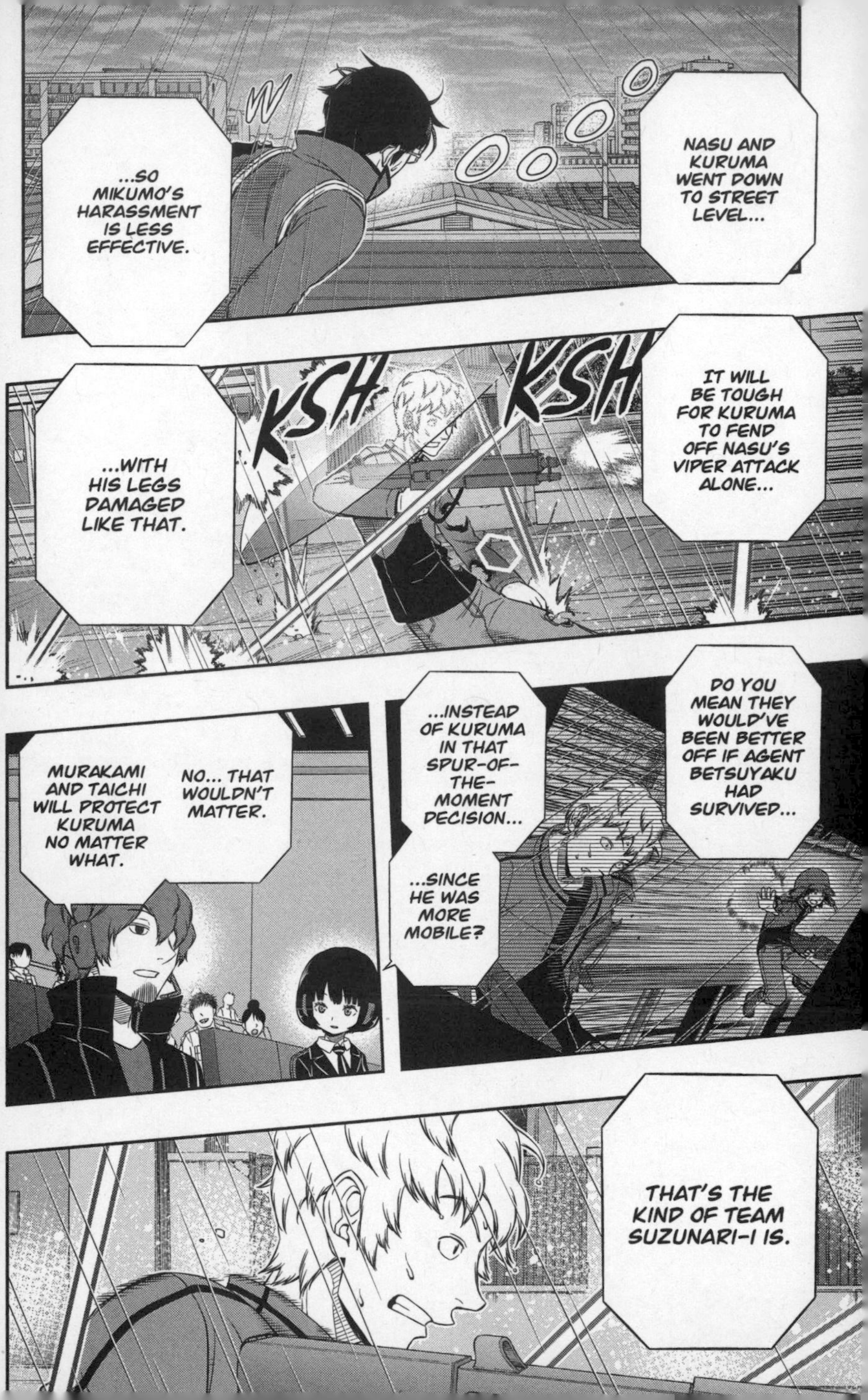
NASU AND KURUMA WENT DOWN TO STREET LEVEL...
WOOOO
...SO MIKUMO'S HARASSMENT IS LESS EFFECTIVE.
IT WILL BE TOUGH FOR KURUMA TO FEND OFF NASU'S VIPER ATTACK ALONE...
KSH
KSH
...WITH HIS LEGS DAMAGED LIKE THAT.
DO YOU MEAN THEY WOULD'VE BEEN BETTER OFF IF AGENT BETSUYAKU HAD SURVIVED...
...INSTEAD OF KURUMA IN THAT SPUR-OF-THE-MOMENT DECISION...
...SINCE HE WAS MORE MOBILE?
NO... THAT WOULDN'T MATTER.
MURAKAMI AND TAICHI WILL PROTECT KURUMA NO MATTER WHAT.
THAT'S THE KIND OF TEAM SUZUNARI-1 IS.

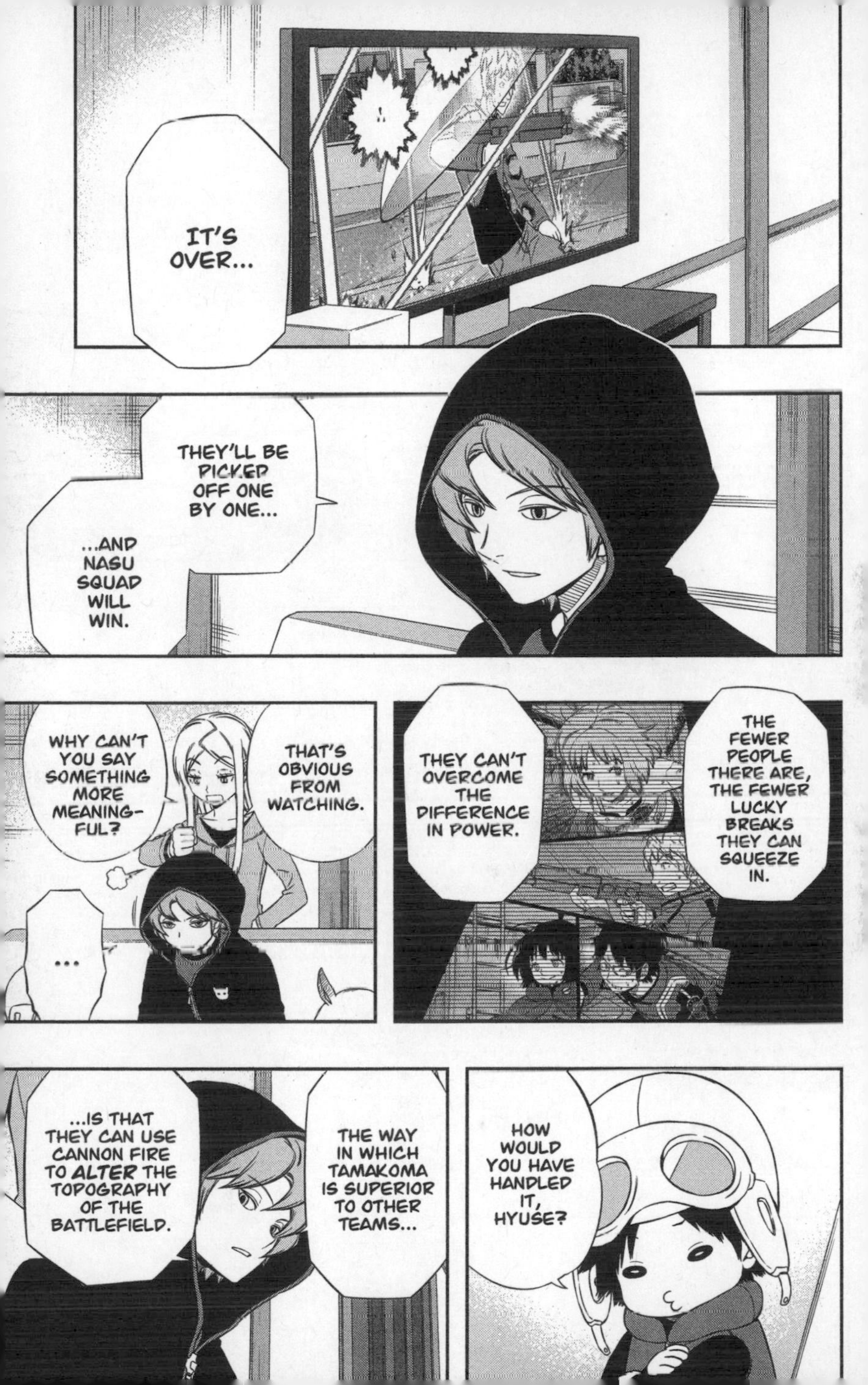
IT'S OVER...
THEY'LL BE PICKED OFF ONE BY ONE...
...AND NASU SQUAD WILL WIN.
THE FEWER PEOPLE THERE ARE, THE FEWER LUCKY BREAKS THEY CAN SQUEEZE IN.
THEY CAN'T OVERCOME THE DIFFERENCE IN POWER.
THAT'S OBVIOUS FROM WATCHING.
WHY CAN'T YOU SAY SOMETHING MORE MEANING-FUL?
...
HOW WOULD YOU HAVE HANDLED IT, HYUSE?
THE WAY IN WHICH TAMAKOMA IS SUPERIOR TO OTHER TEAMS...
...IS THAT THEY CAN USE CANNON FIRE TO ALTER THE TOPOGRAPHY OF THE BATTLEFIELD.

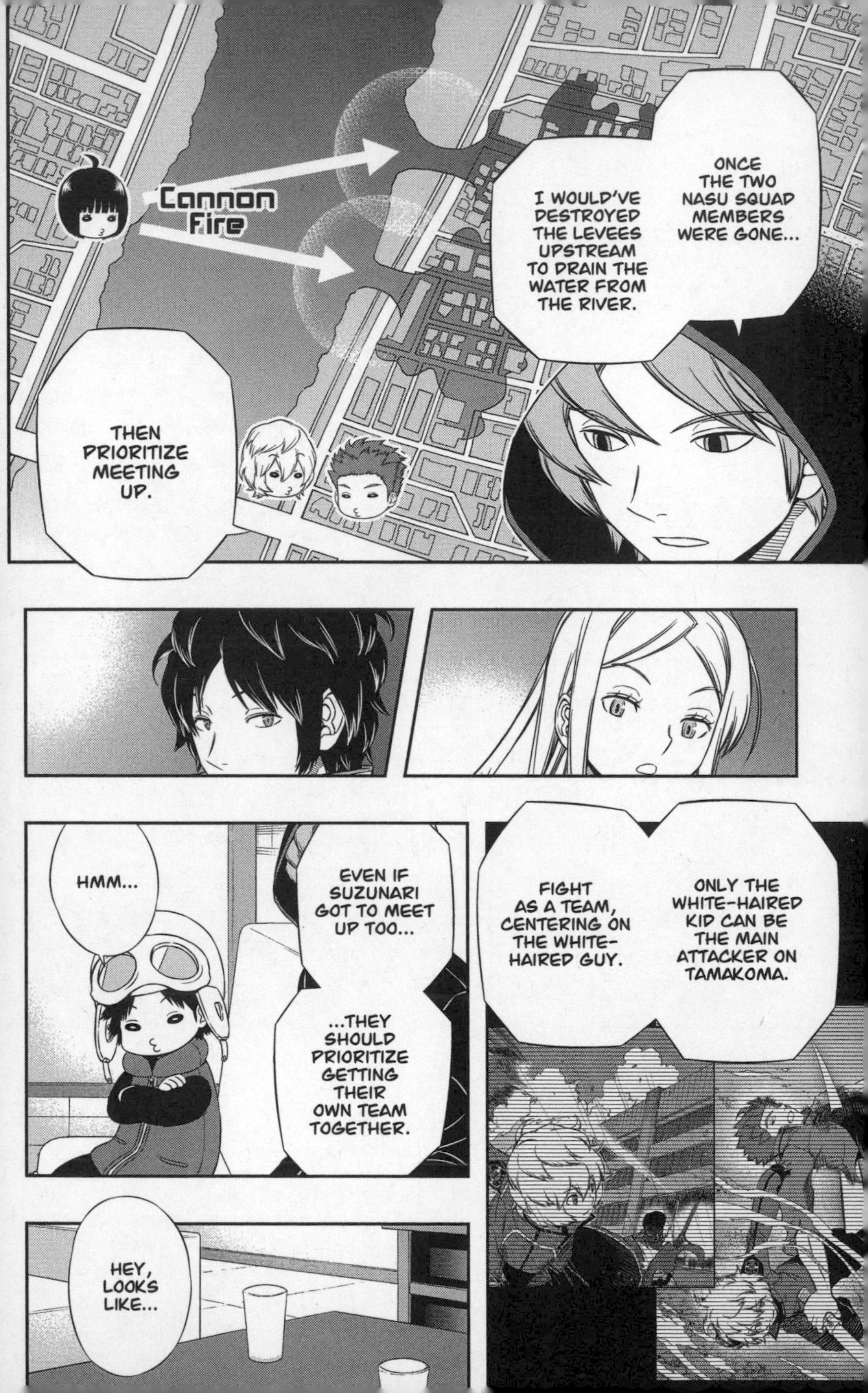
ONCE THE TWO NASU SQUAD MEMBERS WERE GONE...
I WOULD'VE DESTROYED THE LEVEES UPSTREAM TO DRAIN THE WATER FROM THE RIVER.
Cannon Fire
THEN PRIORITIZE MEETING UP.
ONLY THE WHITE-HAIRED KID CAN BE THE MAIN ATTACKER ON TAMAKOMA.
FIGHT AS A TEAM, CENTERING ON THE WHITE-HAIRED GUY.
EVEN IF SUZUNARI GOT TO MEET UP TOO...
...THEY SHOULD PRIORITIZE GETTING THEIR OWN TEAM TOGETHER.
HMM...
HEY, LOOKS LIKE...

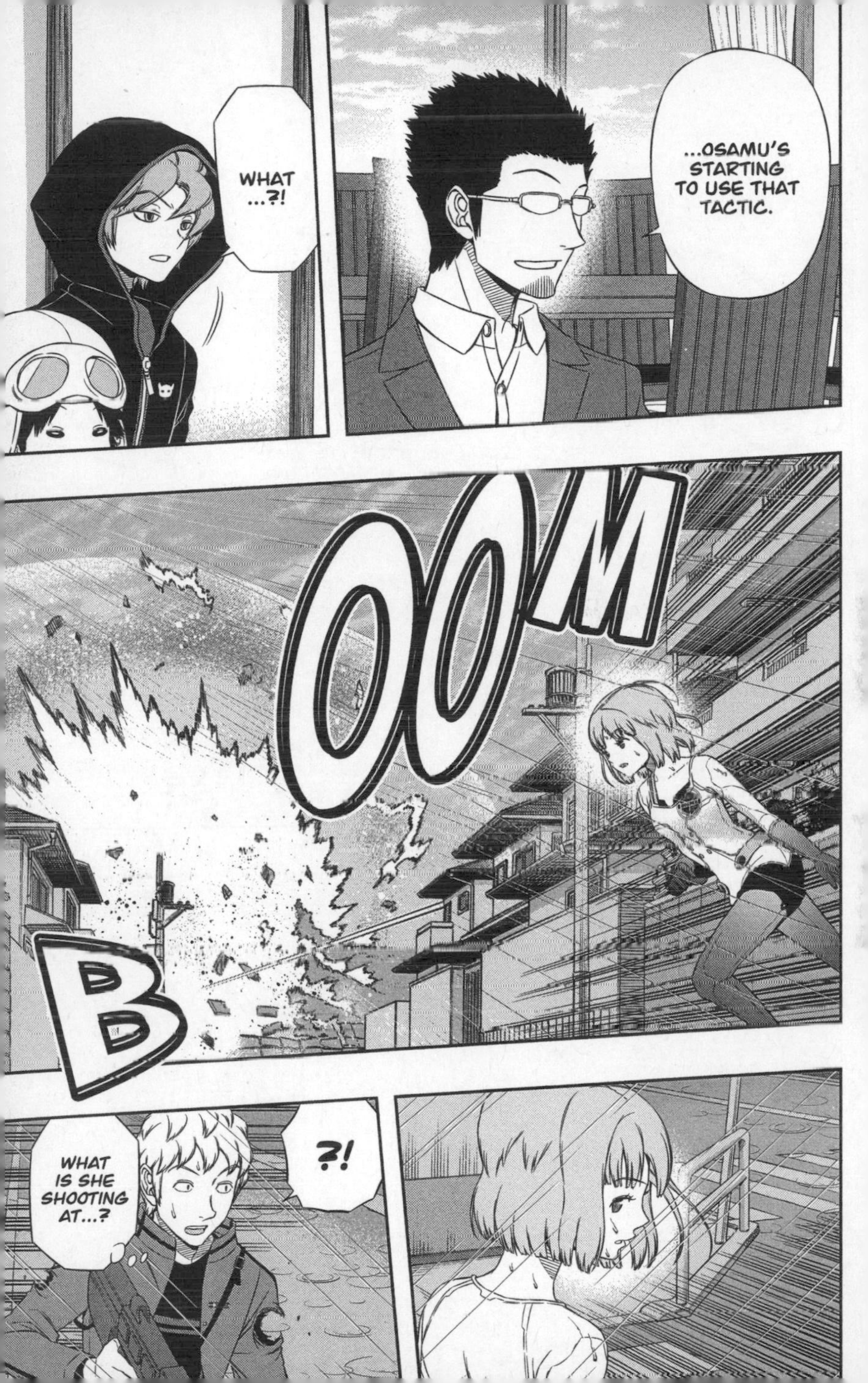
...OSAMU'S STARTING TO USE THAT TACTIC.
WHAT ...?!
BOOM
?!
WHAT IS SHE SHOOTING AT...?

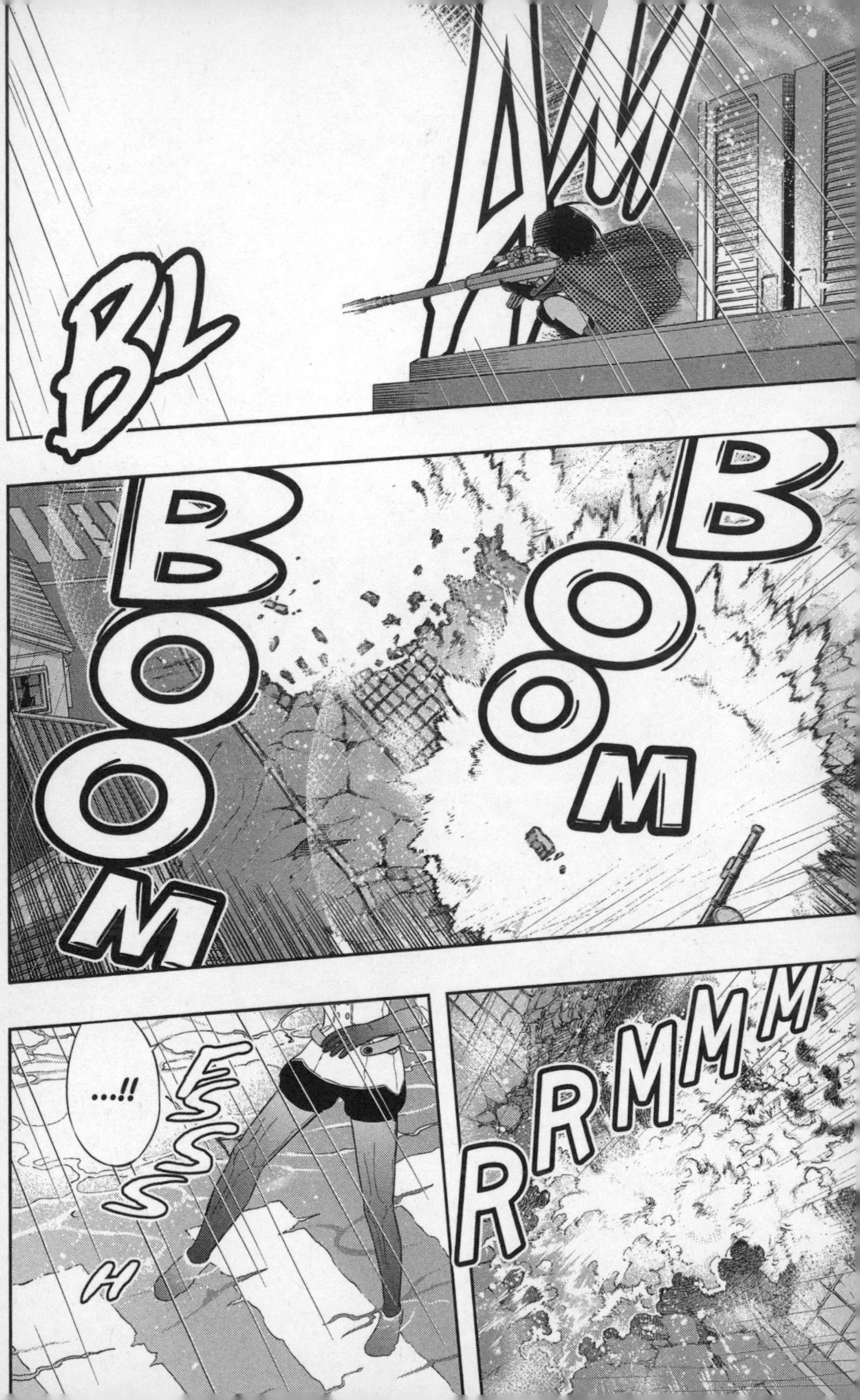
BLAM
BOOM
BOOM
RRMMMM
...!!
FSSSH

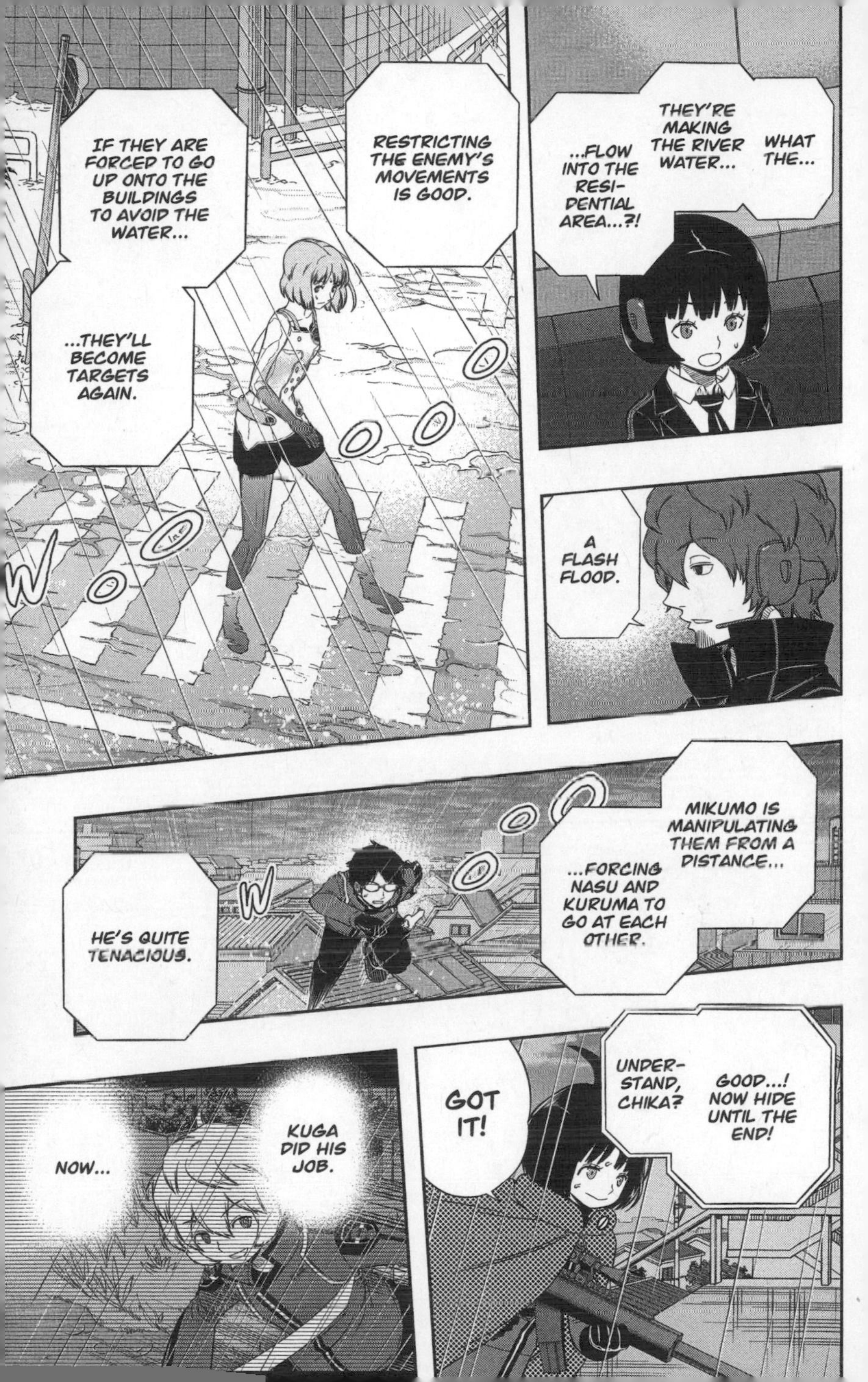
WHAT THE...
THEY'RE MAKING THE RIVER WATER...
...FLOW INTO THE RESI-DENTIAL AREA...?!
A FLASH FLOOD.
RESTRICTING THE ENEMY'S MOVEMENTS IS GOOD.
IF THEY ARE FORCED TO GO UP ONTO THE BUILDINGS TO AVOID THE WATER...
...THEY'LL BECOME TARGETS AGAIN.
W
MIKUMO IS MANIPULATING THEM FROM A DISTANCE...
...FORCING NASU AND KURUMA TO GO AT EACH OTHER.
W
HE'S QUITE TENACIOUS.
GOOD...! NOW HIDE UNTIL THE END!
UNDER-STAND, CHIKA?
GOT IT!
KUGA DID HIS JOB.
NOW...

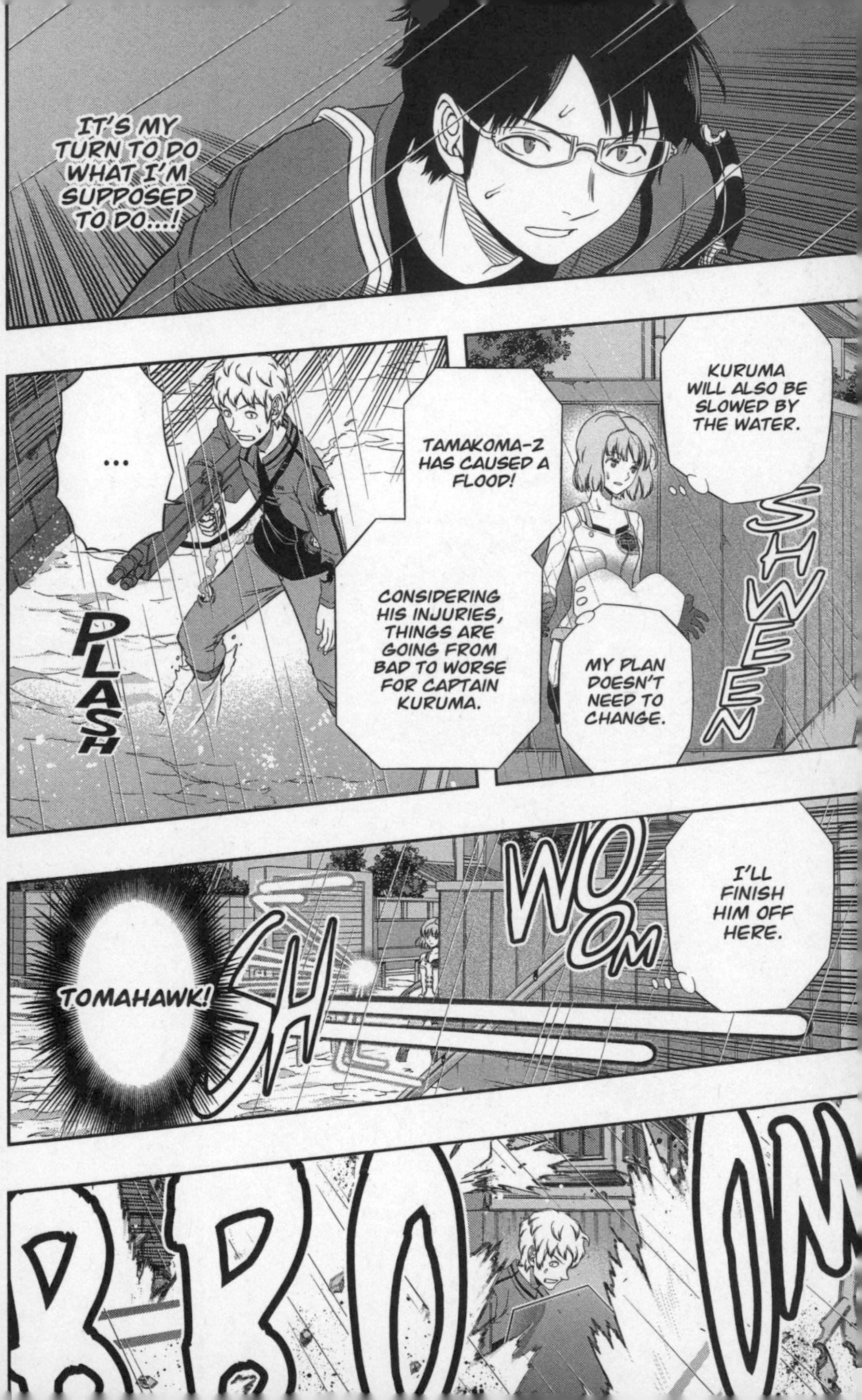
IT'S MY TURN TO DO WHAT I'M SUPPOSED TO DO...!
KURUMA WILL ALSO BE SLOWED BY THE WATER.
TAMAKOMA-2 HAS CAUSED A FLOOD!
CONSIDERING HIS INJURIES, THINGS ARE GOING FROM BAD TO WORSE FOR CAPTAIN KURUMA.
MY PLAN DOESN'T NEED TO CHANGE.
SHWEEN
...
PLASH
I'LL FINISH HIM OFF HERE.
WOOM
SH
TOMAHAWK!
BROOM

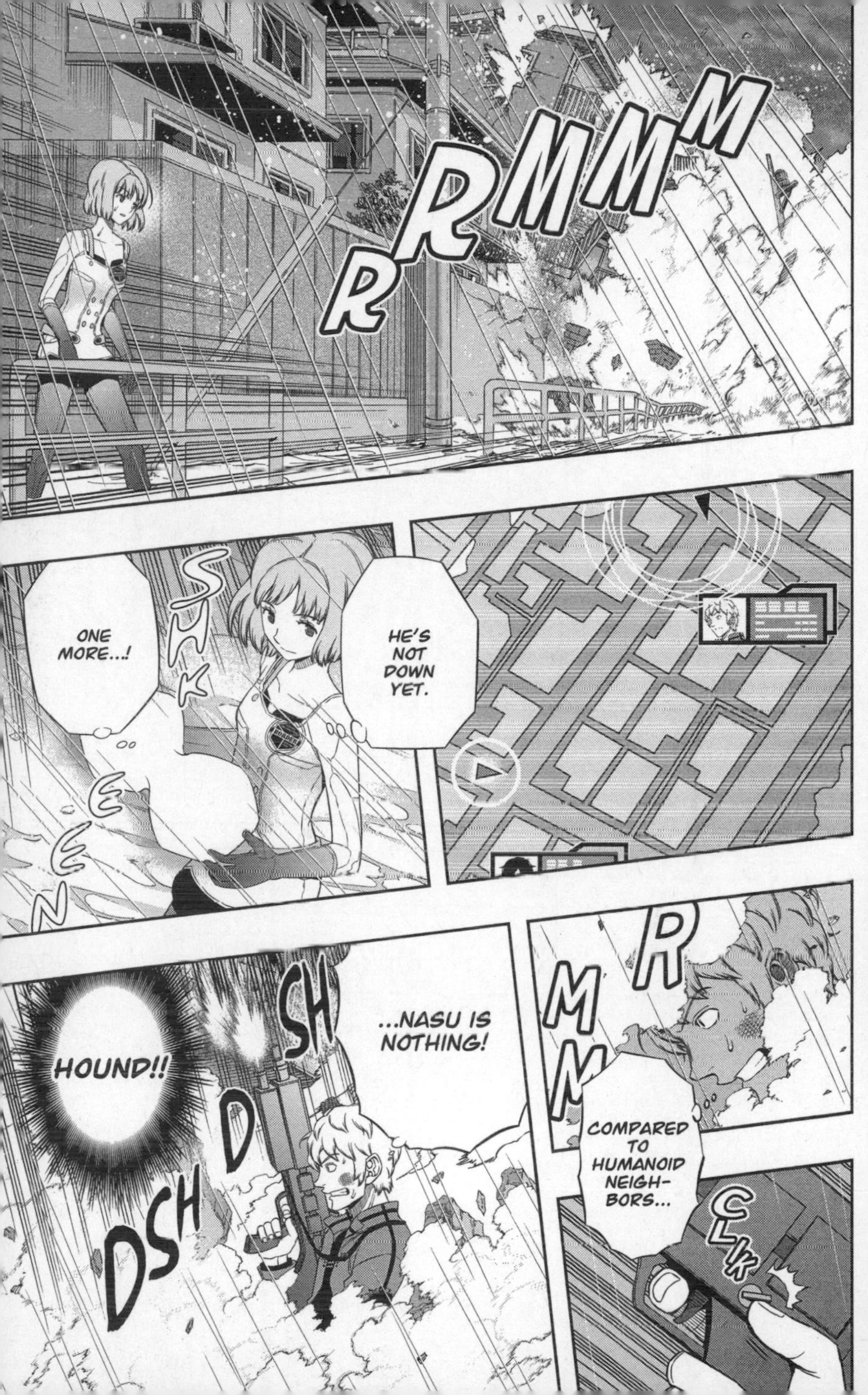

RRMMMM
HE'S NOT DOWN YET.
SHK
ONE MORE...!
EEN
RMM
COMPARED TO HUMANOID NEIGH-BORS...
CLK
...NASU IS NOTHING!
SH
HOUND!!
D
DSH

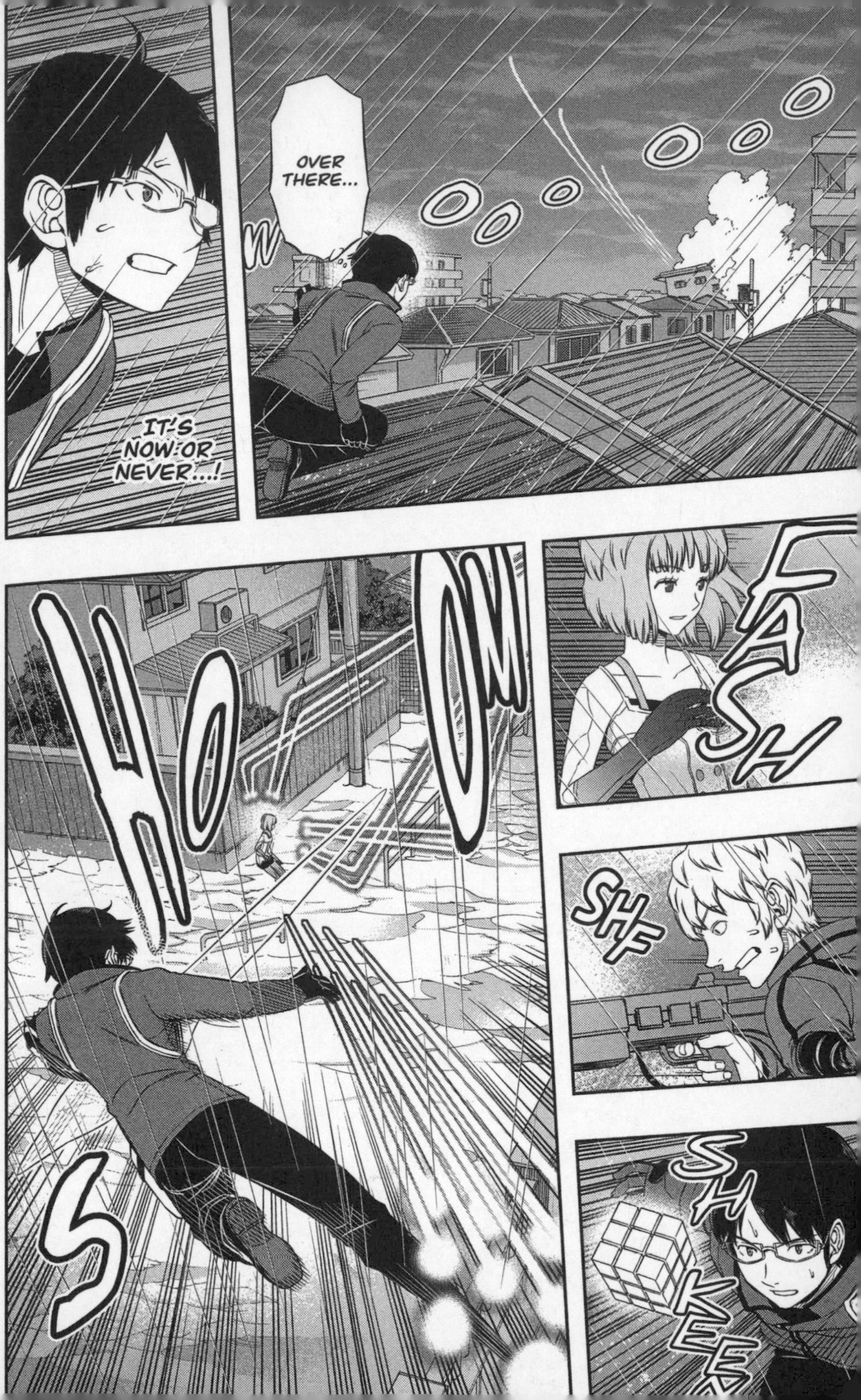
OVER THERE...
IT'S NOW OR NEVER...!
FASH
SHF
SHKEE
HOOM

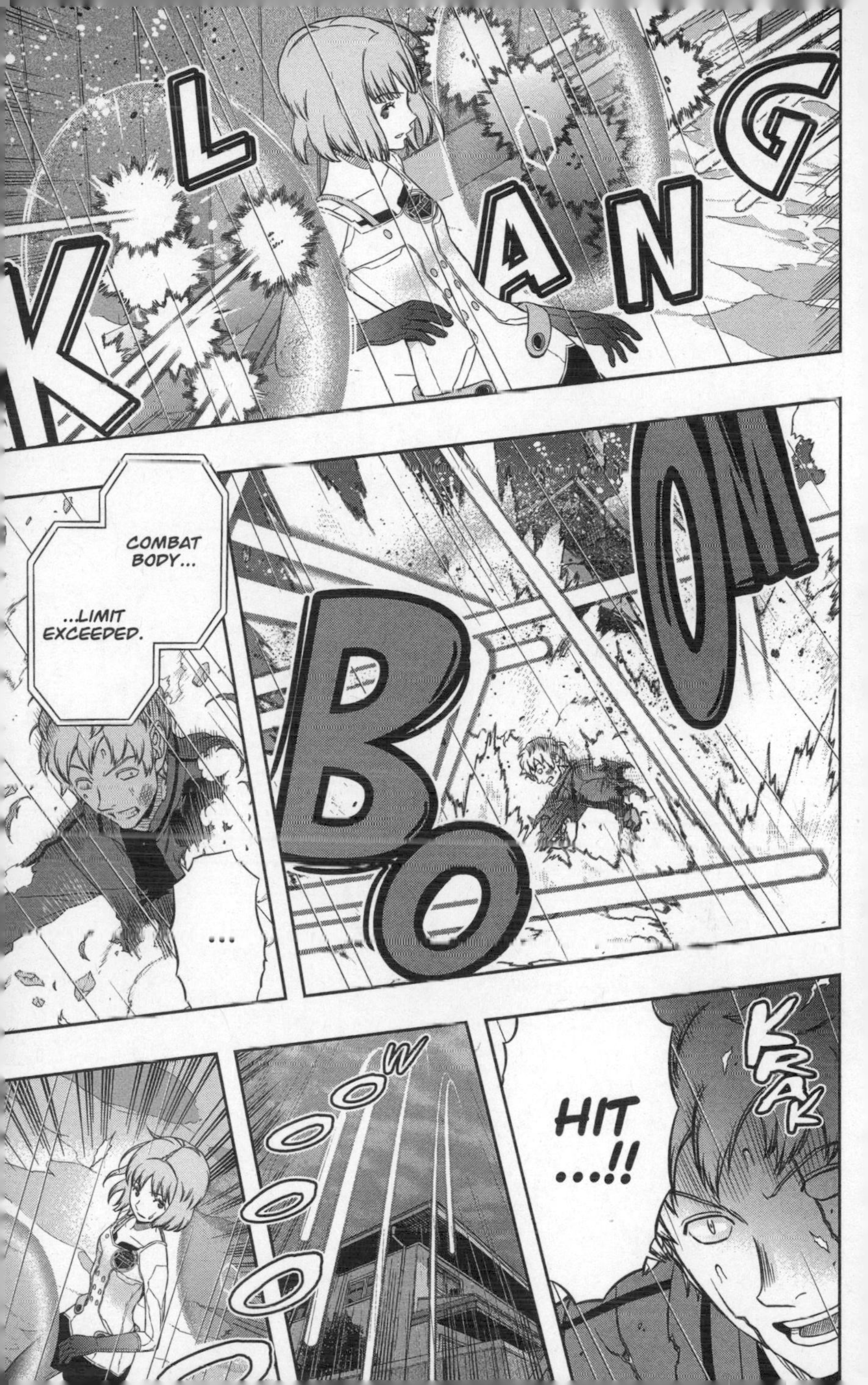
KLANG
BOOM
COMBAT BODY...
...LIMIT EXCEEDED.
...
KRAK
HIT ...!!
WOOOOOOOOW

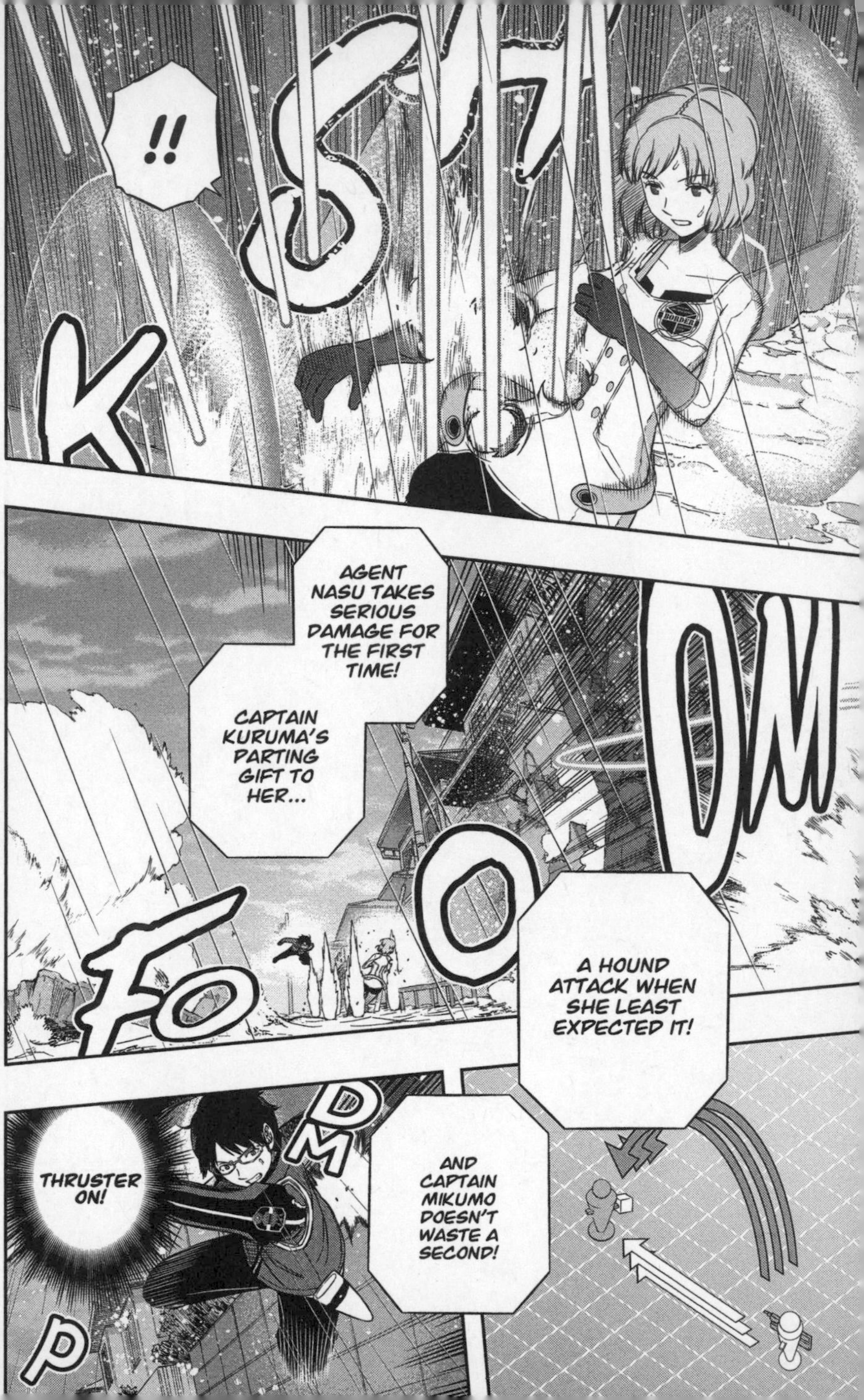
!!
AGENT NASU TAKES SERIOUS DAMAGE FOR THE FIRST TIME!
CAPTAIN KURUMA'S PARTING GIFT TO HER...
A HOUND ATTACK WHEN SHE LEAST EXPECTED IT!
FOOOM
AND CAPTAIN MIKUMO DOESN'T WASTE A SECOND!
THRUSTER ON!

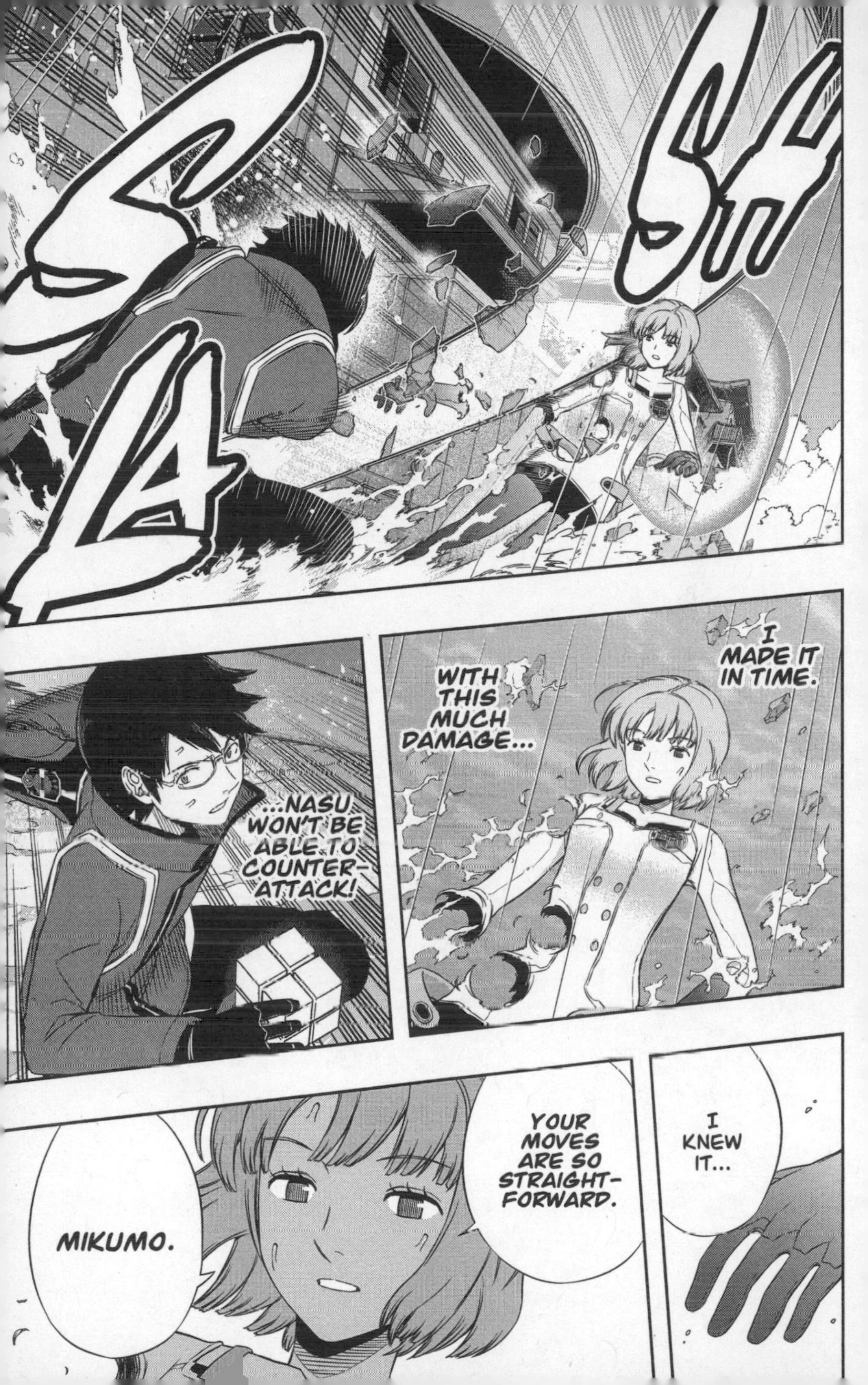
I MADE IT IN TIME.
WITH THIS MUCH DAMAGE...
...NASU WON'T BE ABLE TO COUNTER-ATTACK!
I KNEW IT...
YOUR MOVES ARE SO STRAIGHT-FORWARD.
MIKUMO.

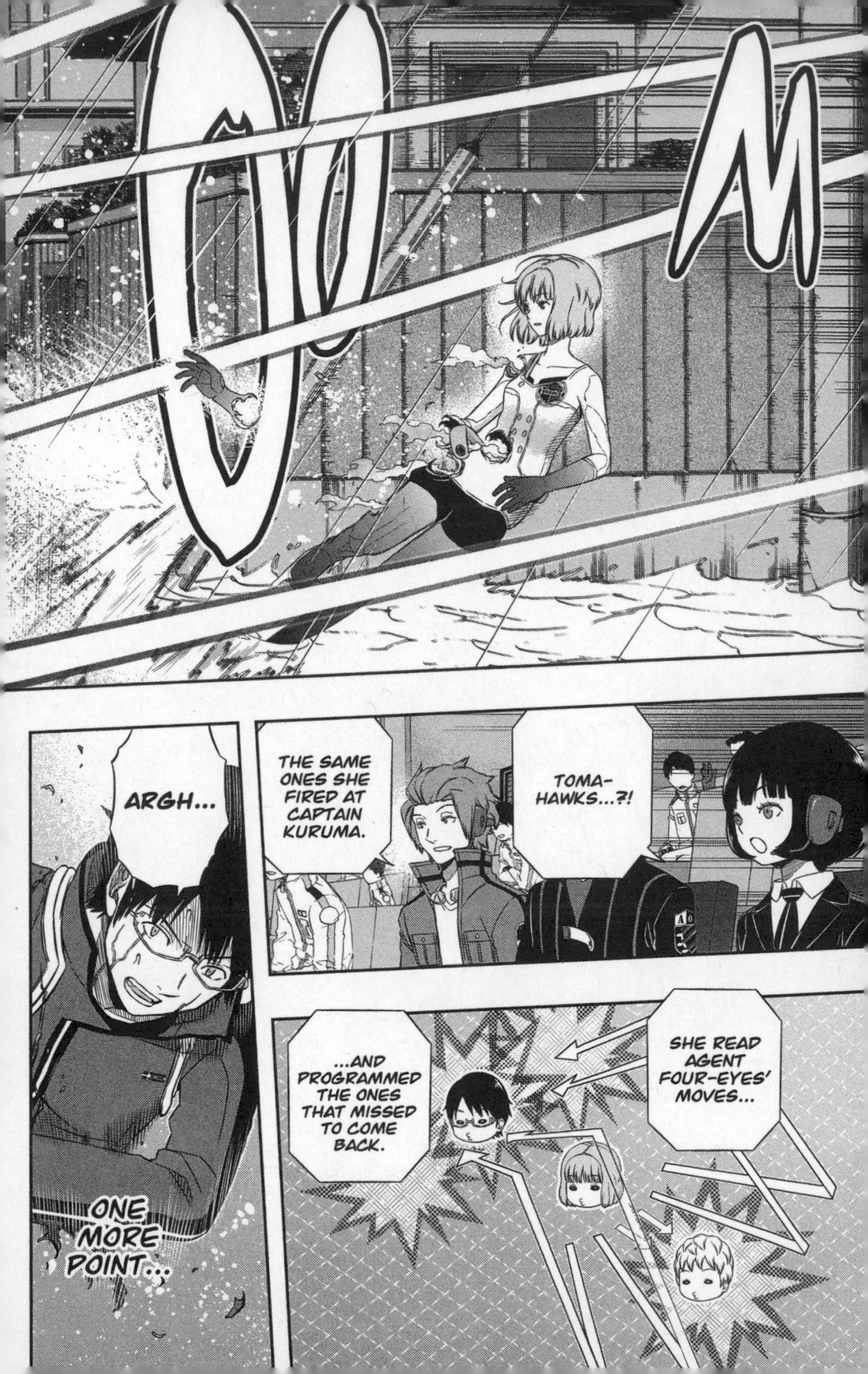
OOM
TOMA-HAWKS...?!
THE SAME ONES SHE FIRED AT CAPTAIN KURUMA.
SHE READ AGENT FOUR-EYES' MOVES...
...AND PROGRAMMED THE ONES THAT MISSED TO COME BACK.
ARGH...
ONE MORE POINT...

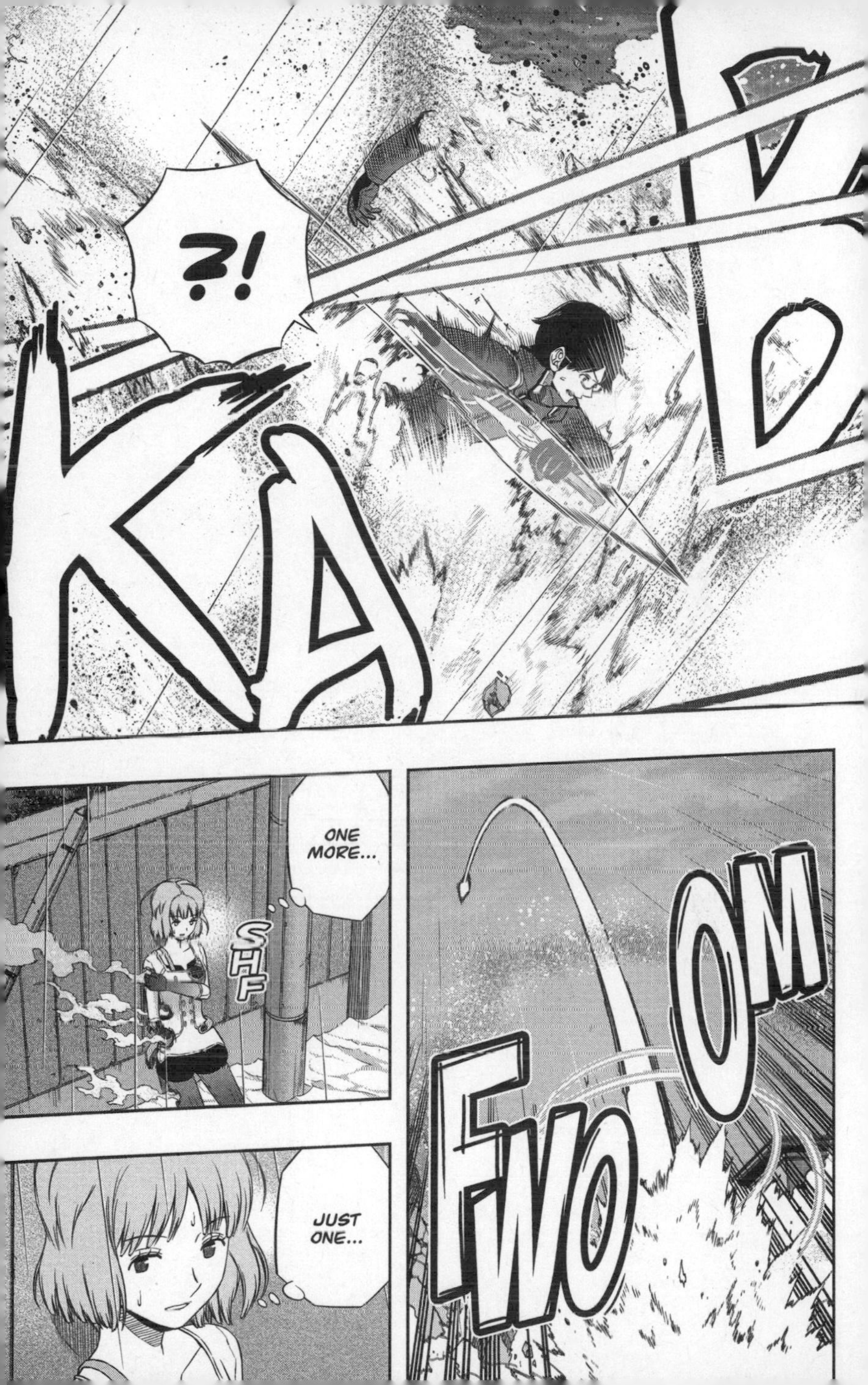
?!
KA
FWOOM
ONE MORE...
SHF
JUST ONE...

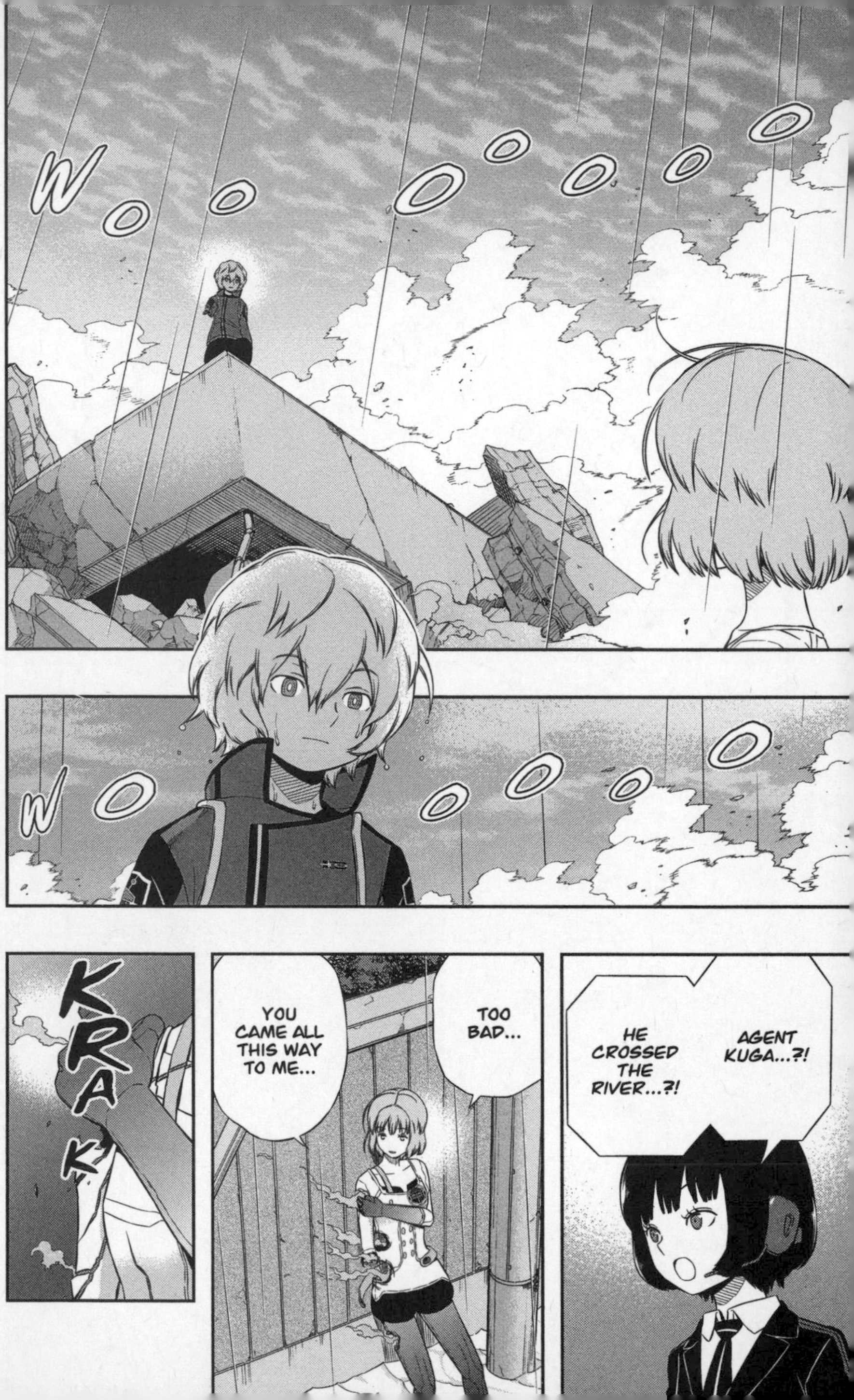
WOOOOOOOO
WOOOOOO
AGENT KUGA...?!
HE CROSSED THE RIVER...?!
TOO BAD...
YOU CAME ALL THIS WAY TO ME...
KRAK

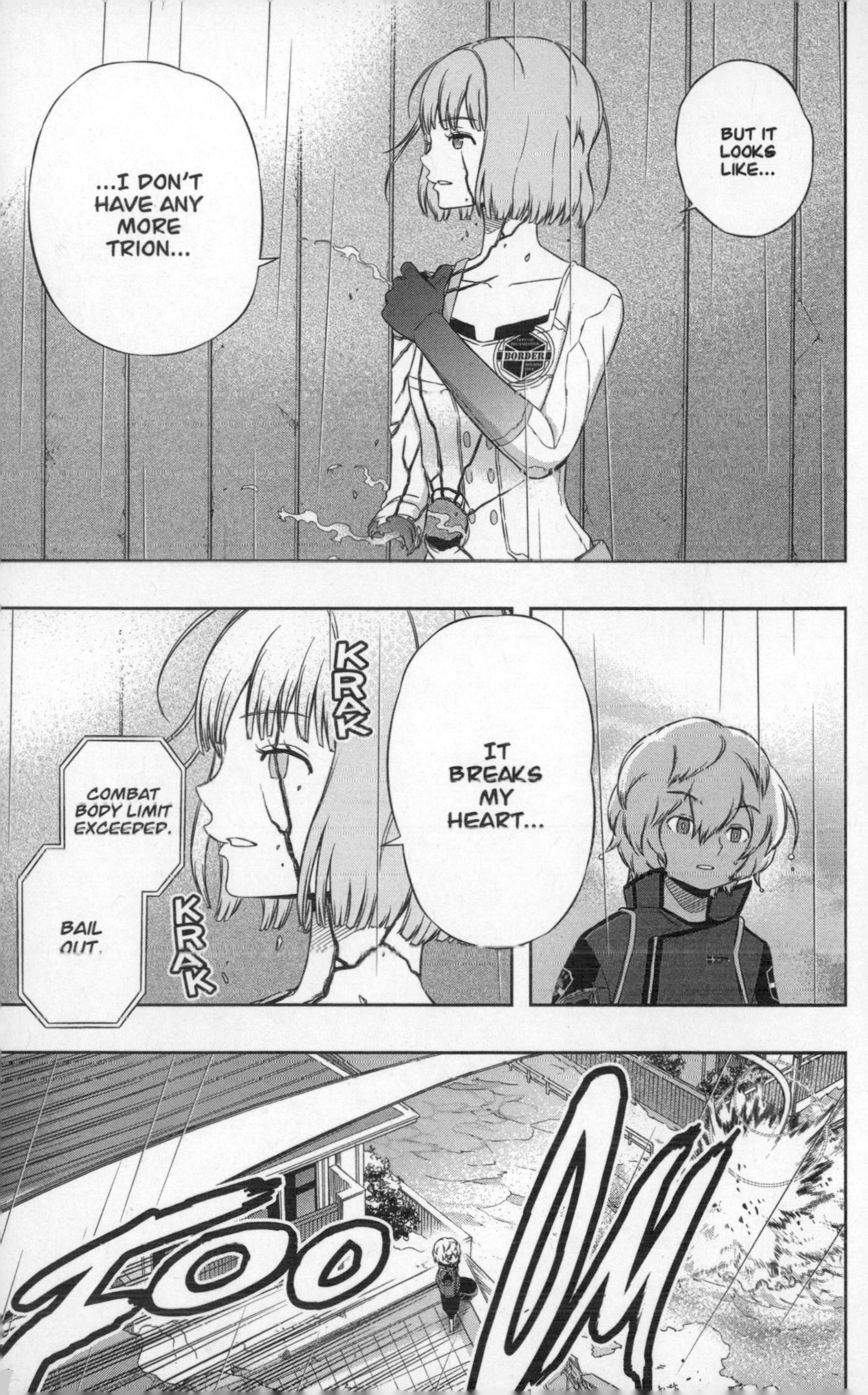
BUT IT LOOKS LIKE...
...I DON'T HAVE ANY MORE TRION...
IT BREAKS MY HEART...
KRAK
KRAK
COMBAT BODY LIMIT EXCEEDED.
BAIL OUT.
ZOOM

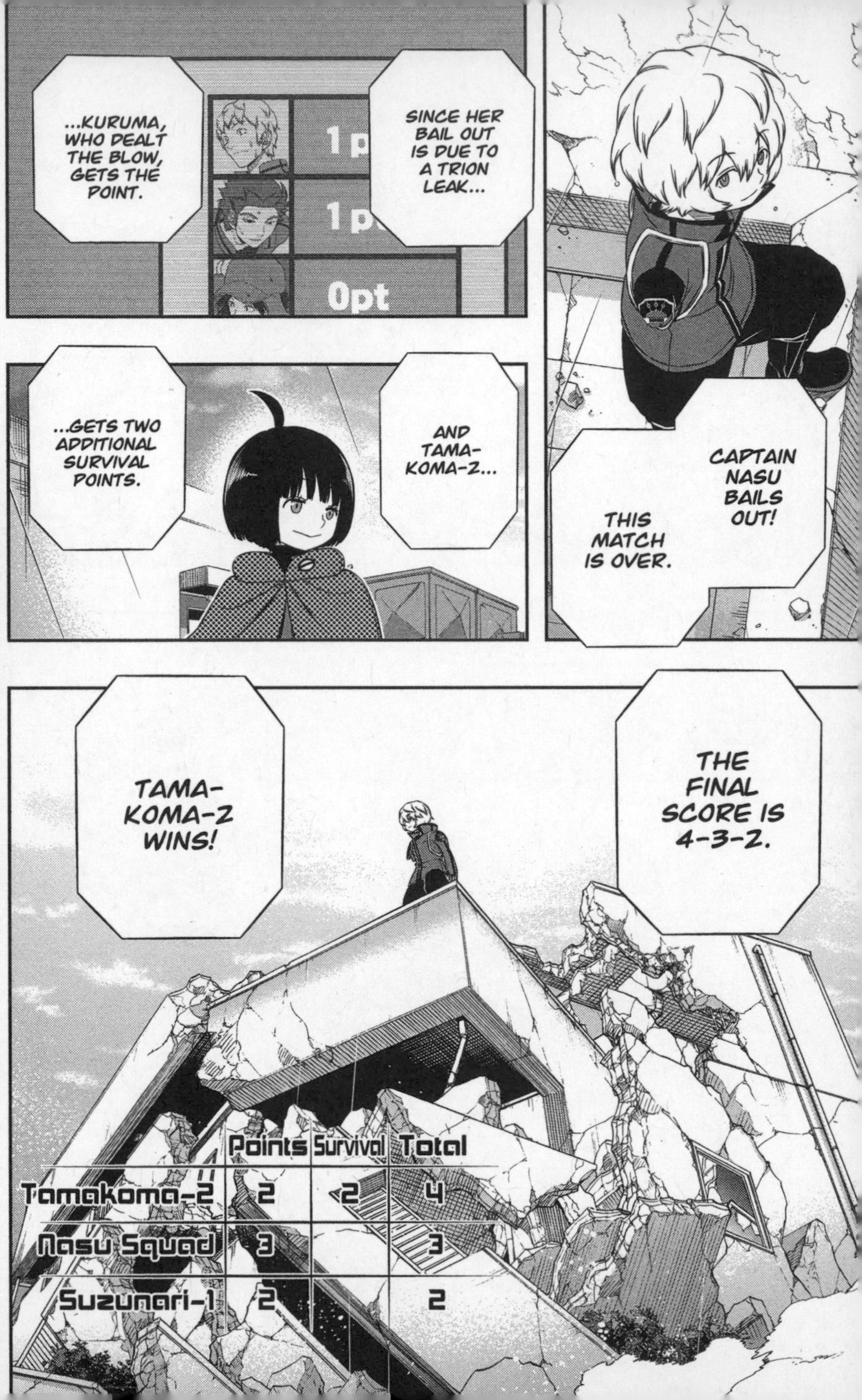
CAPTAIN NASU BAILS OUT!
THIS MATCH IS OVER.
SINCE HER BAIL OUT IS DUE TO A TRION LEAK...
...KURUMA, WHO DEALT THE BLOW, GETS THE POINT.
0pt
AND TAMA-KOMA-2...
...GETS TWO ADDITIONAL SURVIVAL POINTS.
THE FINAL SCORE IS 4-3-2.
TAMA-KOMA-2 WINS!
Points Survival Total
Tamakoma-2 2 2 4
Nasu Squad 3 3
Suzunari-1 2 2

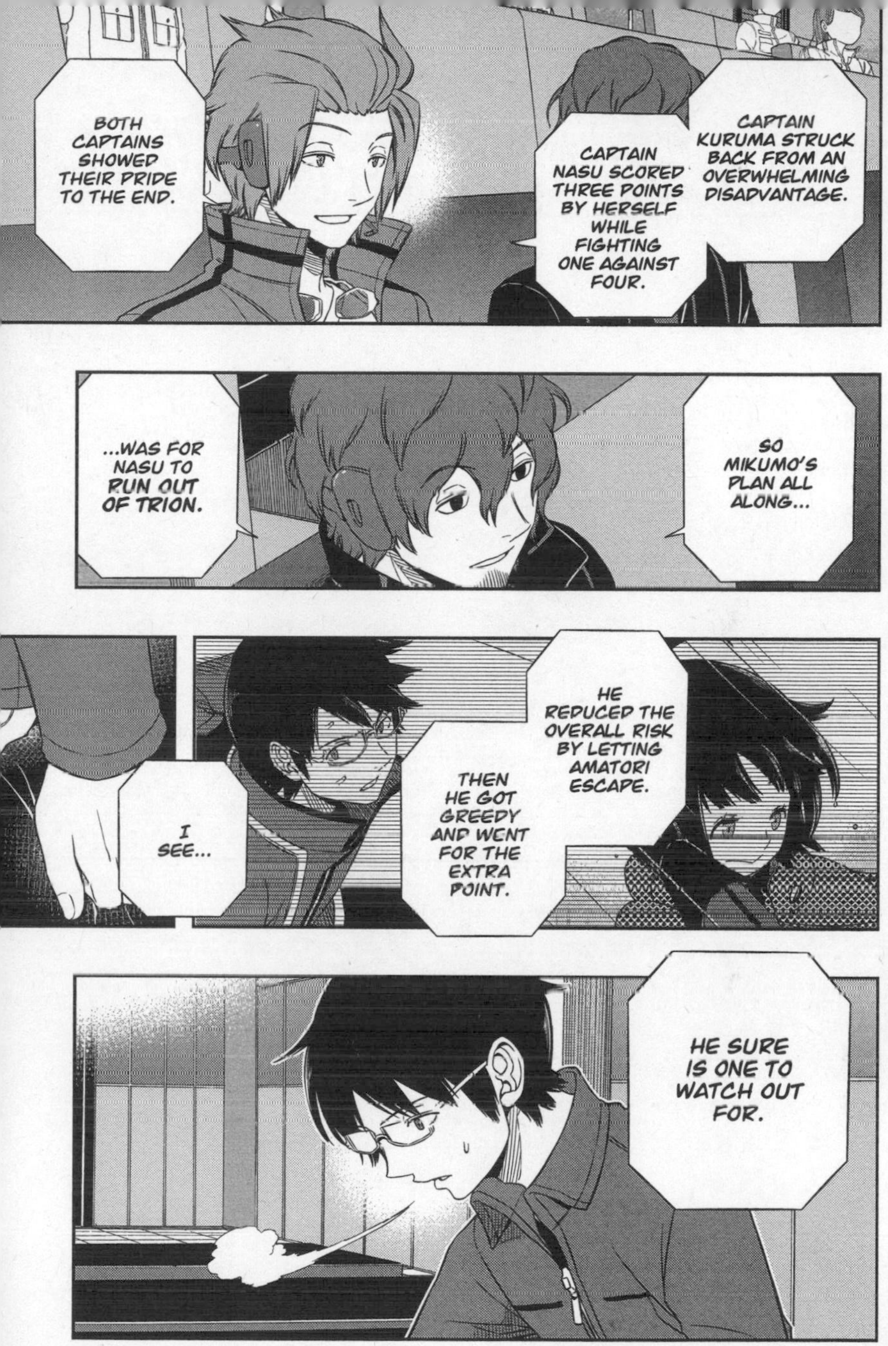
CAPTAIN KURUMA STRUCK BACK FROM AN OVERWHELMING DISADVANTAGE.
CAPTAIN NASU SCORED THREE POINTS BY HERSELF WHILE FIGHTING ONE AGAINST FOUR.
BOTH CAPTAINS SHOWED THEIR PRIDE TO THE END.
SO MIKUMO'S PLAN ALL ALONG...
...WAS FOR NASU TO RUN OUT OF TRION.
HE REDUCED THE OVERALL RISK BY LETTING AMATORI ESCAPE.
THEN HE GOT GREEDY AND WENT FOR THE EXTRA POINT.
I SEE...
HE SURE IS ONE TO WATCH OUT FOR.

Nasu Squad Strategy Room

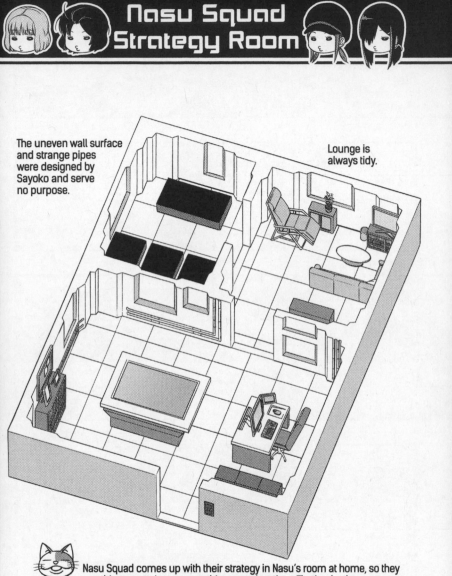

The uneven wall surface and strange pipes were designed by Sayoko and serve no purpose.

Lounge is always tidy.

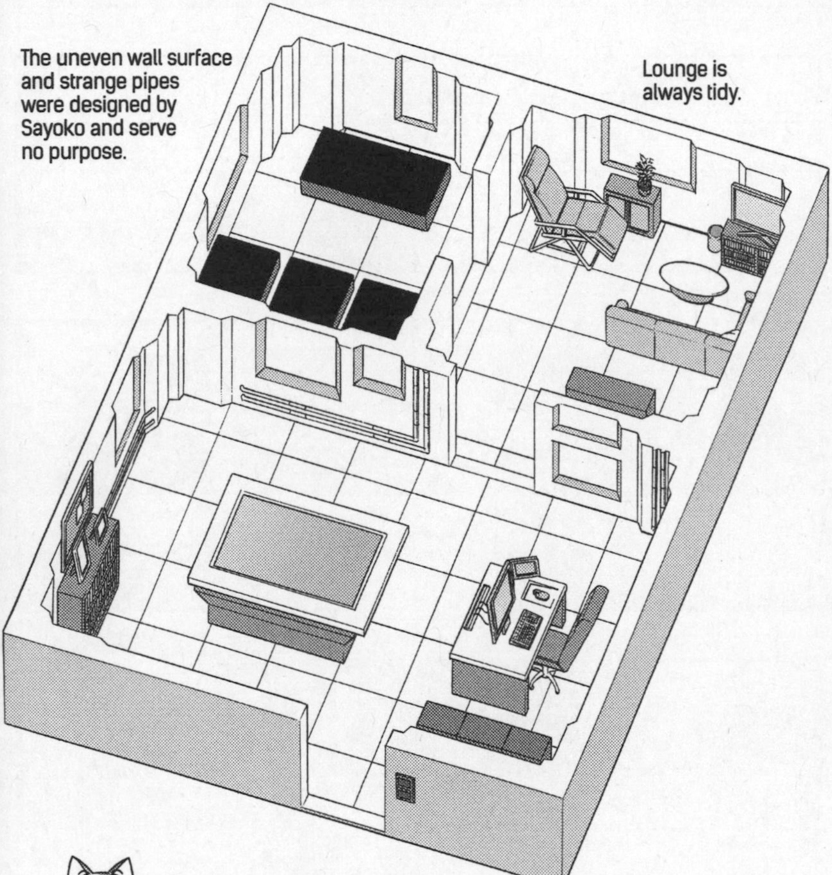

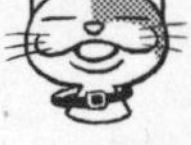

Nasu Squad comes up with their strategy in Nasu's room at home, so they use this room to just go over things one last time. That's why there are no chairs except for Sayoko's in the room. The back room is a lounge where Nasu can rest and everyone can watch TV or movies.

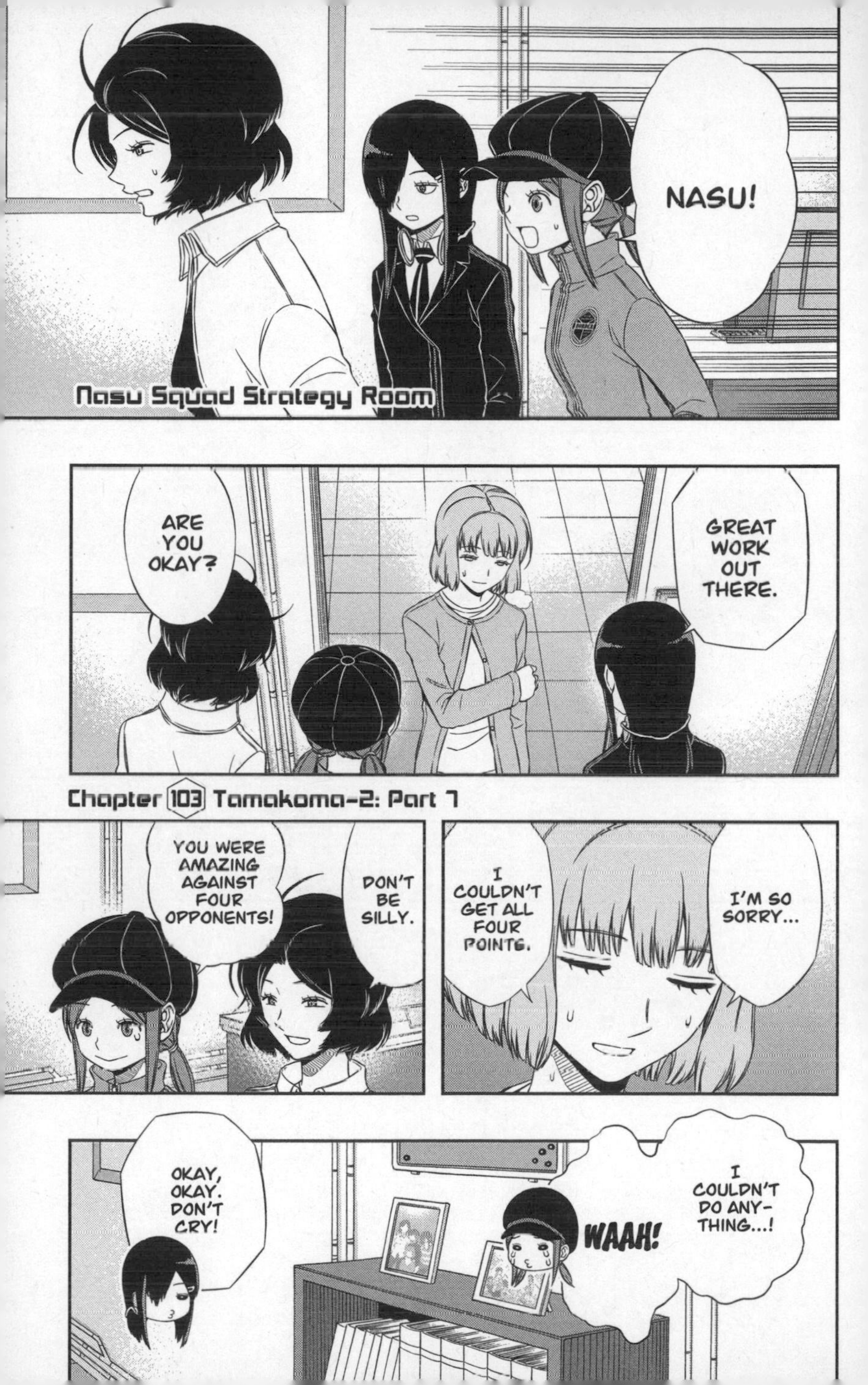
NASU!
Nasu Squad Strategy Room
GREAT WORK OUT THERE.
ARE YOU OKAY?
Chapter 103 Tamakoma-2: Part 7
I'M SO SORRY...
I COULDN'T GET ALL FOUR POINTS.
DON'T BE SILLY.
YOU WERE AMAZING AGAINST FOUR OPPONENTS!
I COULDN'T DO ANY-THING...!
WAAH!
OKAY, OKAY. DON'T CRY!

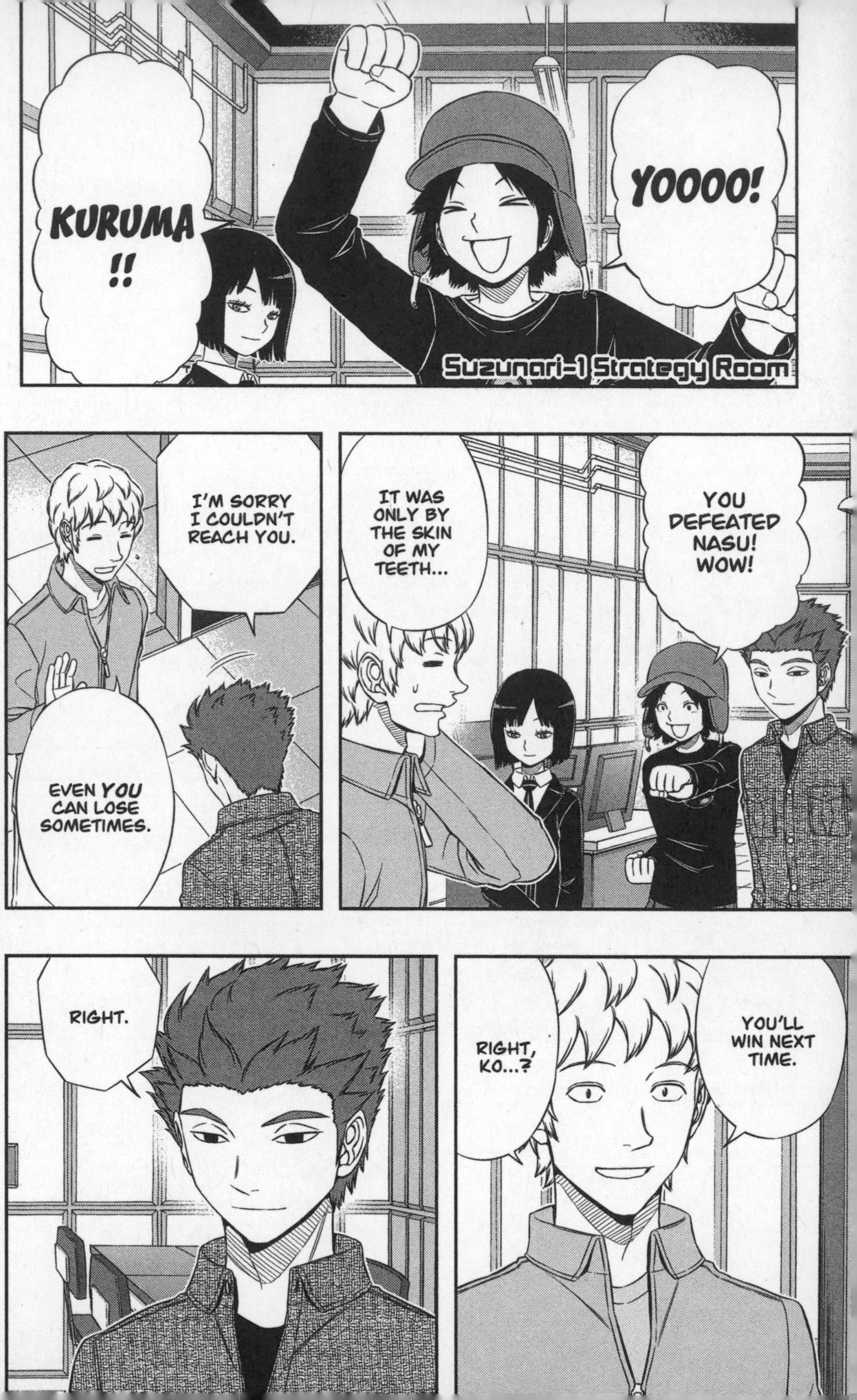
YOOOO!
KURUMA !!
Suzunari-1 Strategy Room
YOU DEFEATED NASU! WOW!
IT WAS ONLY BY THE SKIN OF MY TEETH...
I'M SORRY I COULDN'T REACH YOU.
EVEN YOU CAN LOSE SOMETIMES.
YOU'LL WIN NEXT TIME.
RIGHT, KO...?
RIGHT.

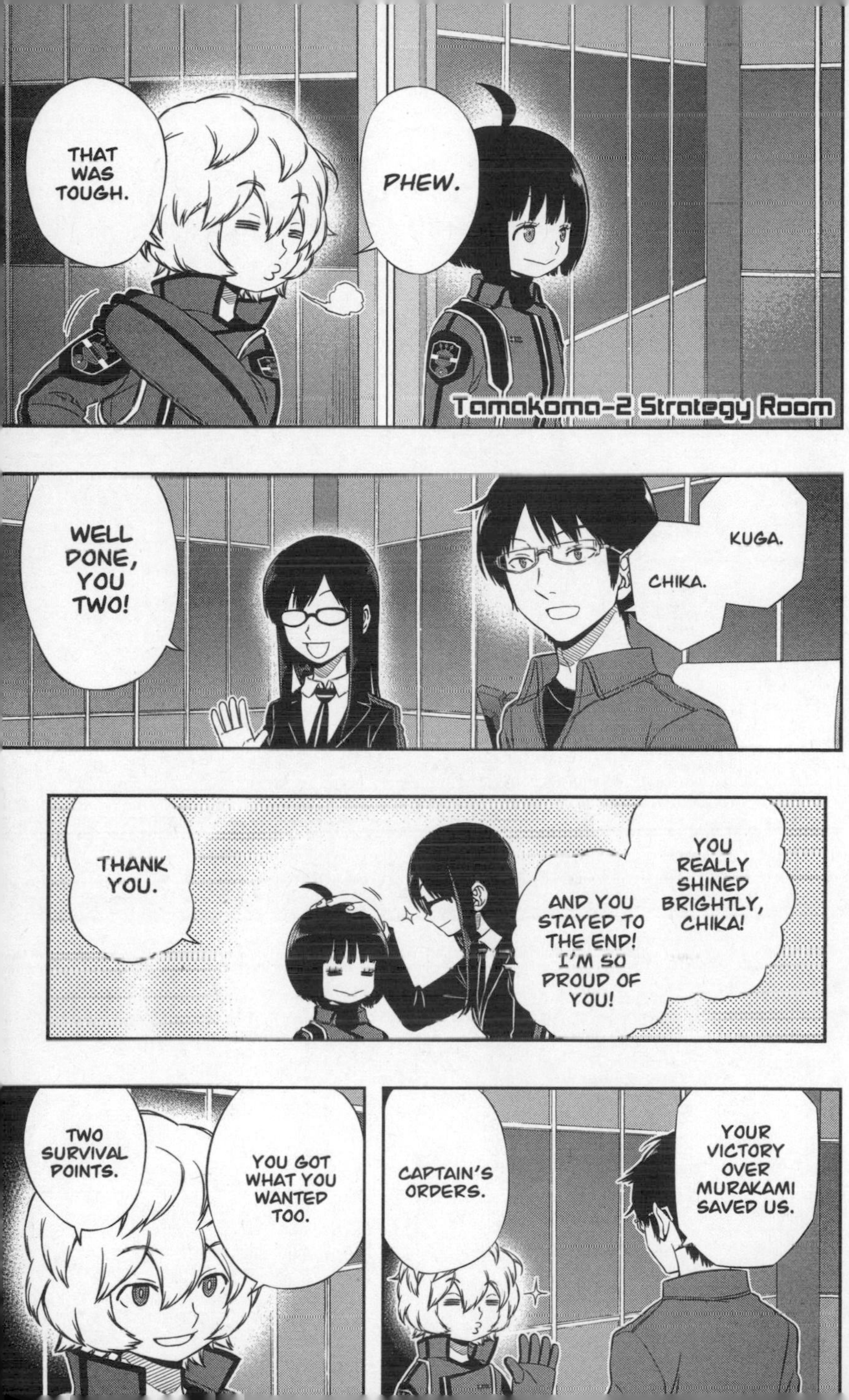
PHEW.
THAT WAS TOUGH.
Tamakoma-2 Strategy Room
KUGA.
CHIKA.
WELL DONE, YOU TWO!
YOU REALLY SHINED BRIGHTLY, CHIKA!
AND YOU STAYED TO THE END! I'M SO PROUD OF YOU!
THANK YOU.
YOUR VICTORY OVER MURAKAMI SAVED US.
CAPTAIN'S ORDERS.
YOU GOT WHAT YOU WANTED TOO.
TWO SURVIVAL POINTS.

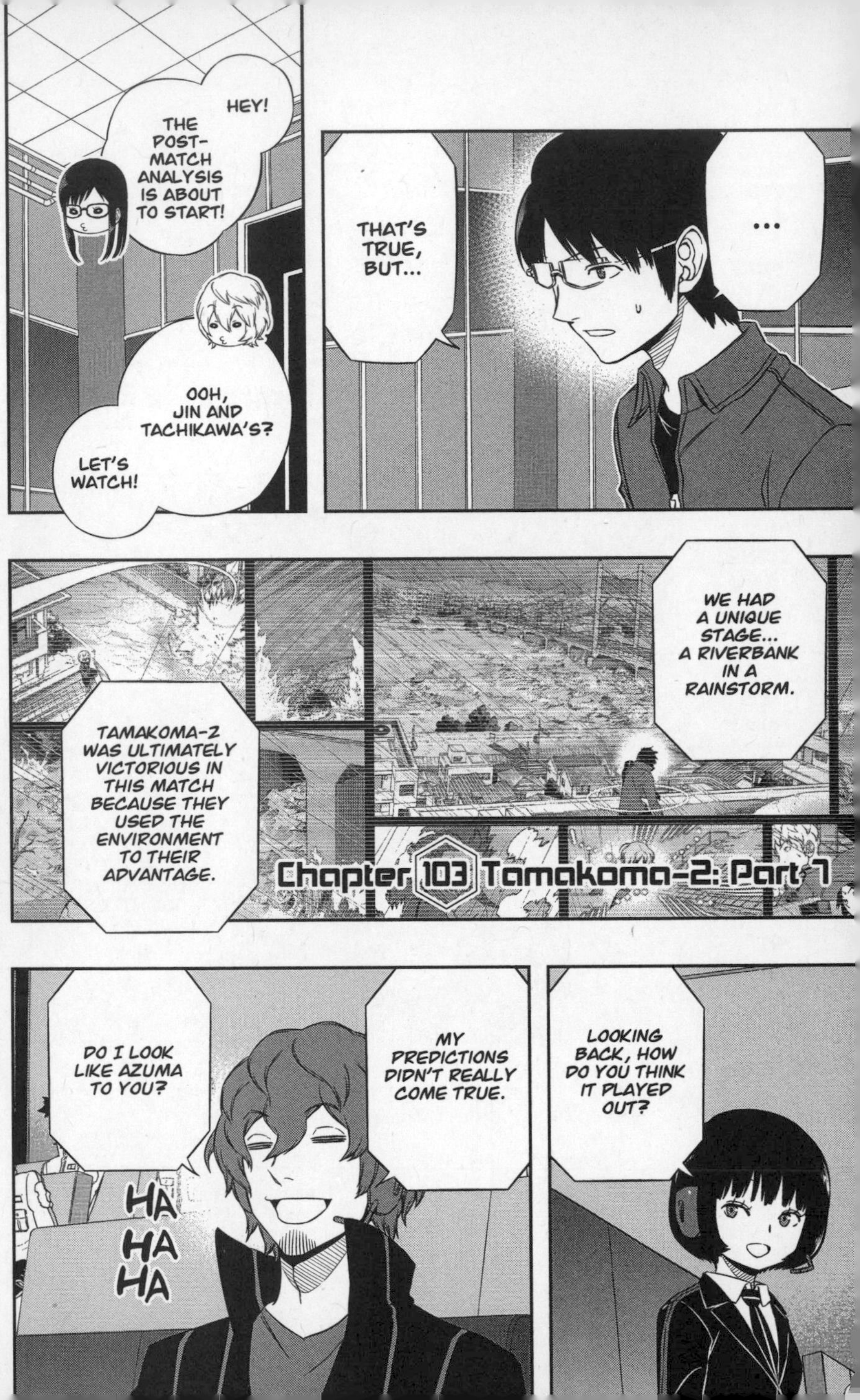
...
THAT'S TRUE, BUT...
HEY! THE POST-MATCH ANALYSIS IS ABOUT TO START!
OOH, JIN AND TACHIKAWA'S?
LET'S WATCH!
WE HAD A UNIQUE STAGE... A RIVERBANK IN A RAINSTORM.
TAMAKOMA-2 WAS ULTIMATELY VICTORIOUS IN THIS MATCH BECAUSE THEY USED THE ENVIRONMENT TO THEIR ADVANTAGE.
Chapter 103 Tamakoma-2: Part 7
LOOKING BACK, HOW DO YOU THINK IT PLAYED OUT?
MY PREDICTIONS DIDN'T REALLY COME TRUE.
DO I LOOK LIKE AZUMA TO YOU?
HA HA HA

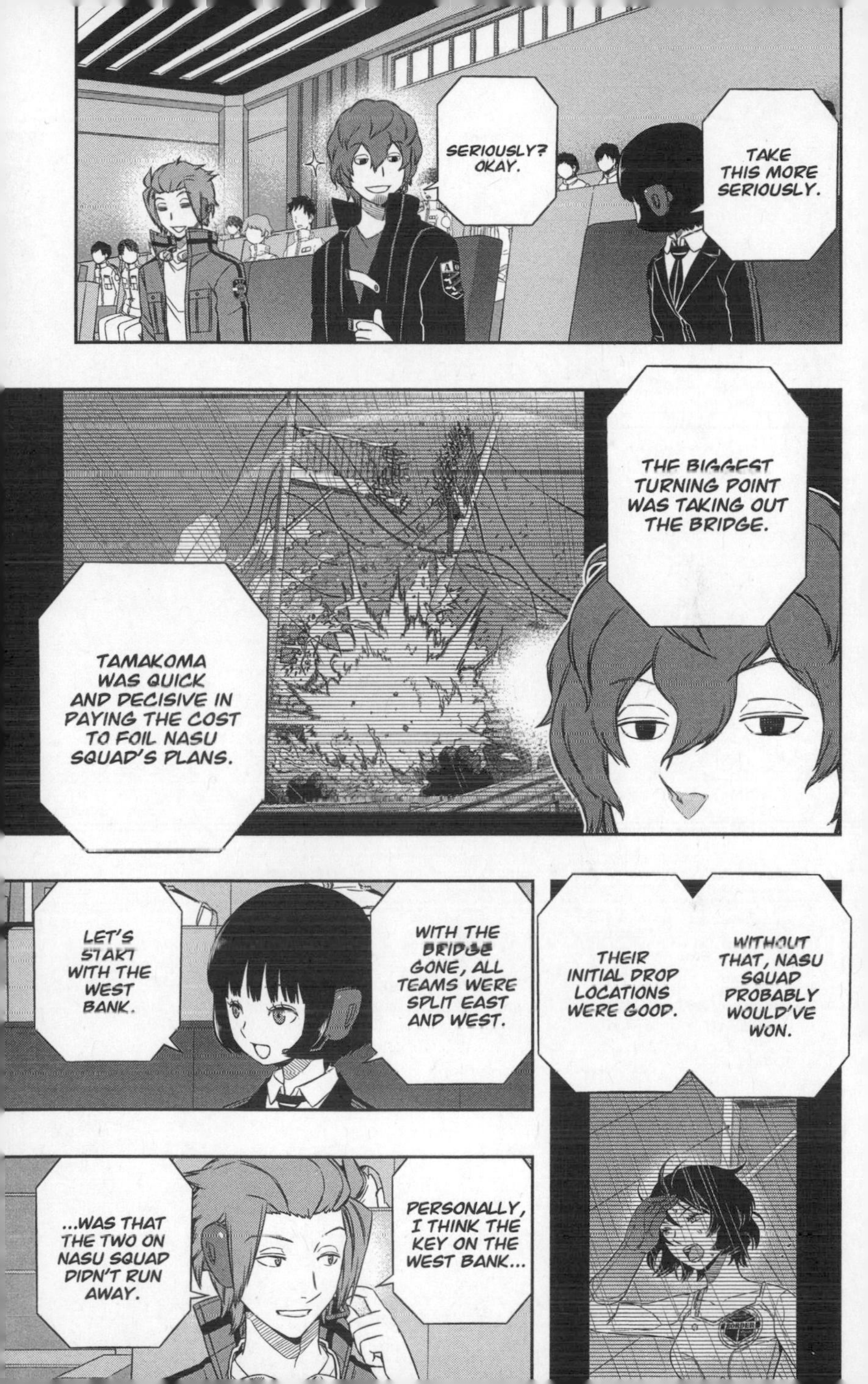
TAKE THIS MORE SERIOUSLY.
SERIOUSLY? OKAY.
THE BIGGEST TURNING POINT WAS TAKING OUT THE BRIDGE.
TAMAKOMA WAS QUICK AND DECISIVE IN PAYING THE COST TO FOIL NASU SQUAD'S PLANS.
WITHOUT THAT, NASU SQUAD PROBABLY WOULD'VE WON.
THEIR INITIAL DROP LOCATIONS WERE GOOD.
WITH THE BRIDGE GONE, ALL TEAMS WERE SPLIT EAST AND WEST.
LET'S START WITH THE WEST BANK.
PERSONALLY, I THINK THE KEY ON THE WEST BANK...
...WAS THAT THE TWO ON NASU SQUAD DIDN'T RUN AWAY.

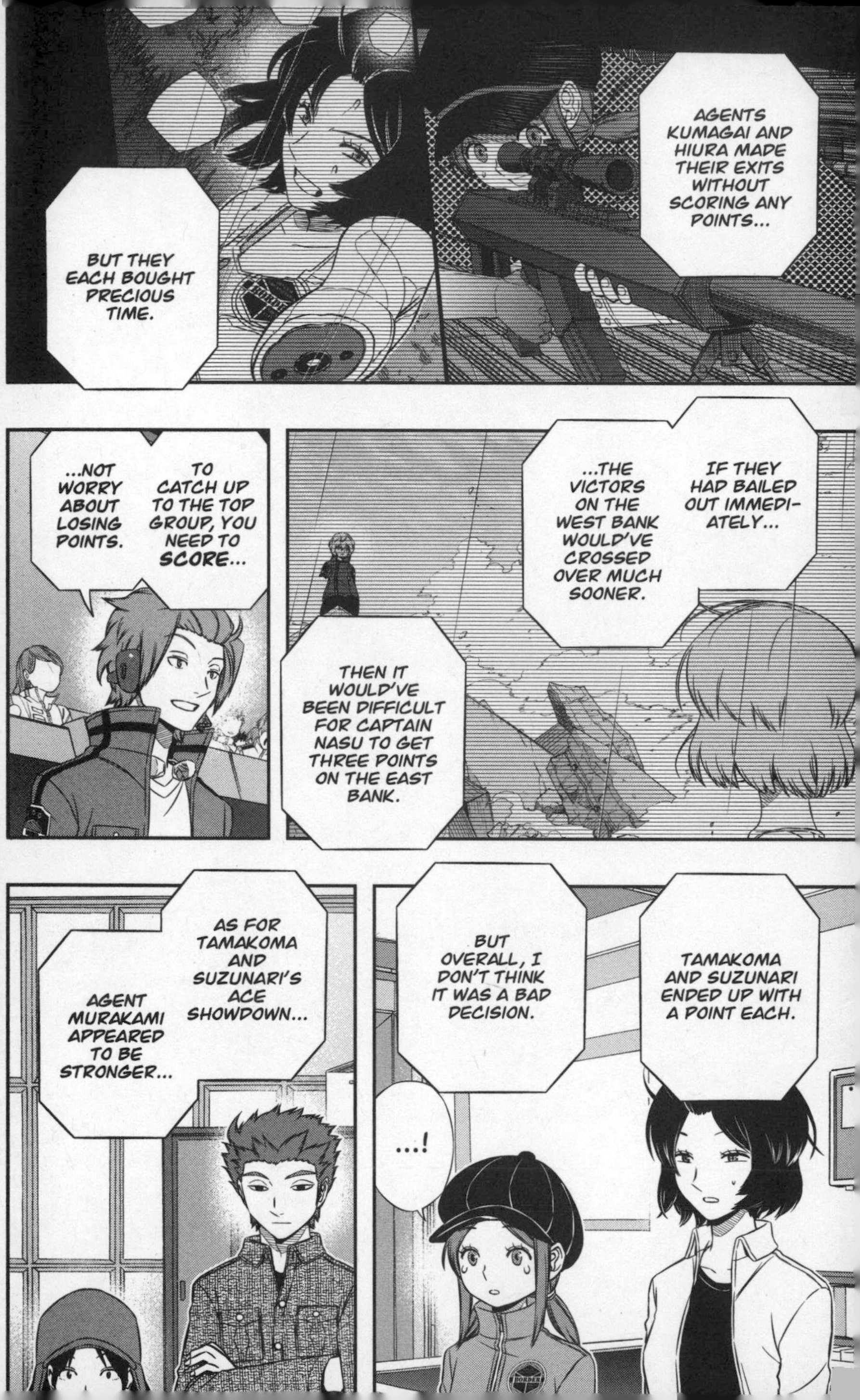
AGENTS KUMAGAI AND HIURA MADE THEIR EXITS WITHOUT SCORING ANY POINTS...
BUT THEY EACH BOUGHT PRECIOUS TIME.
IF THEY HAD BAILED OUT IMMEDIATELY...
...THE VICTORS ON THE WEST BANK WOULD'VE CROSSED OVER MUCH SOONER.
THEN IT WOULD'VE BEEN DIFFICULT FOR CAPTAIN NASU TO GET THREE POINTS ON THE EAST BANK.
TO CATCH UP TO THE TOP GROUP, YOU NEED TO SCORE...
...NOT WORRY ABOUT LOSING POINTS.
TAMAKOMA AND SUZUNARI ENDED UP WITH A POINT EACH.
BUT OVERALL, I DON'T THINK IT WAS A BAD DECISION.
...!
AS FOR TAMAKOMA AND SUZUNARI'S ACE SHOWDOWN...
AGENT MURAKAMI APPEARED TO BE STRONGER...

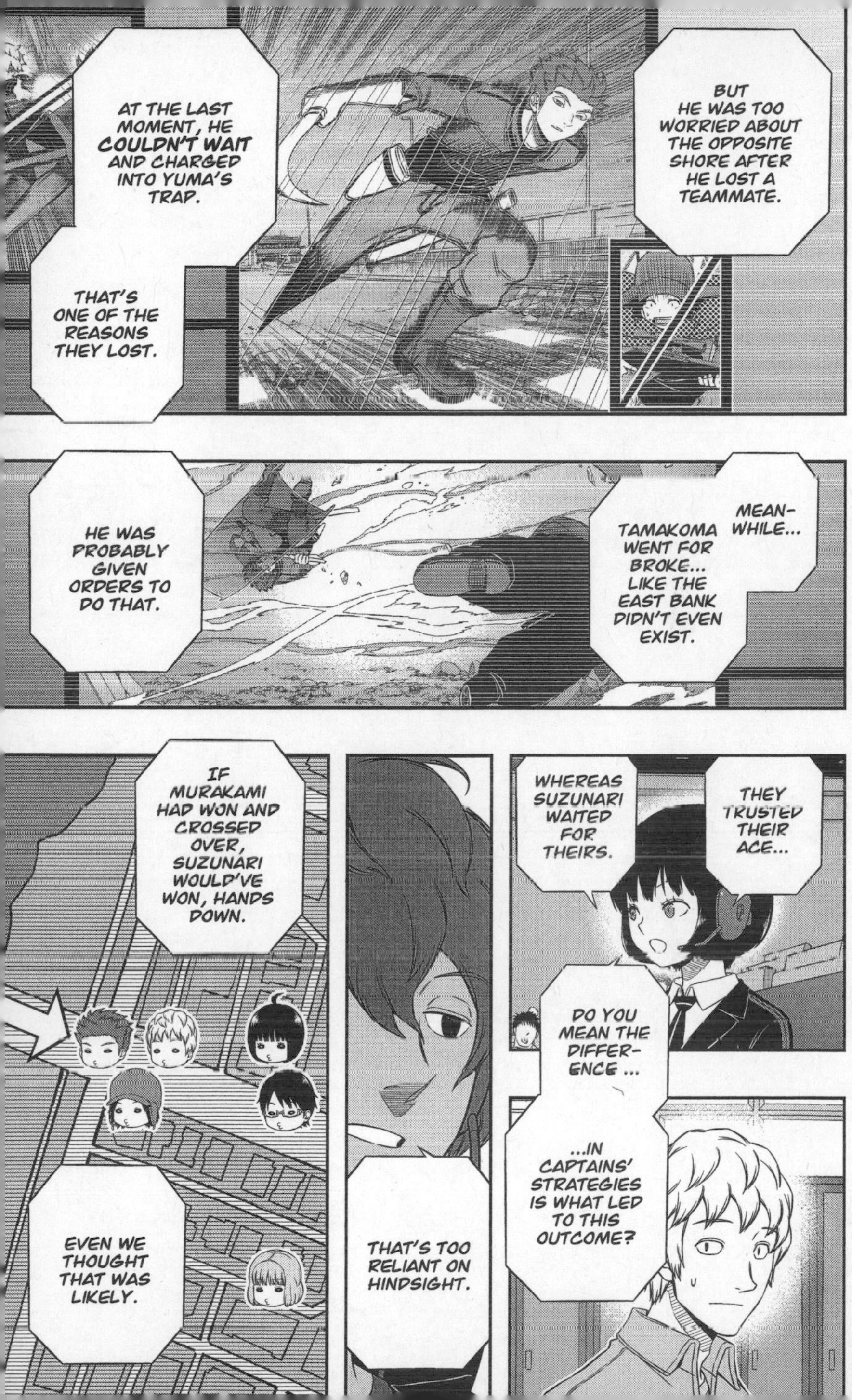
BUT HE WAS TOO WORRIED ABOUT THE OPPOSITE SHORE AFTER HE LOST A TEAMMATE.
AT THE LAST MOMENT, HE COULDN'T WAIT AND CHARGED INTO YUMA'S TRAP.
THAT'S ONE OF THE REASONS THEY LOST.
MEAN-WHILE...
TAMAKOMA WENT FOR BROKE... LIKE THE EAST BANK DIDN'T EVEN EXIST.
HE WAS PROBABLY GIVEN ORDERS TO DO THAT.
THEY TRUSTED THEIR ACE...
WHEREAS SUZUNARI WAITED FOR THEIRS.
DO YOU MEAN THE DIFFER-ENCE ...
...IN CAPTAINS' STRATEGIES IS WHAT LED TO THIS OUTCOME?
THAT'S TOO RELIANT ON HINDSIGHT.
IF MURAKAMI HAD WON AND CROSSED OVER, SUZUNARI WOULD'VE WON, HANDS DOWN.
EVEN WE THOUGHT THAT WAS LIKELY.

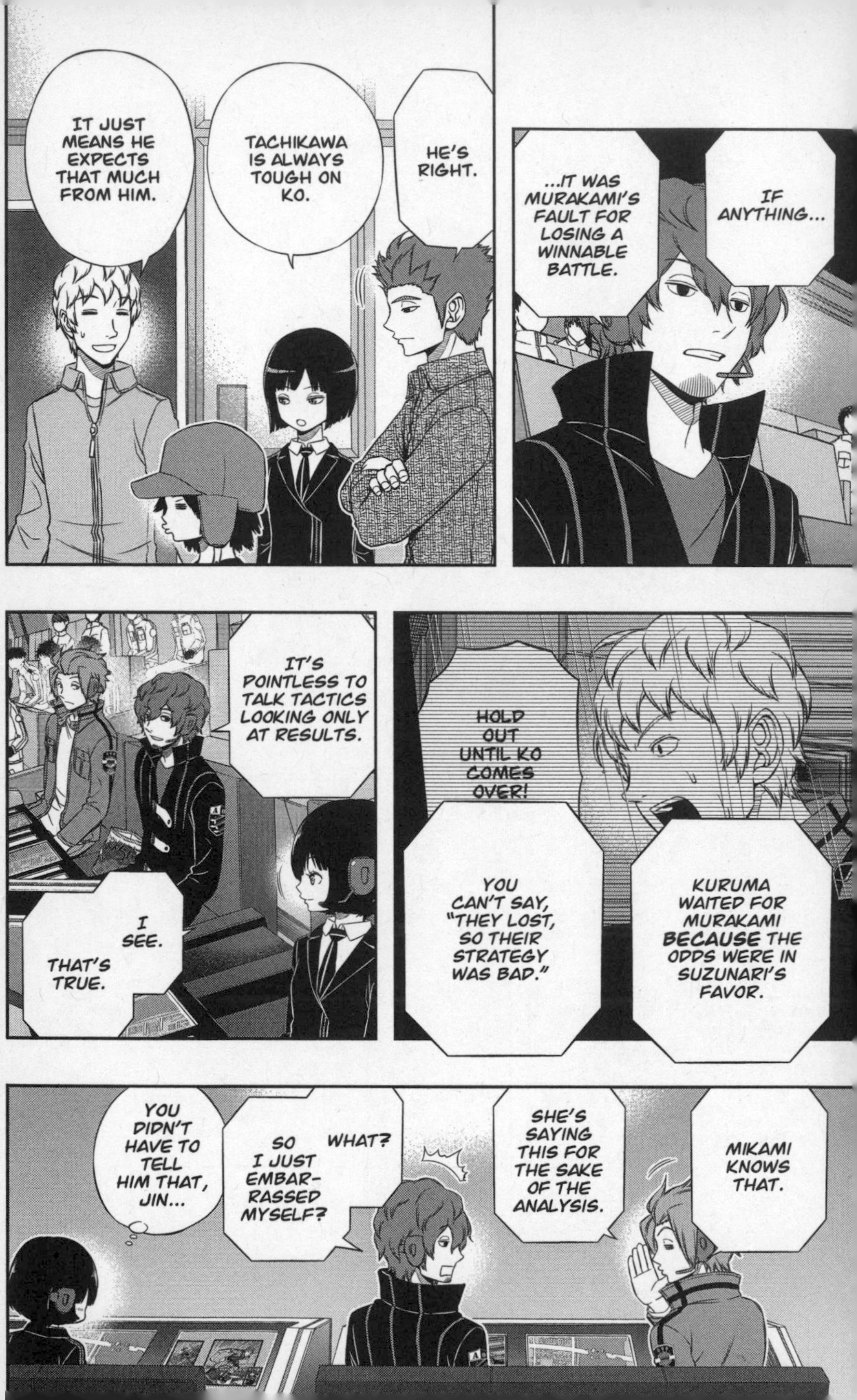
IF ANYTHING...
...IT WAS MURAKAMI'S FAULT FOR LOSING A WINNABLE BATTLE.
HE'S RIGHT.
TACHIKAWA IS ALWAYS TOUGH ON KO.
IT JUST MEANS HE EXPECTS THAT MUCH FROM HIM.
HOLD OUT UNTIL KO COMES OVER!
KURUMA WAITED FOR MURAKAMI **BECAUSE** THE ODDS WERE IN SUZUNARI'S FAVOR.
YOU CAN'T SAY, "THEY LOST, SO THEIR STRATEGY WAS BAD."
IT'S POINTLESS TO TALK TACTICS LOOKING ONLY AT RESULTS.
I SEE.
THAT'S TRUE.
MIKAMI KNOWS THAT.
SHE'S SAYING THIS FOR THE SAKE OF THE ANALYSIS.
WHAT?
SO I JUST EMBARRASSED MYSELF?
YOU DIDN'T HAVE TO TELL HIM THAT, JIN...

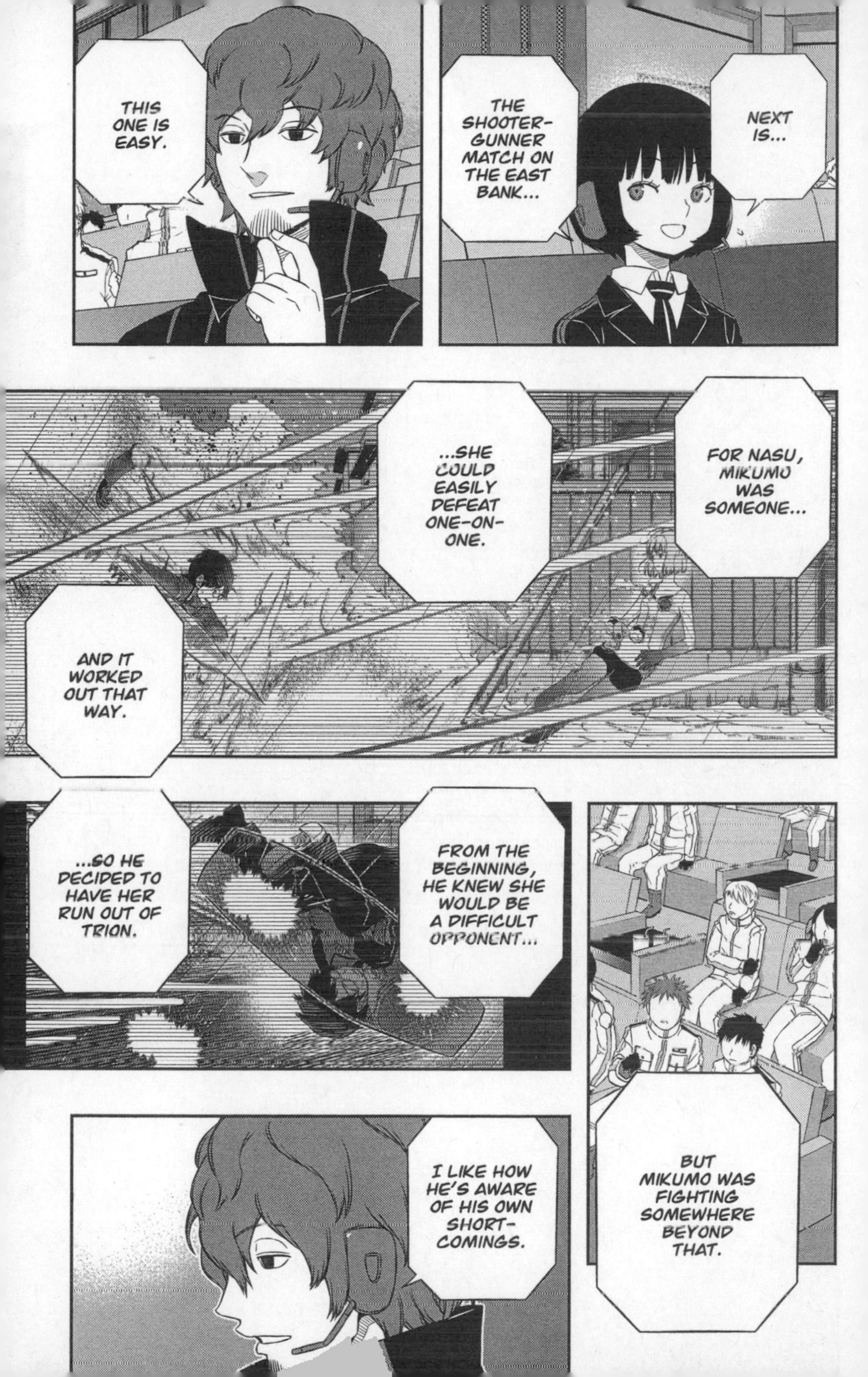
NEXT IS...
THE SHOOTER-GUNNER MATCH ON THE EAST BANK...
THIS ONE IS EASY.
FOR NASU, MIKUMO WAS SOMEONE...
...SHE COULD EASILY DEFEAT ONE-ON-ONE.
AND IT WORKED OUT THAT WAY.
BUT MIKUMO WAS FIGHTING SOMEWHERE BEYOND THAT.
FROM THE BEGINNING, HE KNEW SHE WOULD BE A DIFFICULT OPPONENT...
...SO HE DECIDED TO HAVE HER RUN OUT OF TRION.
I LIKE HOW HE'S AWARE OF HIS OWN SHORT-COMINGS.

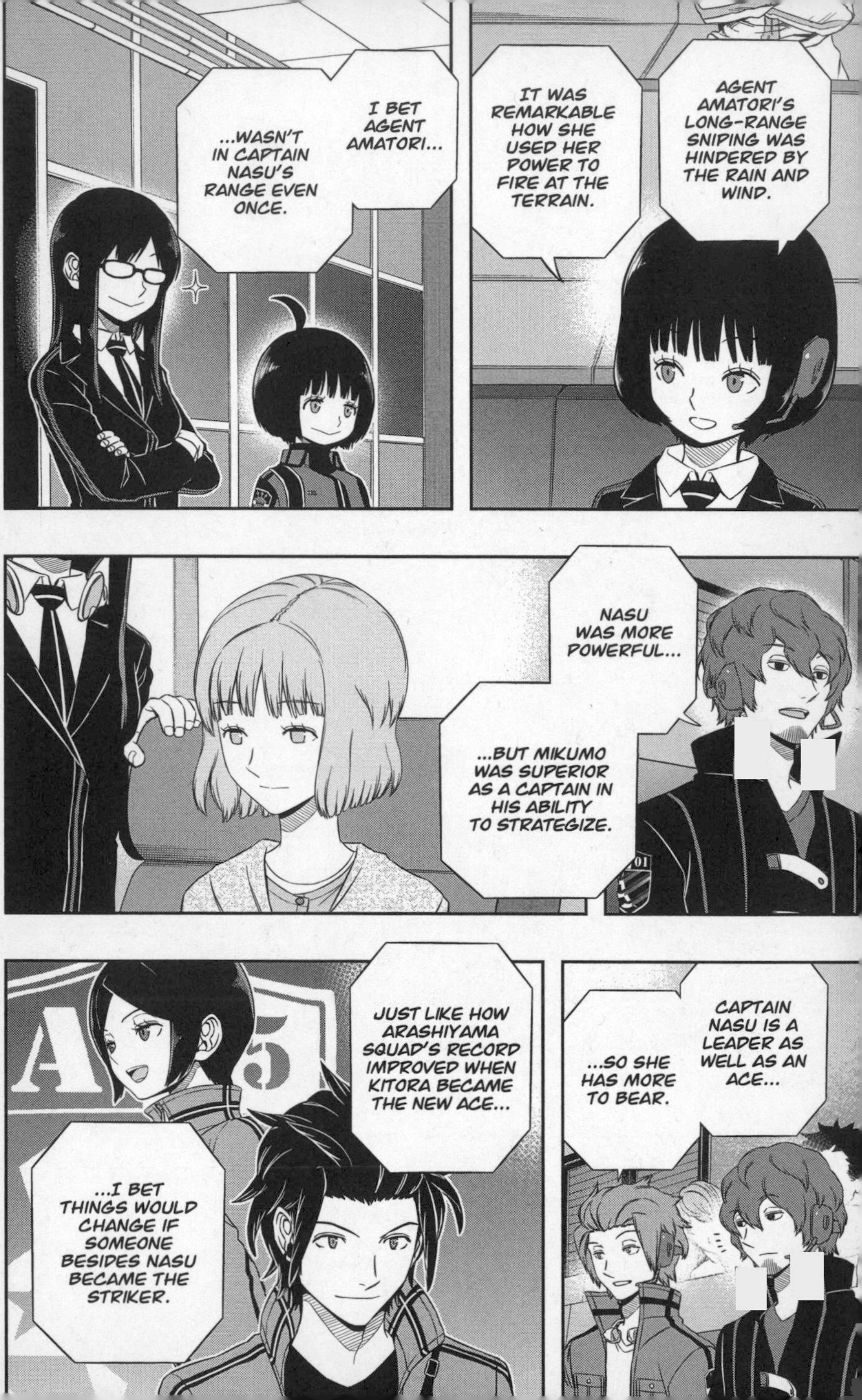
AGENT AMATORI'S LONG-RANGE SNIPING WAS HINDERED BY THE RAIN AND WIND.
IT WAS REMARKABLE HOW SHE USED HER POWER TO FIRE AT THE TERRAIN.
I BET AGENT AMATORI...
...WASN'T IN CAPTAIN NASU'S RANGE EVEN ONCE.
NASU WAS MORE POWERFUL...
...BUT MIKUMO WAS SUPERIOR AS A CAPTAIN IN HIS ABILITY TO STRATEGIZE.
CAPTAIN NASU IS A LEADER AS WELL AS AN ACE...
...SO SHE HAS MORE TO BEAR.
JUST LIKE HOW ARASHIYAMA SQUAD'S RECORD IMPROVED WHEN KITORA BECAME THE NEW ACE...
...I BET THINGS WOULD CHANGE IF SOMEONE BESIDES NASU BECAME THE STRIKER.

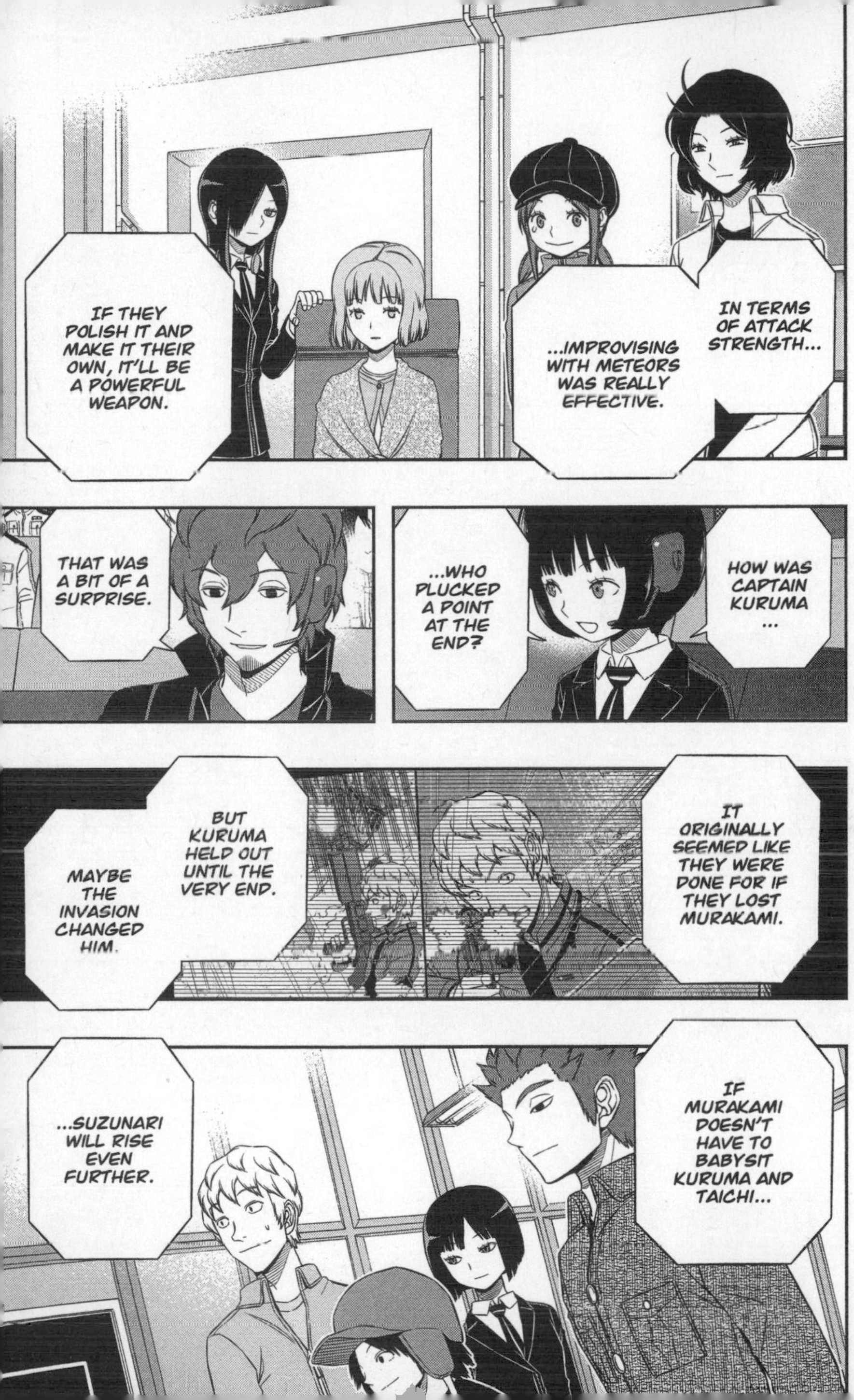
IN TERMS OF ATTACK STRENGTH...
...IMPROVISING WITH METEORS WAS REALLY EFFECTIVE.
IF THEY POLISH IT AND MAKE IT THEIR OWN, IT'LL BE A POWERFUL WEAPON.
HOW WAS CAPTAIN KURUMA ...
...WHO PLUCKED A POINT AT THE END?
THAT WAS A BIT OF A SURPRISE.
IT ORIGINALLY SEEMED LIKE THEY WERE DONE FOR IF THEY LOST MURAKAMI.
BUT KURUMA HELD OUT UNTIL THE VERY END.
MAYBE THE INVASION CHANGED HIM.
IF MURAKAMI DOESN'T HAVE TO BABYSIT KURUMA AND TAICHI...
...SUZUNARI WILL RISE EVEN FURTHER.

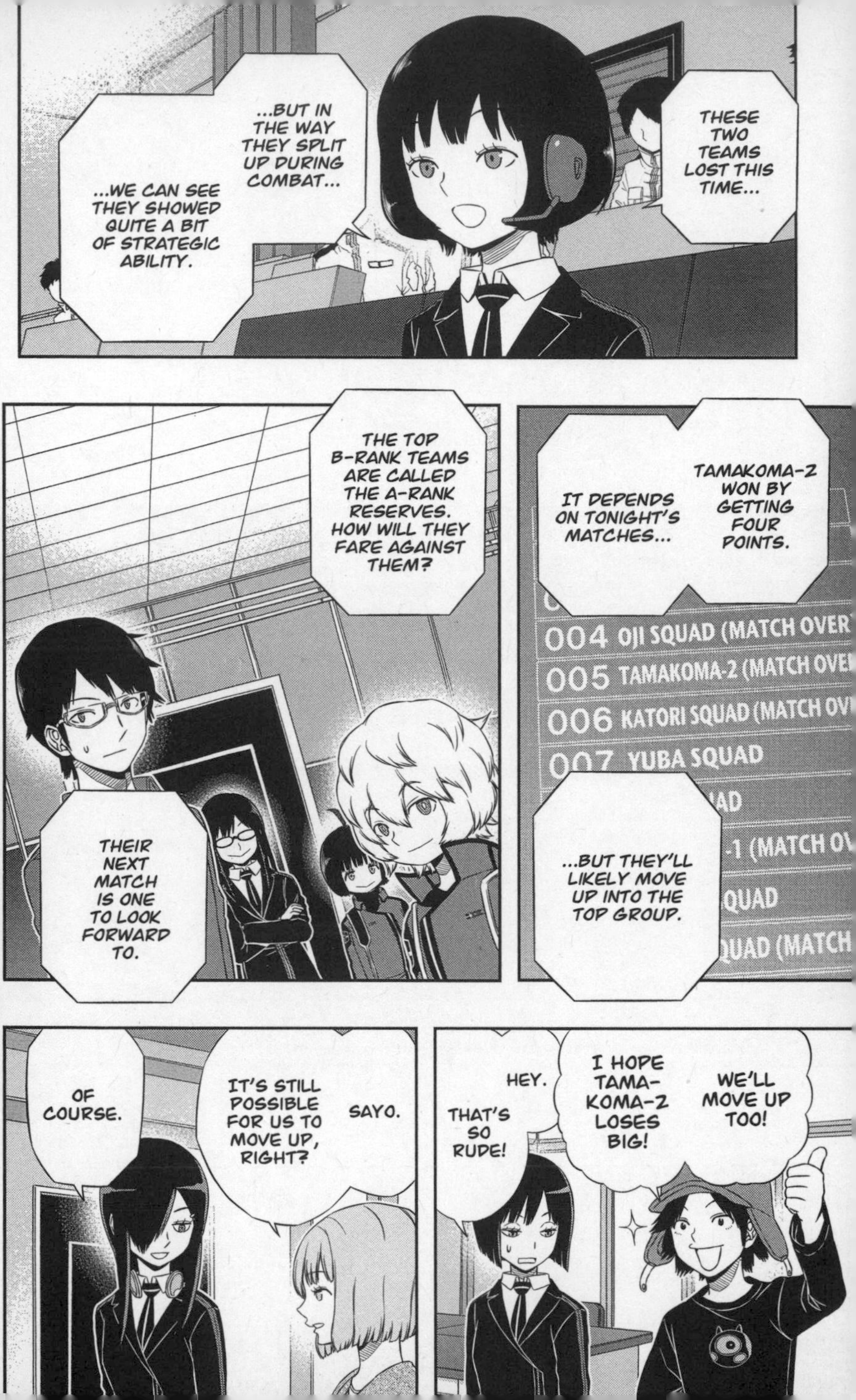
THESE TWO TEAMS LOST THIS TIME...
...BUT IN THE WAY THEY SPLIT UP DURING COMBAT...
...WE CAN SEE THEY SHOWED QUITE A BIT OF STRATEGIC ABILITY.
TAMAKOMA-2 WON BY GETTING FOUR POINTS.
IT DEPENDS ON TONIGHT'S MATCHES...
004 OJI SQUAD (MATCH OVER
005 TAMAKOMA-2 (MATCH OVE
006 KATORI SQUAD (MATCH OV
007 YUBA SQUAD
...BUT THEY'LL LIKELY MOVE UP INTO THE TOP GROUP.
THE TOP B-RANK TEAMS ARE CALLED THE A-RANK RESERVES. HOW WILL THEY FARE AGAINST THEM?
THEIR NEXT MATCH IS ONE TO LOOK FORWARD TO.
WE'LL MOVE UP TOO!
I HOPE TAMA-KOMA-2 LOSES BIG!
HEY.
THAT'S SO RUDE!
SAYO.
IT'S STILL POSSIBLE FOR US TO MOVE UP, RIGHT?
OF COURSE.

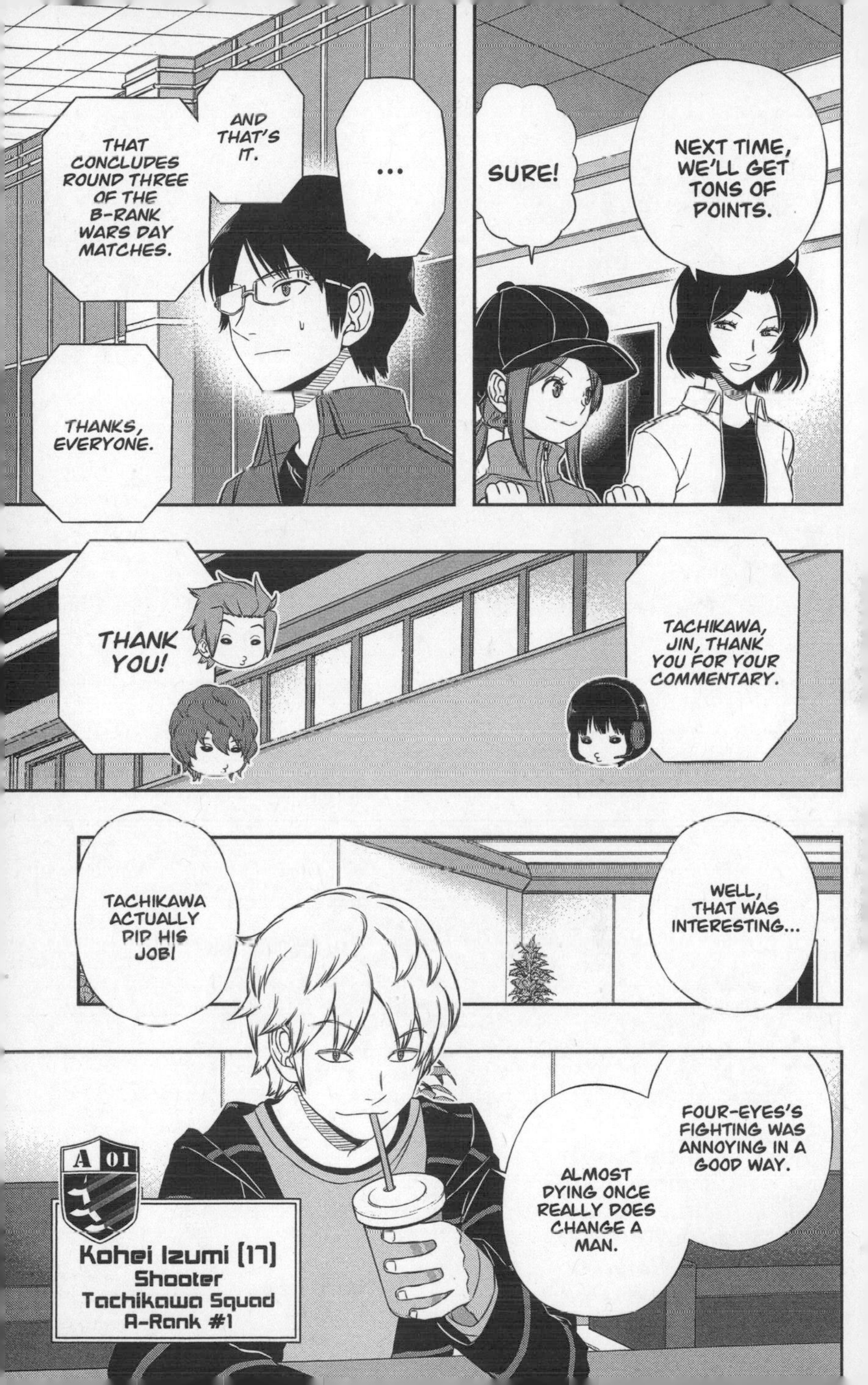
NEXT TIME, WE'LL GET TONS OF POINTS.
SURE!
...
AND THAT'S IT.
THAT CONCLUDES ROUND THREE OF THE B-RANK WARS DAY MATCHES.
THANKS, EVERYONE.
TACHIKAWA, JIN, THANK YOU FOR YOUR COMMENTARY.
THANK YOU!
WELL, THAT WAS INTERESTING...
TACHIKAWA ACTUALLY DID HIS JOB!
FOUR-EYES'S FIGHTING WAS ANNOYING IN A GOOD WAY.
ALMOST DYING ONCE REALLY DOES CHANGE A MAN.
A 01
Kohei Izumi (17)
Shooter
Tachikawa Squad
A-Rank #1

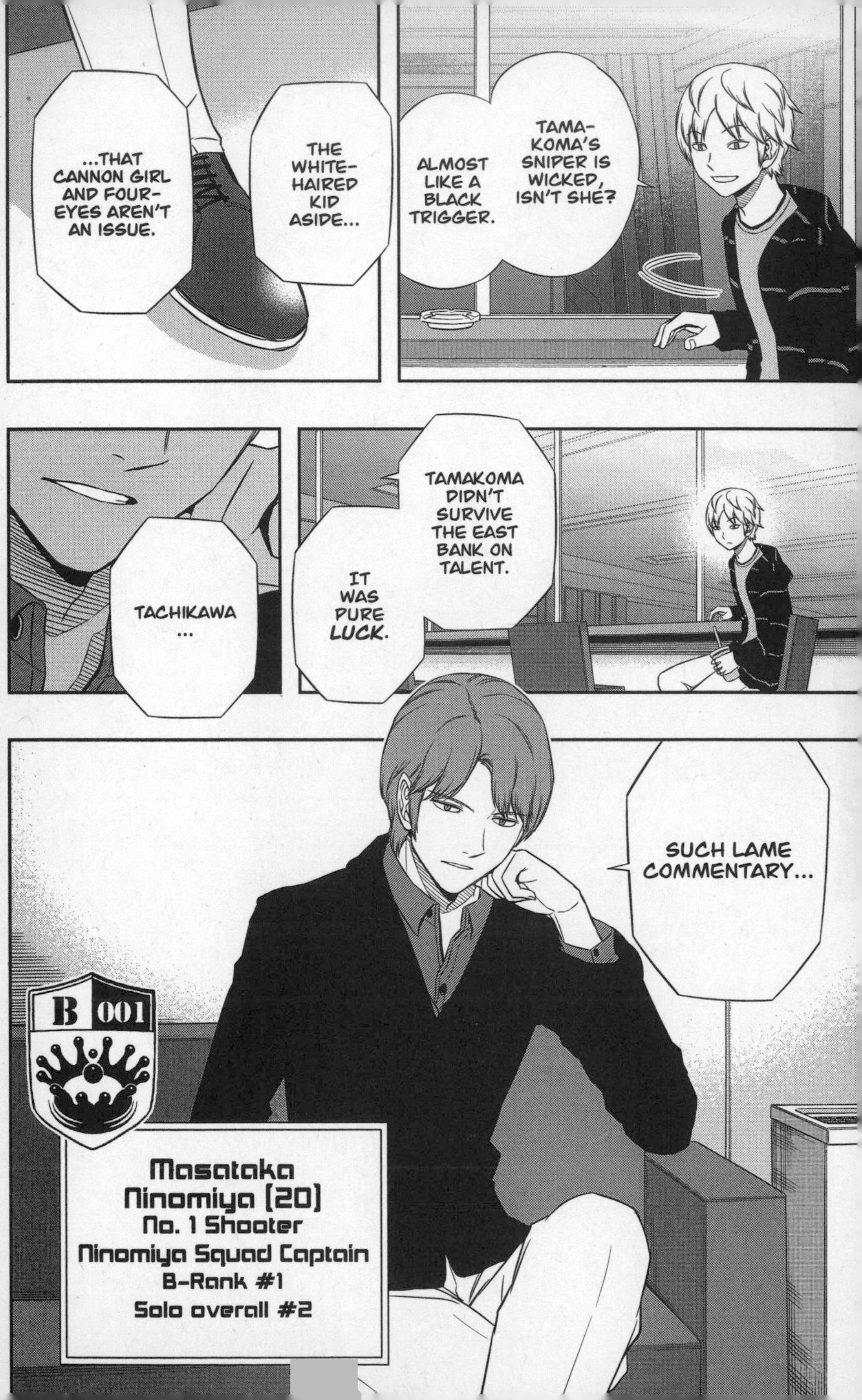
TAMA-KOMA'S SNIPER IS WICKED, ISN'T SHE?
ALMOST LIKE A BLACK TRIGGER.
THE WHITE-HAIRED KID ASIDE...
...THAT CANNON GIRL AND FOUR-EYES AREN'T AN ISSUE.
TAMAKOMA DIDN'T SURVIVE THE EAST BANK ON TALENT.
IT WAS PURE LUCK.
TACHIKAWA...
SUCH LAME COMMENTARY...
B 001
Masataka Ninomiya (20)
No. 1 Shooter
Ninomiya Squad Captain
B-Rank #1
Solo overall #2

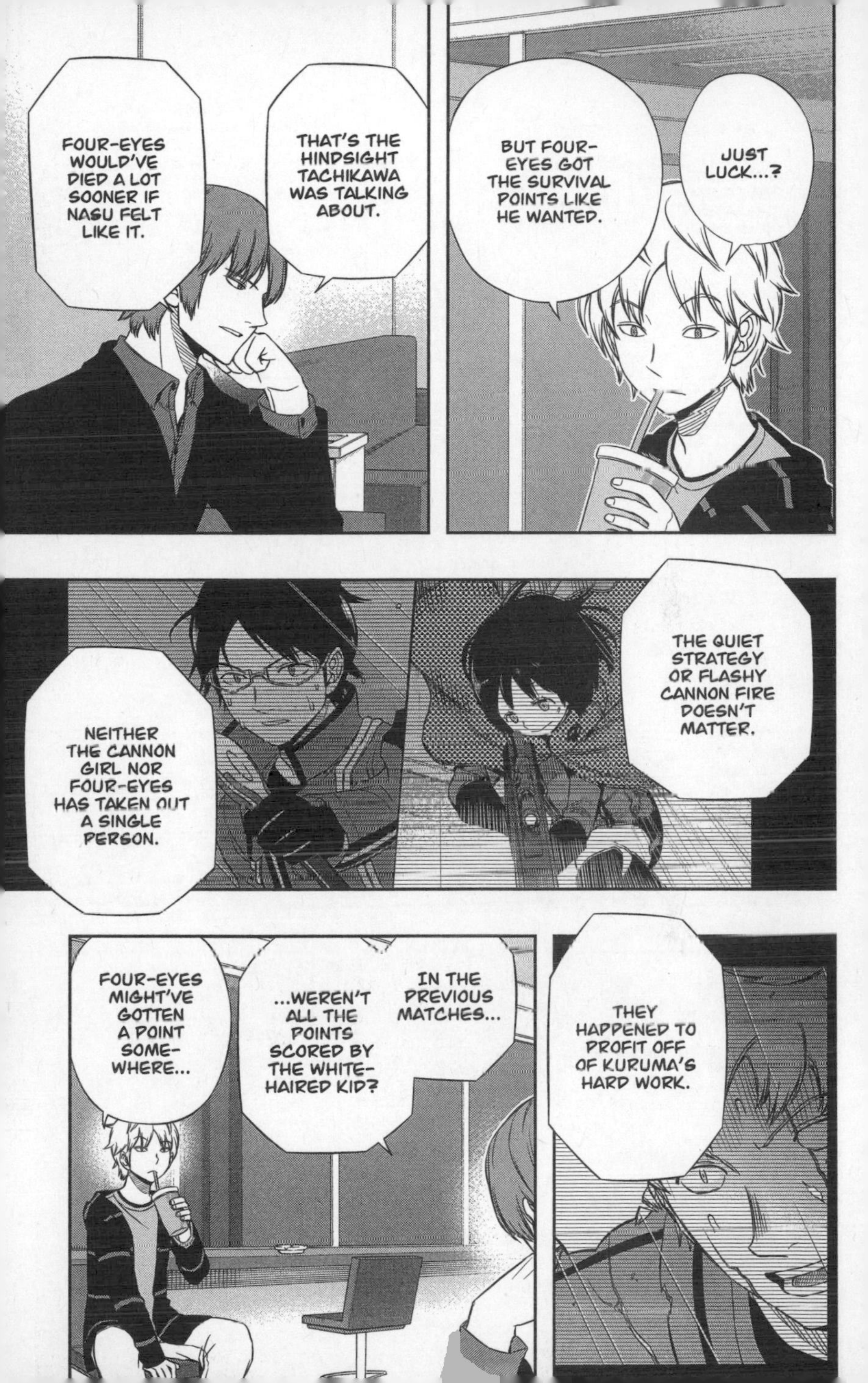
JUST LUCK...?
BUT FOUR-EYES GOT THE SURVIVAL POINTS LIKE HE WANTED.
THAT'S THE HINDSIGHT TACHIKAWA WAS TALKING ABOUT.
FOUR-EYES WOULD'VE DIED A LOT SOONER IF NASU FELT LIKE IT.
THE QUIET STRATEGY OR FLASHY CANNON FIRE DOESN'T MATTER.
NEITHER THE CANNON GIRL NOR FOUR-EYES HAS TAKEN OUT A SINGLE PERSON.
THEY HAPPENED TO PROFIT OFF OF KURUMA'S HARD WORK.
IN THE PREVIOUS MATCHES...
...WEREN'T ALL THE POINTS SCORED BY THE WHITE-HAIRED KID?
FOUR-EYES MIGHT'VE GOTTEN A POINT SOME-WHERE...

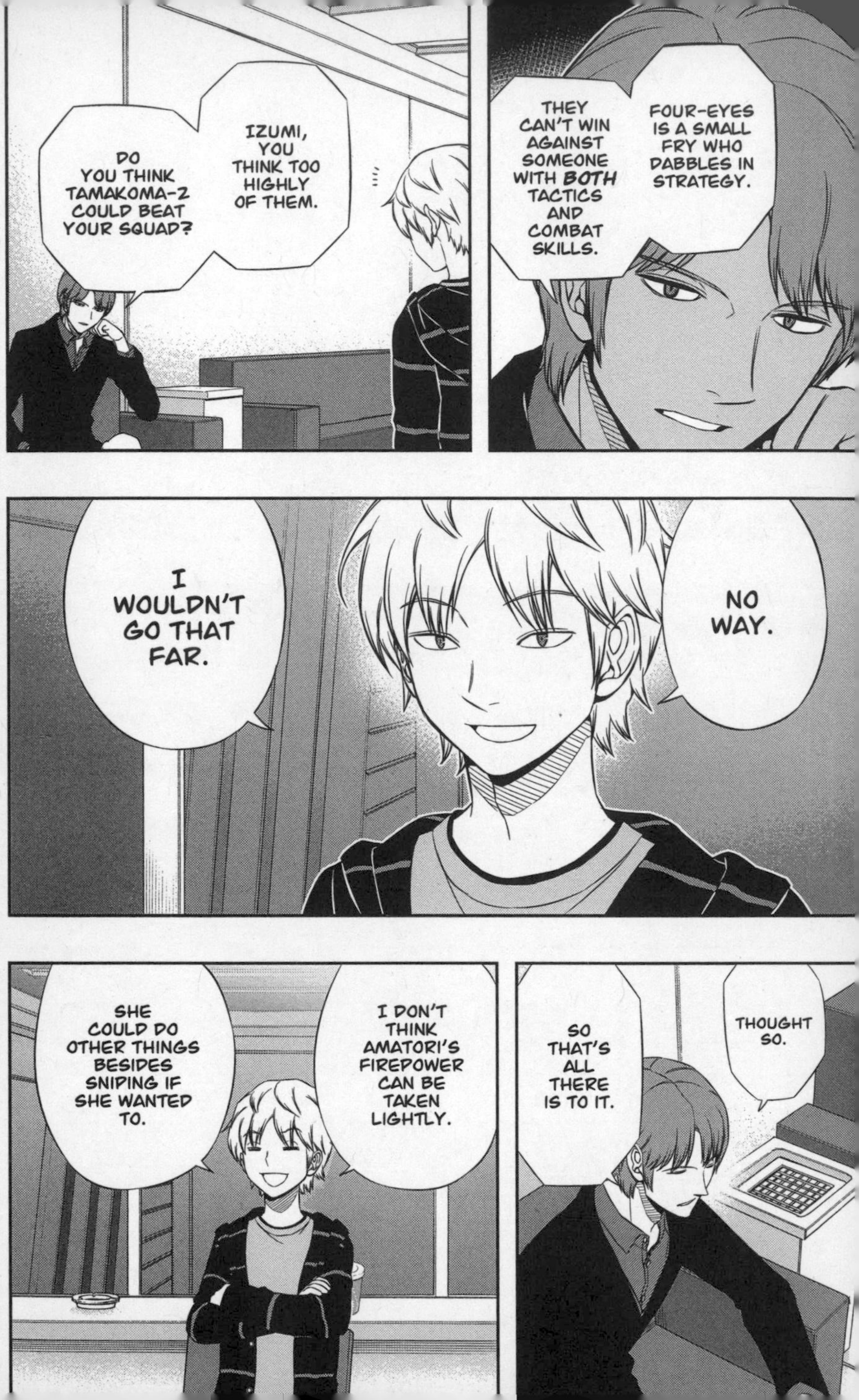
FOUR-EYES IS A SMALL FRY WHO DABBLES IN STRATEGY.
THEY CAN'T WIN AGAINST SOMEONE WITH **BOTH** TACTICS AND COMBAT SKILLS.
IZUMI, YOU THINK TOO HIGHLY OF THEM.
DO YOU THINK TAMAKOMA-2 COULD BEAT YOUR SQUAD?
NO WAY.
I WOULDN'T GO THAT FAR.
THOUGHT SO.
SO THAT'S ALL THERE IS TO IT.
I DON'T THINK AMATORI'S FIREPOWER CAN BE TAKEN LIGHTLY.
SHE COULD DO OTHER THINGS BESIDES SNIPING IF SHE WANTED TO.

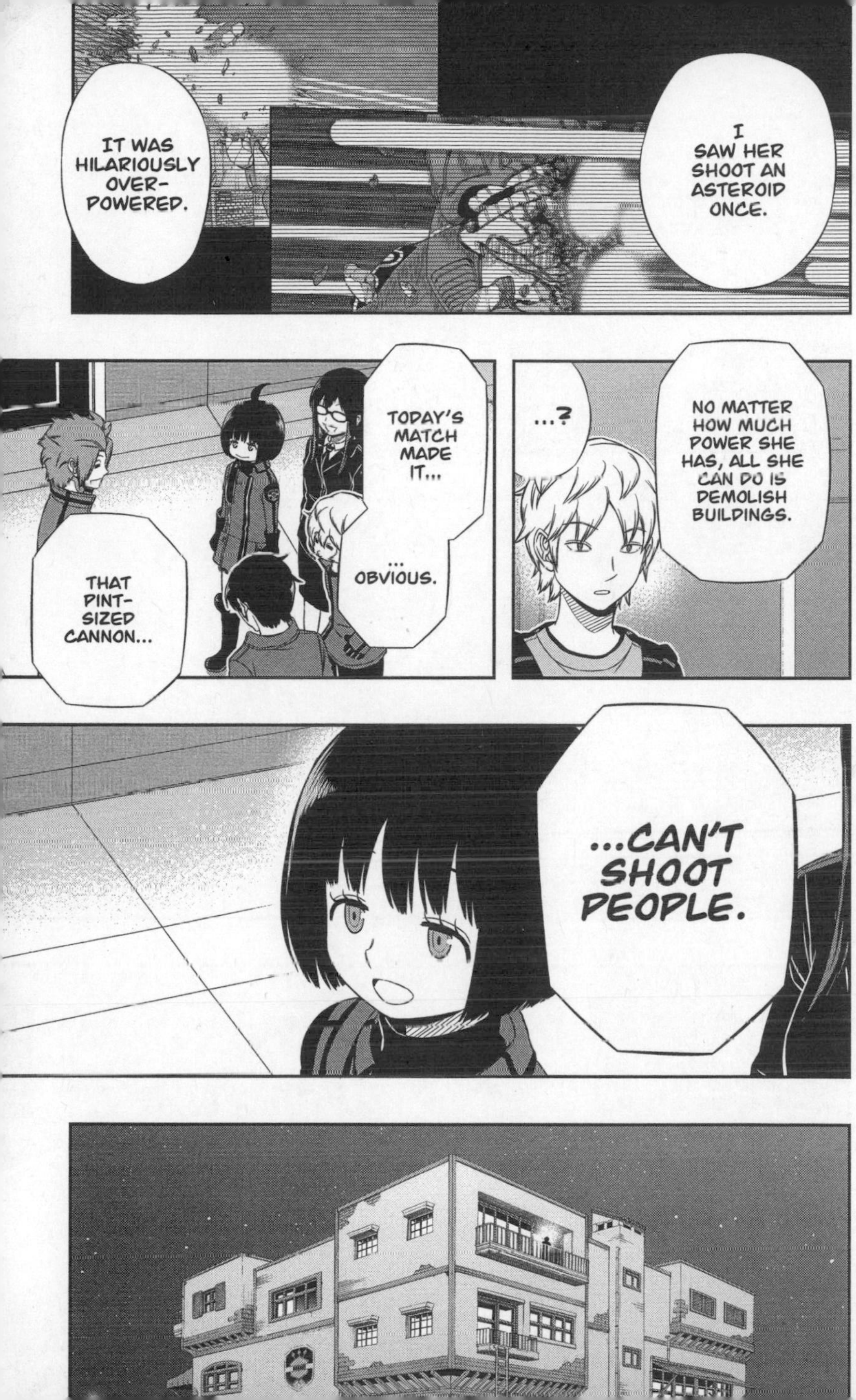
I SAW HER SHOOT AN ASTEROID ONCE.
IT WAS HILARIOUSLY OVER-POWERED.
NO MATTER HOW MUCH POWER SHE HAS, ALL SHE CAN DO IS DEMOLISH BUILDINGS.
...?
TODAY'S MATCH MADE IT...
...OBVIOUS.
THAT PINT-SIZED CANNON...
...CAN'T SHOOT PEOPLE.

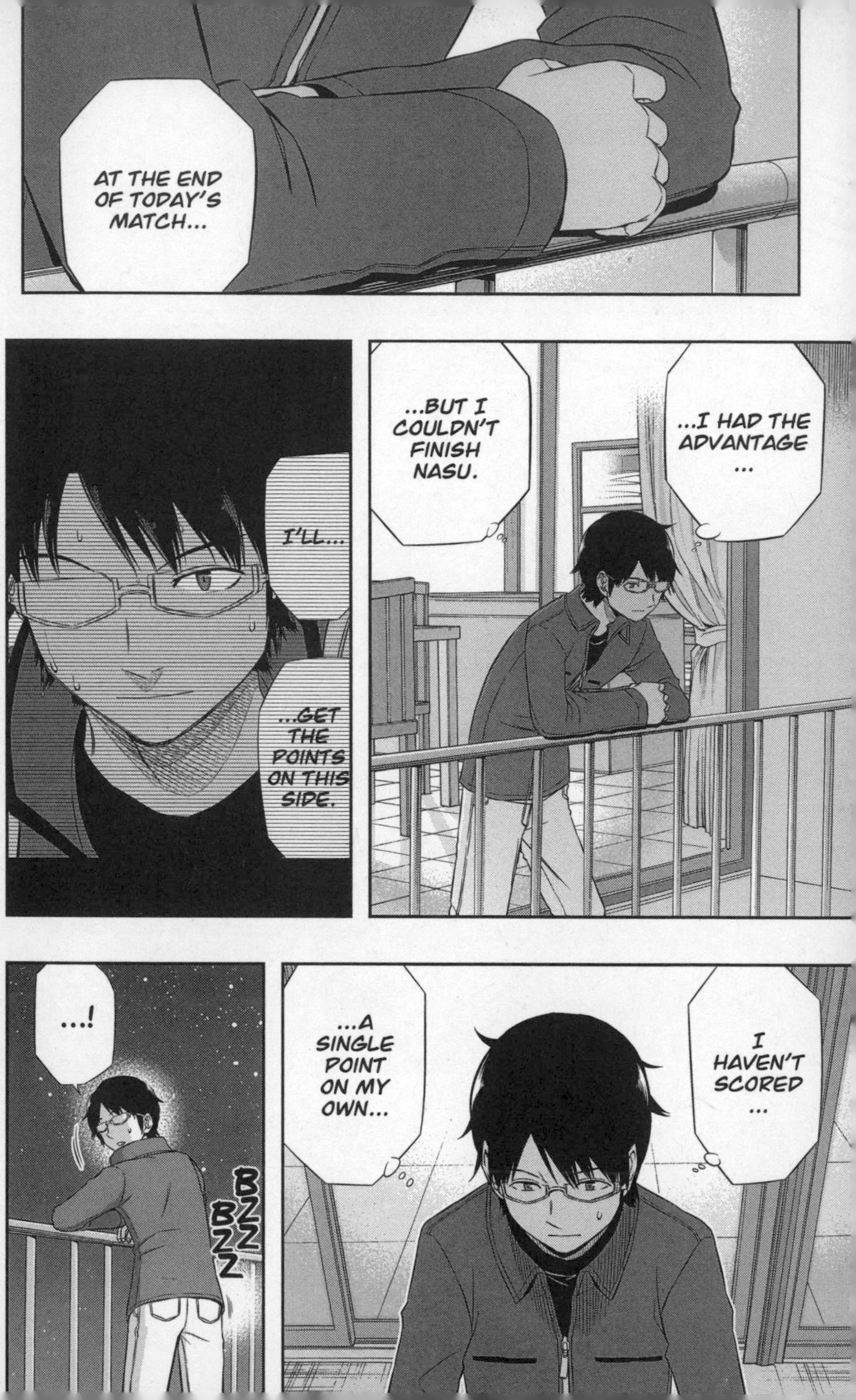
AT THE END OF TODAY'S MATCH...
...I HAD THE ADVANTAGE ...
...BUT I COULDN'T FINISH NASU.
I'LL...
...GET THE POINTS ON THIS SIDE.
I HAVEN'T SCORED ...
...A SINGLE POINT ON MY OWN...
...!
BZZ BZZ

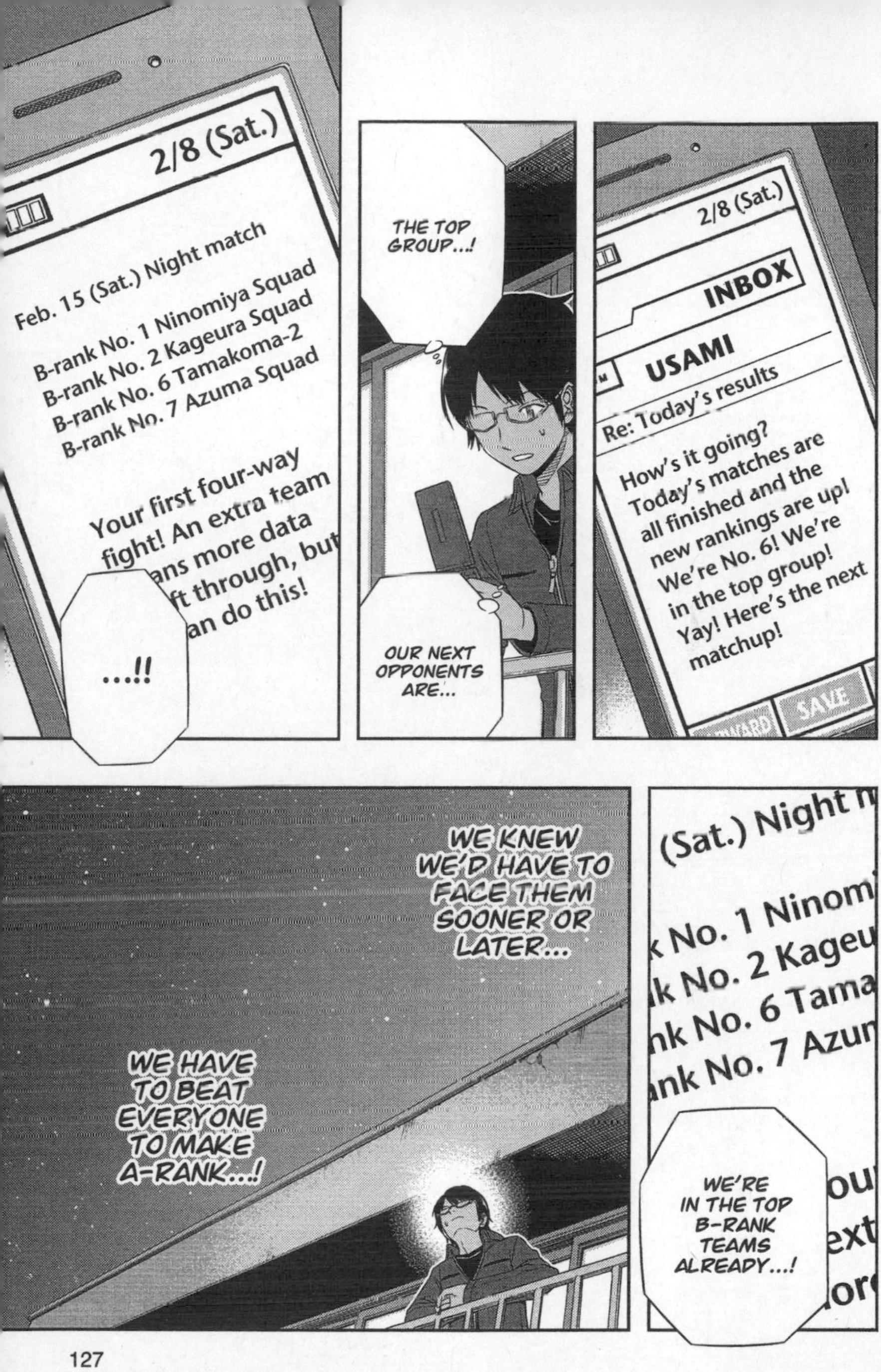
2/8 (Sat.)
INBOX
USAMI
Re: Today's results
How's it going? Today's matches are all finished and the new rankings are up! We're No. 6! We're in the top group! Yay! Here's the next matchup!
SAVE
THE TOP GROUP...!
OUR NEXT OPPONENTS ARE...
2/8 (Sat.)
Feb. 15 (Sat.) Night match
B-rank No. 1 Ninomiya Squad
B-rank No. 2 Kageura Squad
B-rank No. 6 Tamakoma-2
B-rank No. 7 Azuma Squad
Your first four-way fight! An extra team
...!!
(Sat.) Night
WE'RE IN THE TOP B-RANK TEAMS ALREADY...!
WE KNEW WE'D HAVE TO FACE THEM SOONER OR LATER...
WE HAVE TO BEAT EVERYONE TO MAKE A-RANK...!

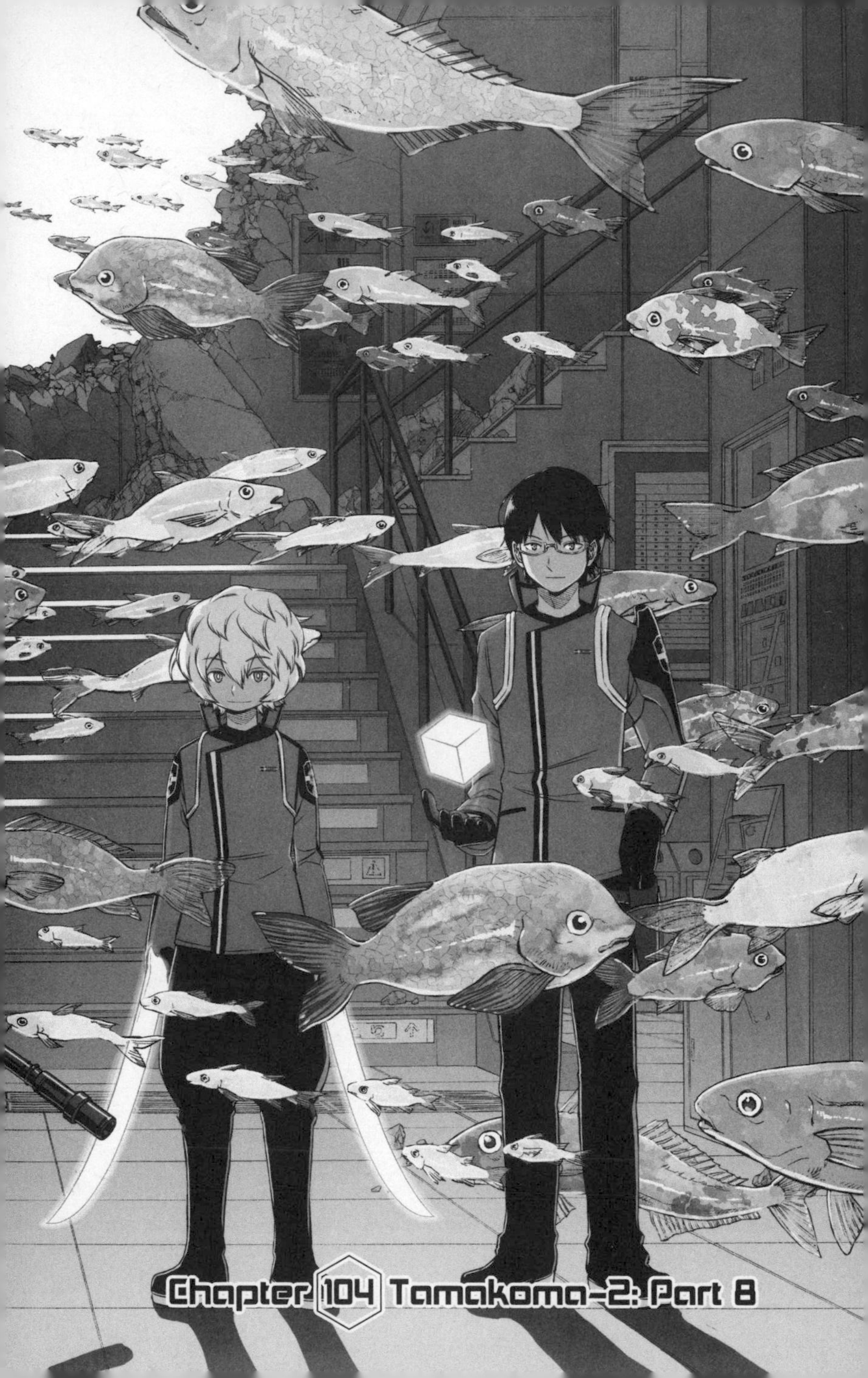
Chapter 104 Tamakoma-2: Part 8

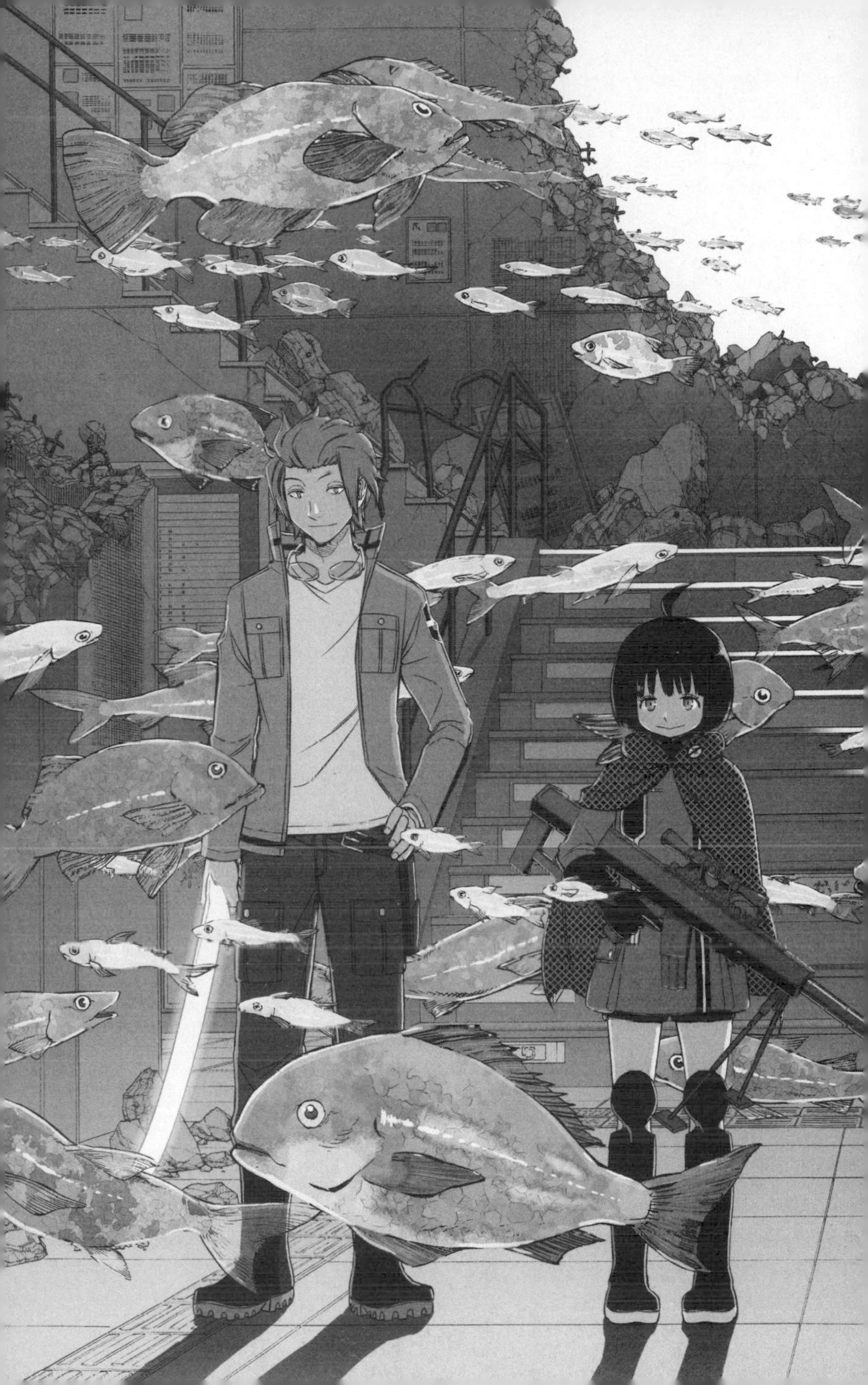

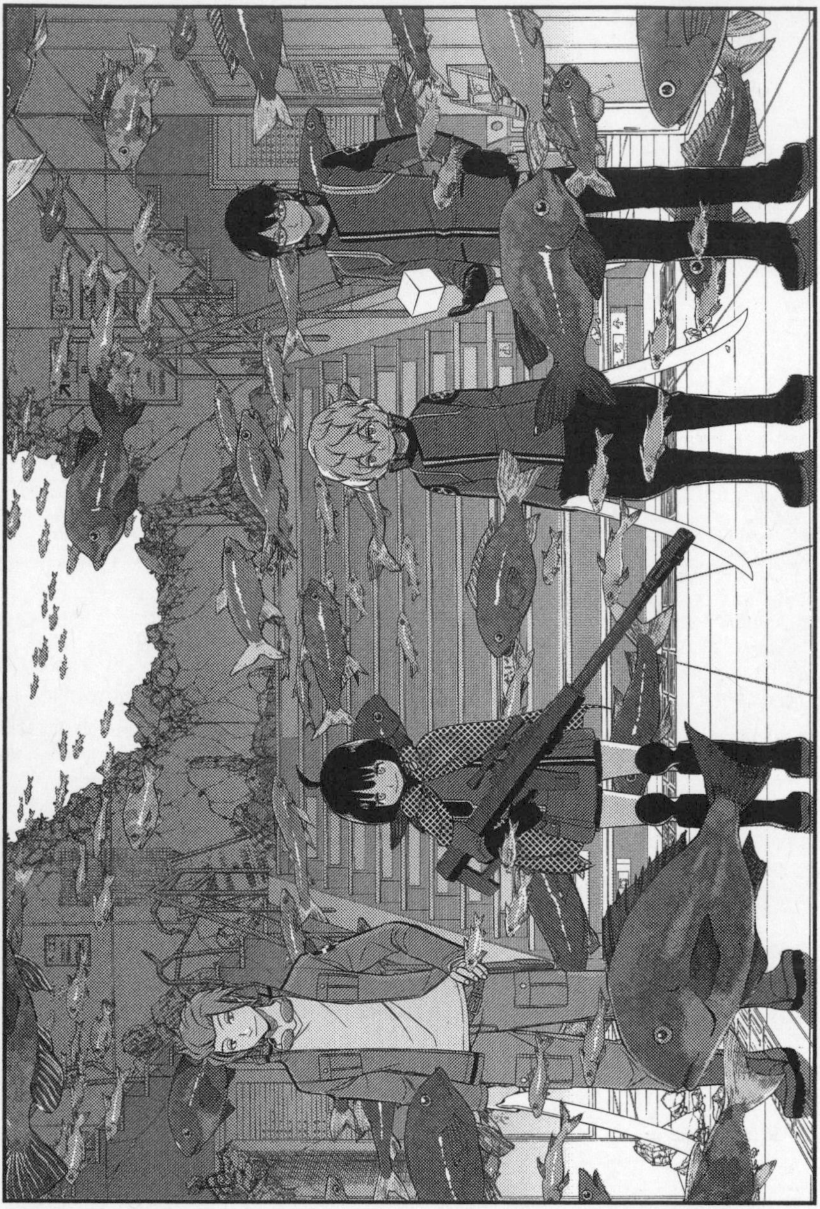

■ **2015 *Weekly Shonen Jump* Issue 27 initial color page (fifth time)**

The second anniversary opening color page. In volume 6 I wrote that I wanted to do the same composition next time, and I managed to pull it off. Thank you everyone for your continued support. What should I do for the third anniversary?

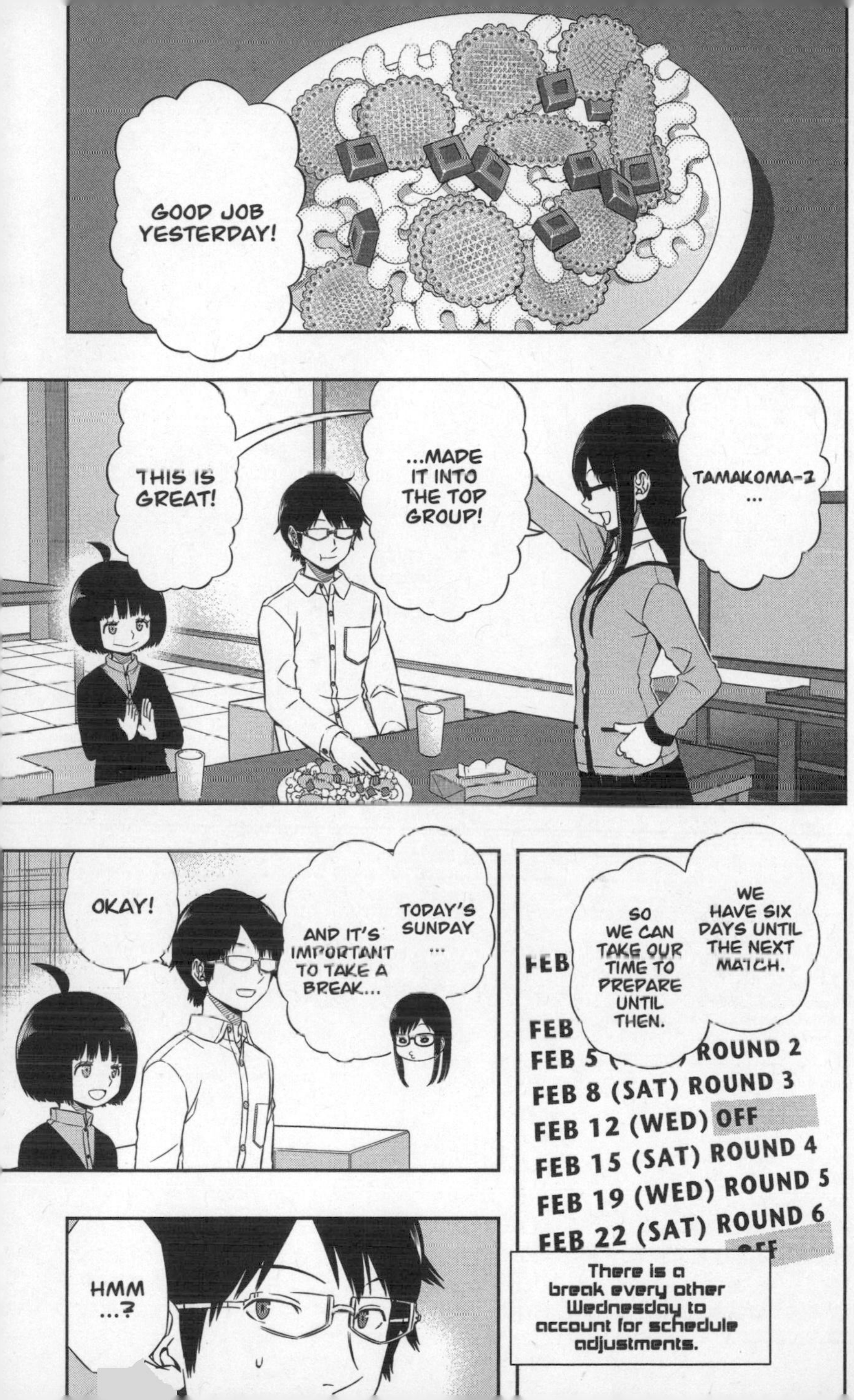
GOOD JOB YESTERDAY!
TAMAKOMA-2 ...
...MADE IT INTO THE TOP GROUP!
THIS IS GREAT!
WE HAVE SIX DAYS UNTIL THE NEXT MATCH.
SO WE CAN TAKE OUR TIME TO PREPARE UNTIL THEN.
FEB
FEB
FEB 5
ROUND 2
FEB 8 (SAT) ROUND 3
FEB 12 (WED) OFF
FEB 15 (SAT) ROUND 4
FEB 19 (WED) ROUND 5
FEB 22 (SAT) ROUND 6
There is a break every other Wednesday to account for schedule adjustments.
TODAY'S SUNDAY ...
AND IT'S IMPORTANT TO TAKE A BREAK...
OKAY!
HMM ...?

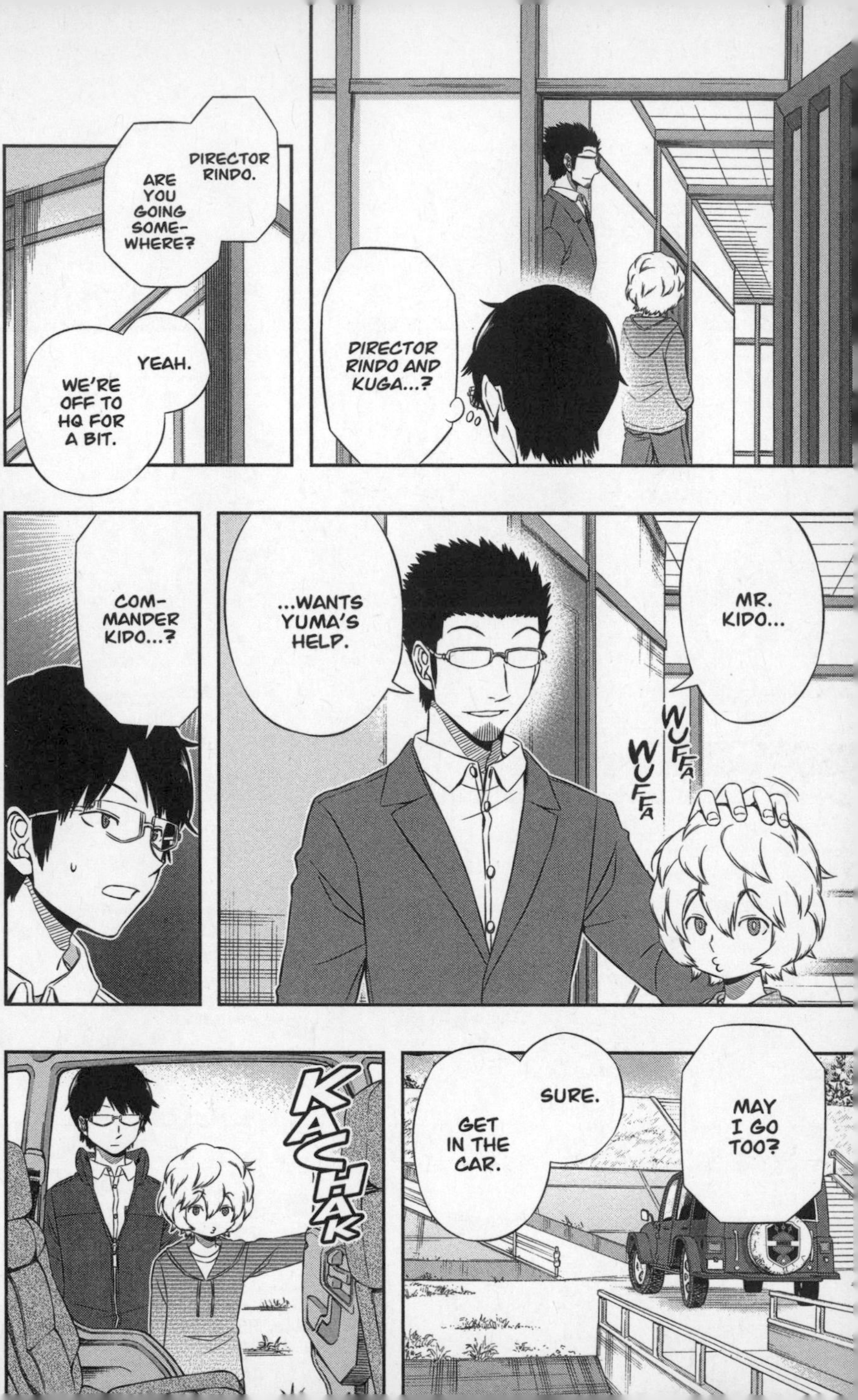
DIRECTOR RINDO AND KUGA...?
DIRECTOR RINDO. ARE YOU GOING SOME-WHERE?
YEAH. WE'RE OFF TO HQ FOR A BIT.
MR. KIDO...
WUFFA WUFFA
...WANTS YUMA'S HELP.
COM-MANDER KIDO...?
MAY I GO TOO?
SURE. GET IN THE CAR.
KACHAK

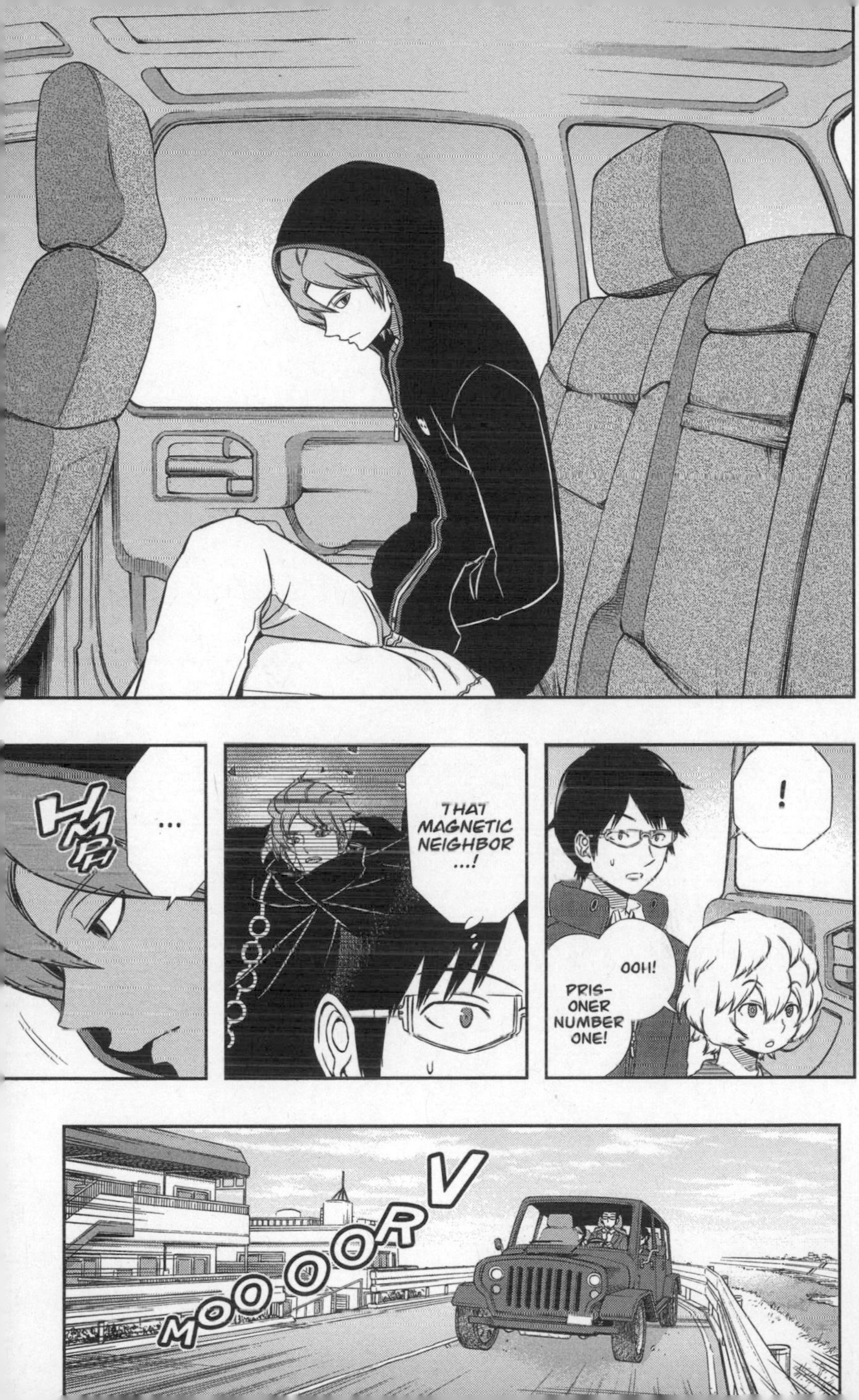
!
OOH! PRIS-ONER NUMBER ONE!
THAT MAGNETIC NEIGHBOR ....!
HMPH
...
MOOOOORV

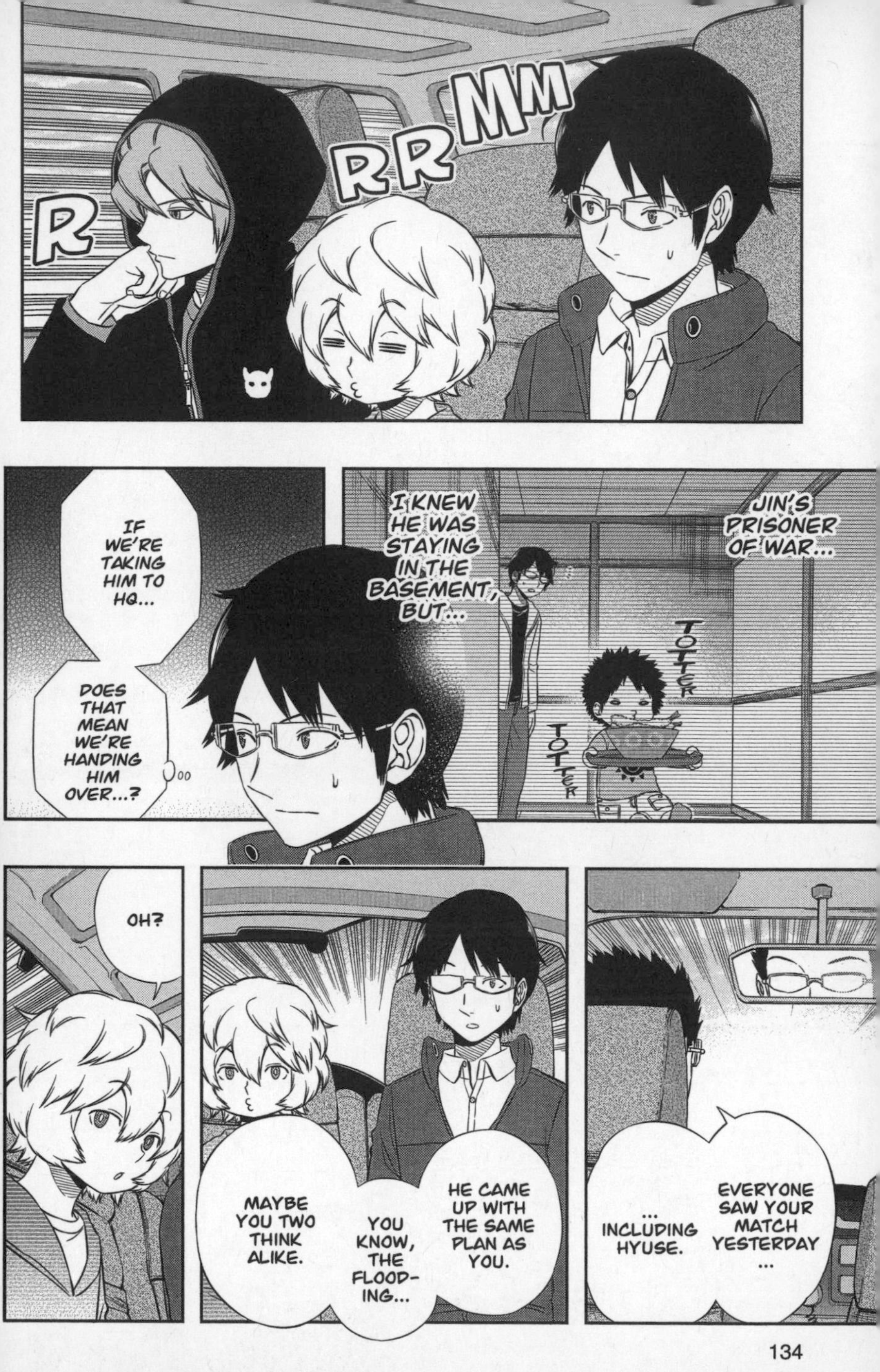
R
RR
MM
JIN'S PRISONER OF WAR...
I KNEW HE WAS STAYING IN THE BASEMENT, BUT...
TOTTER
TOTTER
IF WE'RE TAKING HIM TO HQ...
DOES THAT MEAN WE'RE HANDING HIM OVER...?
EVERYONE SAW YOUR MATCH YESTERDAY...
...INCLUDING HYUSE.
HE CAME UP WITH THE SAME PLAN AS YOU.
YOU KNOW, THE FLOODING...
MAYBE YOU TWO THINK ALIKE.
OH?

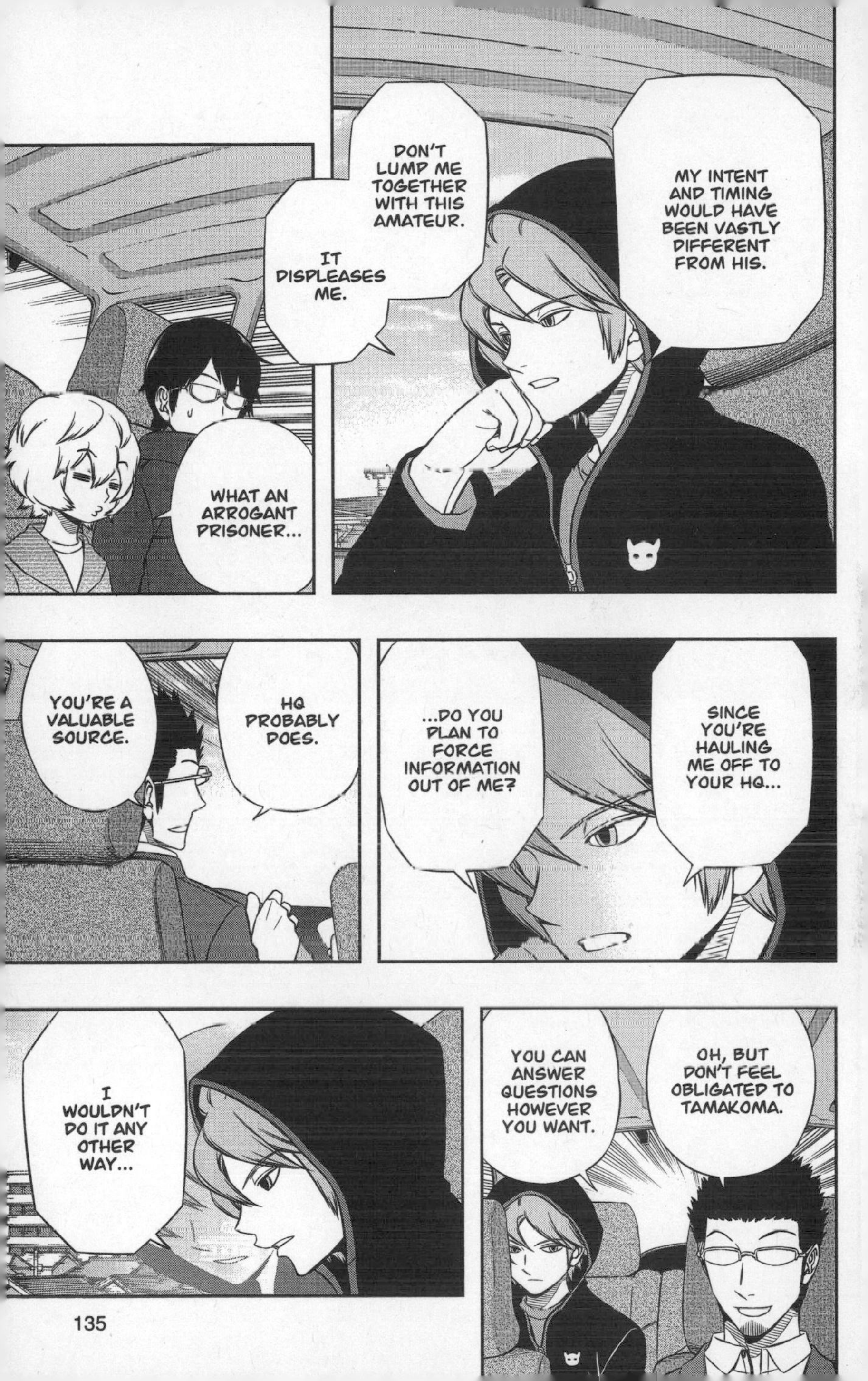
MY INTENT AND TIMING WOULD HAVE BEEN VASTLY DIFFERENT FROM HIS.
DON'T LUMP ME TOGETHER WITH THIS AMATEUR.
IT DISPLEASES ME.
WHAT AN ARROGANT PRISONER...
SINCE YOU'RE HAULING ME OFF TO YOUR HQ...
...DO YOU PLAN TO FORCE INFORMATION OUT OF ME?
HQ PROBABLY DOES.
YOU'RE A VALUABLE SOURCE.
OH, BUT DON'T FEEL OBLIGATED TO TAMAKOMA.
YOU CAN ANSWER QUESTIONS HOWEVER YOU WANT.
I WOULDN'T DO IT ANY OTHER WAY...

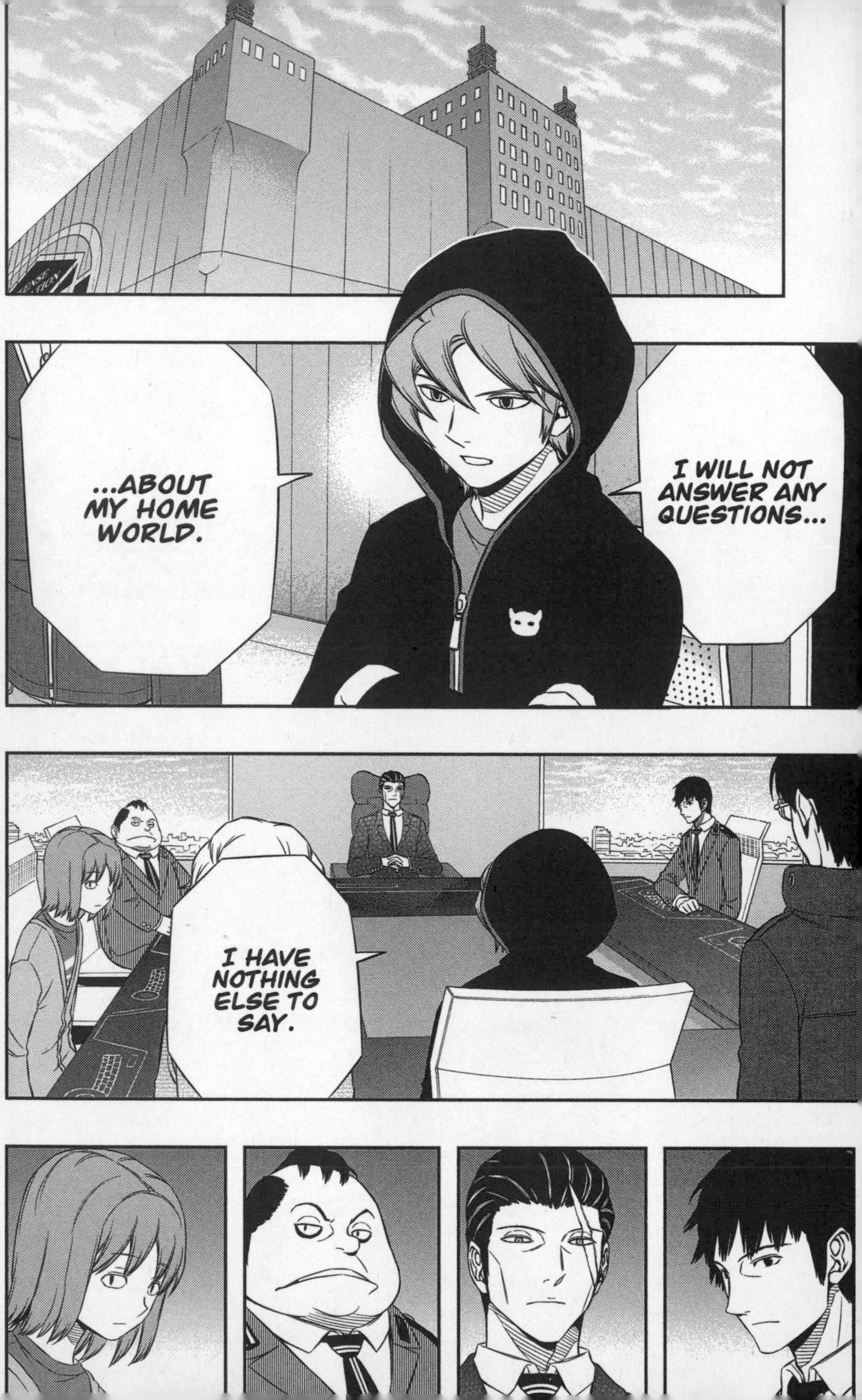
I WILL NOT ANSWER ANY QUESTIONS...
...ABOUT MY HOME WORLD.
I HAVE NOTHING ELSE TO SAY.

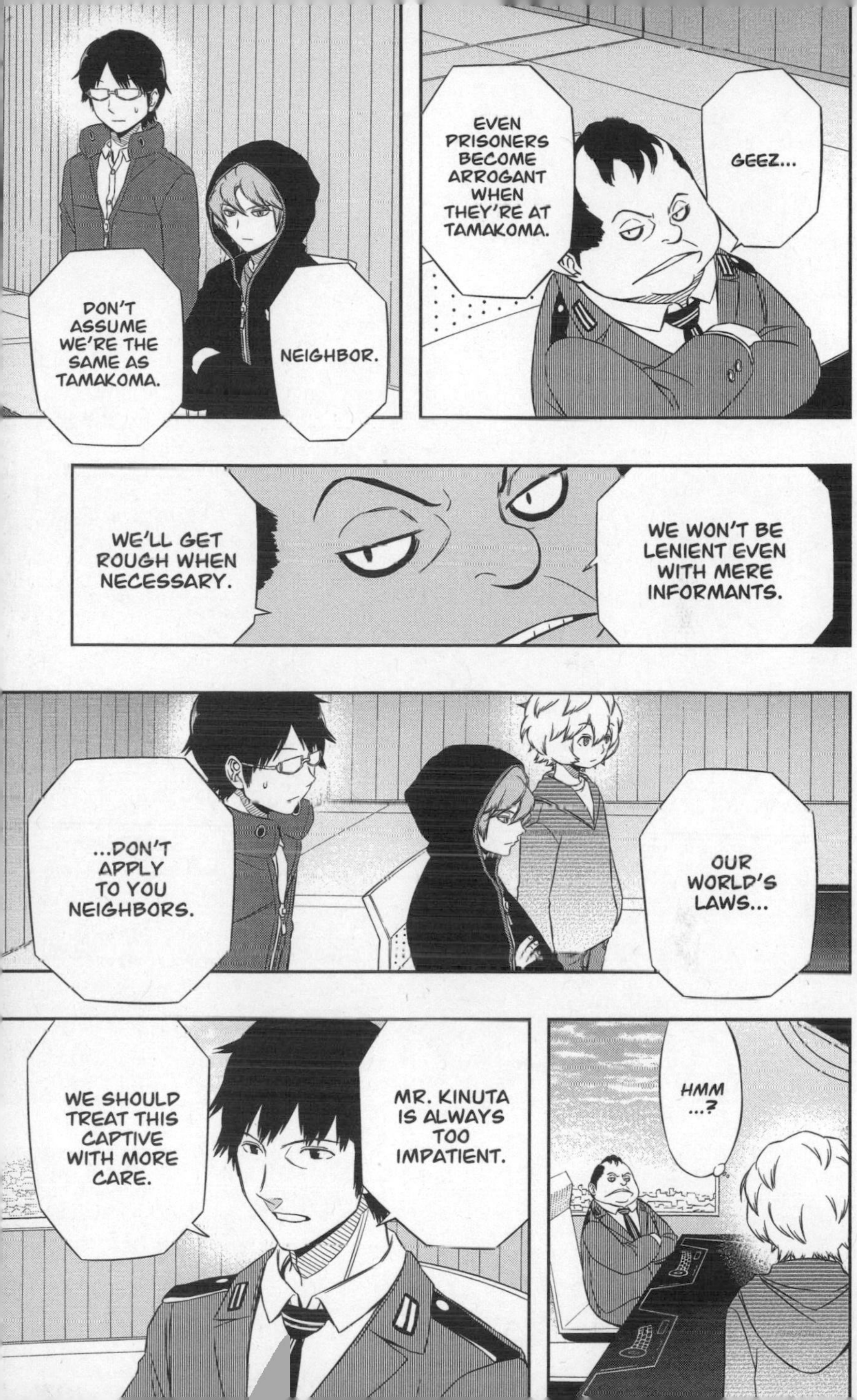
GEEZ...
EVEN PRISONERS BECOME ARROGANT WHEN THEY'RE AT TAMAKOMA.
NEIGHBOR.
DON'T ASSUME WE'RE THE SAME AS TAMAKOMA.
WE WON'T BE LENIENT EVEN WITH MERE INFORMANTS.
WE'LL GET ROUGH WHEN NECESSARY.
OUR WORLD'S LAWS...
...DON'T APPLY TO YOU NEIGHBORS.
HMM ...?
MR. KINUTA IS ALWAYS TOO IMPATIENT.
WE SHOULD TREAT THIS CAPTIVE WITH MORE CARE.

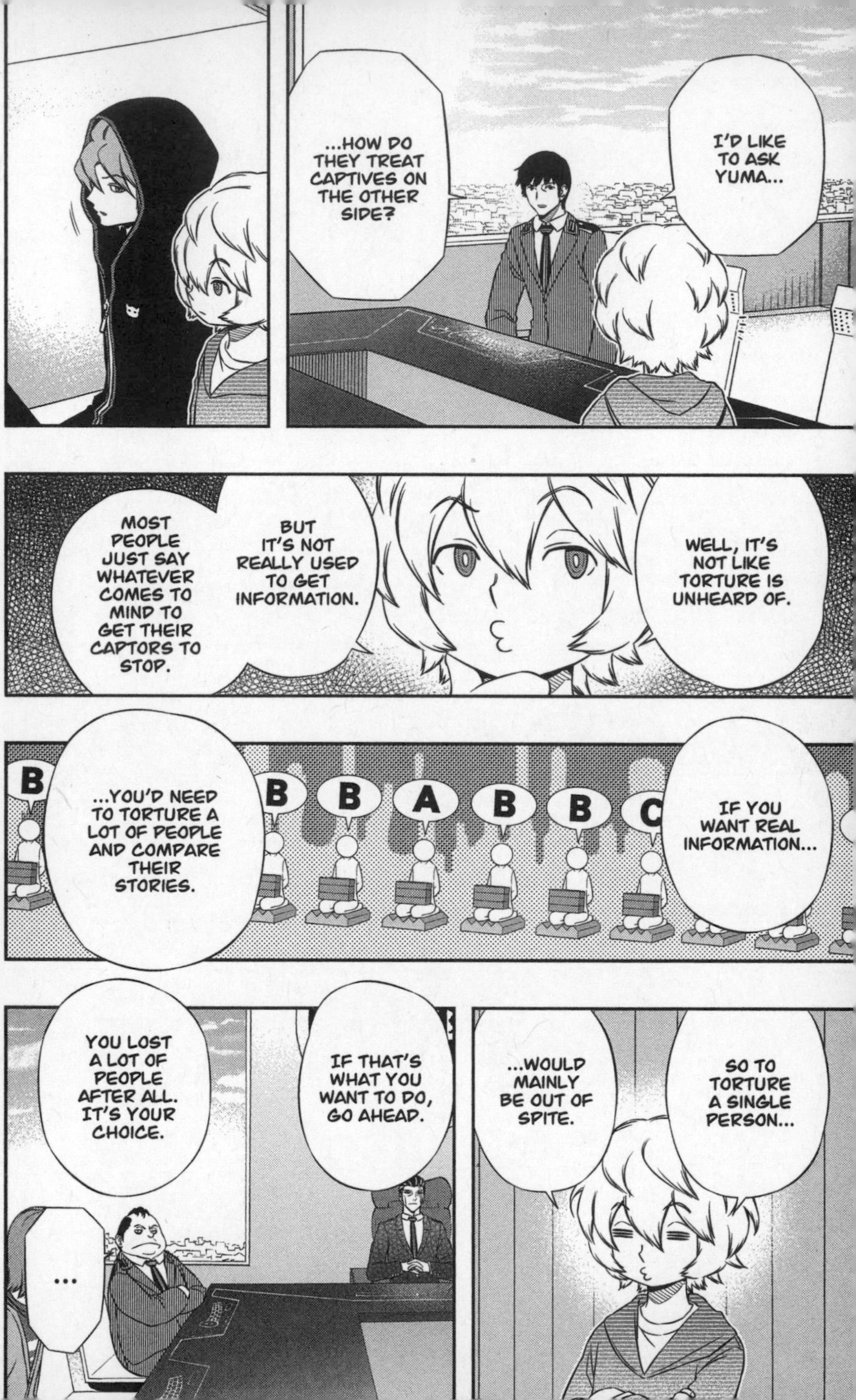
I'D LIKE TO ASK YUMA...
...HOW DO THEY TREAT CAPTIVES ON THE OTHER SIDE?
WELL, IT'S NOT LIKE TORTURE IS UNHEARD OF.
BUT IT'S NOT REALLY USED TO GET INFORMATION.
MOST PEOPLE JUST SAY WHATEVER COMES TO MIND TO GET THEIR CAPTORS TO STOP.
IF YOU WANT REAL INFORMATION...
C
B
B
A
B
B
B
...YOU'D NEED TO TORTURE A LOT OF PEOPLE AND COMPARE THEIR STORIES.
SO TO TORTURE A SINGLE PERSON...
...WOULD MAINLY BE OUT OF SPITE.
IF THAT'S WHAT YOU WANT TO DO, GO AHEAD.
YOU LOST A LOT OF PEOPLE AFTER ALL. IT'S YOUR CHOICE.
...

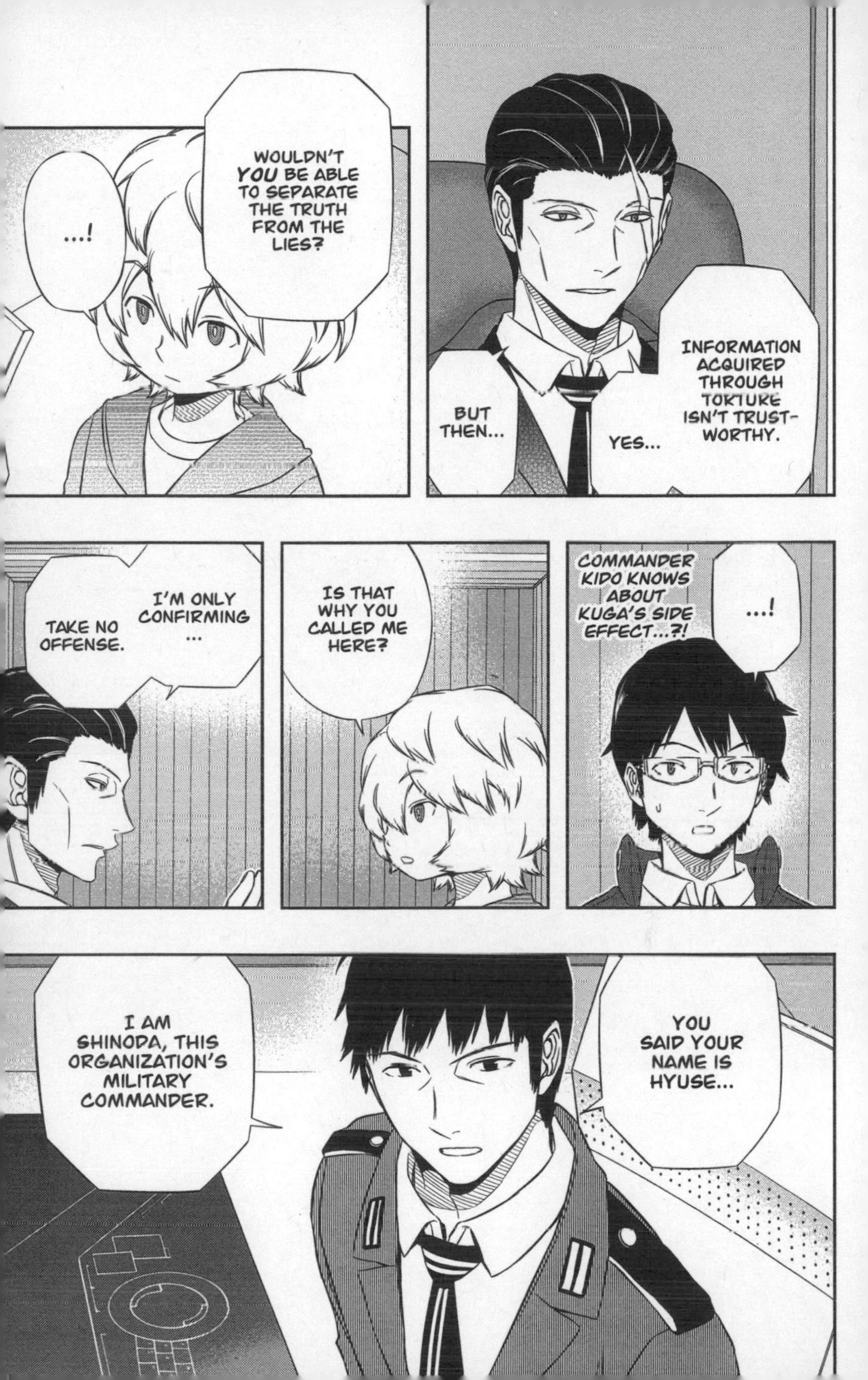
INFORMATION ACQUIRED THROUGH TORTURE ISN'T TRUST-WORTHY.
YES...
BUT THEN...
WOULDN'T *YOU* BE ABLE TO SEPARATE THE TRUTH FROM THE LIES?
...!
...!
COMMANDER KIDO KNOWS ABOUT KUGA'S SIDE EFFECT...?!
IS THAT WHY YOU CALLED ME HERE?
I'M ONLY CONFIRMING ...
TAKE NO OFFENSE.
YOU SAID YOUR NAME IS HYUSE...
I AM SHINODA, THIS ORGANIZATION'S MILITARY COMMANDER.

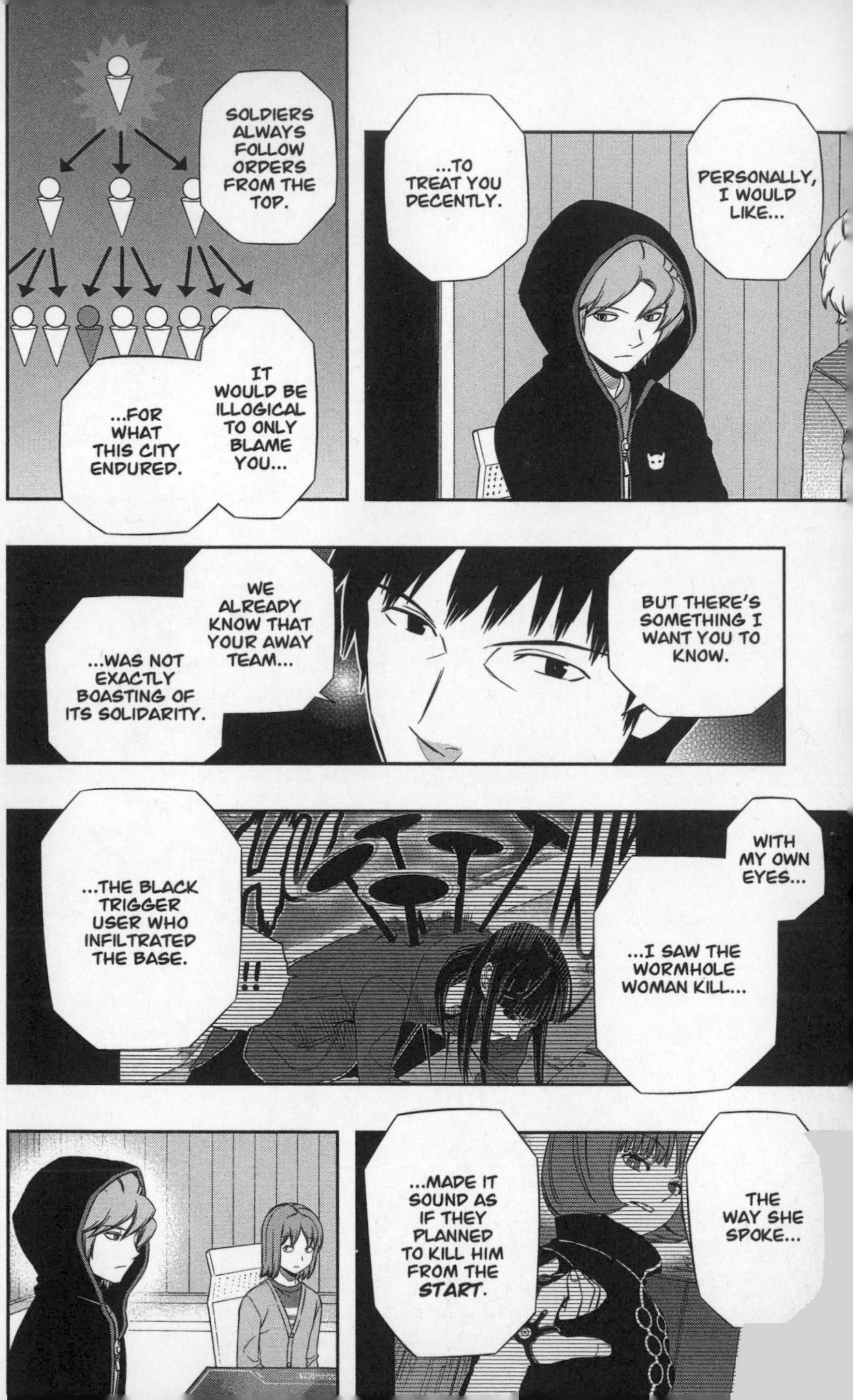
PERSONALLY, I WOULD LIKE...
...TO TREAT YOU DECENTLY.
SOLDIERS ALWAYS FOLLOW ORDERS FROM THE TOP.
IT WOULD BE ILLOGICAL TO ONLY BLAME YOU...
...FOR WHAT THIS CITY ENDURED.
BUT THERE'S SOMETHING I WANT YOU TO KNOW.
WE ALREADY KNOW THAT YOUR AWAY TEAM...
...WAS NOT EXACTLY BOASTING OF ITS SOLIDARITY.
WITH MY OWN EYES...
...I SAW THE WORMHOLE WOMAN KILL...
!!
...THE BLACK TRIGGER USER WHO INFILTRATED THE BASE.
THE WAY SHE SPOKE...
...MADE IT SOUND AS IF THEY PLANNED TO KILL HIM FROM THE START.

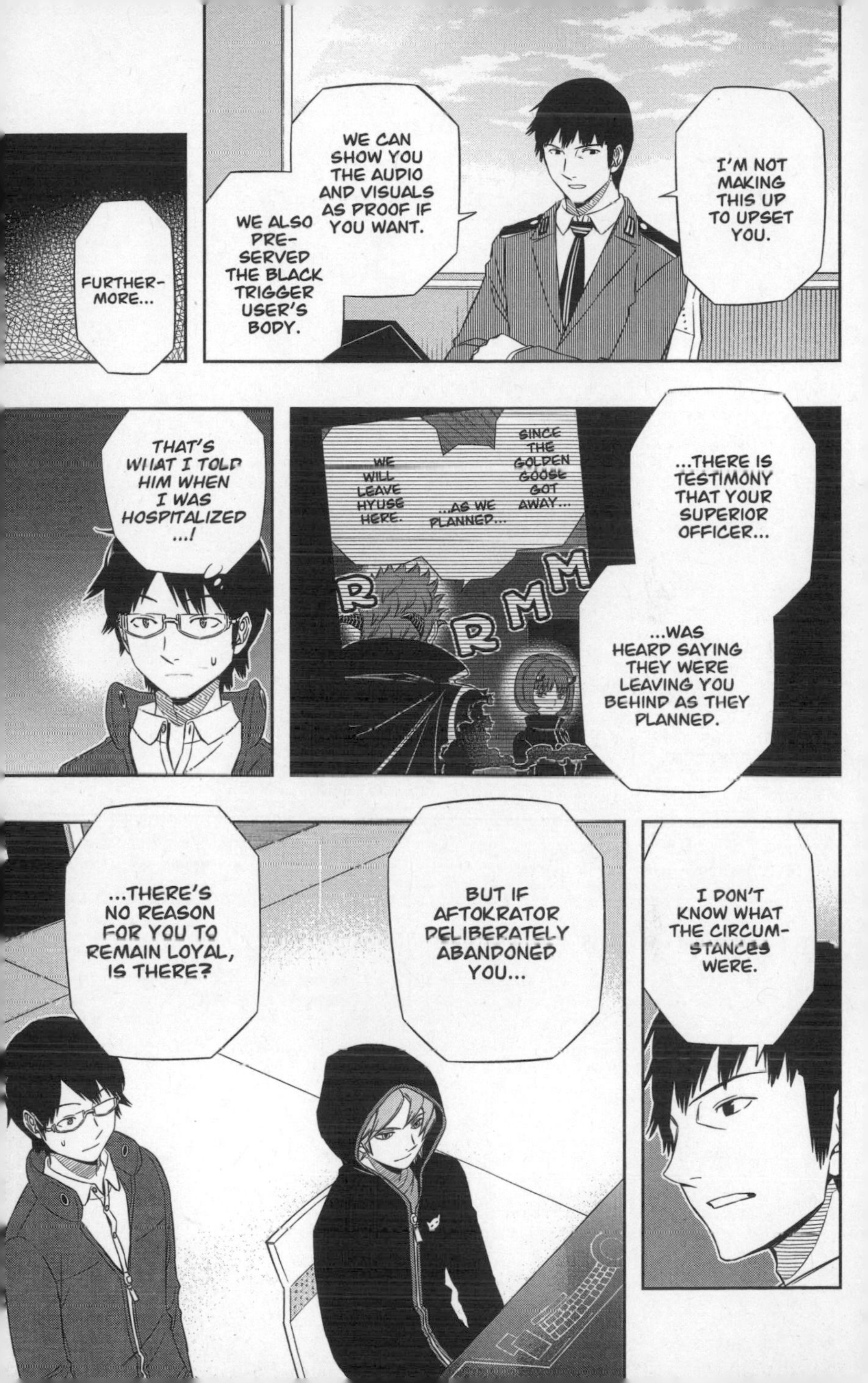
I'M NOT MAKING THIS UP TO UPSET YOU.
WE CAN SHOW YOU THE AUDIO AND VISUALS AS PROOF IF YOU WANT.
WE ALSO PRE-SERVED THE BLACK TRIGGER USER'S BODY.
FURTHER-MORE...
...THERE IS TESTIMONY THAT YOUR SUPERIOR OFFICER...
SINCE THE GOLDEN GOOSE GOT AWAY...
...AS WE PLANNED...
WE WILL LEAVE HYUSE HERE.
R RMMM
...WAS HEARD SAYING THEY WERE LEAVING YOU BEHIND AS THEY PLANNED.
THAT'S WHAT I TOLD HIM WHEN I WAS HOSPITALIZED ...!
I DON'T KNOW WHAT THE CIRCUM-STANCES WERE.
BUT IF AFTOKRATOR DELIBERATELY ABANDONED YOU...
...THERE'S NO REASON FOR YOU TO REMAIN LOYAL, IS THERE?

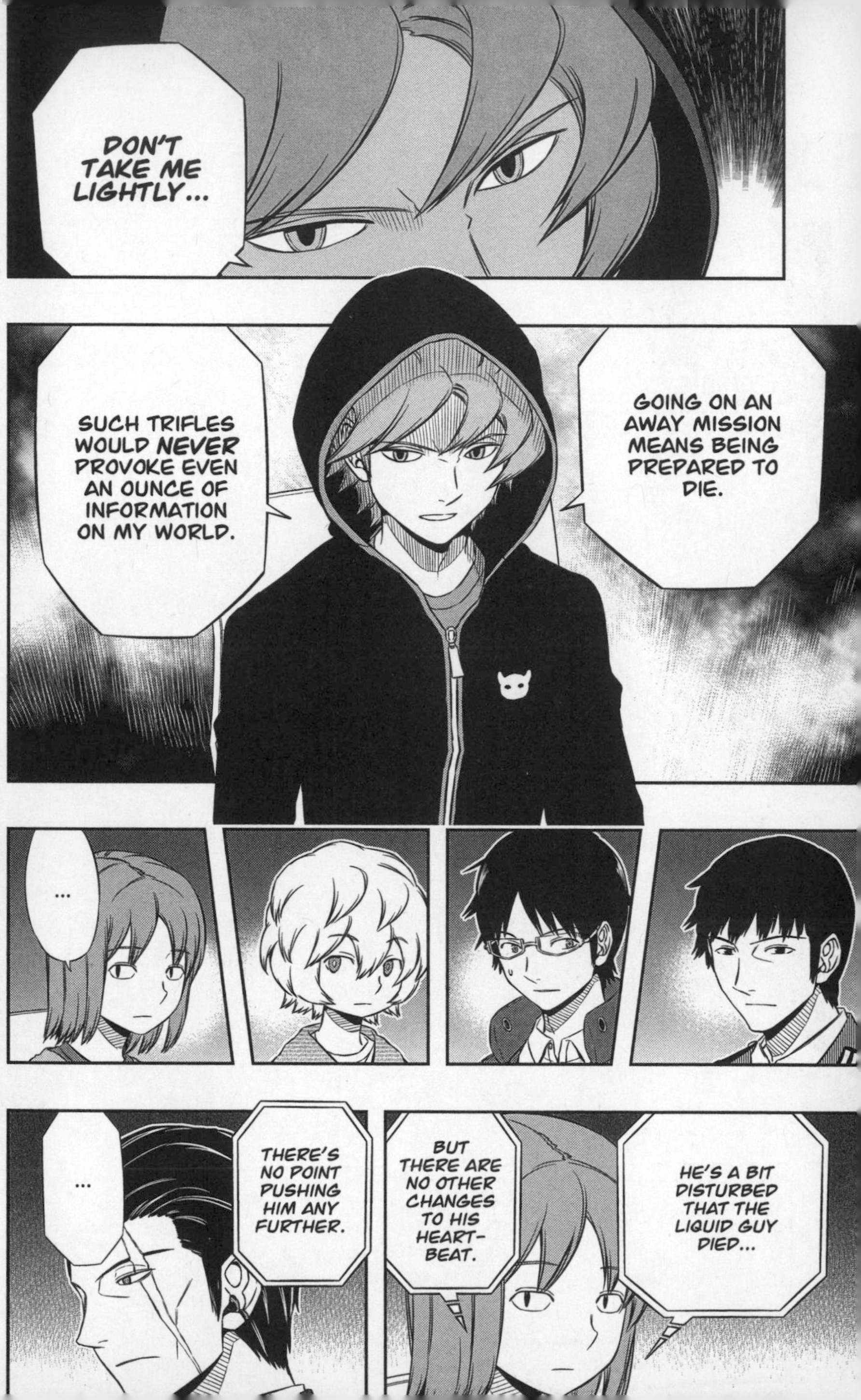
DON'T TAKE ME LIGHTLY...
GOING ON AN AWAY MISSION MEANS BEING PREPARED TO DIE.
SUCH TRIFLES WOULD NEVER PROVOKE EVEN AN OUNCE OF INFORMATION ON MY WORLD.
...
HE'S A BIT DISTURBED THAT THE LIQUID GUY DIED...
BUT THERE ARE NO OTHER CHANGES TO HIS HEART-BEAT.
THERE'S NO POINT PUSHING HIM ANY FURTHER.
...

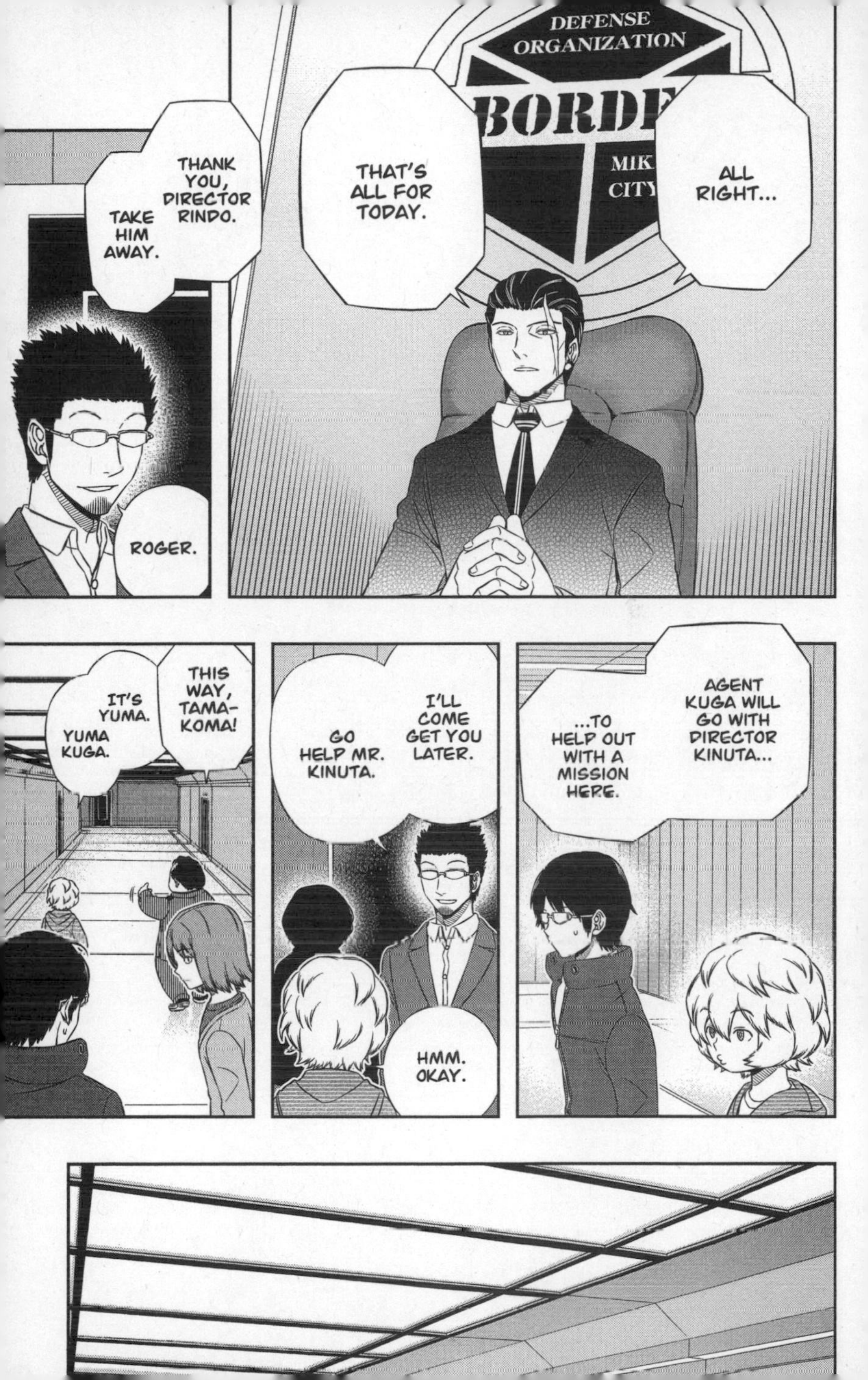
DEFENSE ORGANIZATION
BORDE
ALL RIGHT...
THAT'S ALL FOR TODAY.
THANK YOU, DIRECTOR RINDO.
TAKE HIM AWAY.
ROGER.
AGENT KUGA WILL GO WITH DIRECTOR KINUTA...
...TO HELP OUT WITH A MISSION HERE.
I'LL COME GET YOU LATER.
GO HELP MR. KINUTA.
HMM. OKAY.
THIS WAY, TAMA-KOMA!
IT'S YUMA.
YUMA KUGA.

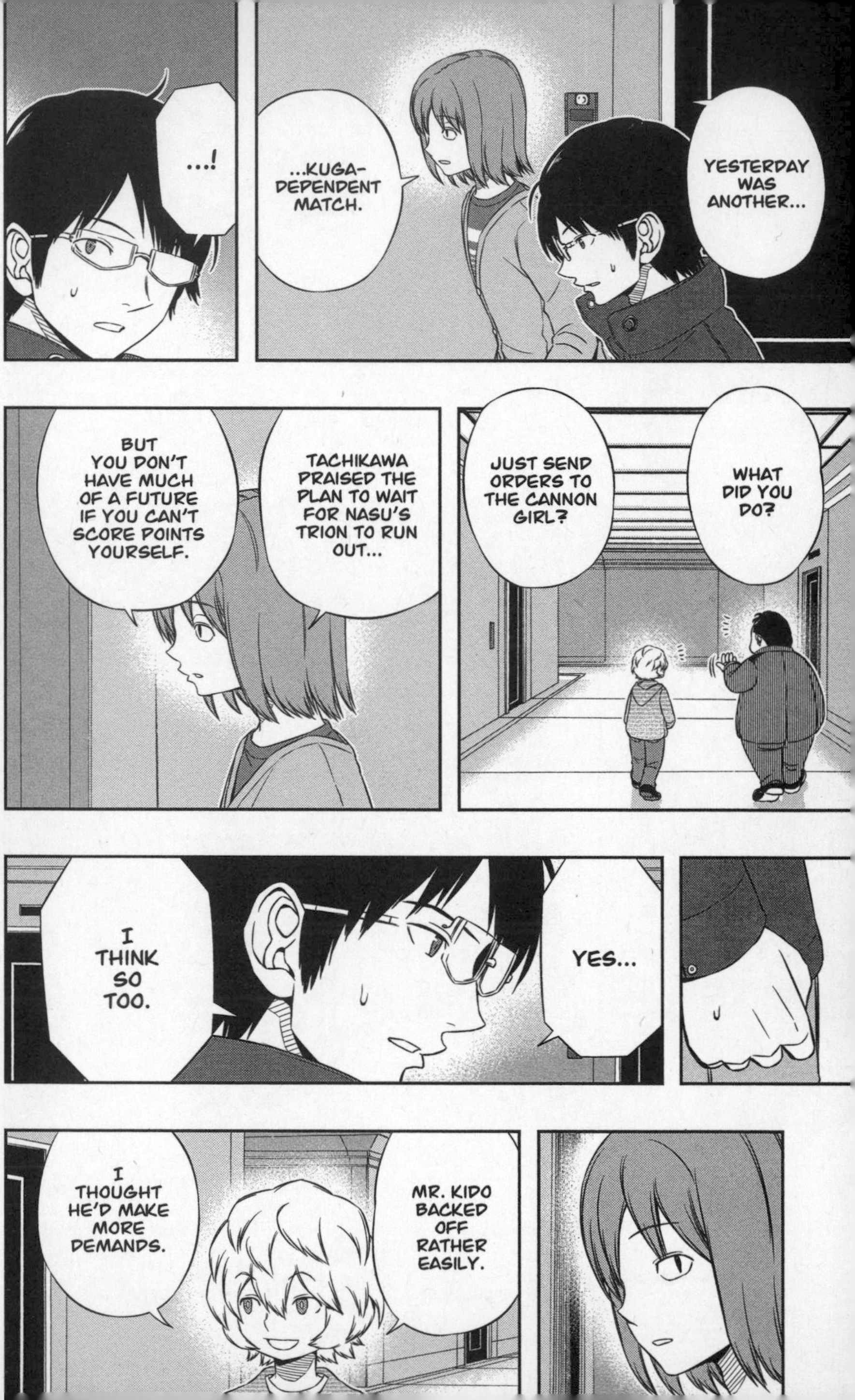
YESTERDAY WAS ANOTHER...
...KUGA-DEPENDENT MATCH.
...!
WHAT DID YOU DO?
JUST SEND ORDERS TO THE CANNON GIRL?
TACHIKAWA PRAISED THE PLAN TO WAIT FOR NASU'S TRION TO RUN OUT...
BUT YOU DON'T HAVE MUCH OF A FUTURE IF YOU CAN'T SCORE POINTS YOURSELF.
YES...
I THINK SO TOO.
MR. KIDO BACKED OFF RATHER EASILY.
I THOUGHT HE'D MAKE MORE DEMANDS.

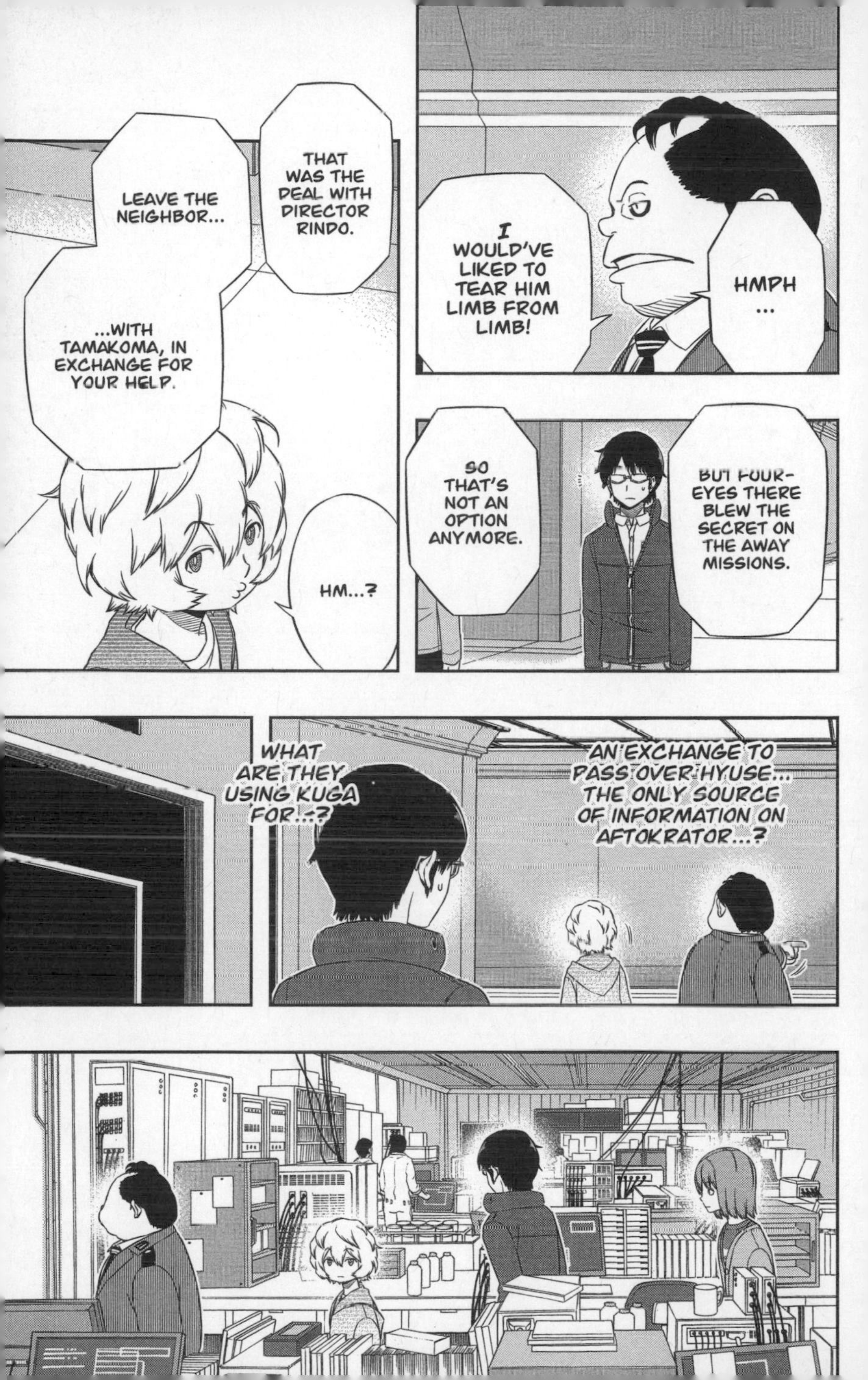
HMPH
...
I WOULD'VE LIKED TO TEAR HIM LIMB FROM LIMB!
BUT FOUR-EYES THERE BLEW THE SECRET ON THE AWAY MISSIONS.
SO THAT'S NOT AN OPTION ANYMORE.
THAT WAS THE DEAL WITH DIRECTOR RINDO.
LEAVE THE NEIGHBOR...
...WITH TAMAKOMA, IN EXCHANGE FOR YOUR HELP.
HM...?
AN EXCHANGE TO PASS OVER HYUSE... THE ONLY SOURCE OF INFORMATION ON AFTOKRATOR...?
WHAT ARE THEY USING KUGA FOR...?

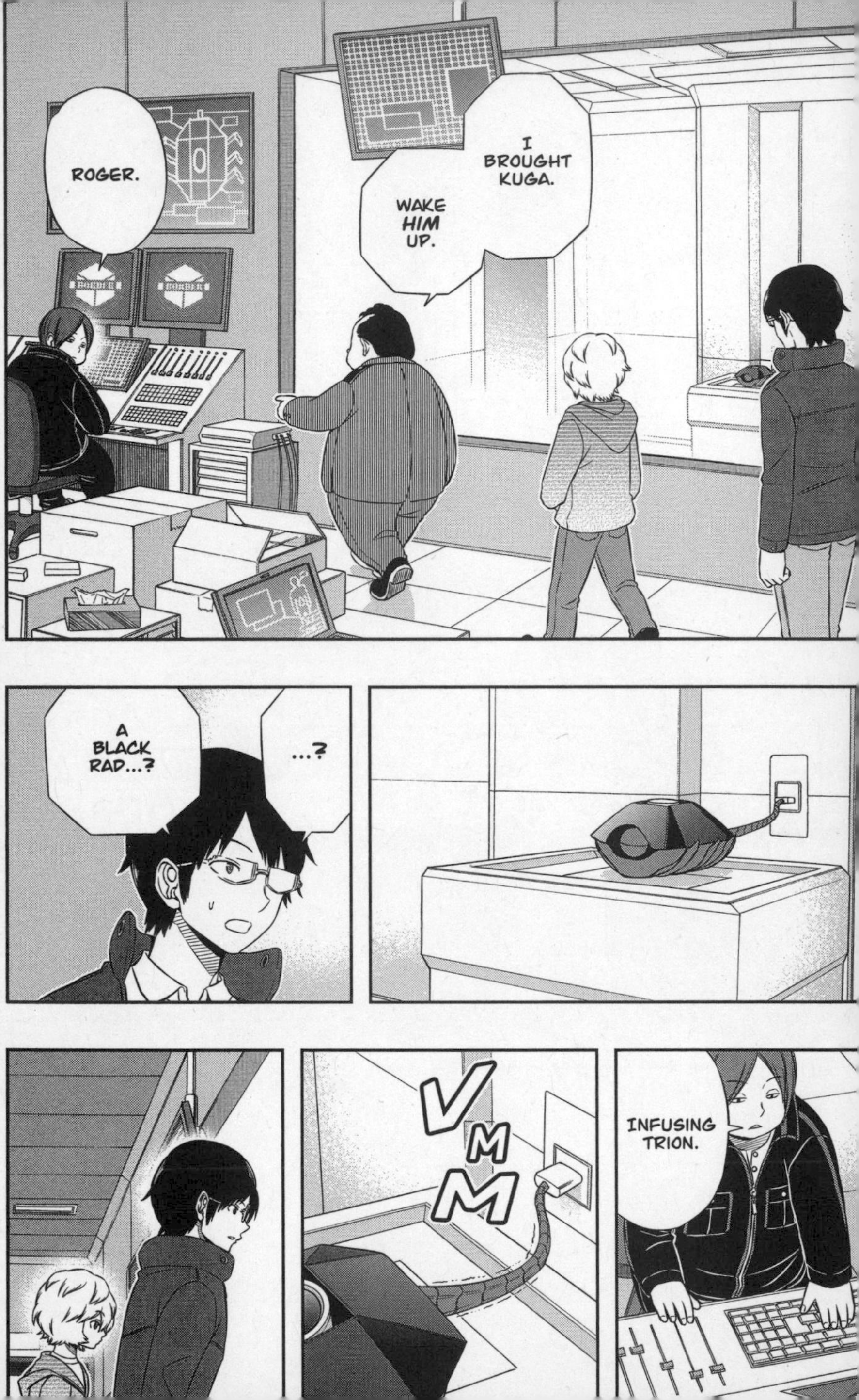
I BROUGHT KUGA.
WAKE HIM UP.
ROGER.
...?
A BLACK RAD...?
INFUSING TRION.
VMM

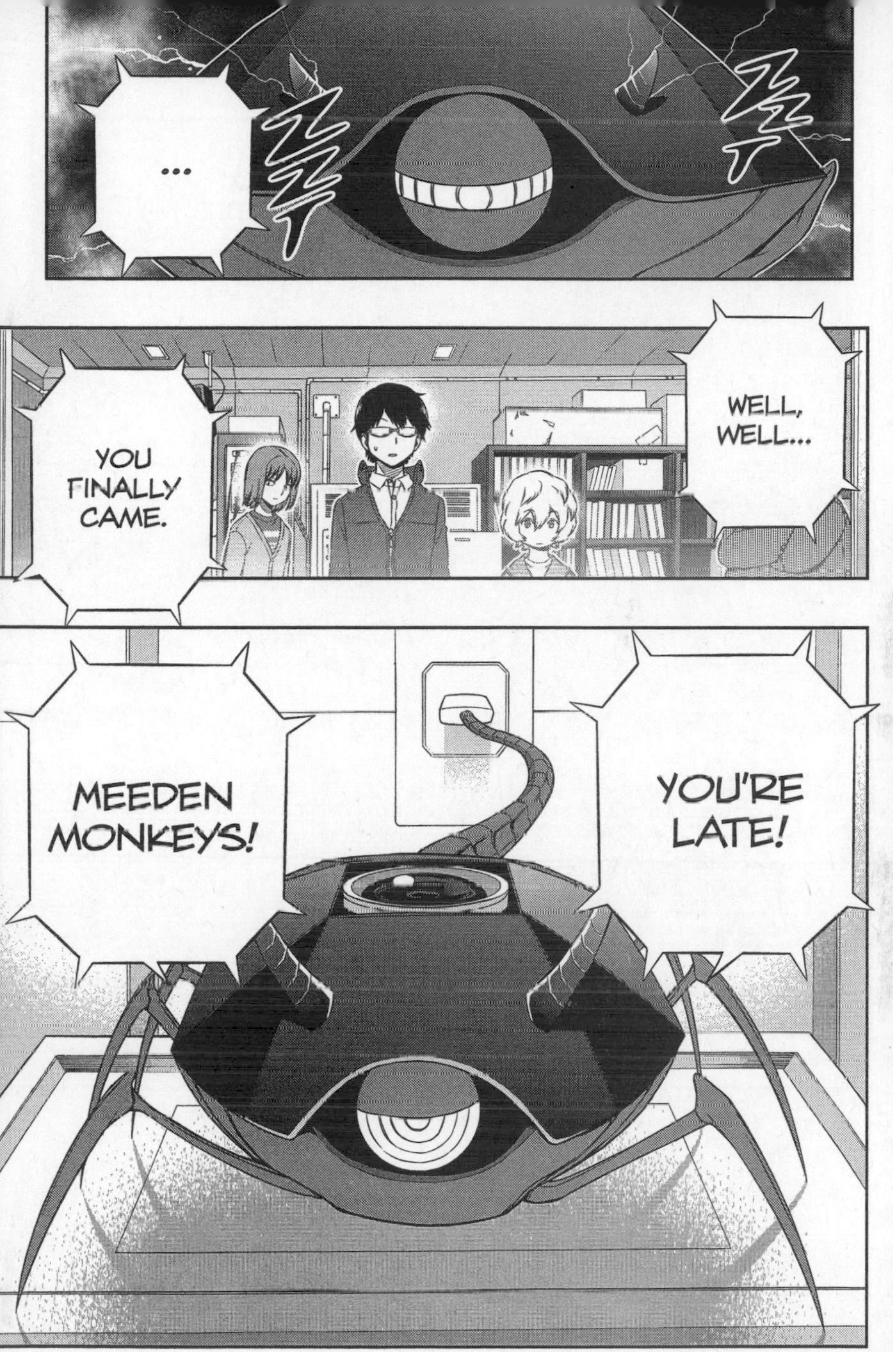
...
WELL, WELL...
YOU FINALLY CAME.
YOU'RE LATE!
MEEDEN MONKEYS!

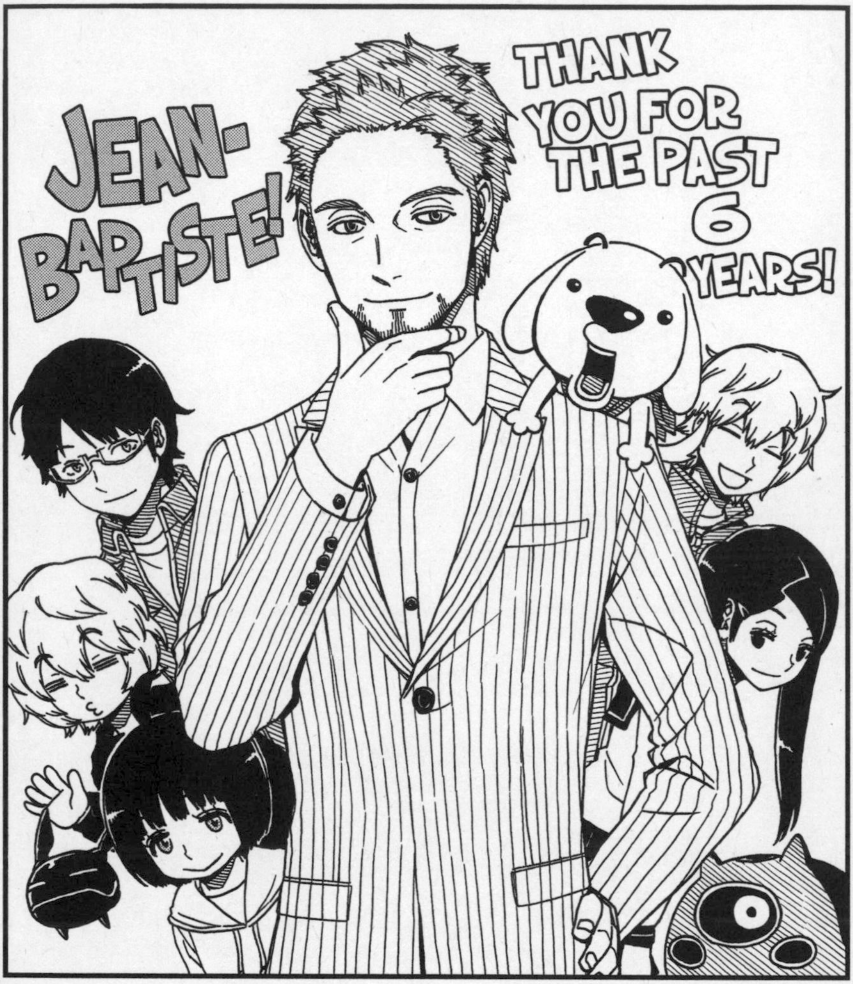
JEAN-BAPTISTE!
THANK YOU FOR THE PAST 6 YEARS!

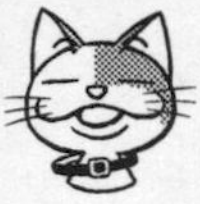

Jean-Baptiste had been my editor since my debut, but due to his transfer to a different department, I got a new editor. Bapti was very good to me for six long years. Without him, *Rilienthal* and *World Trigger* might not have existed. The above picture is the autograph board I gave him at his farewell party (which my manager scanned and digitized).

Thank you so much. I'll keep working hard.

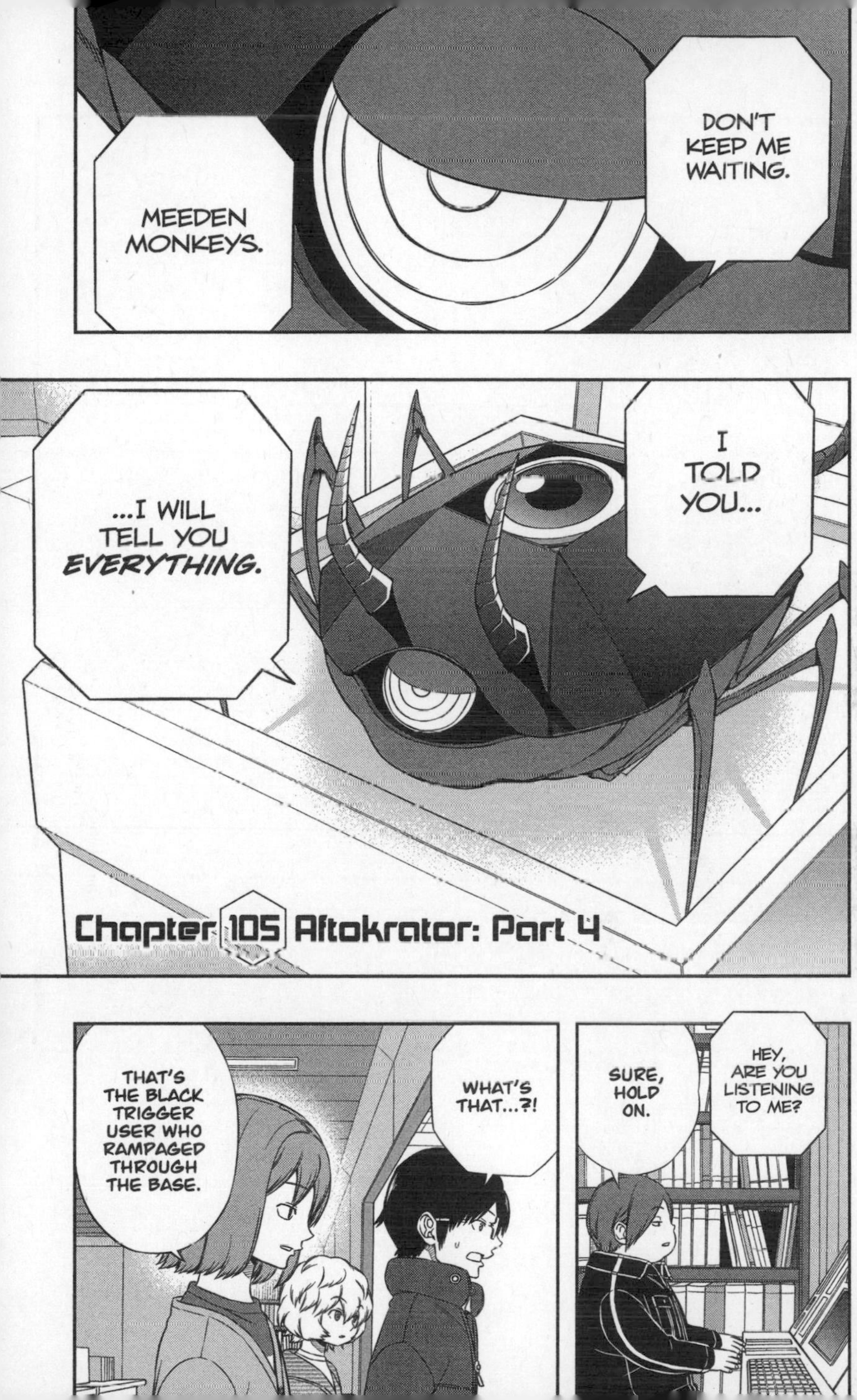
DON'T KEEP ME WAITING.
MEEDEN MONKEYS.
I TOLD YOU...
...I WILL TELL YOU EVERYTHING.
Chapter 105 Aftokrator: Part 4
HEY, ARE YOU LISTENING TO ME?
SURE, HOLD ON.
WHAT'S THAT...?!
THAT'S THE BLACK TRIGGER USER WHO RAMPAGED THROUGH THE BASE.

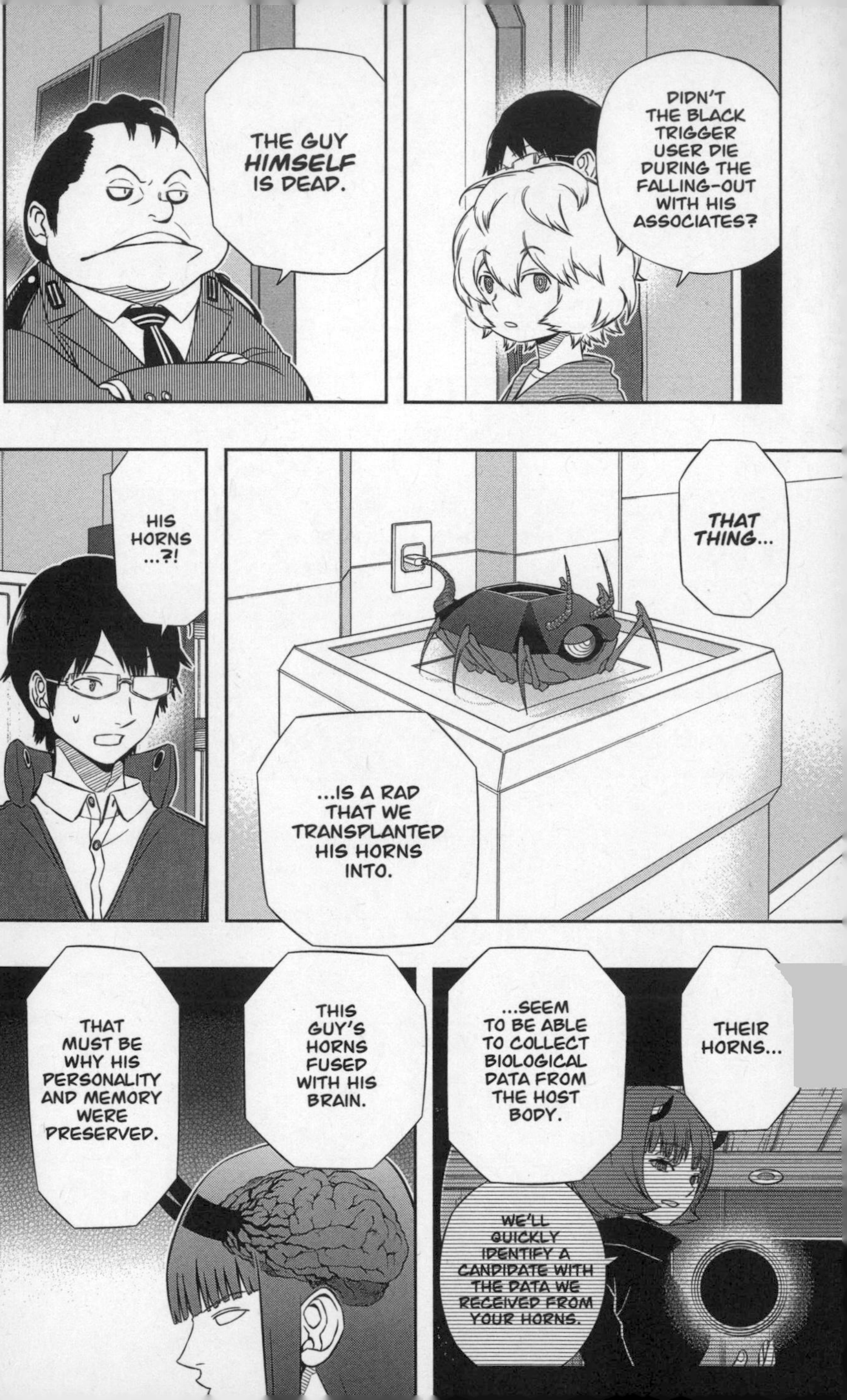
DIDN'T THE BLACK TRIGGER USER DIE DURING THE FALLING-OUT WITH HIS ASSOCIATES?
THE GUY *HIMSELF* IS DEAD.
THAT THING...
...IS A RAD THAT WE TRANSPLANTED HIS HORNS INTO.
HIS HORNS ...?!
THEIR HORNS...
...SEEM TO BE ABLE TO COLLECT BIOLOGICAL DATA FROM THE HOST BODY.
WE'LL QUICKLY IDENTIFY A CANDIDATE WITH THE DATA WE RECEIVED FROM YOUR HORNS.
THIS GUY'S HORNS FUSED WITH HIS BRAIN.
THAT MUST BE WHY HIS PERSONALITY AND MEMORY WERE PRESERVED.

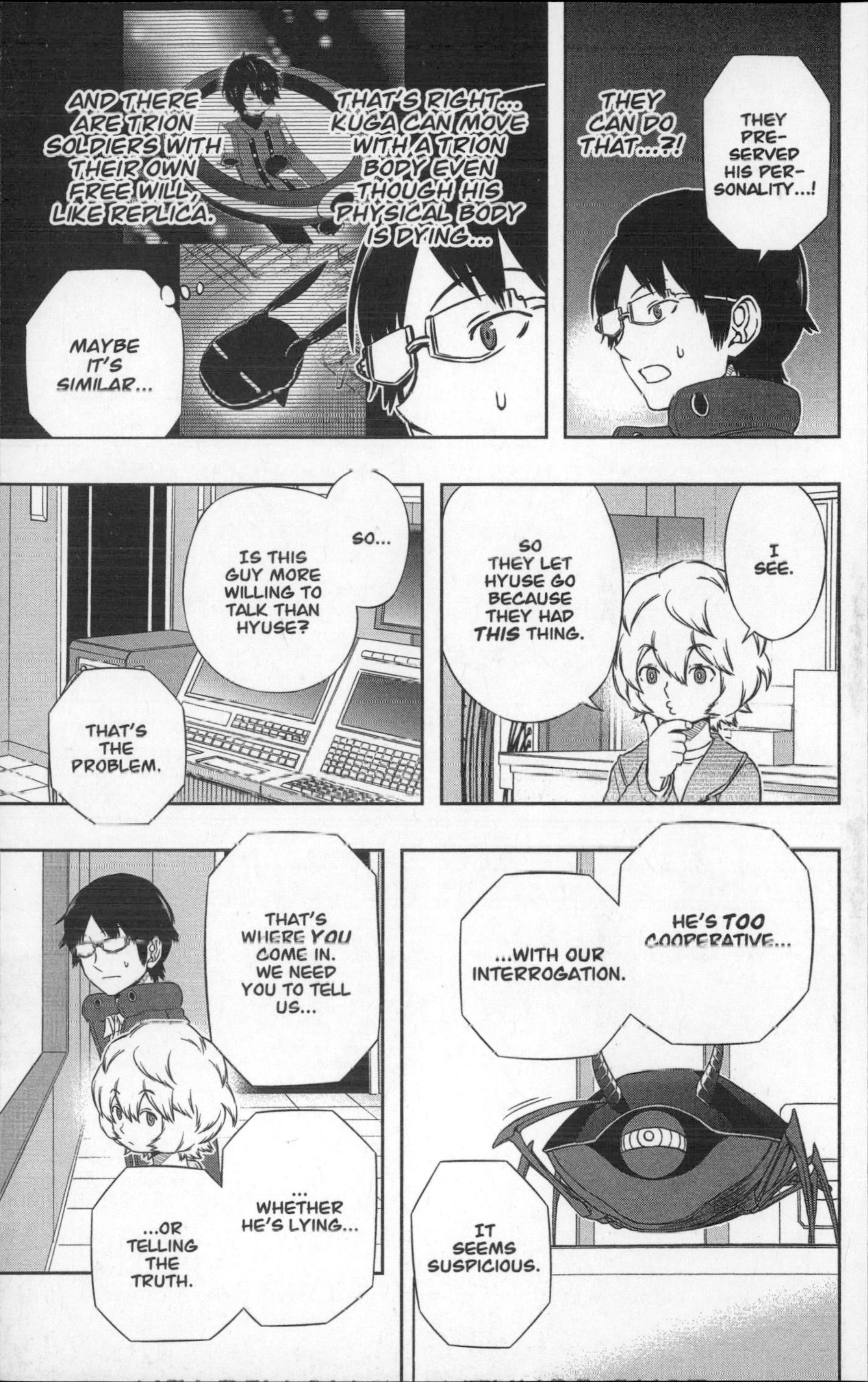
THEY PRE-SERVED HIS PER-SONALITY...!
THEY CAN DO THAT...?!
THAT'S RIGHT... KUGA CAN MOVE WITH A TRION BODY EVEN THOUGH HIS PHYSICAL BODY IS DYING...
AND THERE ARE TRION SOLDIERS WITH THEIR OWN FREE WILL, LIKE REPLICA.
MAYBE IT'S SIMILAR...
I SEE.
SO THEY LET HYUSE GO BECAUSE THEY HAD *THIS* THING.
SO...
IS THIS GUY MORE WILLING TO TALK THAN HYUSE?
THAT'S THE PROBLEM.
HE'S *TOO* COOPERATIVE...
...WITH OUR INTERROGATION.
IT SEEMS SUSPICIOUS.
THAT'S WHERE *YOU* COME IN. WE NEED YOU TO TELL US...
...WHETHER HE'S LYING...
...OR TELLING THE TRUTH.

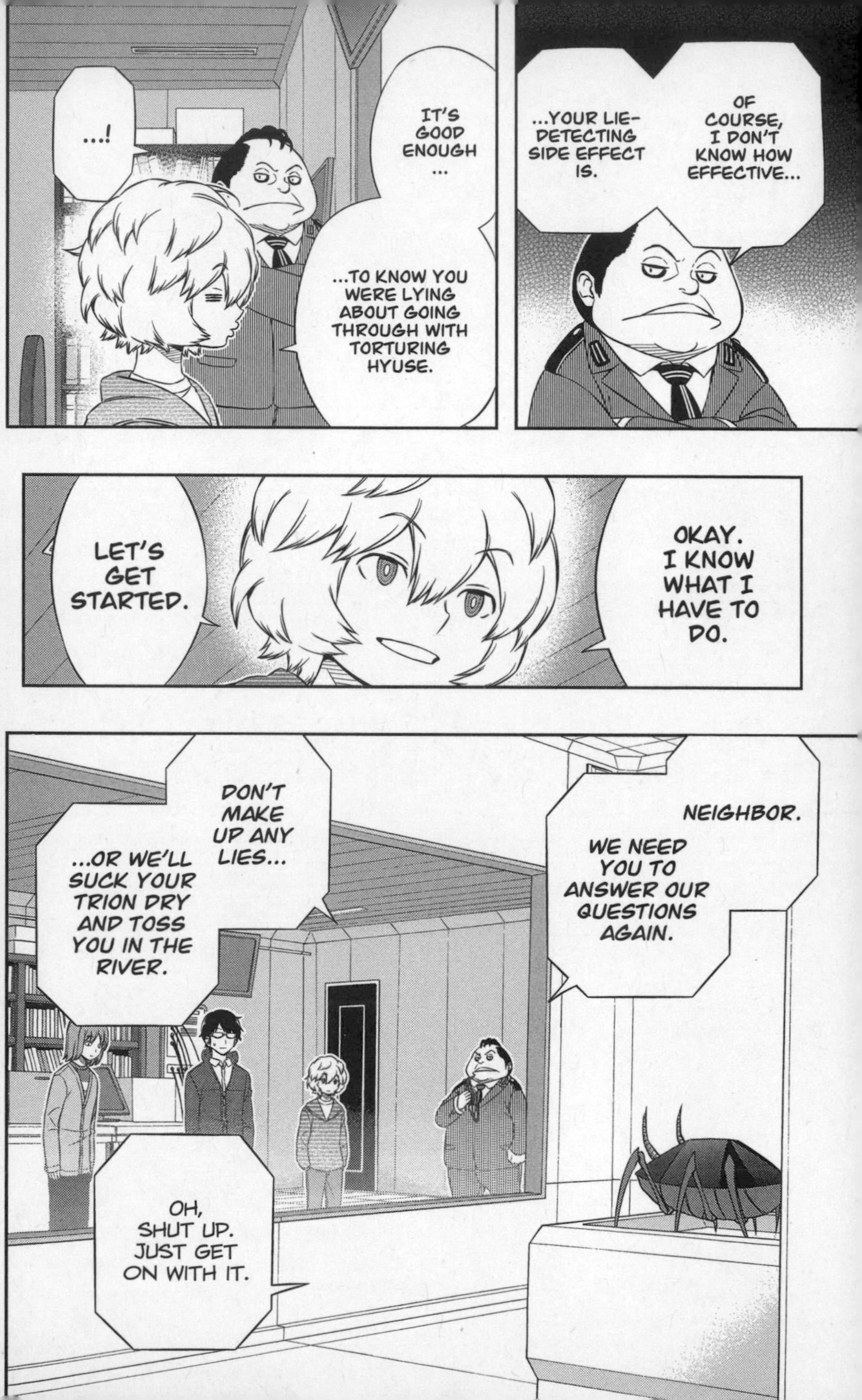
OF COURSE, I DON'T KNOW HOW EFFECTIVE...
...YOUR LIE-DETECTING SIDE EFFECT IS.
IT'S GOOD ENOUGH ...
...!
...TO KNOW YOU WERE LYING ABOUT GOING THROUGH WITH TORTURING HYUSE.
OKAY. I KNOW WHAT I HAVE TO DO.
LET'S GET STARTED.
NEIGHBOR.
WE NEED YOU TO ANSWER OUR QUESTIONS AGAIN.
DON'T MAKE UP ANY LIES...
...OR WE'LL SUCK YOUR TRION DRY AND TOSS YOU IN THE RIVER.
OH, SHUT UP. JUST GET ON WITH IT.

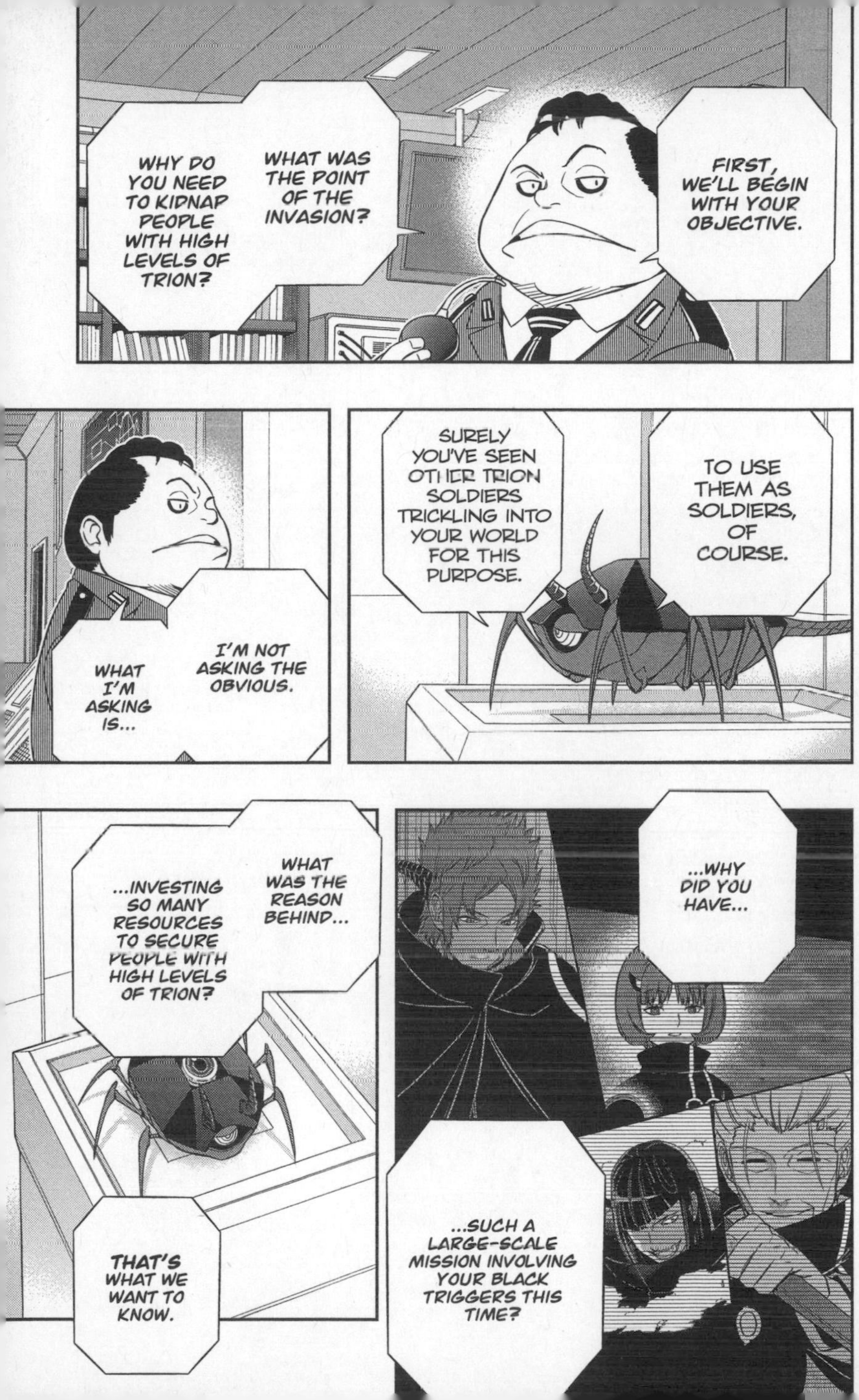
FIRST, WE'LL BEGIN WITH YOUR OBJECTIVE.
WHAT WAS THE POINT OF THE INVASION?
WHY DO YOU NEED TO KIDNAP PEOPLE WITH HIGH LEVELS OF TRION?
TO USE THEM AS SOLDIERS, OF COURSE.
SURELY YOU'VE SEEN OTHER TRION SOLDIERS TRICKLING INTO YOUR WORLD FOR THIS PURPOSE.
I'M NOT ASKING THE OBVIOUS.
WHAT I'M ASKING IS...
...WHY DID YOU HAVE...
...SUCH A LARGE-SCALE MISSION INVOLVING YOUR BLACK TRIGGERS THIS TIME?
WHAT WAS THE REASON BEHIND...
...INVESTING SO MANY RESOURCES TO SECURE PEOPLE WITH HIGH LEVELS OF TRION?
THAT'S WHAT WE WANT TO KNOW.

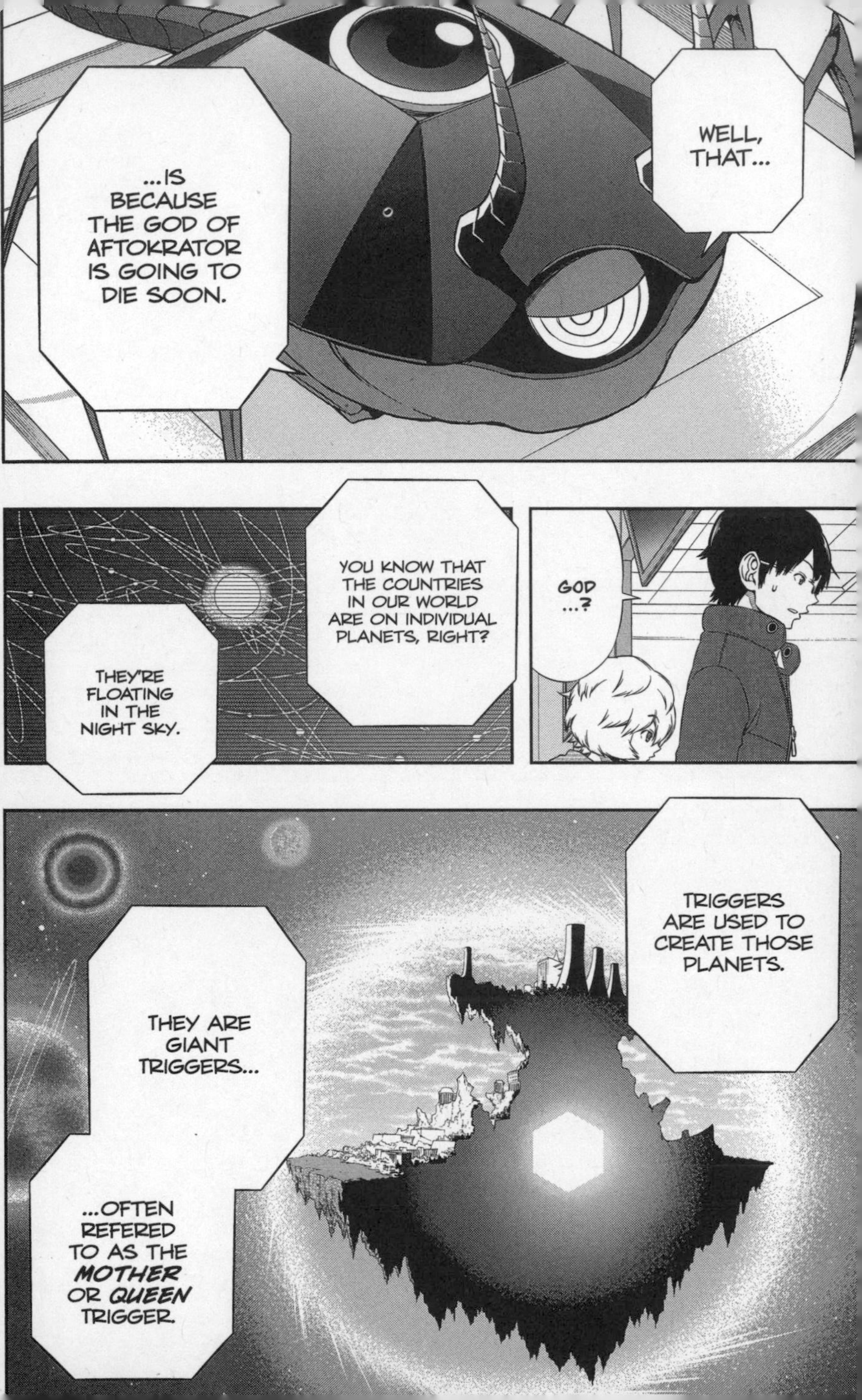
WELL, THAT...
...IS BECAUSE THE GOD OF AFTOKRATOR IS GOING TO DIE SOON.
GOD ...?
YOU KNOW THAT THE COUNTRIES IN OUR WORLD ARE ON INDIVIDUAL PLANETS, RIGHT?
THEY'RE FLOATING IN THE NIGHT SKY.
TRIGGERS ARE USED TO CREATE THOSE PLANETS.
THEY ARE GIANT TRIGGERS...
...OFTEN REFERED TO AS THE *MOTHER* OR *QUEEN* TRIGGER.

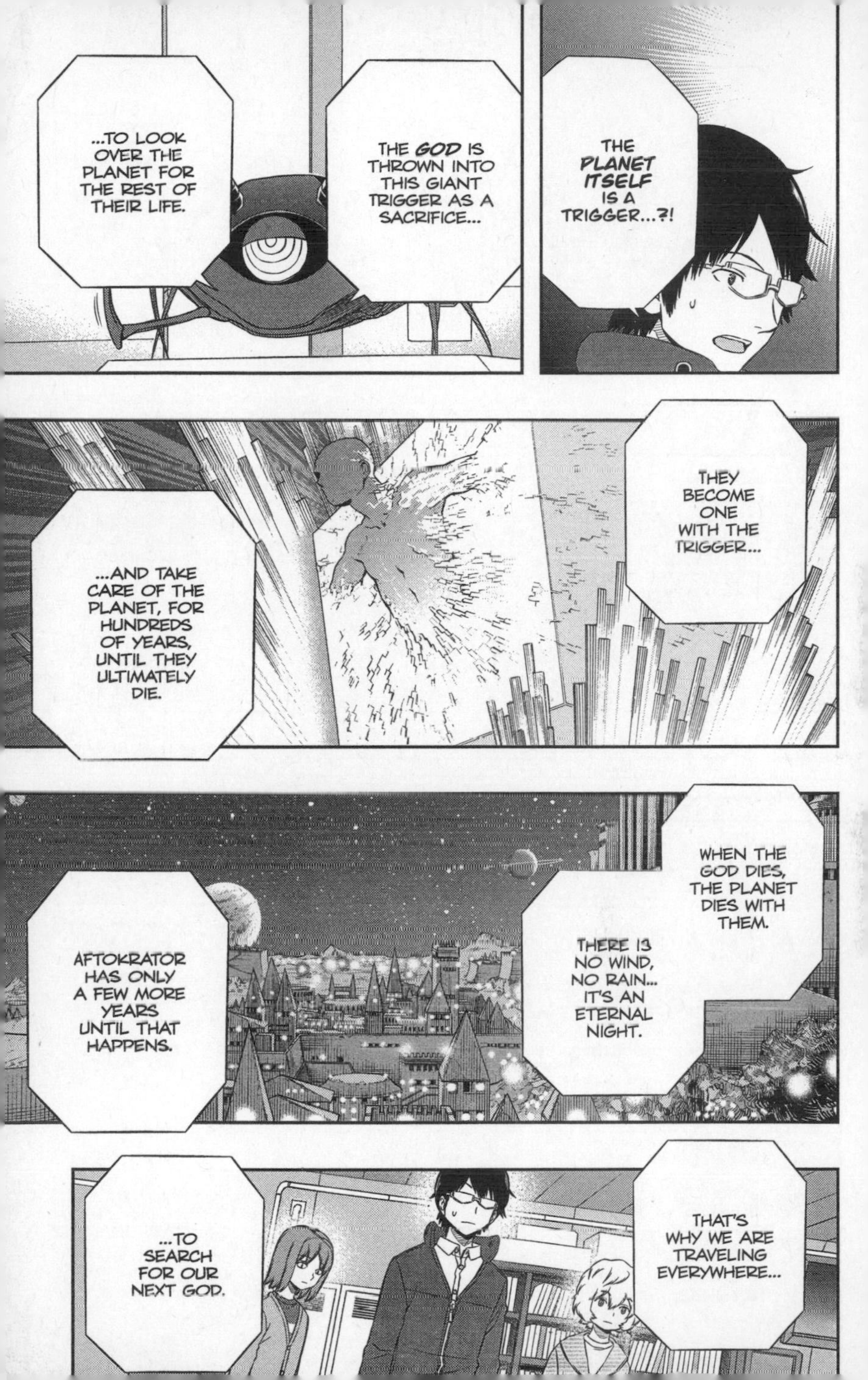
THE PLANET ITSELF IS A TRIGGER...?!
THE GOD IS THROWN INTO THIS GIANT TRIGGER AS A SACRIFICE...
...TO LOOK OVER THE PLANET FOR THE REST OF THEIR LIFE.
THEY BECOME ONE WITH THE TRIGGER...
...AND TAKE CARE OF THE PLANET, FOR HUNDREDS OF YEARS, UNTIL THEY ULTIMATELY DIE.
WHEN THE GOD DIES, THE PLANET DIES WITH THEM.
THERE IS NO WIND, NO RAIN... IT'S AN ETERNAL NIGHT.
AFTOKRATOR HAS ONLY A FEW MORE YEARS UNTIL THAT HAPPENS.
THAT'S WHY WE ARE TRAVELING EVERYWHERE...
...TO SEARCH FOR OUR NEXT GOD.

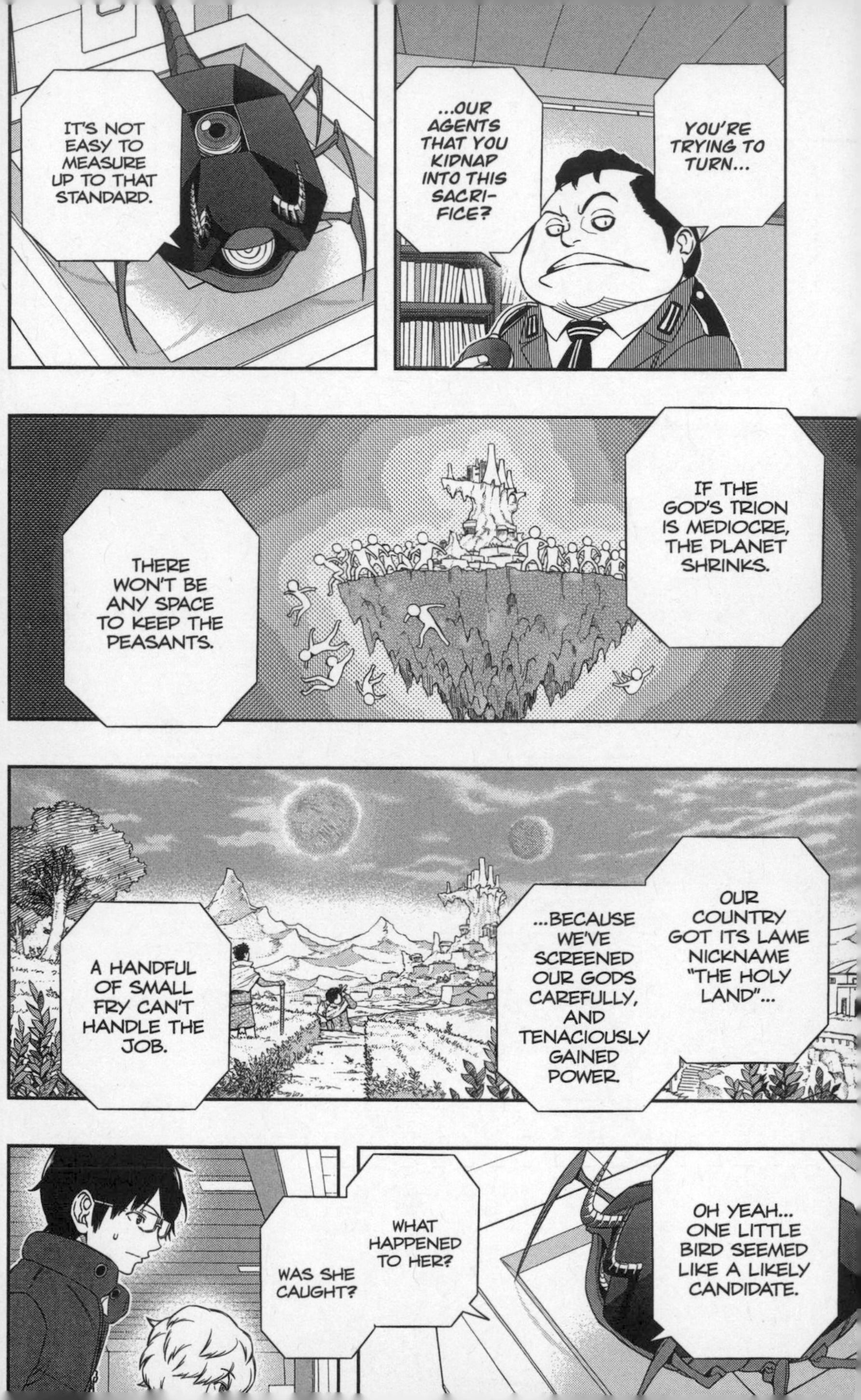
YOU'RE TRYING TO TURN...
...OUR AGENTS THAT YOU KIDNAP INTO THIS SACRI-FICE?
IT'S NOT EASY TO MEASURE UP TO THAT STANDARD.
IF THE GOD'S TRION IS MEDIOCRE, THE PLANET SHRINKS.
THERE WON'T BE ANY SPACE TO KEEP THE PEASANTS.
OUR COUNTRY GOT ITS LAME NICKNAME "THE HOLY LAND"...
...BECAUSE WE'VE SCREENED OUR GODS CAREFULLY, AND TENACIOUSLY GAINED POWER.
A HANDFUL OF SMALL FRY CAN'T HANDLE THE JOB.
OH YEAH... ONE LITTLE BIRD SEEMED LIKE A LIKELY CANDIDATE.
WHAT HAPPENED TO HER?
WAS SHE CAUGHT?

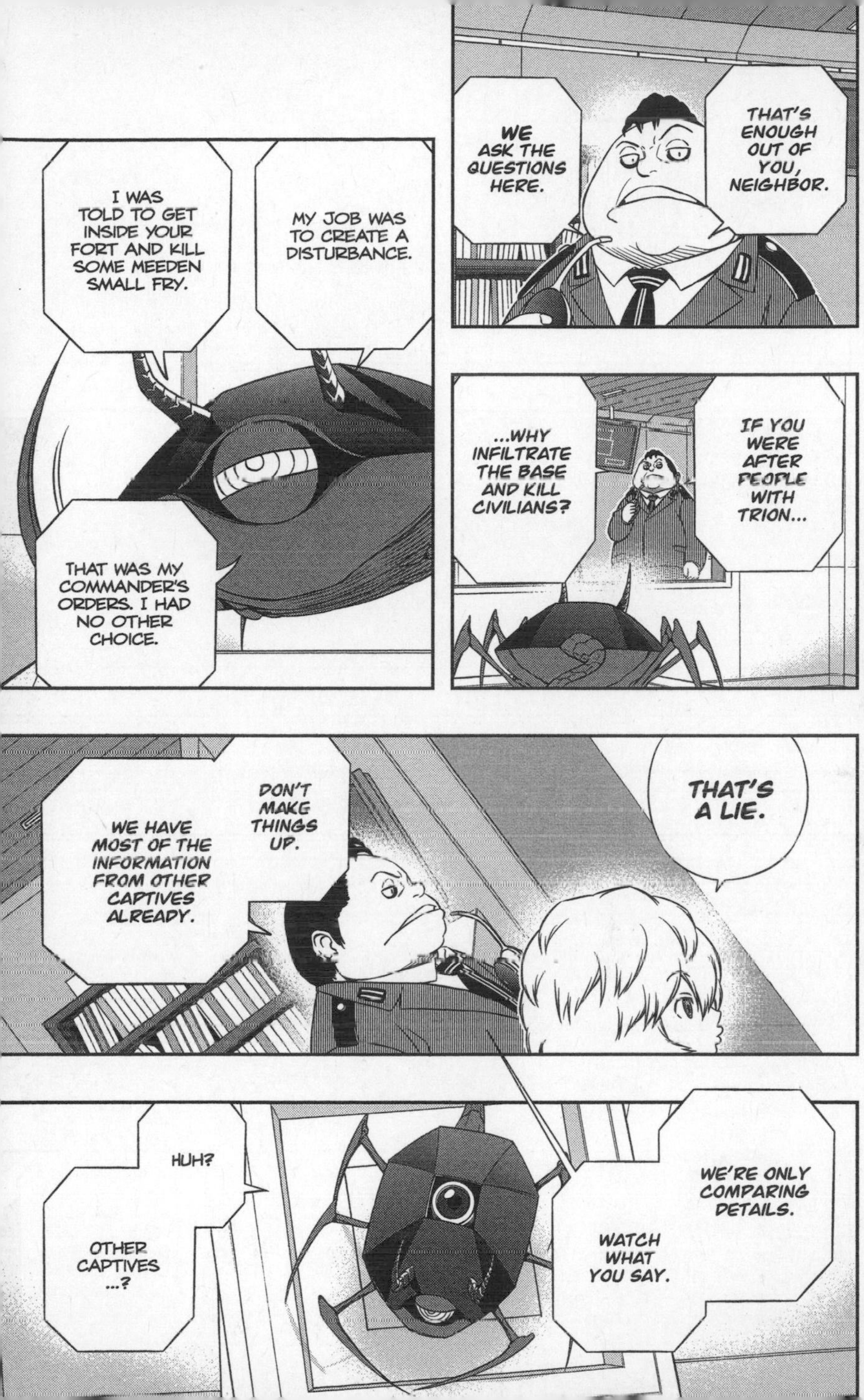
THAT'S ENOUGH OUT OF YOU, NEIGHBOR.
WE ASK THE QUESTIONS HERE.
IF YOU WERE AFTER PEOPLE WITH TRION...
...WHY INFILTRATE THE BASE AND KILL CIVILIANS?
MY JOB WAS TO CREATE A DISTURBANCE.
I WAS TOLD TO GET INSIDE YOUR FORT AND KILL SOME MEEDEN SMALL FRY.
THAT WAS MY COMMANDER'S ORDERS. I HAD NO OTHER CHOICE.
THAT'S A LIE.
DON'T MAKE THINGS UP.
WE HAVE MOST OF THE INFORMATION FROM OTHER CAPTIVES ALREADY.
WE'RE ONLY COMPARING DETAILS.
WATCH WHAT YOU SAY.
HUH?
OTHER CAPTIVES ...?

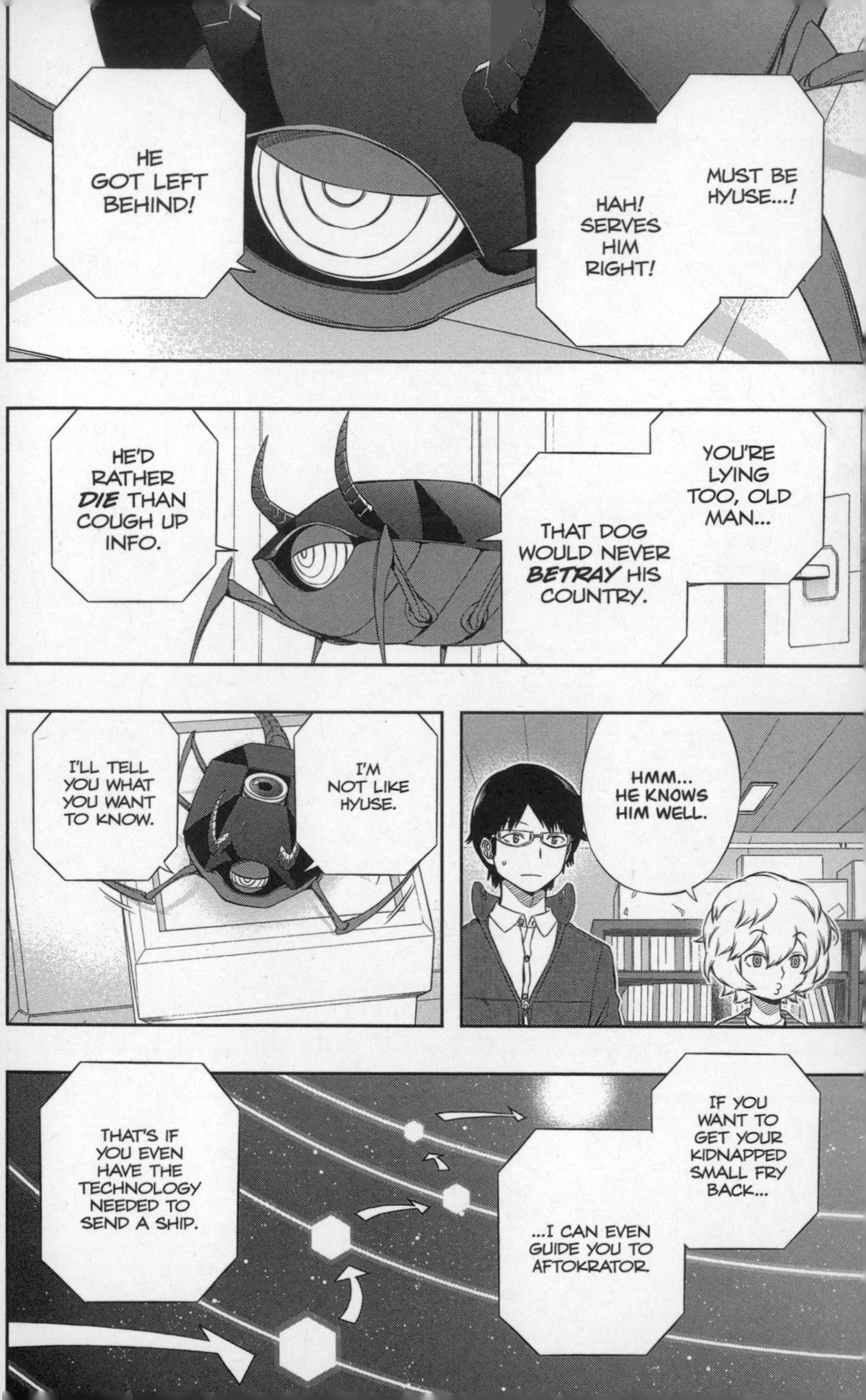
MUST BE HYUSE...!
HAH! SERVES HIM RIGHT!
HE GOT LEFT BEHIND!
YOU'RE LYING TOO, OLD MAN...
THAT DOG WOULD NEVER *BETRAY* HIS COUNTRY.
HE'D RATHER *DIE* THAN COUGH UP INFO.
HMM... HE KNOWS HIM WELL.
I'M NOT LIKE HYUSE.
I'LL TELL YOU WHAT YOU WANT TO KNOW.
IF YOU WANT TO GET YOUR KIDNAPPED SMALL FRY BACK...
...I CAN EVEN GUIDE YOU TO AFTOKRATOR.
THAT'S IF YOU EVEN HAVE THE TECHNOLOGY NEEDED TO SEND A SHIP.

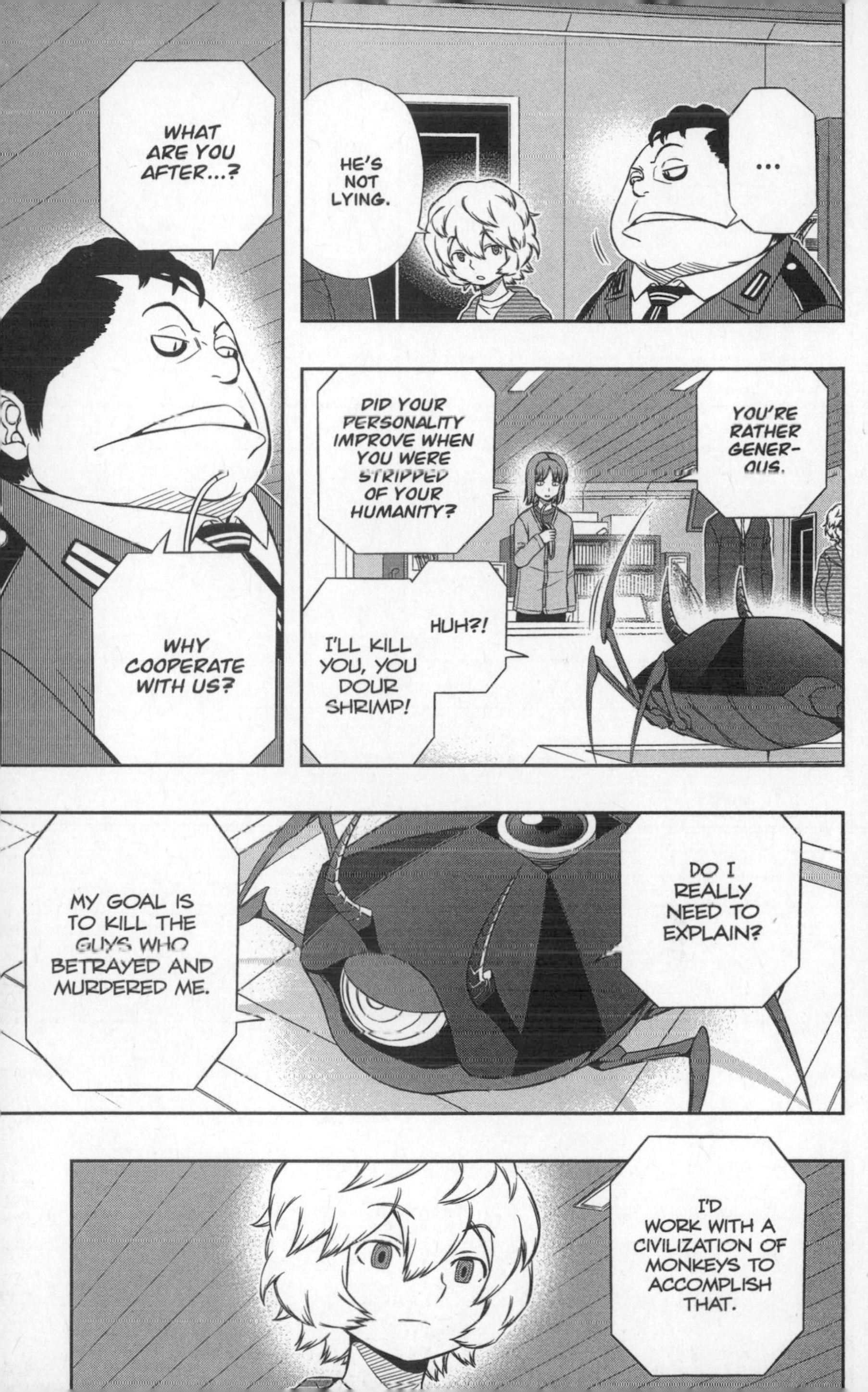
...
HE'S NOT LYING.
YOU'RE RATHER GENER-OUS.
DID YOUR PERSONALITY IMPROVE WHEN YOU WERE STRIPPED OF YOUR HUMANITY?
HUH?!
I'LL KILL YOU, YOU DOUR SHRIMP!
WHAT ARE YOU AFTER...?
WHY COOPERATE WITH US?
DO I REALLY NEED TO EXPLAIN?
MY GOAL IS TO KILL THE GUYS WHO BETRAYED AND MURDERED ME.
I'D WORK WITH A CIVILIZATION OF MONKEYS TO ACCOMPLISH THAT.

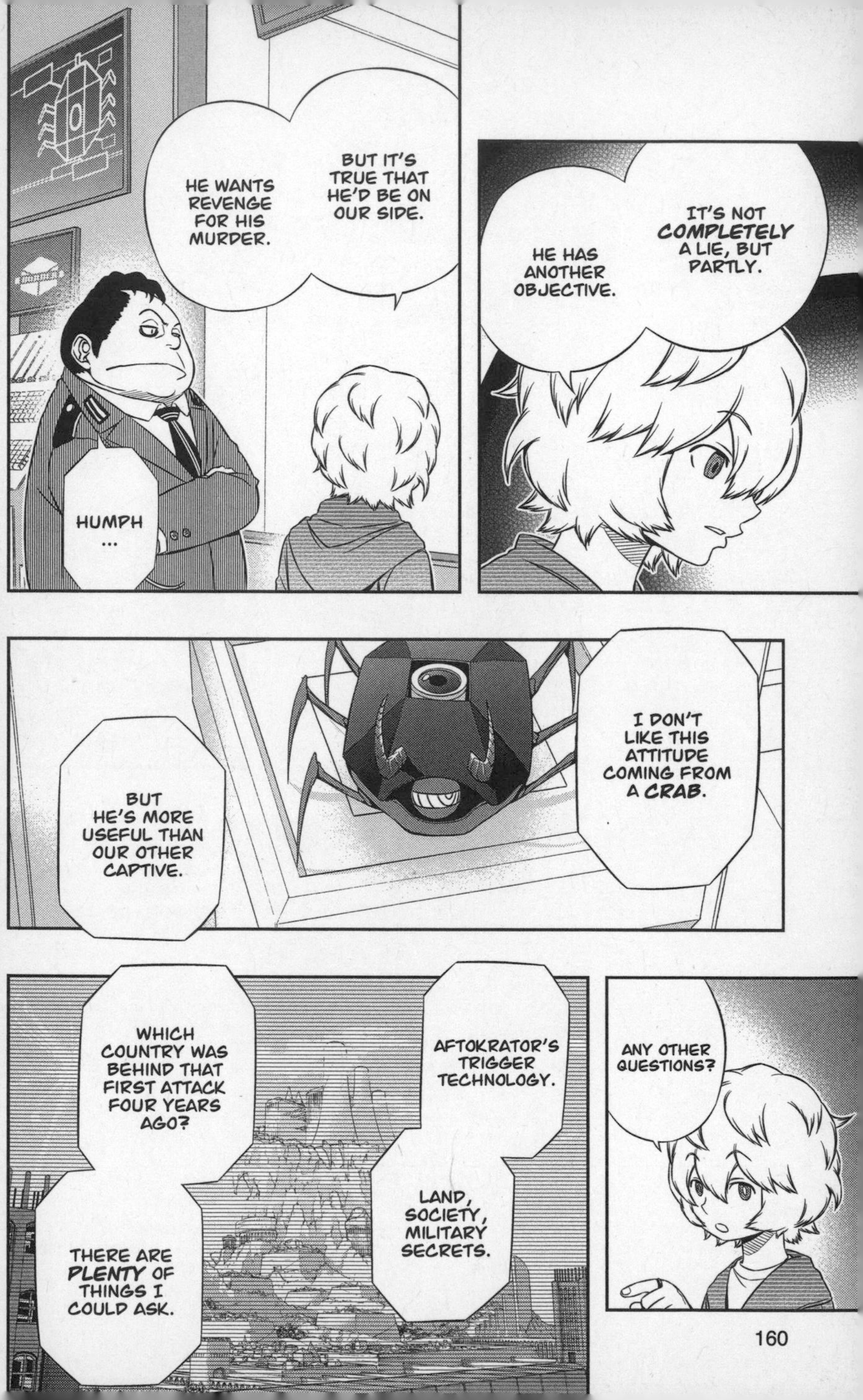
IT'S NOT COMPLETELY A LIE, BUT PARTLY.
HE HAS ANOTHER OBJECTIVE.
BUT IT'S TRUE THAT HE'D BE ON OUR SIDE.
HE WANTS REVENGE FOR HIS MURDER.
HUMPH ...
I DON'T LIKE THIS ATTITUDE COMING FROM A CRAB.
BUT HE'S MORE USEFUL THAN OUR OTHER CAPTIVE.
ANY OTHER QUESTIONS?
AFTOKRATOR'S TRIGGER TECHNOLOGY.
WHICH COUNTRY WAS BEHIND THAT FIRST ATTACK FOUR YEARS AGO?
LAND, SOCIETY, MILITARY SECRETS.
THERE ARE PLENTY OF THINGS I COULD ASK.

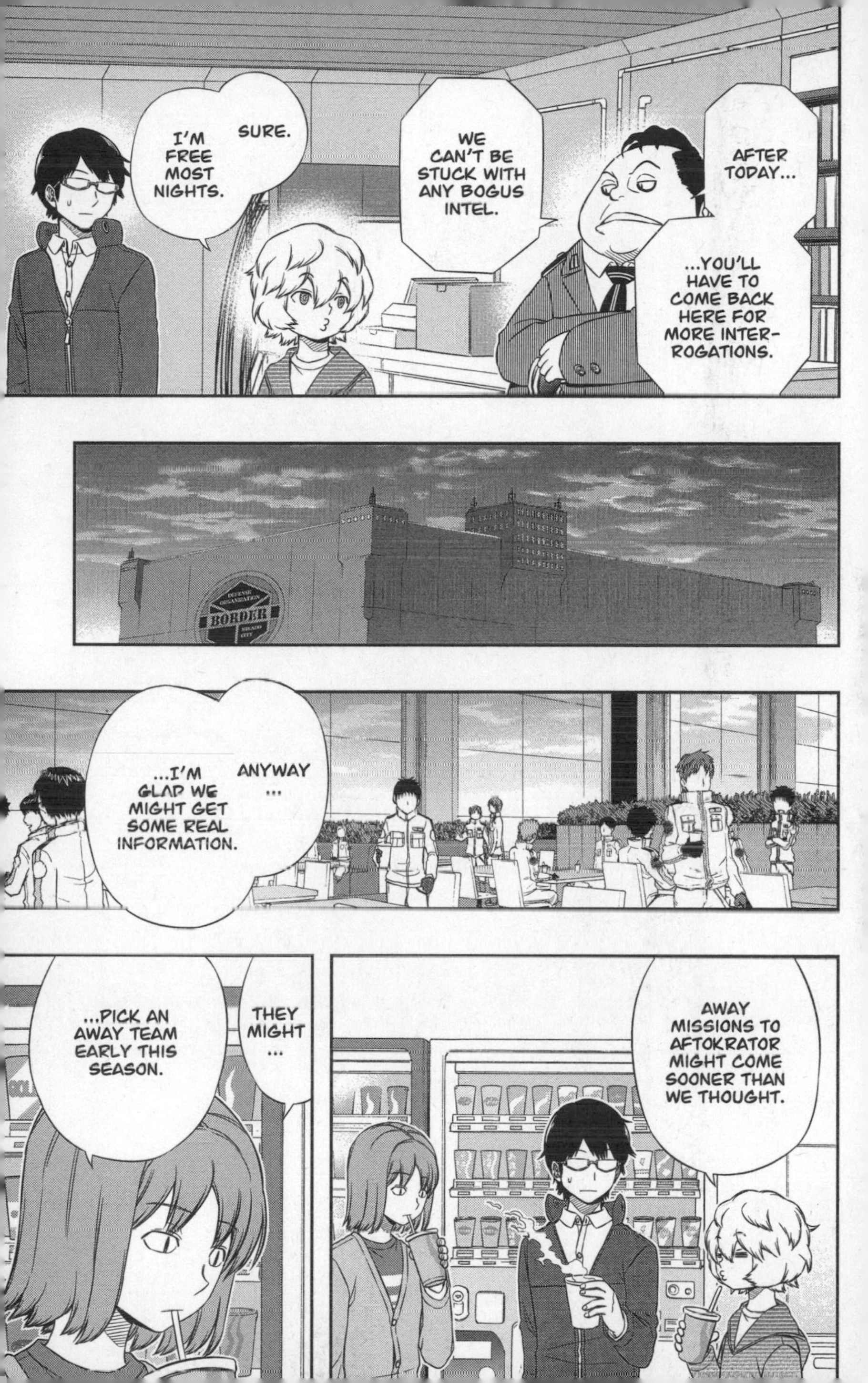
AFTER TODAY...
...YOU'LL HAVE TO COME BACK HERE FOR MORE INTER-ROGATIONS.
WE CAN'T BE STUCK WITH ANY BOGUS INTEL.
SURE.
I'M FREE MOST NIGHTS.
BORDER
ANYWAY ...
...I'M GLAD WE MIGHT GET SOME REAL INFORMATION.
AWAY MISSIONS TO AFTOKRATOR MIGHT COME SOONER THAN WE THOUGHT.
THEY MIGHT ...
...PICK AN AWAY TEAM EARLY THIS SEASON.

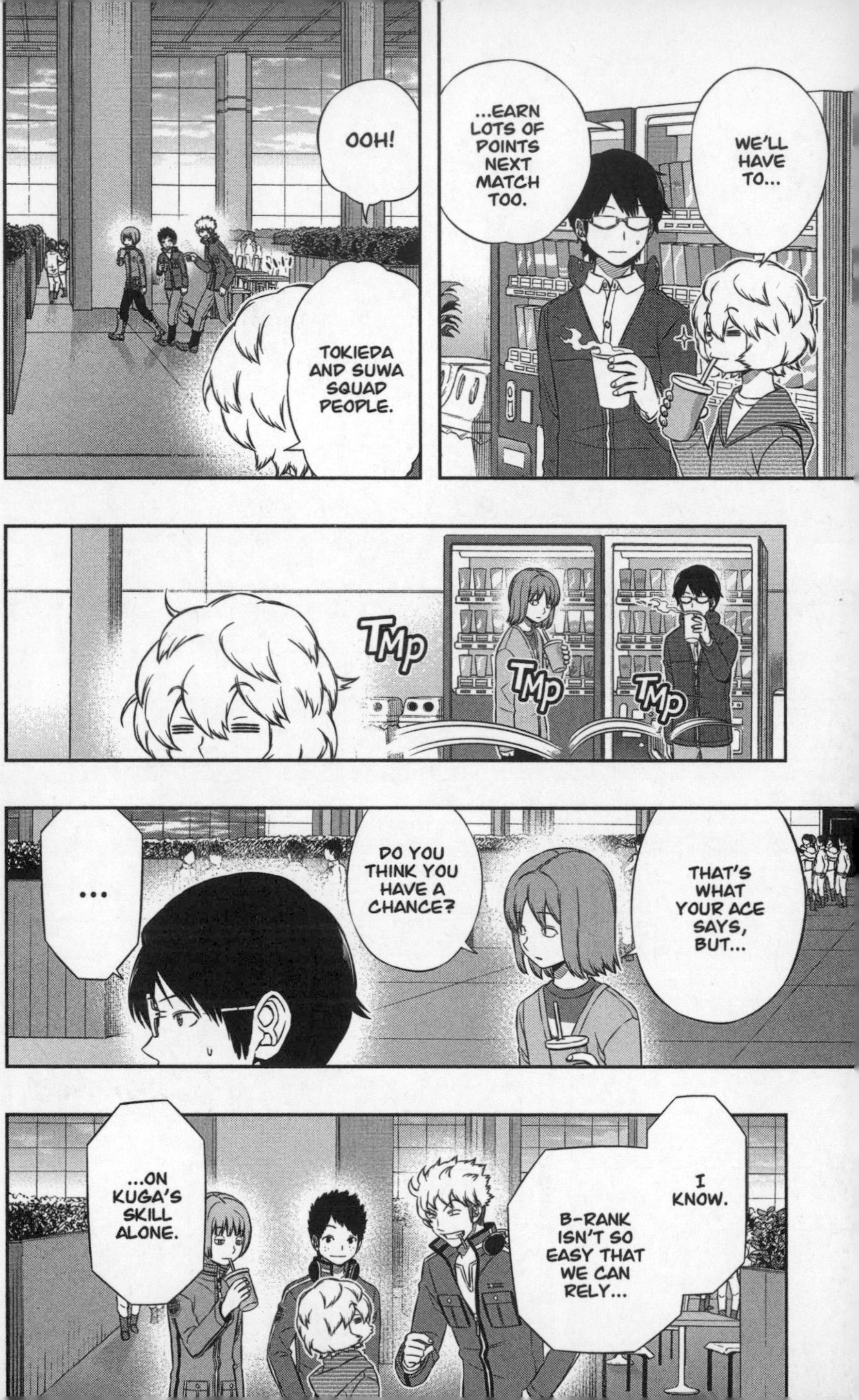
WE'LL HAVE TO...
...EARN LOTS OF POINTS NEXT MATCH TOO.
OOH!
TOKIEDA AND SUWA SQUAD PEOPLE.
TMp
TMp
TMp
THAT'S WHAT YOUR ACE SAYS, BUT...
DO YOU THINK YOU HAVE A CHANCE?
...
I KNOW.
B-RANK ISN'T SO EASY THAT WE CAN RELY...
...ON KUGA'S SKILL ALONE.

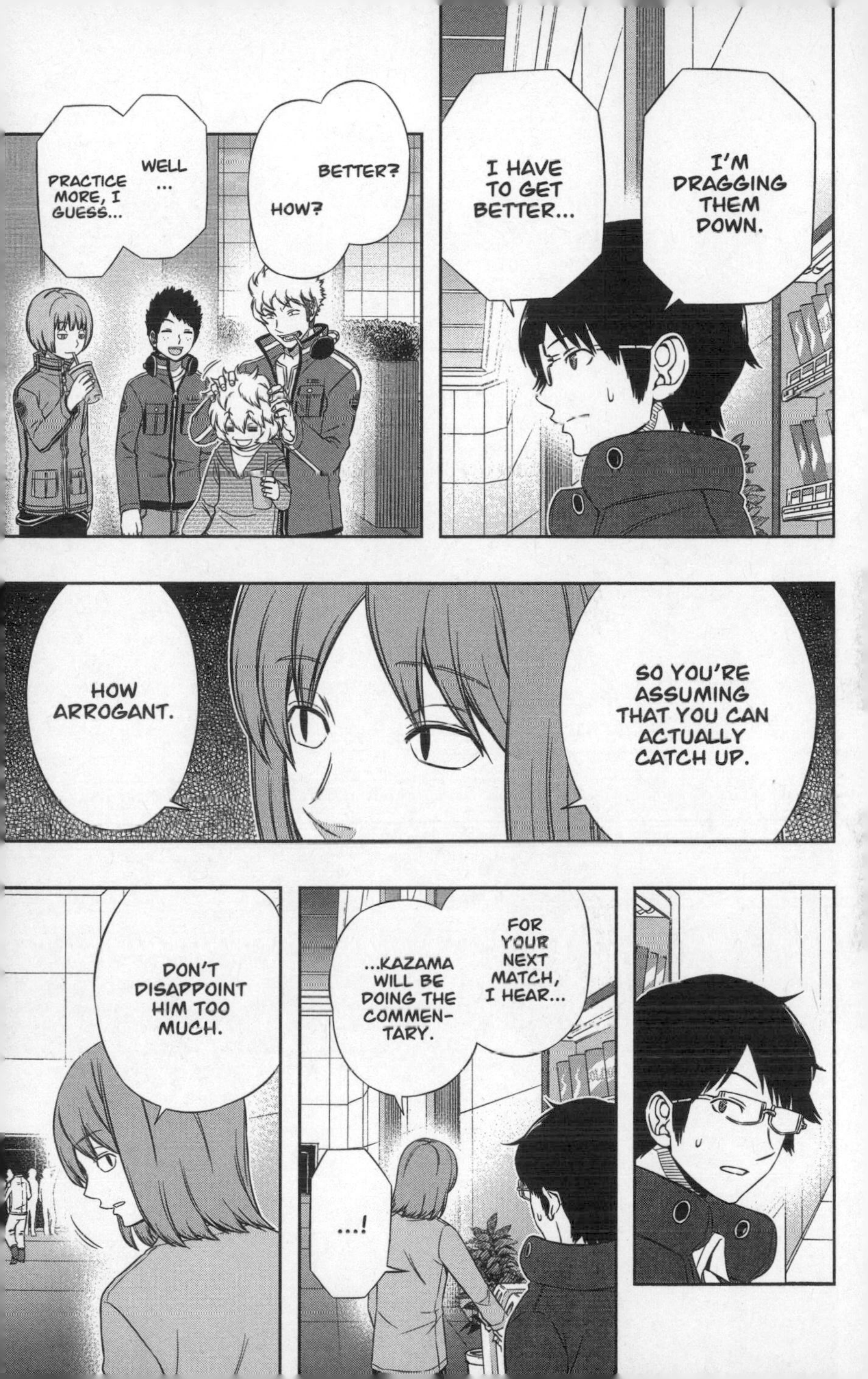
I'M DRAGGING THEM DOWN.
I HAVE TO GET BETTER...
BETTER?
HOW?
WELL ...
PRACTICE MORE, I GUESS...
SO YOU'RE ASSUMING THAT YOU CAN ACTUALLY CATCH UP.
HOW ARROGANT.
FOR YOUR NEXT MATCH, I HEAR...
...KAZAMA WILL BE DOING THE COMMENTARY.
...!
DON'T DISAPPOINT HIM TOO MUCH.

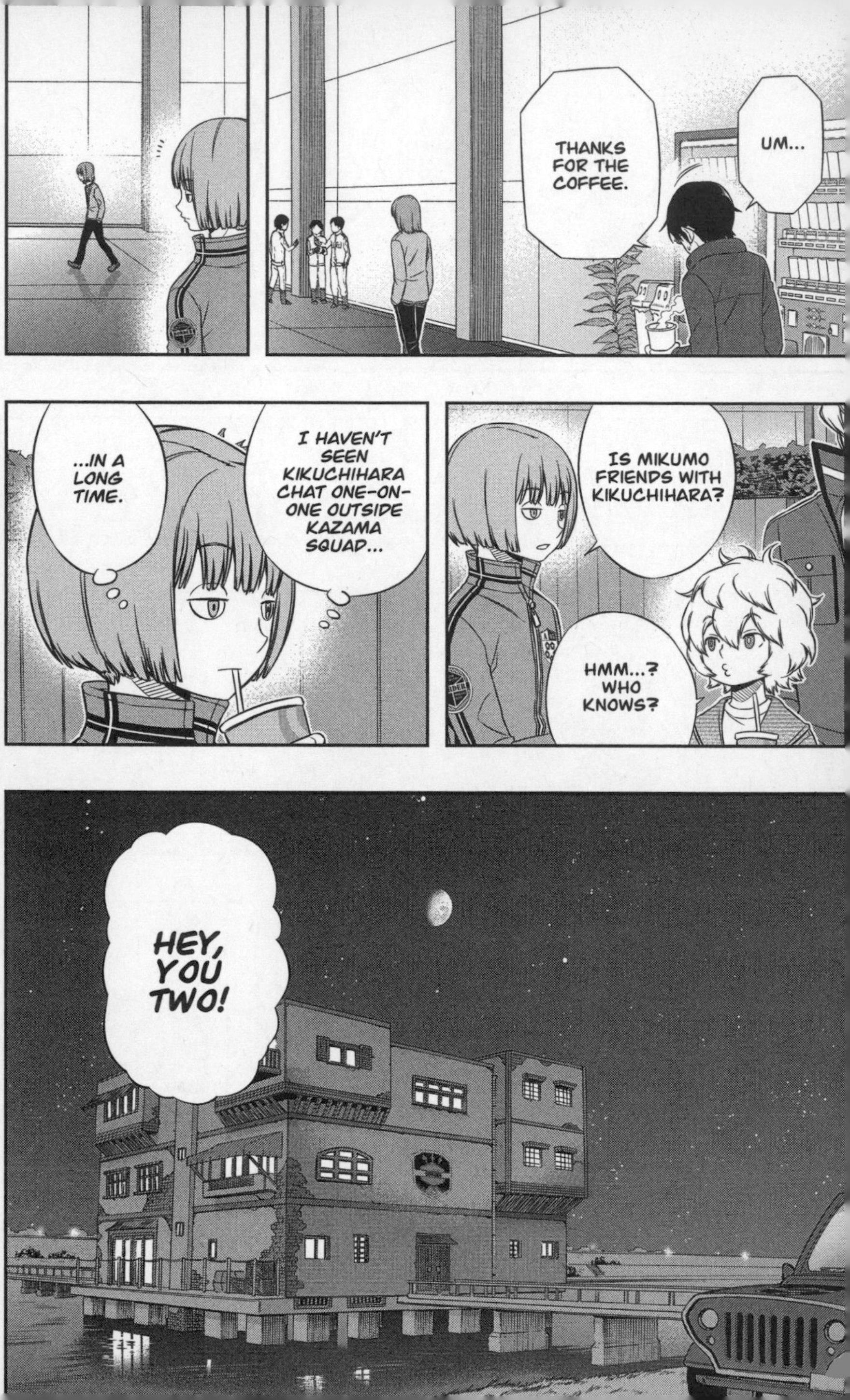
UM...
THANKS FOR THE COFFEE.
IS MIKUMO FRIENDS WITH KIKUCHIHARA?
HMM...? WHO KNOWS?
I HAVEN'T SEEN KIKUCHIHARA CHAT ONE-ON-ONE OUTSIDE KAZAMA SQUAD...
...IN A LONG TIME.
HEY, YOU TWO!

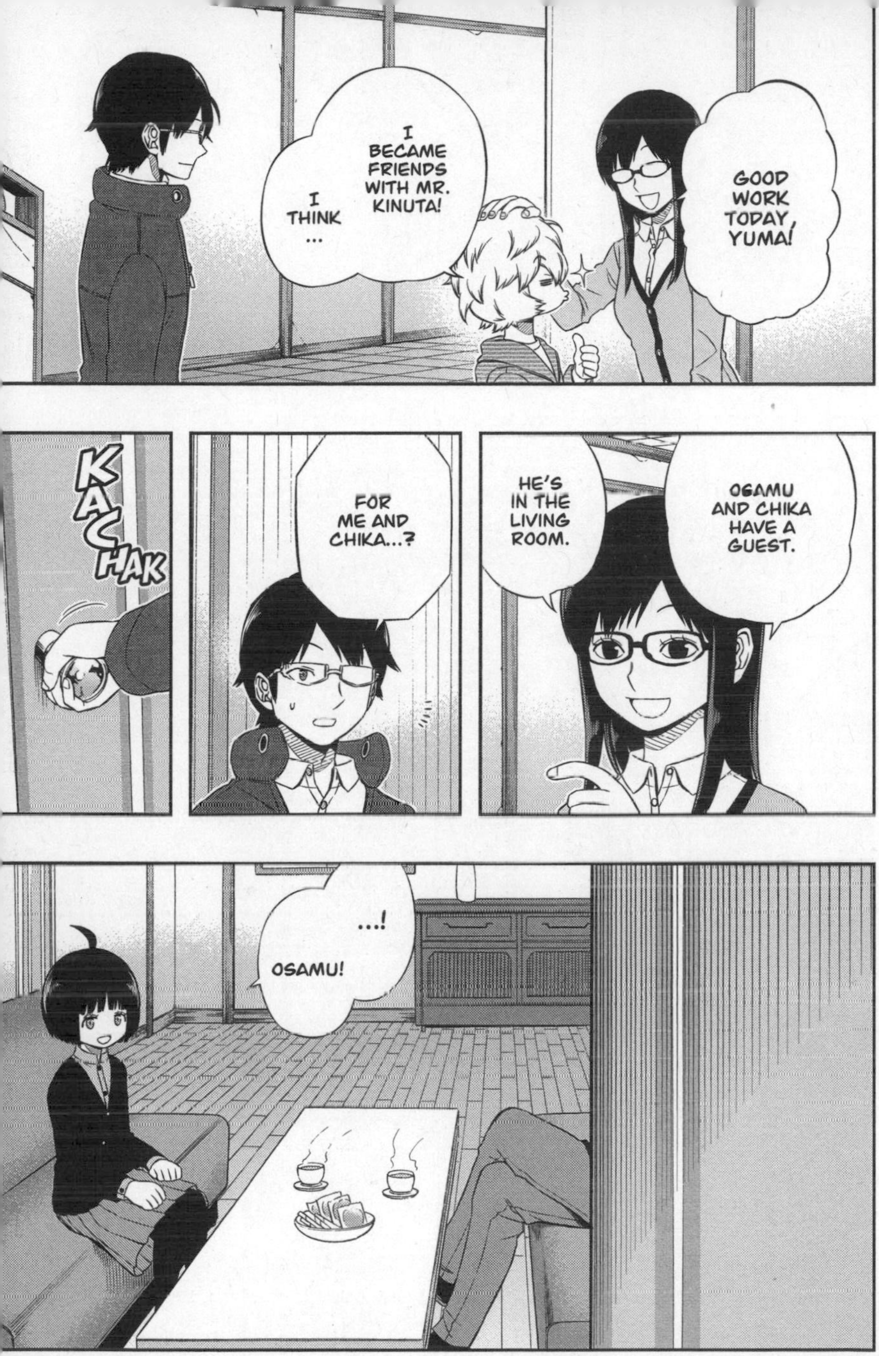
GOOD WORK TODAY, YUMA!
I BECAME FRIENDS WITH MR. KINUTA!
I THINK...
OSAMU AND CHIKA HAVE A GUEST.
HE'S IN THE LIVING ROOM.
FOR ME AND CHIKA...?
KACHAK
...!
OSAMU!

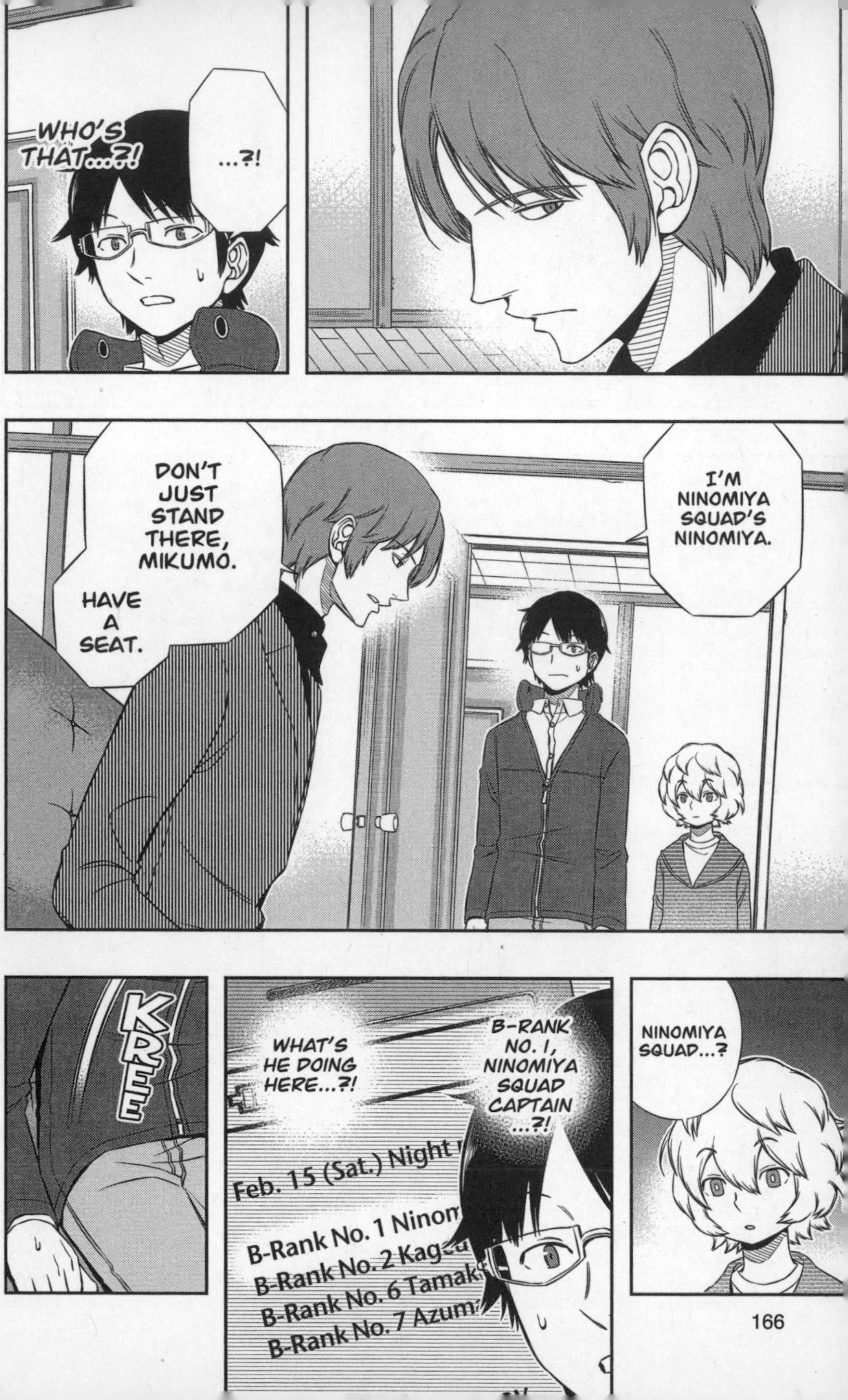
...?!
WHO'S THAT...?!
I'M NINOMIYA SQUAD'S NINOMIYA.
DON'T JUST STAND THERE, MIKUMO.
HAVE A SEAT.
NINOMIYA SQUAD...?
B-RANK NO. 1, NINOMIYA SQUAD CAPTAIN...?!
WHAT'S HE DOING HERE...?!
Feb. 15 (Sat.) Night
B-Rank No. 1 Ninom
B-Rank No. 2 Kage
B-Rank No. 6 Tamak
B-Rank No. 7 Azum
KREE

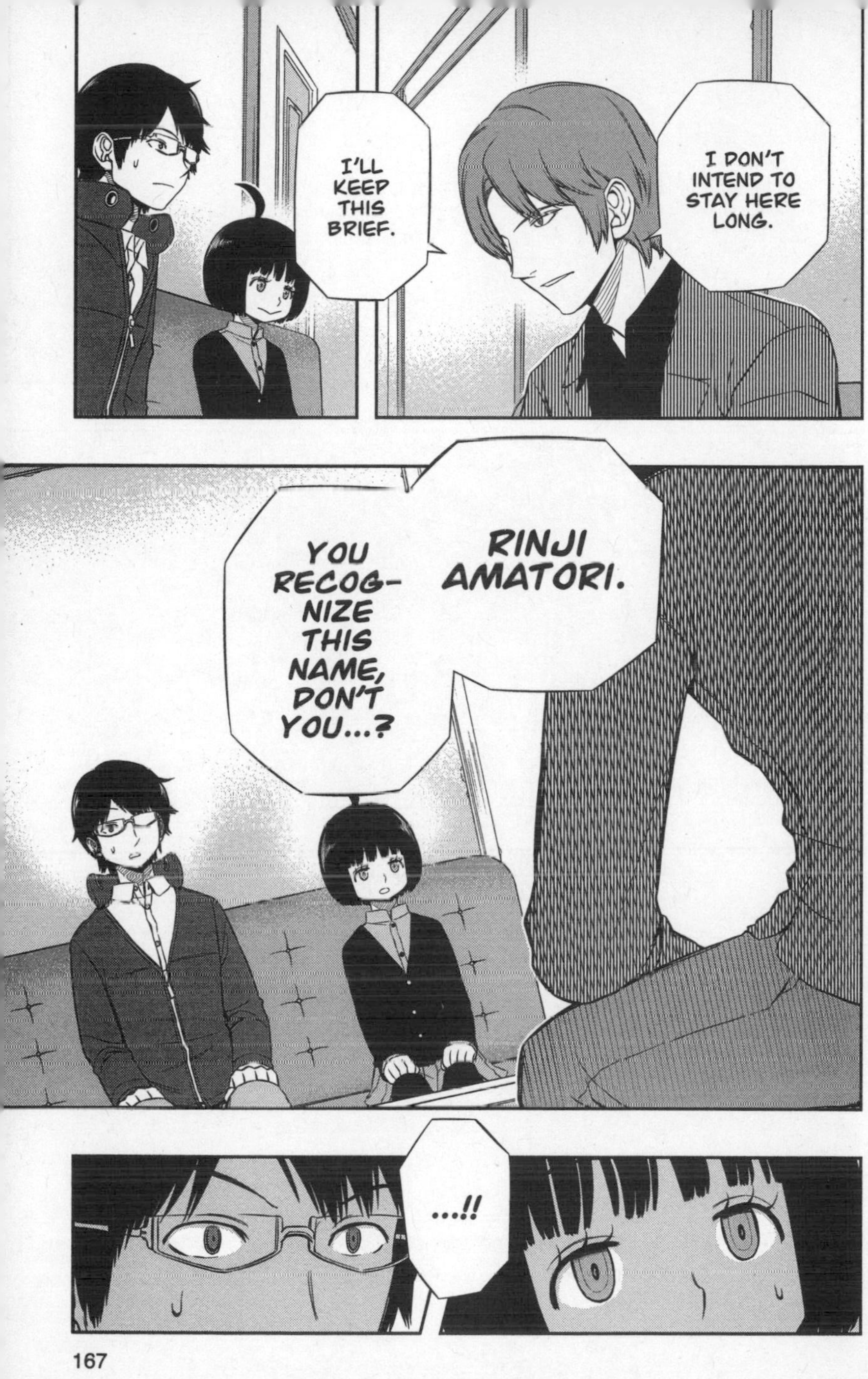
I DON'T INTEND TO STAY HERE LONG.
I'LL KEEP THIS BRIEF.
RINJI AMATORI.
YOU RECOG-NIZE THIS NAME, DON'T YOU...?
...!!

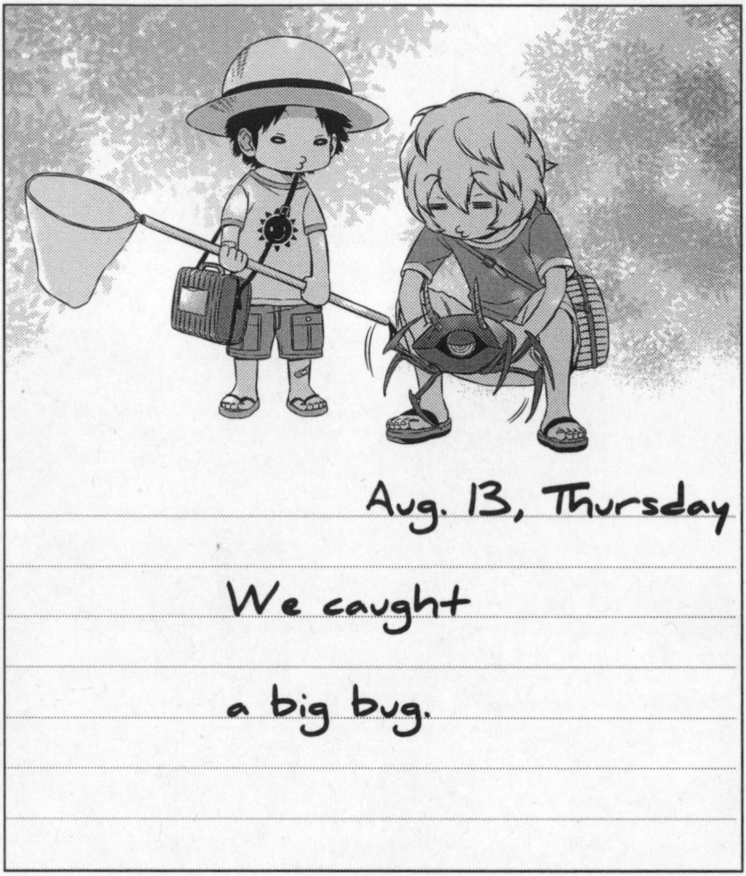
Aug. 13, Thursday
We caught
a big bug.

■ 2015 *Weekly Shonen Jump* 37/38 combined issue illustration for reader extras
I drew this for the "Jump characters doing a picture diary" event. There was a theme for each series, and *World Trigger's* was bug collecting. I decided on this in about five seconds. Captured Enedorad.

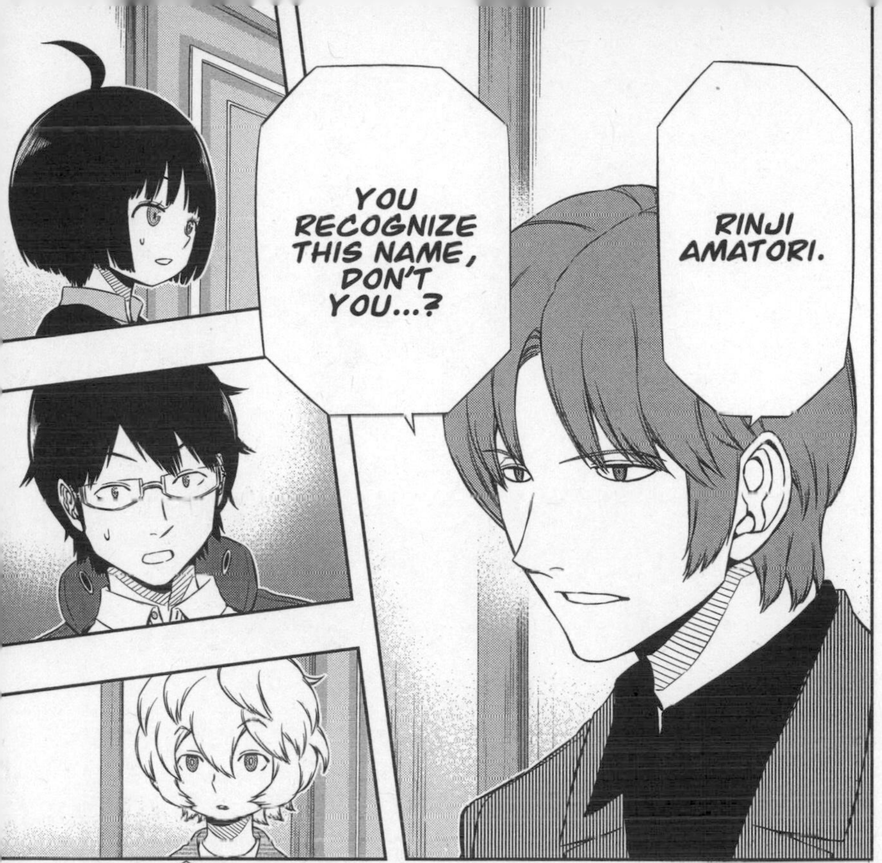
RINJI AMATORI.
YOU RECOGNIZE THIS NAME, DON'T YOU...?

Chapter 106 Masataka Ninomiya

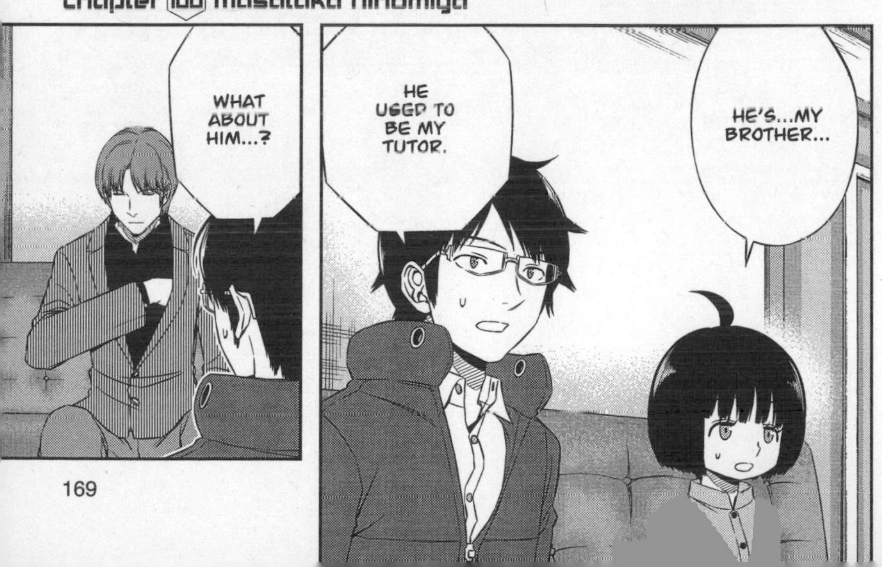
HE'S...MY BROTHER...
HE USED TO BE MY TUTOR.
WHAT ABOUT HIM...?

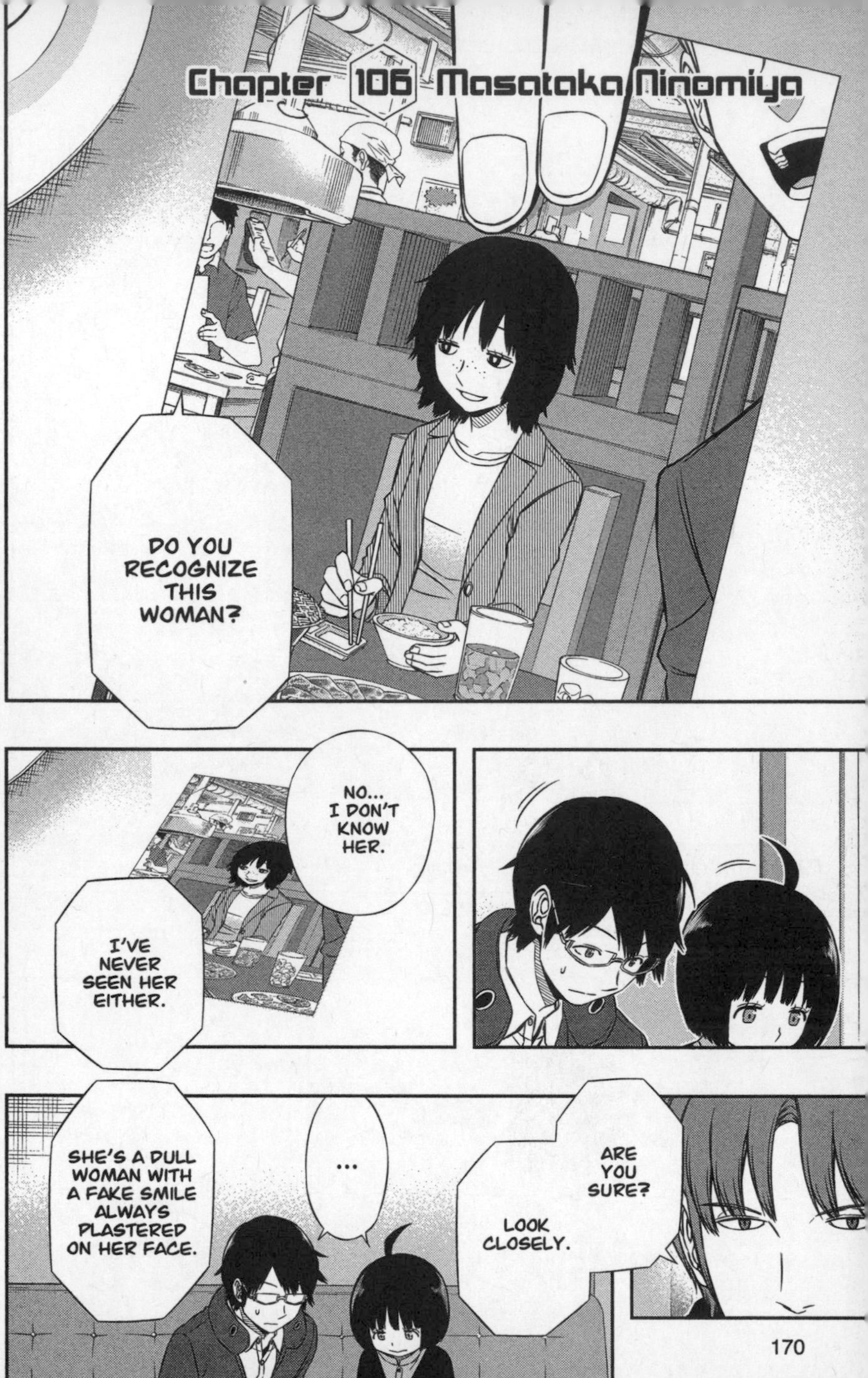
Chapter 106 Masataka Ninomiya
DO YOU RECOGNIZE THIS WOMAN?
NO... I DON'T KNOW HER.
I'VE NEVER SEEN HER EITHER.
ARE YOU SURE?
LOOK CLOSELY.
...
SHE'S A DULL WOMAN WITH A FAKE SMILE ALWAYS PLASTERED ON HER FACE.

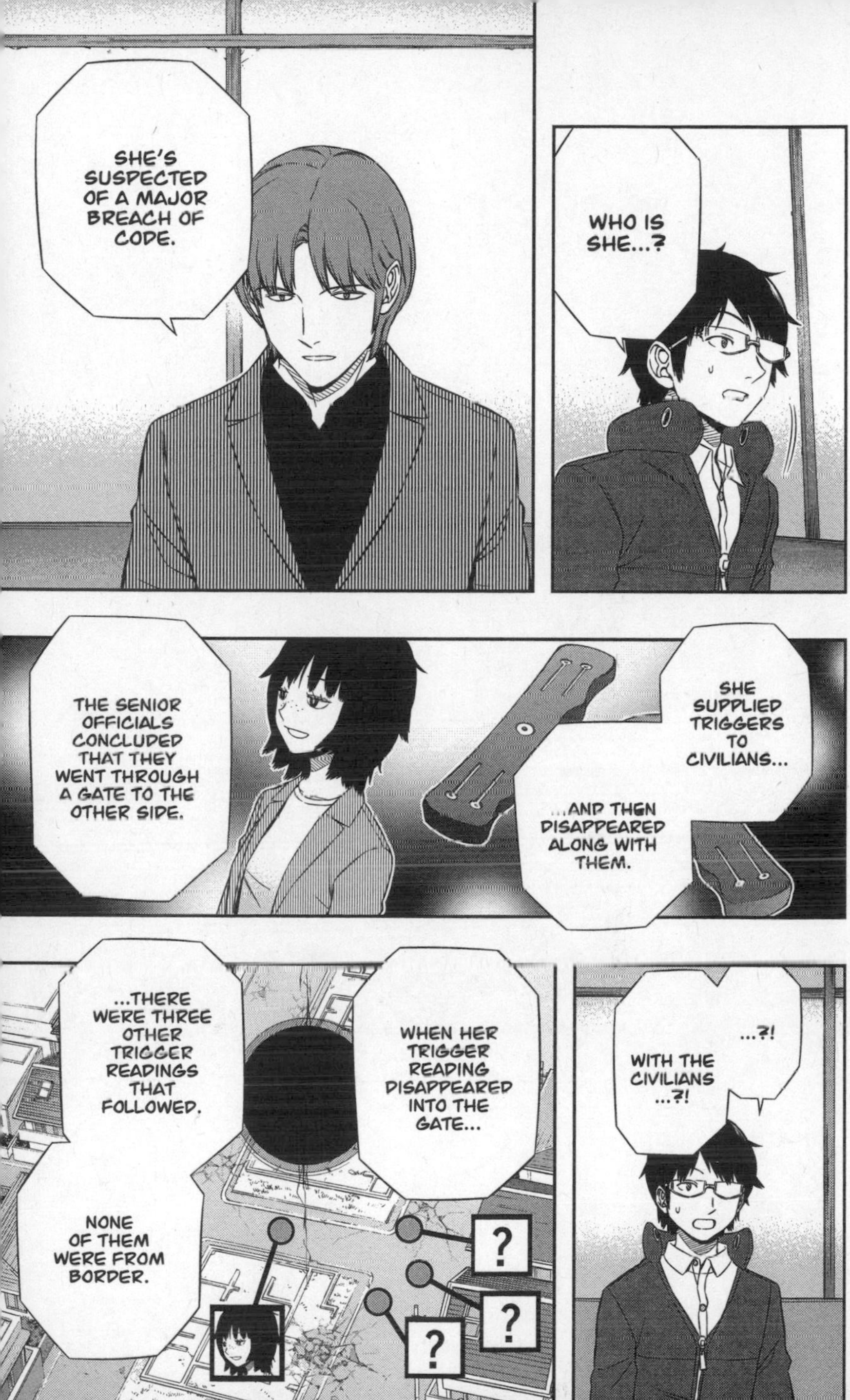
WHO IS SHE...?
SHE'S SUSPECTED OF A MAJOR BREACH OF CODE.
SHE SUPPLIED TRIGGERS TO CIVILIANS...
...AND THEN DISAPPEARED ALONG WITH THEM.
THE SENIOR OFFICIALS CONCLUDED THAT THEY WENT THROUGH A GATE TO THE OTHER SIDE.
...?!
WITH THE CIVILIANS ...?!
WHEN HER TRIGGER READING DISAPPEARED INTO THE GATE...
...THERE WERE THREE OTHER TRIGGER READINGS THAT FOLLOWED.
NONE OF THEM WERE FROM BORDER.

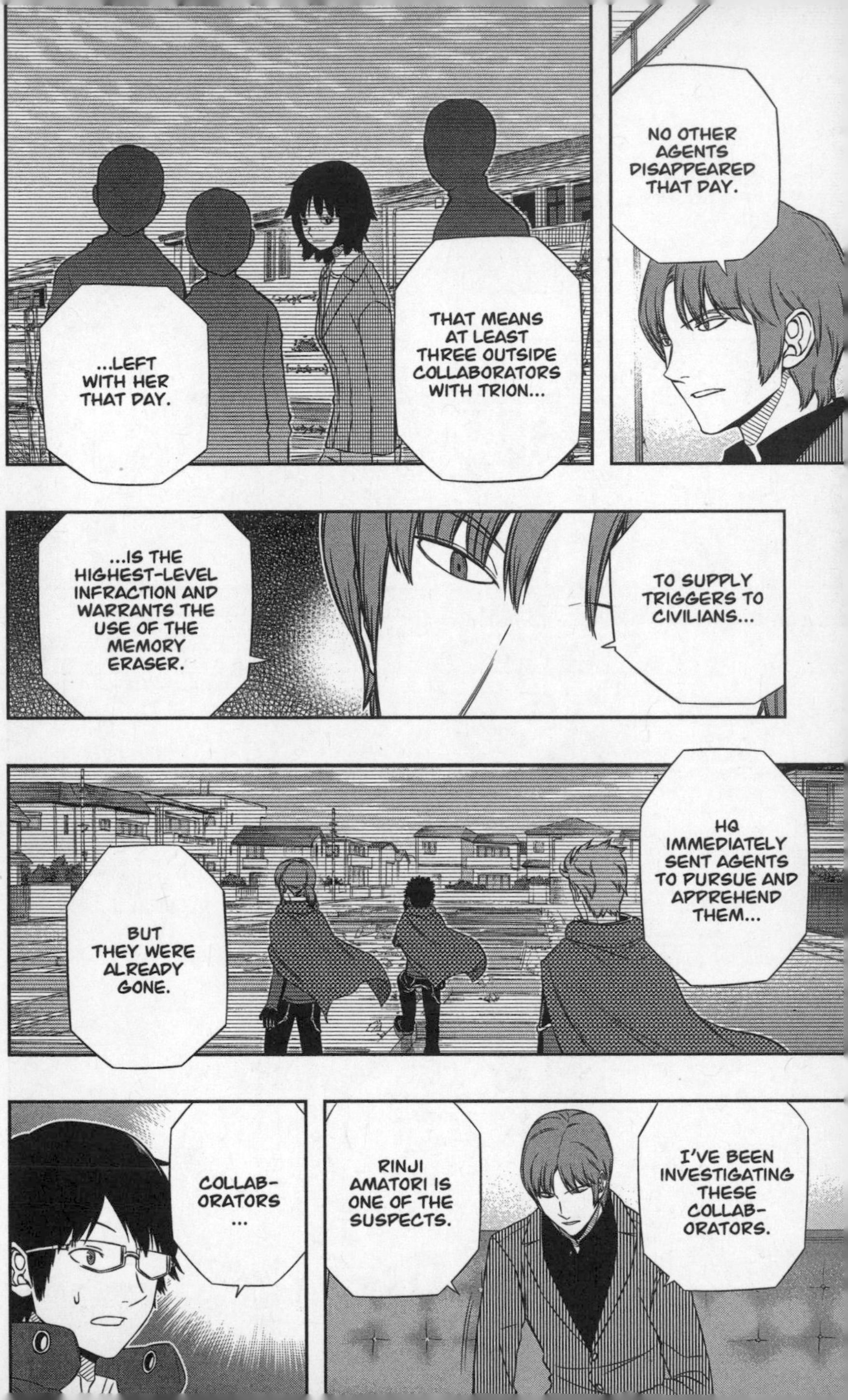
NO OTHER AGENTS DISAPPEARED THAT DAY.
THAT MEANS AT LEAST THREE OUTSIDE COLLABORATORS WITH TRION...
...LEFT WITH HER THAT DAY.
TO SUPPLY TRIGGERS TO CIVILIANS...
...IS THE HIGHEST-LEVEL INFRACTION AND WARRANTS THE USE OF THE MEMORY ERASER.
HQ IMMEDIATELY SENT AGENTS TO PURSUE AND APPREHEND THEM...
BUT THEY WERE ALREADY GONE.
I'VE BEEN INVESTIGATING THESE COLLAB-ORATORS.
RINJI AMATORI IS ONE OF THE SUSPECTS.
COLLAB-ORATORS ...

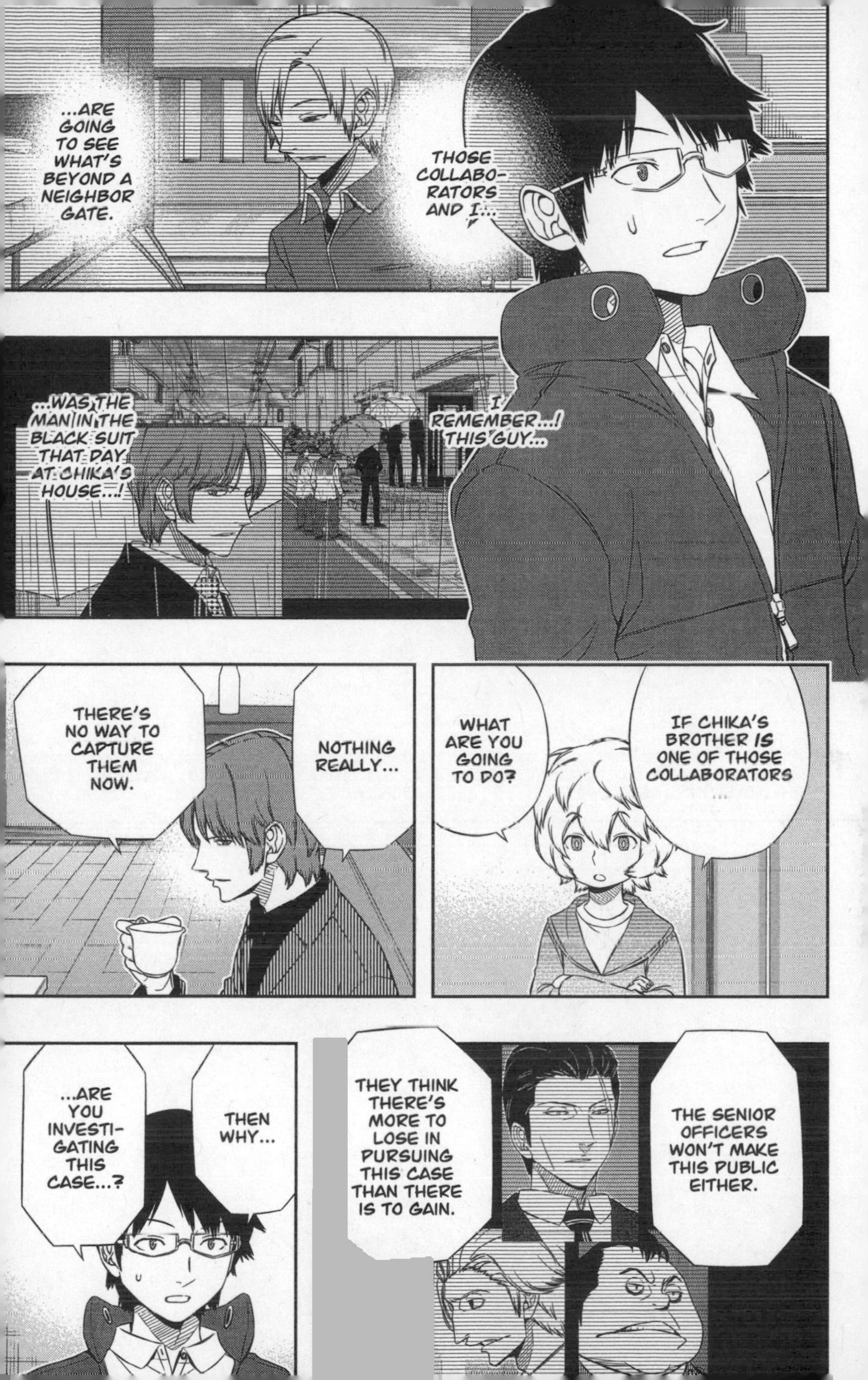
THOSE COLLABORATORS AND I...
...ARE GOING TO SEE WHAT'S BEYOND A NEIGHBOR GATE.
I REMEMBER...! THIS GUY...
...WAS THE MAN IN THE BLACK SUIT THAT DAY AT CHIKA'S HOUSE...!
IF CHIKA'S BROTHER IS ONE OF THOSE COLLABORATORS ...
WHAT ARE YOU GOING TO DO?
NOTHING REALLY...
THERE'S NO WAY TO CAPTURE THEM NOW.
THE SENIOR OFFICERS WON'T MAKE THIS PUBLIC EITHER.
THEY THINK THERE'S MORE TO LOSE IN PURSUING THIS CASE THAN THERE IS TO GAIN.
THEN WHY...
...ARE YOU INVESTIGATING THIS CASE...?

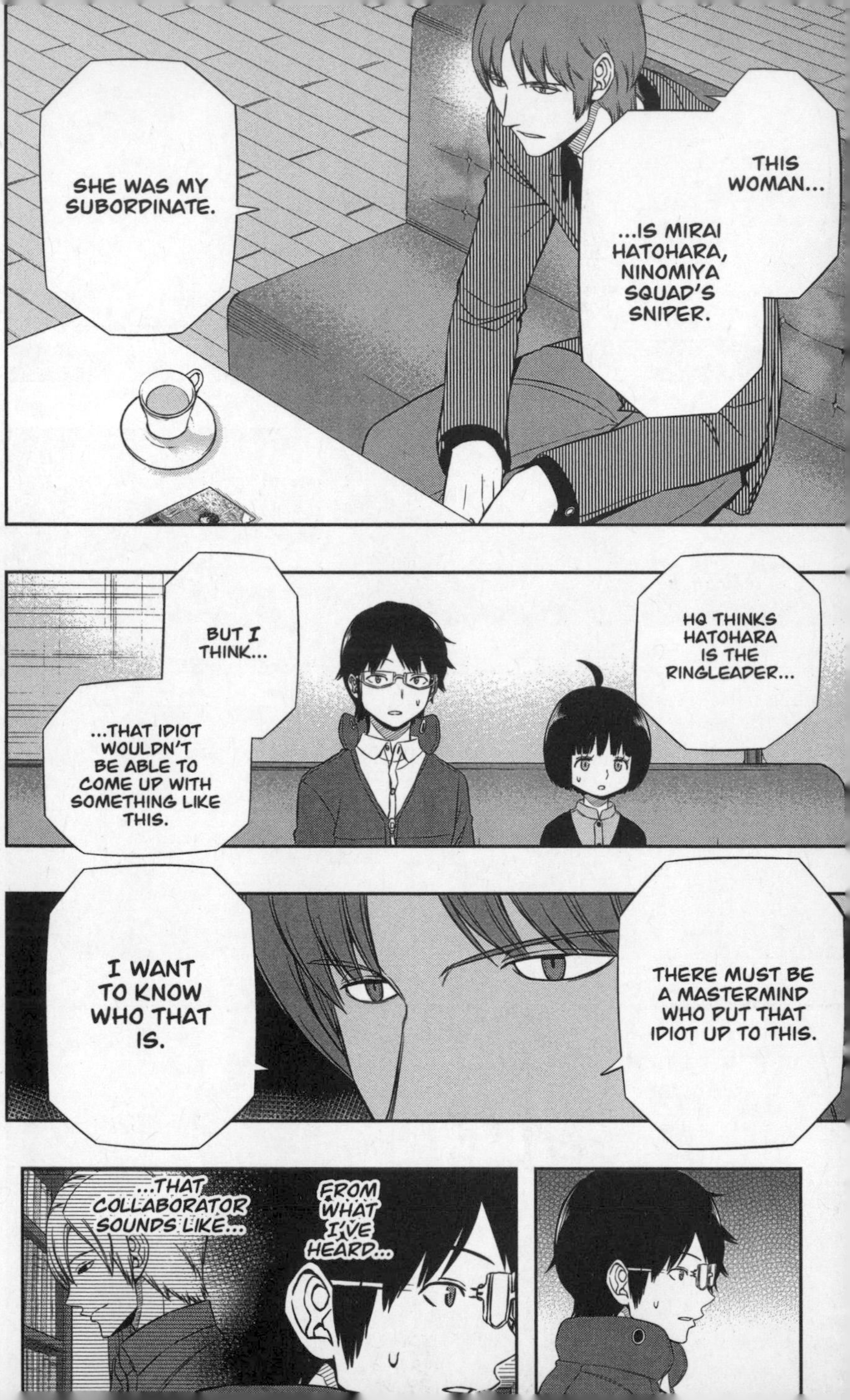
THIS WOMAN...
...IS MIRAI HATOHARA, NINOMIYA SQUAD'S SNIPER.
SHE WAS MY SUBORDINATE.
HQ THINKS HATOHARA IS THE RINGLEADER...
BUT I THINK...
...THAT IDIOT WOULDN'T BE ABLE TO COME UP WITH SOMETHING LIKE THIS.
THERE MUST BE A MASTERMIND WHO PUT THAT IDIOT UP TO THIS.
I WANT TO KNOW WHO THAT IS.
FROM WHAT I'VE HEARD...
...THAT COLLABORATOR SOUNDS LIKE...

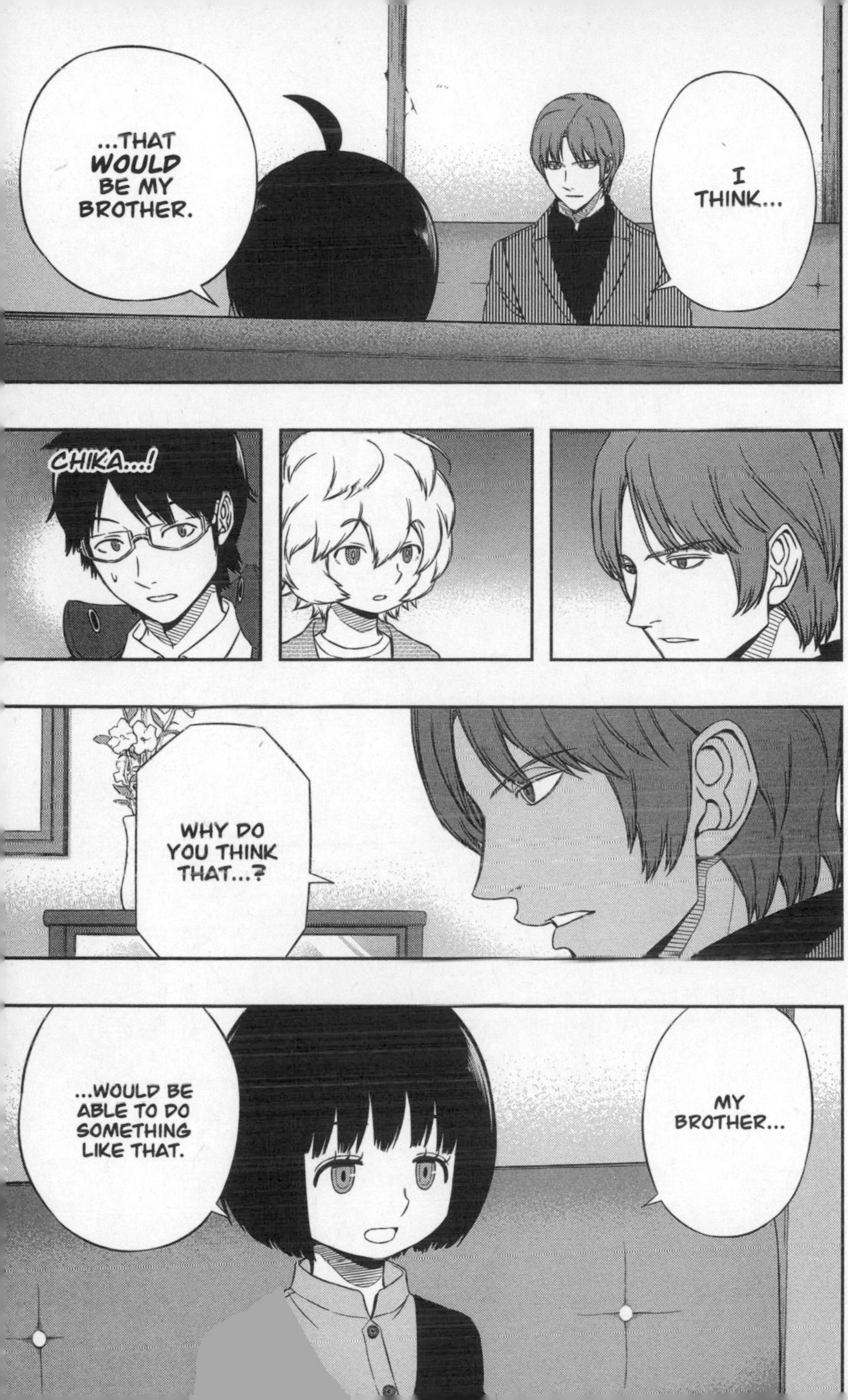
I THINK...
...THAT WOULD BE MY BROTHER.
CHIKA...!
WHY DO YOU THINK THAT...?
MY BROTHER...
...WOULD BE ABLE TO DO SOMETHING LIKE THAT.

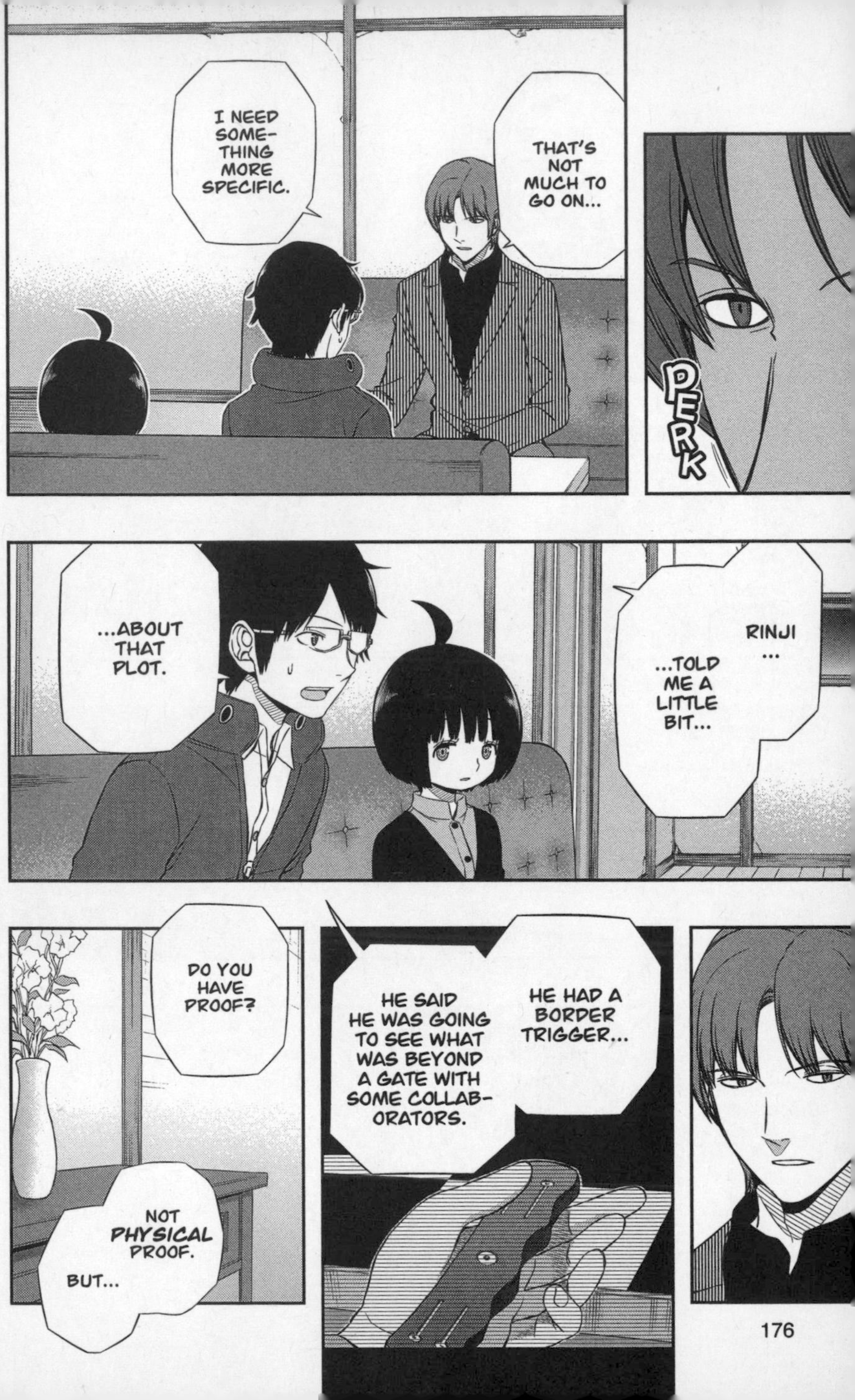
PERK
THAT'S NOT MUCH TO GO ON...
I NEED SOME-THING MORE SPECIFIC.
RINJI...
...TOLD ME A LITTLE BIT...
...ABOUT THAT PLOT.
HE HAD A BORDER TRIGGER...
HE SAID HE WAS GOING TO SEE WHAT WAS BEYOND A GATE WITH SOME COLLAB-ORATORS.
DO YOU HAVE PROOF?
NOT PHYSICAL PROOF.
BUT...

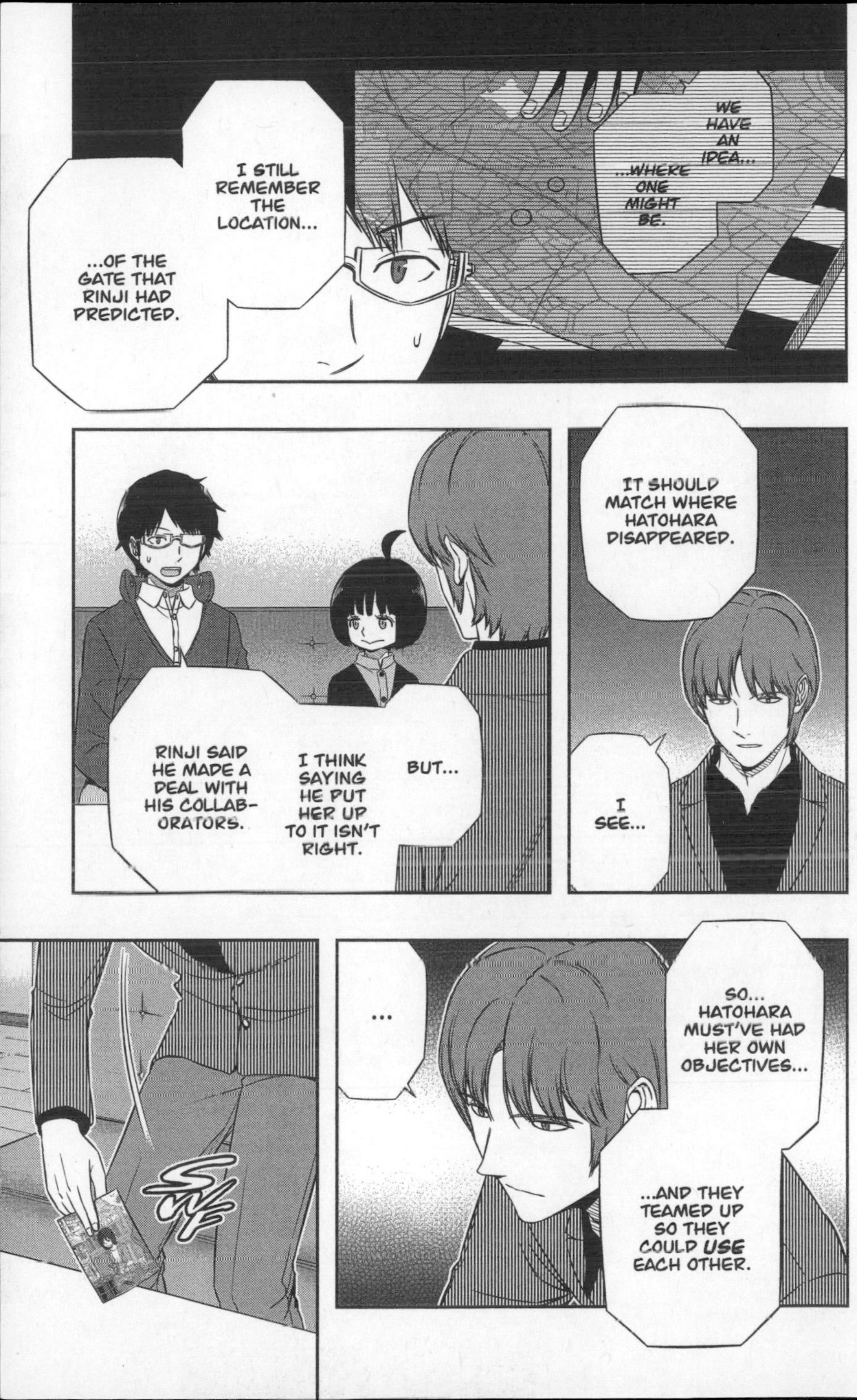
WE HAVE AN IDEA... ...WHERE ONE MIGHT BE.
I STILL REMEMBER THE LOCATION...
...OF THE GATE THAT RINJI HAD PREDICTED.
IT SHOULD MATCH WHERE HATOHARA DISAPPEARED.
I SEE...
RINJI SAID HE MADE A DEAL WITH HIS COLLAB-ORATORS. I THINK SAYING HE PUT HER UP TO IT ISN'T RIGHT. BUT...
SO... HATOHARA MUST'VE HAD HER OWN OBJECTIVES...
...
...AND THEY TEAMED UP SO THEY COULD *USE* EACH OTHER.
SWF

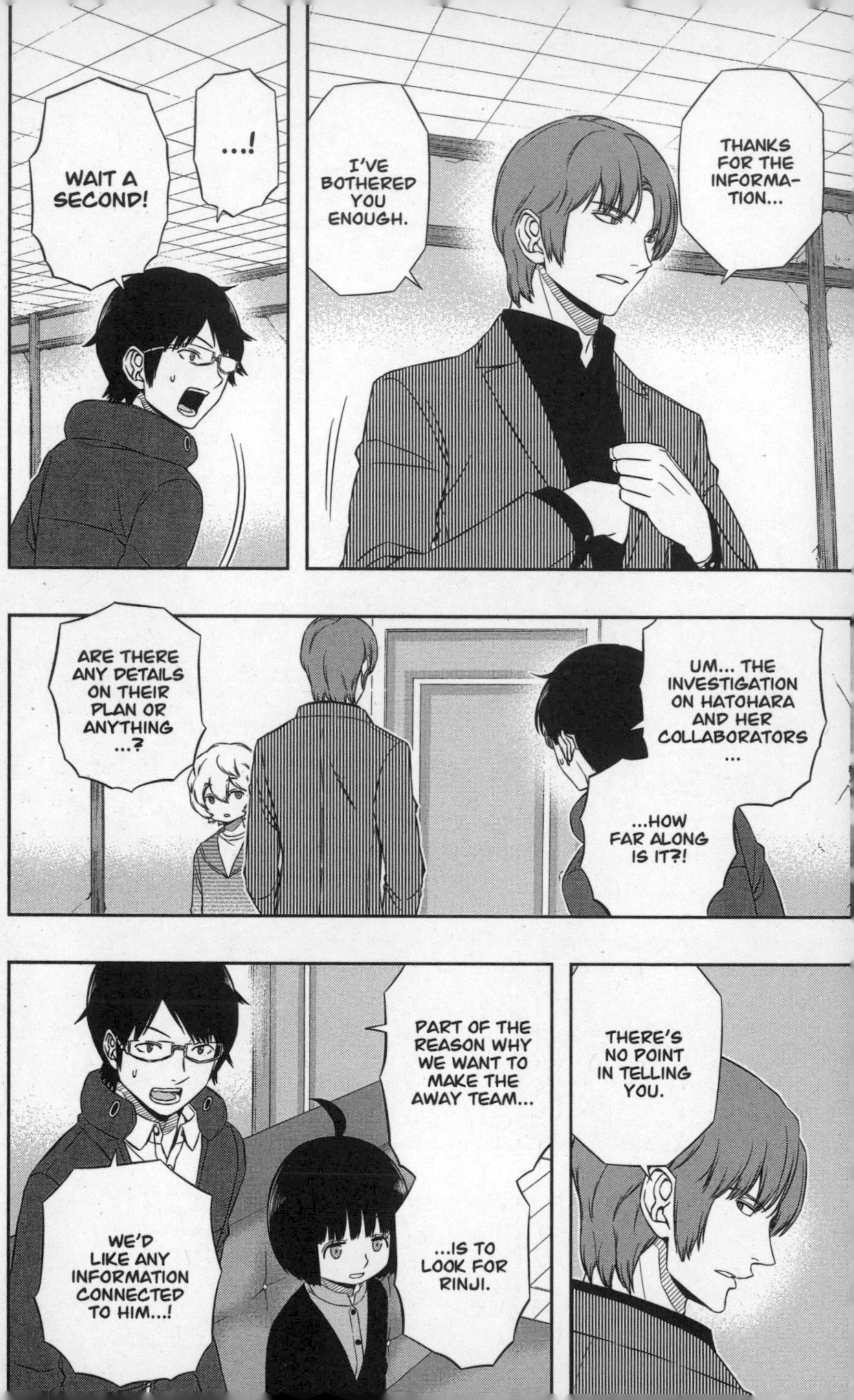
THANKS FOR THE INFORMATION...
I'VE BOTHERED YOU ENOUGH.
...!
WAIT A SECOND!
UM... THE INVESTIGATION ON HATOHARA AND HER COLLABORATORS ...
...HOW FAR ALONG IS IT?!
ARE THERE ANY DETAILS ON THEIR PLAN OR ANYTHING ...?
THERE'S NO POINT IN TELLING YOU.
PART OF THE REASON WHY WE WANT TO MAKE THE AWAY TEAM...
...IS TO LOOK FOR RINJI.
WE'D LIKE ANY INFORMATION CONNECTED TO HIM...!

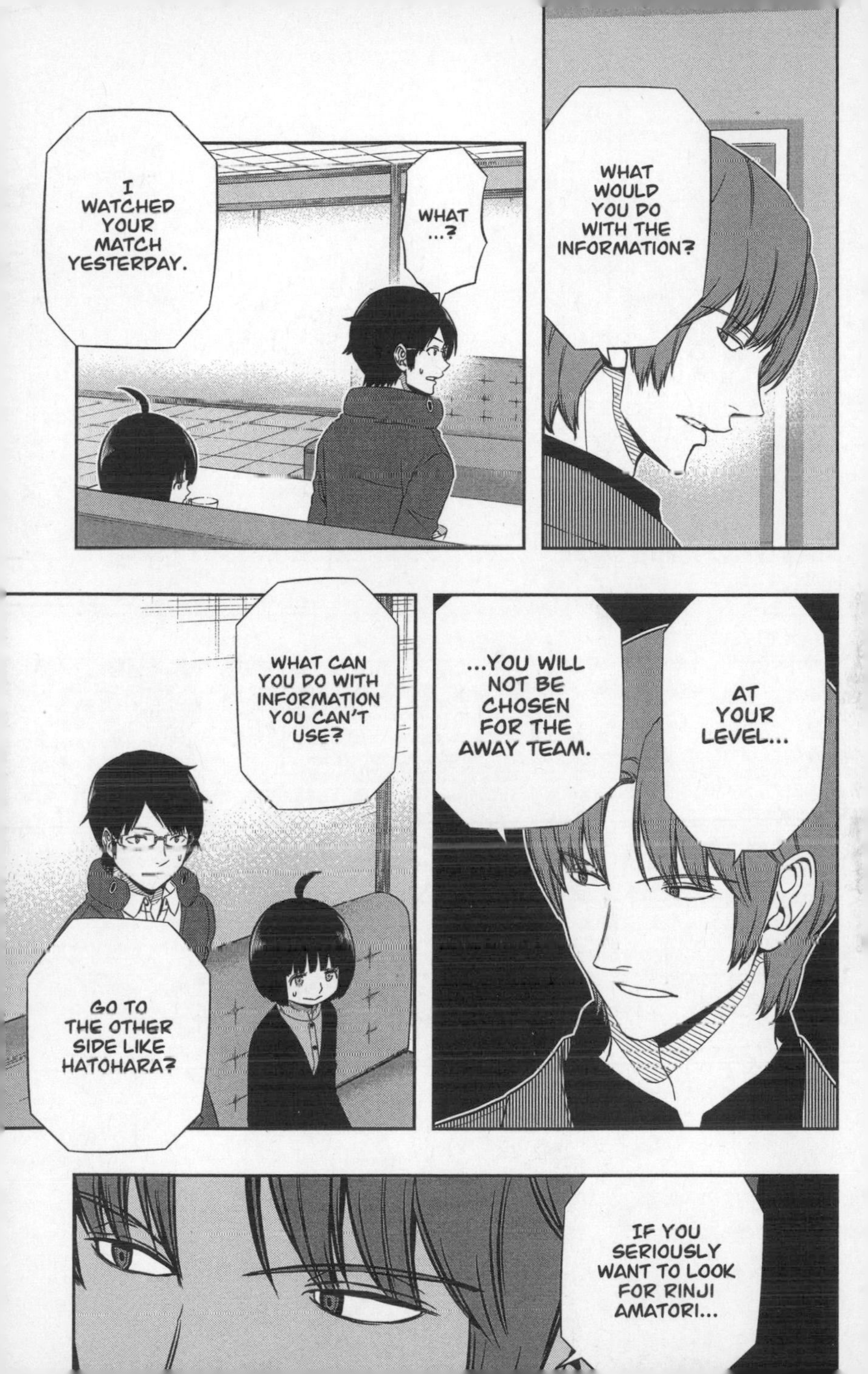
WHAT WOULD YOU DO WITH THE INFORMATION?
I WATCHED YOUR MATCH YESTERDAY.
WHAT ...?
AT YOUR LEVEL...
...YOU WILL NOT BE CHOSEN FOR THE AWAY TEAM.
WHAT CAN YOU DO WITH INFORMATION YOU CAN'T USE?
GO TO THE OTHER SIDE LIKE HATOHARA?
IF YOU SERIOUSLY WANT TO LOOK FOR RINJI AMATORI...

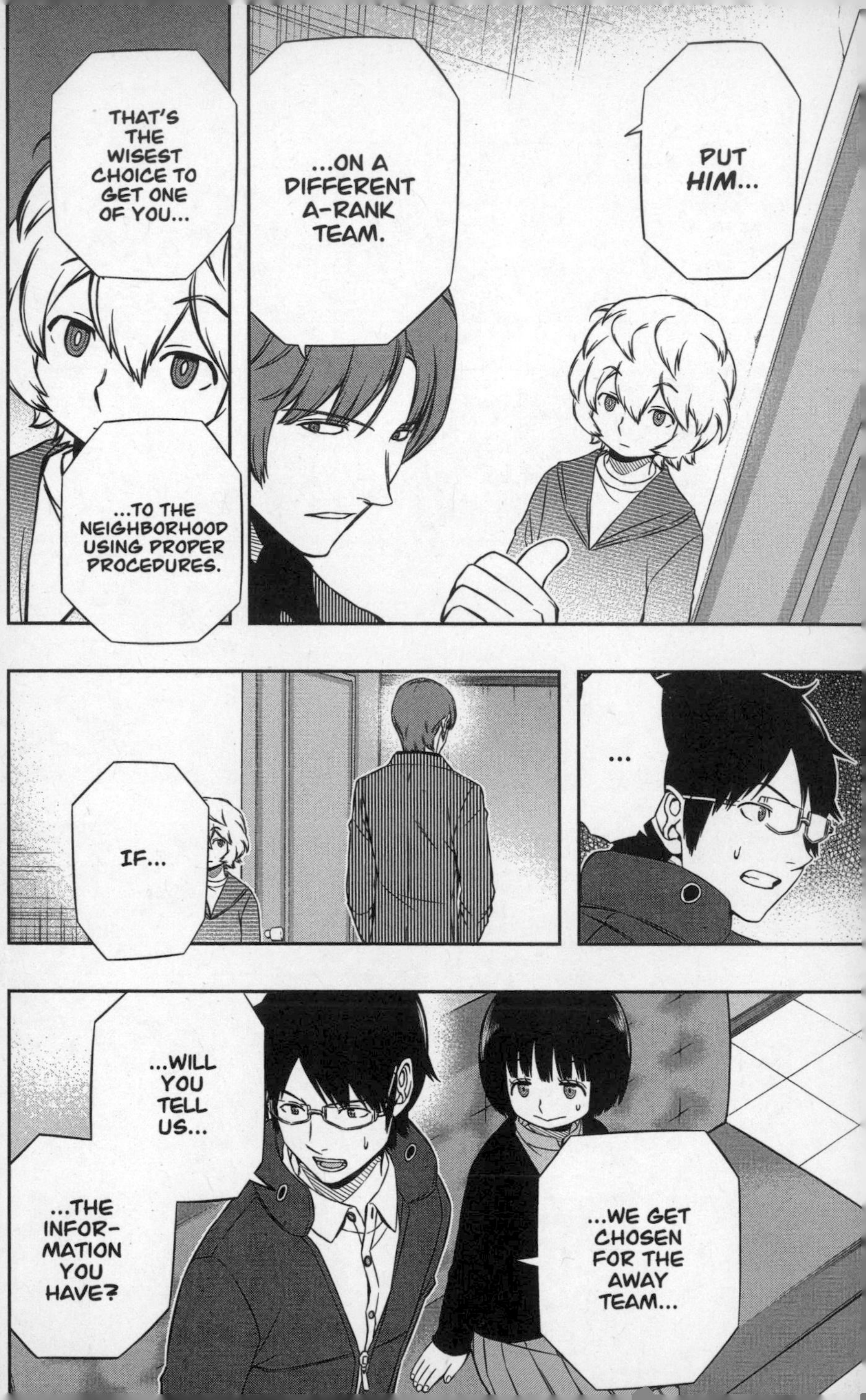
PUT HIM...
...ON A DIFFERENT A-RANK TEAM.
THAT'S THE WISEST CHOICE TO GET ONE OF YOU...
...TO THE NEIGHBORHOOD USING PROPER PROCEDURES.
...
IF...
...WE GET CHOSEN FOR THE AWAY TEAM...
...WILL YOU TELL US...
...THE INFOR-MATION YOU HAVE?

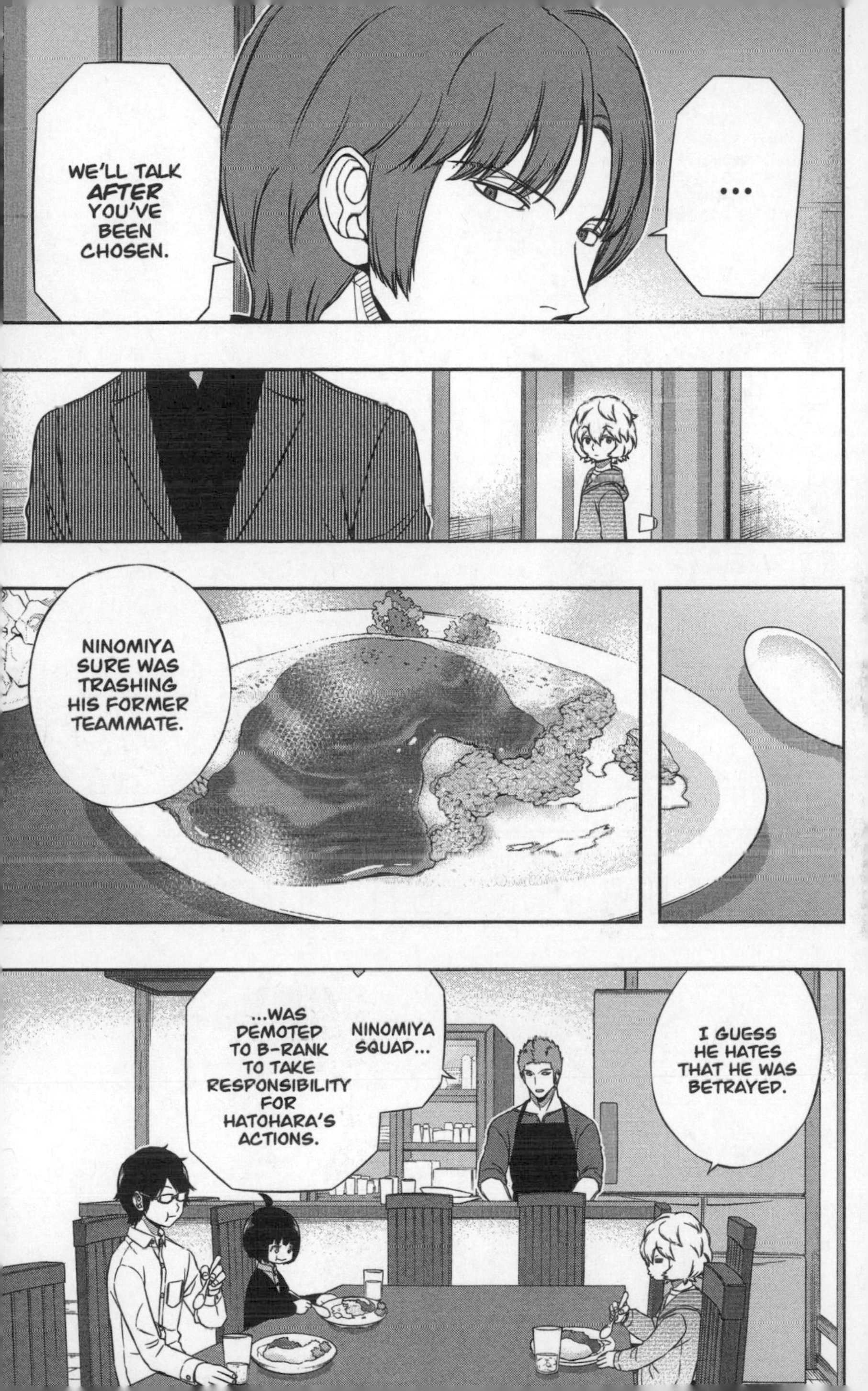
...
WE'LL TALK AFTER YOU'VE BEEN CHOSEN.
NINOMIYA SURE WAS TRASHING HIS FORMER TEAMMATE.
I GUESS HE HATES THAT HE WAS BETRAYED.
NINOMIYA SQUAD...
...WAS DEMOTED TO B-RANK TO TAKE RESPONSIBILITY FOR HATOHARA'S ACTIONS.

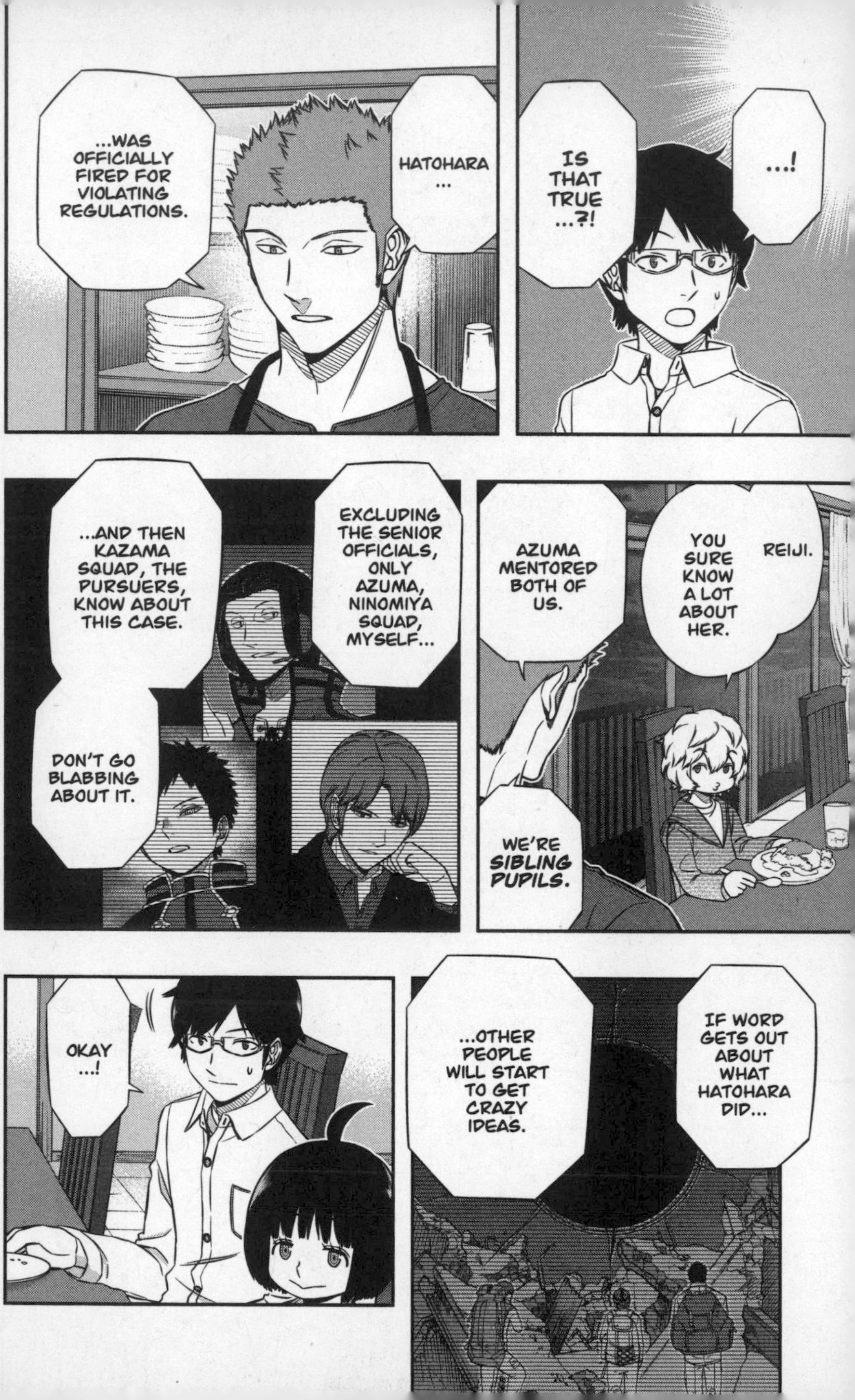
...!
IS THAT TRUE ...?!
HATOHARA ...
...WAS OFFICIALLY FIRED FOR VIOLATING REGULATIONS.
REIJI.
YOU SURE KNOW A LOT ABOUT HER.
AZUMA MENTORED BOTH OF US.
WE'RE *SIBLING PUPILS.*
EXCLUDING THE SENIOR OFFICIALS, ONLY AZUMA, NINOMIYA SQUAD, MYSELF...
...AND THEN KAZAMA SQUAD, THE PURSUERS, KNOW ABOUT THIS CASE.
DON'T GO BLABBING ABOUT IT.
IF WORD GETS OUT ABOUT WHAT HATOHARA DID...
...OTHER PEOPLE WILL START TO GET CRAZY IDEAS.
OKAY ...!

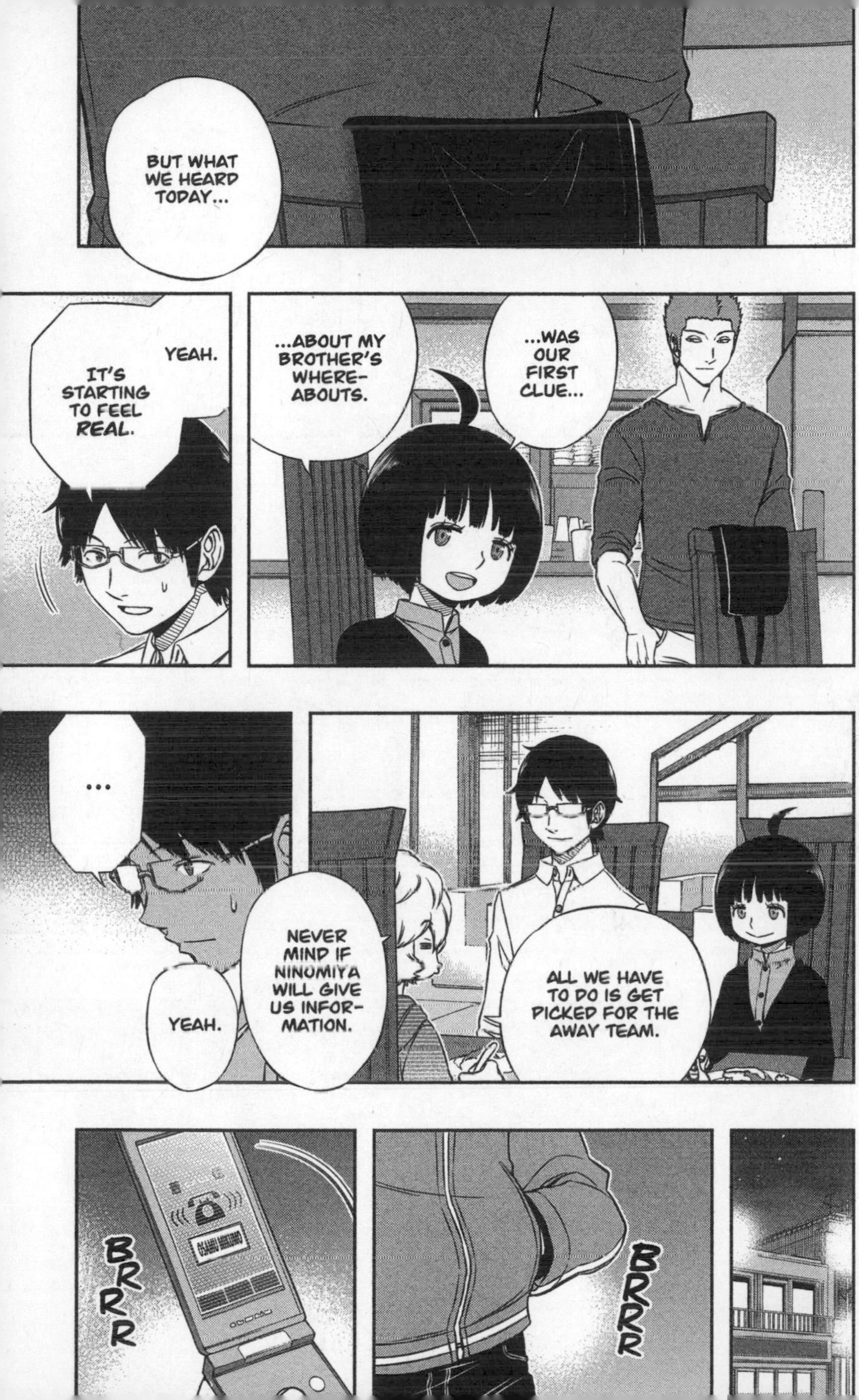
BUT WHAT WE HEARD TODAY...
...WAS OUR FIRST CLUE...
...ABOUT MY BROTHER'S WHERE-ABOUTS.
YEAH.
IT'S STARTING TO FEEL REAL.
ALL WE HAVE TO DO IS GET PICKED FOR THE AWAY TEAM.
...
NEVER MIND IF NINOMIYA WILL GIVE US INFORMATION.
YEAH.
BRRR
BRRR

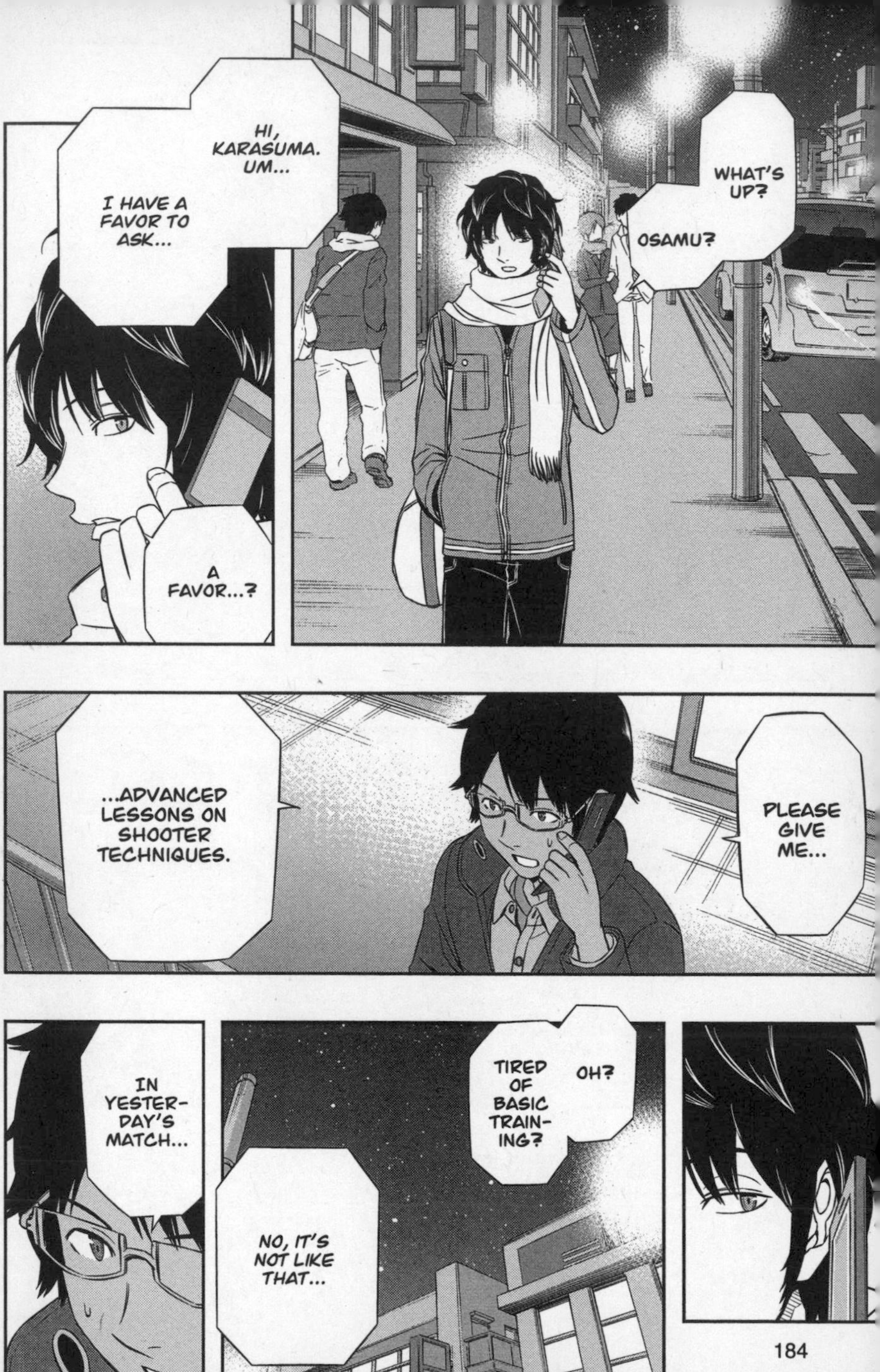
WHAT'S UP?
OSAMU?
HI, KARASUMA. UM...
I HAVE A FAVOR TO ASK...
A FAVOR...?
PLEASE GIVE ME...
...ADVANCED LESSONS ON SHOOTER TECHNIQUES.
OH?
TIRED OF BASIC TRAIN-ING?
NO, IT'S NOT LIKE THAT...
IN YESTER-DAY'S MATCH...

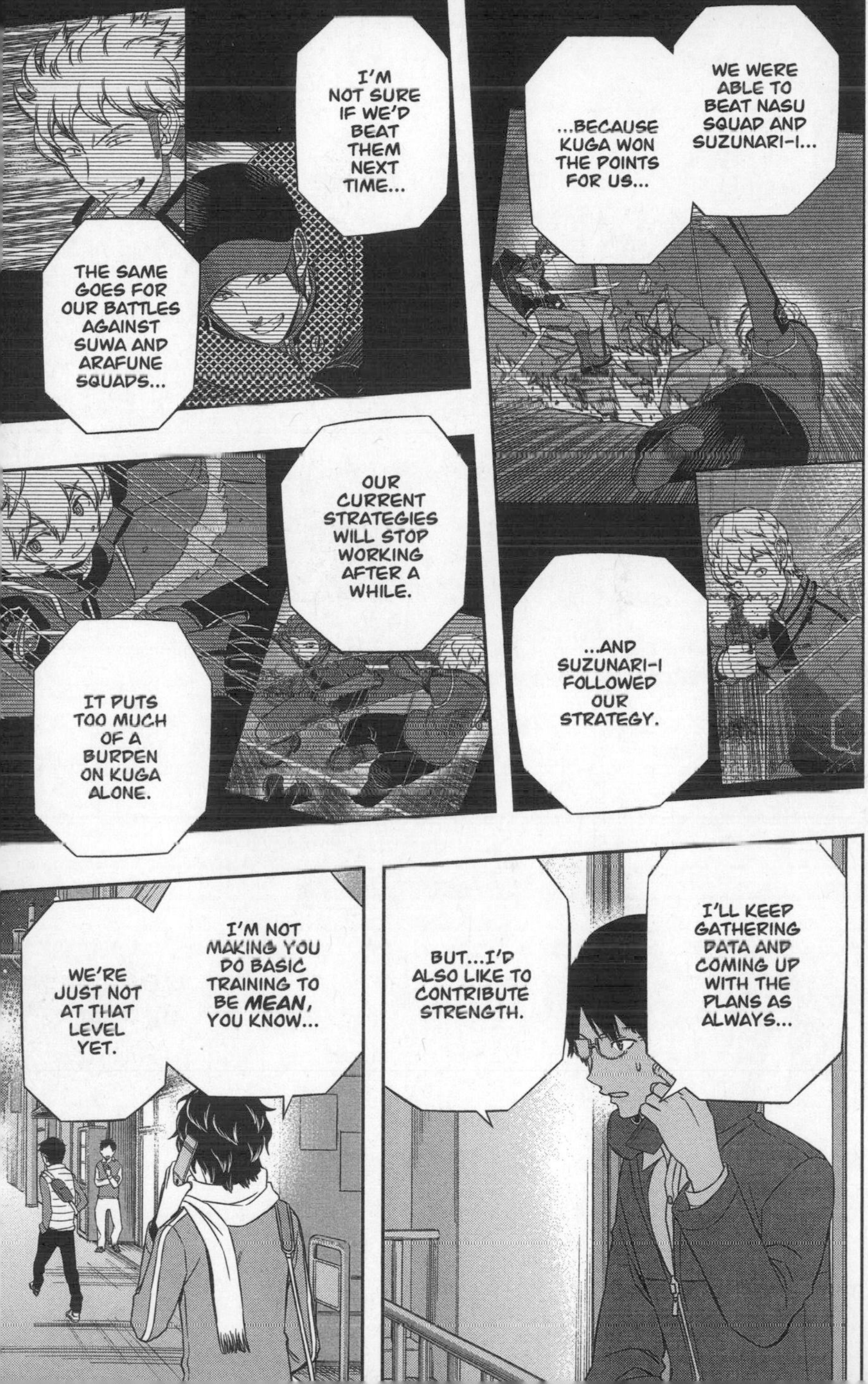
WE WERE ABLE TO BEAT NASU SQUAD AND SUZUNARI-1...
...BECAUSE KUGA WON THE POINTS FOR US...
...AND SUZUNARI-1 FOLLOWED OUR STRATEGY.
I'M NOT SURE IF WE'D BEAT THEM NEXT TIME...
THE SAME GOES FOR OUR BATTLES AGAINST SUWA AND ARAFUNE SQUADS...
OUR CURRENT STRATEGIES WILL STOP WORKING AFTER A WHILE.
IT PUTS TOO MUCH OF A BURDEN ON KUGA ALONE.
I'LL KEEP GATHERING DATA AND COMING UP WITH THE PLANS AS ALWAYS...
BUT...I'D ALSO LIKE TO CONTRIBUTE STRENGTH.
I'M NOT MAKING YOU DO BASIC TRAINING TO BE *MEAN*, YOU KNOW...
WE'RE JUST NOT AT THAT LEVEL YET.

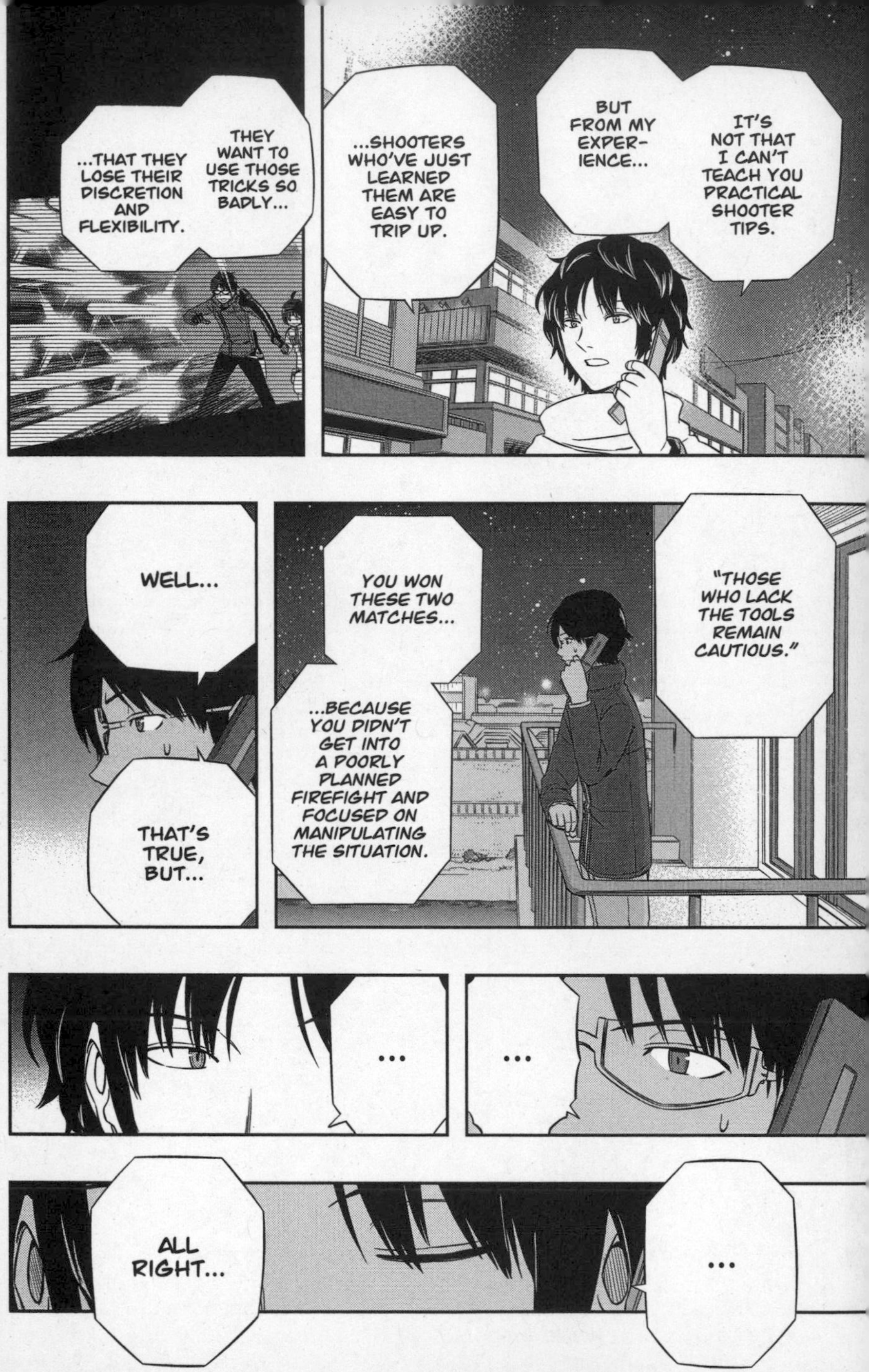
IT'S NOT THAT I CAN'T TEACH YOU PRACTICAL SHOOTER TIPS.
BUT FROM MY EXPERIENCE...
...SHOOTERS WHO'VE JUST LEARNED THEM ARE EASY TO TRIP UP.
THEY WANT TO USE THOSE TRICKS SO BADLY...
...THAT THEY LOSE THEIR DISCRETION AND FLEXIBILITY.
"THOSE WHO LACK THE TOOLS REMAIN CAUTIOUS."
YOU WON THESE TWO MATCHES...
...BECAUSE YOU DIDN'T GET INTO A POORLY PLANNED FIREFIGHT AND FOCUSED ON MANIPULATING THE SITUATION.
WELL...
THAT'S TRUE, BUT...
...
...
...
ALL RIGHT...

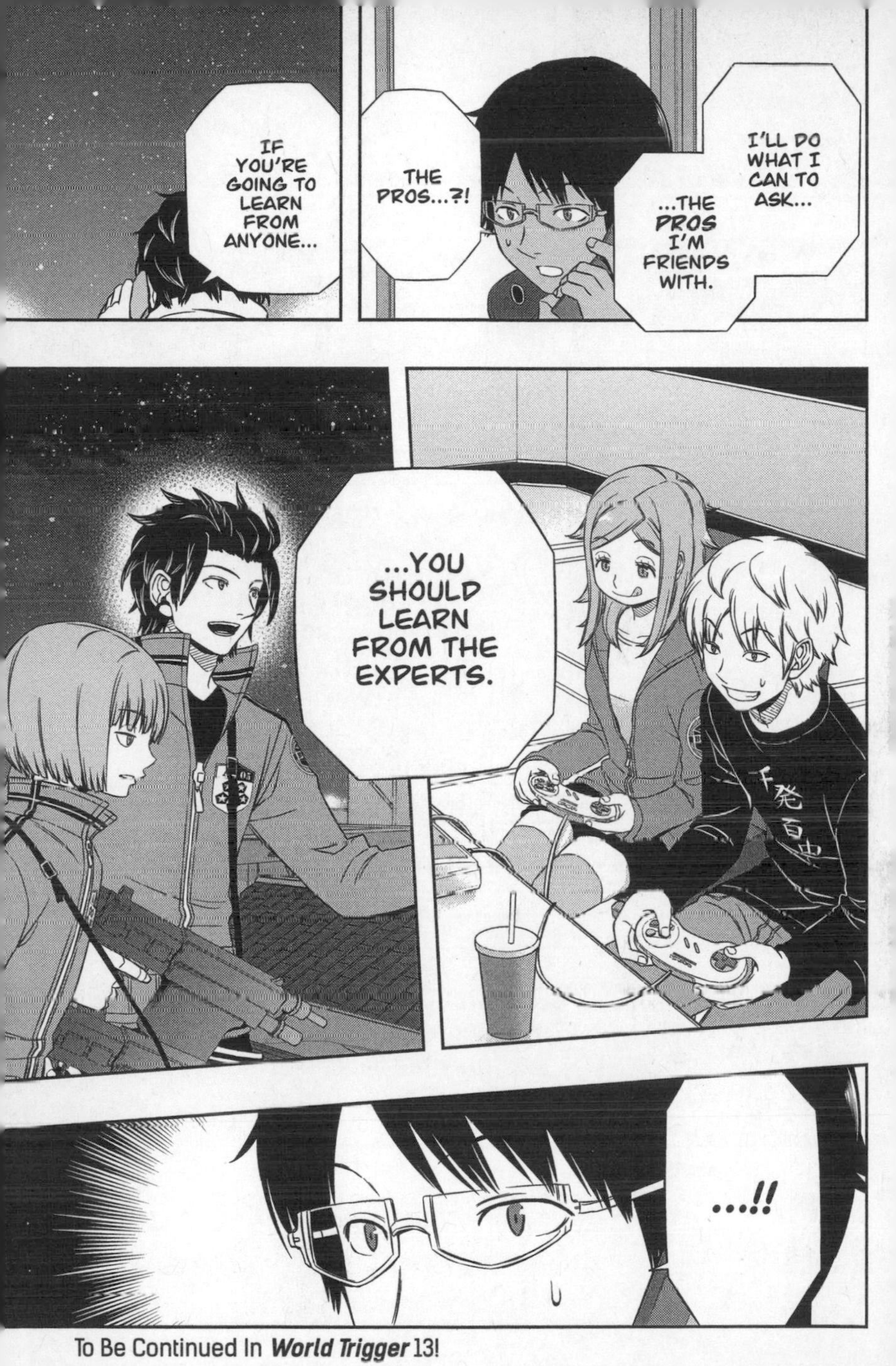
I'LL DO WHAT I CAN TO ASK...
...THE PROS I'M FRIENDS WITH.
THE PROS...?!
IF YOU'RE GOING TO LEARN FROM ANYONE...
...YOU SHOULD LEARN FROM THE EXPERTS.
...!!

To Be Continued In ***World Trigger*** 13!

B-Rank Wars Rules

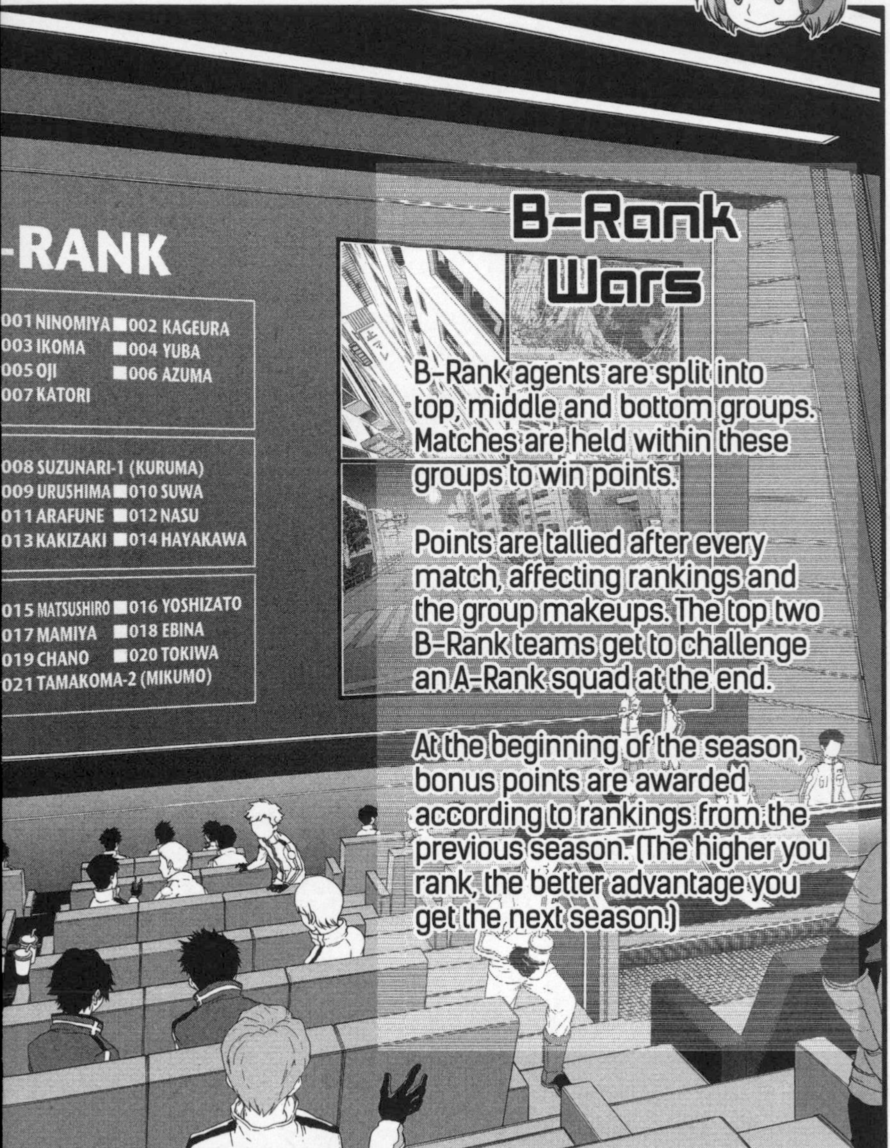

-RANK
001 NINOMIYA
002 KAGEURA
003 IKOMA
004 YUBA
005 OJI
006 AZUMA
007 KATORI
008 SUZUNARI-1 (KURUMA)
009 URUSHIMA
010 SUWA
011 ARAFUNE
012 NASU
013 KAKIZAKI
014 HAYAKAWA
015 MATSUSHIRO
016 YOSHIZATO
017 MAMIYA
018 EBINA
019 CHANO
020 TOKIWA
021 TAMAKOMA-2 (MIKUMO)

B-Rank Wars

B-Rank agents are split into top, middle and bottom groups. Matches are held within these groups to win points.

Points are tallied after every match, affecting rankings and the group makeups. The top two B-Rank teams get to challenge an A-Rank squad at the end.

At the beginning of the season, bonus points are awarded according to rankings from the previous season. (The higher you rank, the better advantage you get the next season.)

Basic rules

1

Three to four teams fight in a melee-style battle.

(One squad consists of an Operator and 1-4 agents.)

2

Defeating an opposing squad member earns you one point.

(Points for a bail out due to excessive Trion loss is awarded to the agent who dealt the most damage.)

3

Surviving nets two points.

(There is no survival bonus when the match runs out of time with no winner.)

4

One match has a 45- to 60-minute time limit.

(Depends on the size of the map—the bigger it is, the longer the match.)

5

The lowest-ranked team in each match gets to pick the stage.

6

Solo points in team Rank Wars work the same as the points in the solo Rank Wars.

7-1

You may only bail out while there are no enemy agents within a 60-meter radius of you.

(You can escape without awarding points to the enemy.)

7-2

Leaving the combat area on the map also counts as bailing out.

WORLD TRIGGER

Bonus Character Pages

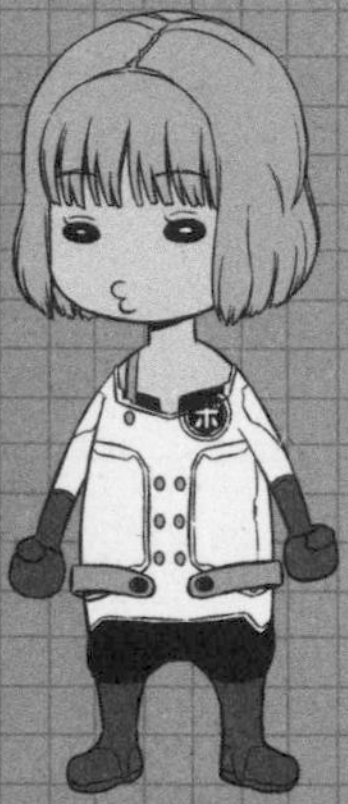

NASU

Sickly Girl (Tomahawk)

The No. 2 trigger-happy idiot with flashy attacks. She joined Border to participate in research to see whether a sickly person can get better with a Trion body. Six months later, she's jumping around blowing holes in her opponents. I think she's the prettiest character I've drawn recently. She has many secret fans within Border. Also, it's not important, but she's Narasaka's cousin.

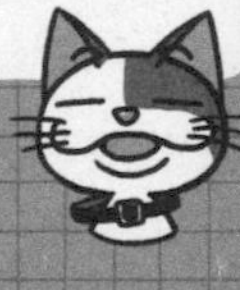

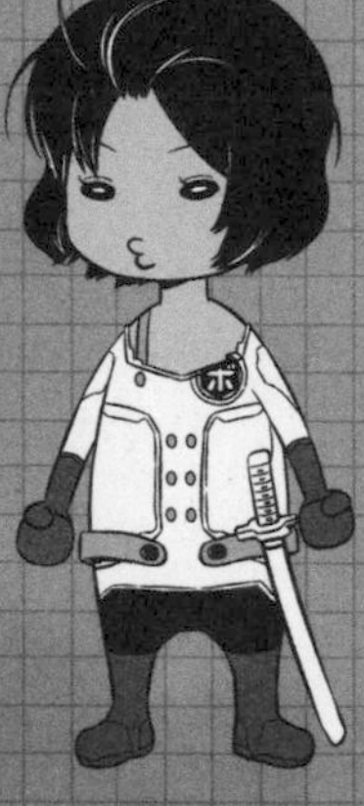

KUMA

Katana + High School Student

Due to my manager tenaciously adding screentone shadow to her chest, she became one of the bustiest female characters in Nasu squad. She was the driving force behind the formation of Nasu squad. She often focuses on guarding Nasu, so she doesn't have many solo points, but her counterattacks are quite impressive, earning the respect of male Attackers. She's been the most fun to draw recently.

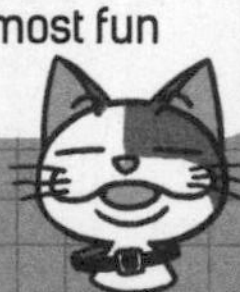

*Badge: Bo

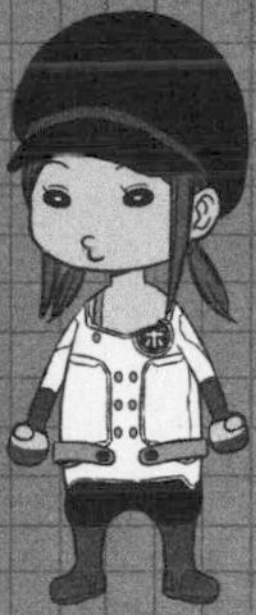

AKANE

Waaah!

She's in middle school and fond of fingerless gloves—an intrepid girl. Her older brother is Kuma's classmate, but she doesn't know that he has a crush on Kuma. She was popular as the youngest female Sniper until Chika and Izuho showed up. She doesn't know that though. She's generally clueless. She's the most stereotypical cartoony character in the series. She's originally from one of my one-shots.

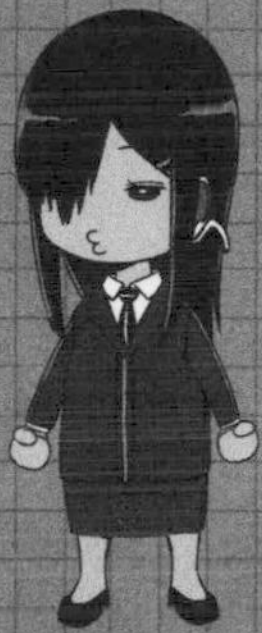

SAYOKO

Cardboard Boxes in Her Room

A recluse who designed Nasu squad's current uniform, earning the praise and respect of some of the guys. She's not good at handling the opposite sex, especially older guys, to the extent that it affects her life. She stays at home and was living on water and pickled kelp sent by her family when she was scouted by Kuma. She now has her financial situation in check and gets her supply over the internet. A slouching B-cup.

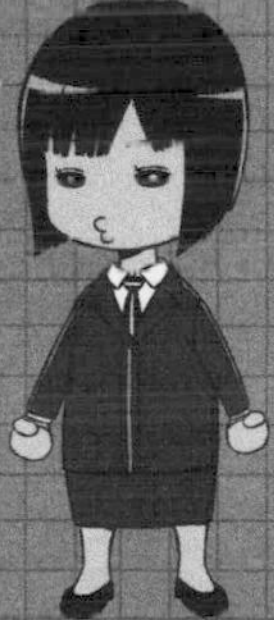

KON

No. 1 Bob Hair

An unfortunate Operator who can claim the pointless stat of having no waist. Is it the result of eating too many sweets to neutralize her stress from dealing with Taichi? She goes to a normal school, but gets good grades and is a good cook. She once rescued Toma and Kunichika from their atrocious grades. She's a character for the people with discriminating taste who know what's up. She's the ideal traditional Japanese woman, with an A-cup.

YOU'RE READING THE WRONG WAY!

World Trigger reads from right to left, starting in the upper-right corner. Japanese is read from right to left, meaning that action, sound effects, and word-balloon order are completely reversed from the English order.

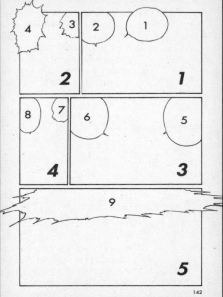